When Art meets Money

Encounters at the Art Basel

Kunstwissenschaftliche Bibliothek 44

Edited by Christian Posthofen

Verlag der Buchhandlung Walther König, Köln

Franz Schultheis
Erwin Single
Stephan Egger
Thomas Mazzurana

When Art meets Money
Encounters at the Art Basel

Translated by
James Fearns

Translated and published with the support of the Dr. Albert Bühler-Reindl-Fund of the University of St. Gallen.

Layout Conny Jelitte, Druckhaus Zanker, Markdorf
Print bookfactory, Bad Münder

Verlag der Buchhandlung Walther König, Köln
Ehrenstr. 4, 50672 Köln

Bibliographic information published by the Deutsche Nationalbibliothek
The Deutsche Nationalbibliothek lists this publication in the Deutsche Nationalbibligrafie; detailed bibliographic data are available in the Internet at http://dnb.d-nb.de.

Printed in Germany

Distribution:

Germany & Europe
Buchhandlung Walther König, Köln
Fon +49 (0) 221 / 20 59 6-53
Fax +49 (0) 221 / 20 59 6-60
verlag@buchhandlung-walther-koenig.de

UK & Eire
Cornerhouse Publications
70 Oxford Street
GB-Manchester M1 5NH
Fon +44 (0) 161 200 15 03
Fax +44 (0) 161 200 15 04
publications@cornerhouse.org

USA & Canada
D.A.P., Distributed Art Publishers
55 Sixth Avenue/ 2nd Floor
USA-New York, NY 10013
Fon +1 (0) 212 627 1999
Fax +1 (0) 212 627 9484
eleshowitz@dapinc.com

ISBN 978-3-86335-744-3

Contents

Preliminary remarks

The most expensive painting of all time, the most valuable living artist, new sales records at Christie's, purchases running into millions in Basel, huge yachts in Venice, fountains of champagne at Miami Beach, UBS, Deutsche Bank, Louis Vuitton – for some years now the relationship between „art" and „money" has been thematized with mounting criticism. The discussions create the impression that this relationship has entered into a new stadium, as if one were the witness of at least the engagement if not the wedding of two worlds. But even if the impression is not deceptive, will this ever turn out to be a love relationship?

Why is it that the sensation-conscious depictions of these superlatives are at the same time accompanied by a certain degree of moral indignation, which is often only scantily clad as an attempt to show ironic distance? The ambivalence of this constellation becomes intelligible when one takes into account the enormous claims which the art of the present day not only makes but is also confronted with – it should achieve scarcely less than the shaping of a different truth and reality beyond the banality of everyday life and our entanglement in the world. And what is more, it should do so independently of this claim, committed only to its own ideal and exclusively obeying its own laws.

It is easy to understand why the barefaced appearance of money in this scenario seems disturbing, even shameless. We are, however, faced here, in the first place, with a very classical script. Modern art, as we wish to know and experience it, has lived since the end of the nineteenth century from precisely this realized myth, from a repression of the economic world, from its increasingly radical distancing from the demands of the state, of bourgeois tastes, of all kinds of affirmative and decorative needs – and it can only be converted into money when „worldly" tastes have submitted to its aesthetic regime.

Is this script still valid today? What could make more sense than to pursue this question by examining a phenomenon which epitomizes this relationship between art and money, its structures and mechanisms, its claims and contradictions as scarcely any other does – the most significant art fair worldwide, the Art Basel. The phenomenon Art Basel gives voice to the tendencies of modern art events in an incomparably succinct fashion and it does so just within the framework of that semantics which to this today feeds on the historically achieved autonomy of the arts over „the world", of the sacred over the profane.

The Art Basel is more than just a fair in the commercial sense of the word, more than a temporally and spatially concentrated gathering of dealers offering their goods for sale to interested buyers. It is at the same time the site of a display of „holy" goods in the presence of thousands and thousands of believers, a pilgrim's goal for the ritualized adoration of traditional relics of art history and the forecourt of the consecration of their contemporary manifestations. The Art Basel is also, and for the very same reason, the decisive witness of the upheaval marking a radical change in that relationship between „art" and „money" which has increasingly become a subject of discussion – with all the consequences, not at least for the evaluation of what is to be regarded „globally" as „genuine" art.

That is the reason behind the choice of this setting and this book. It is the result of a research project stretching over several years, of an „ethnography" of the fairs in Basel and Miami Beach; and it is supported by an abundance of material. A decisive source is provided by more than a hundred detailed interviews with the most important actors at the fairs, with the management and „staff", with gallery owners and collectors, with museum directors and curators, art consultants and artists. In addition there are findings deriving from an intensive observation of what goes on at the fair, conversations in the galleries, the initiation of purchasing negotiations, the behaviour of the visitors, which has also been recorded photographically a thousandfold. Of course secondary material must also find a place in such a publication, primarily the results of previous research, statistical sources, the relevant press reports – but the emphasis of the study lies on the precise interpretation and understanding observation of the phenomenon observed, on the social practice.

Within the framework of this publication it was by no means possible to exploit the abundant material exhaustively. This results in a certain degree of heterogeneity in the individual chapters. This is not only because four authors have worked on the text, whose personal handwriting clearly remains recognizable. The treatment of the „actual" givens, often a presentation of facts on the contemporary art market and then the reproduction of „stories" followed by an attempt to reflect systematically on the perceptions of the actors – the difficult bridgebuilding between the empirical, the practical and the theoretical – has without doubt also left its traces.

And nevertheless the reading of the text quickly makes it clear that the conception and interpretation of the ethnography of an exemplary segment of the contemporary art market presented in this case study owes its approach to a perspective which has made decisive fruitful contributions to the discourse on art in the last twenty years – to the many works of Pierre Bourdieu, who can be regarded at the latest since his epochal study *Les règles de l'art* as one of the leading representatives of a theoretically advanced and yet empirically saturated sociology of art.

This circumstance has some consequences, among others for the style of the argumentation. If one wished to proceed only at the theoretical level the book would, in spite of many concrete examples, turn into an academic treatise. But this was not its purpose. Instead the publication is addressed to the actors in the art world themselves, without however being able to blend out completely the discussion at the level of art theory.

There are also consequences in regard to the degree of possible disagreement. If the concrete findings of this study can be generalized then a position comes to the fore which, in spite of all the overlapping, can in a certain fashion be perceived as „uncomfortable". One reason is that the talk of the „commercialization" of art formulates concepts whose suggestive character tends to contradict the requirements of an unbiased understanding. But the dimensions of the processes involved are greater.

This is, above all, the case because the discourse in art theory has long bid farewell to „modernism", although all the indications are that this is a premature departure, if one does not mean by it a sclerosis of the social configurations of the modern art field, but its „modernist" logic as a whole. The line of argumentation in this book is different and moves in a different direction.

And finally there are consequences for the self-perception of the participants in the field. If one does not understand this publication as „socio-analysis", not as an attempt to describe the logic of the phenomena in the art field with all their immense powers of „devotion" to art, then this normative constellation can very quickly turn into a „personal" one and give rise to feelings of hurt.

But this also was not our purpose. The disclosure of the ways the „magical" functions in our profane world puts belief to the test. But it can also help us to better understand ourselves and the world in which we are imprisoned. This is a walk on a tight-rope. The reader must decide if it has been successful.

St. Gallen, in June 2015

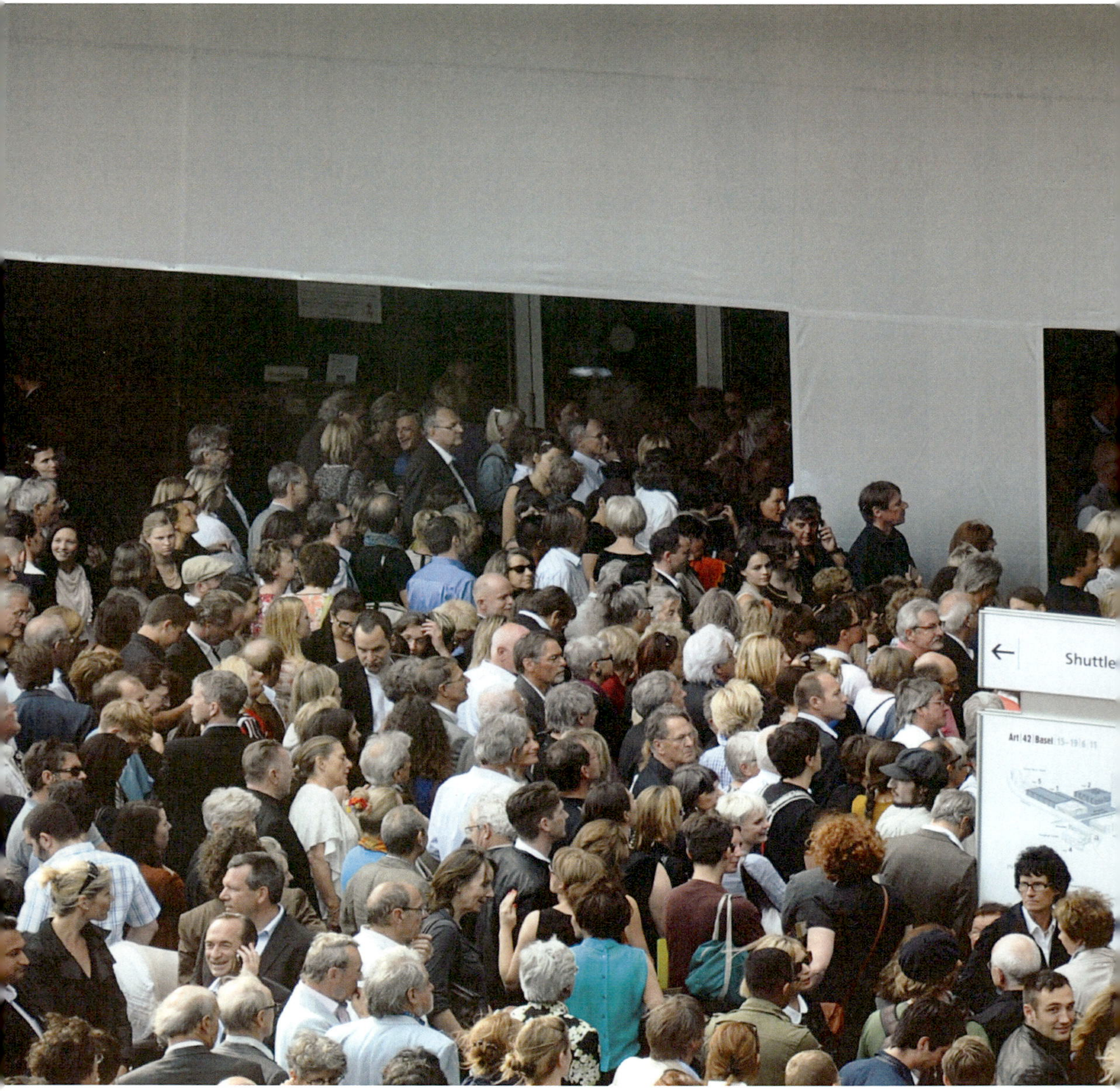
Shuttle

1 At the Fair

The event and its narrations

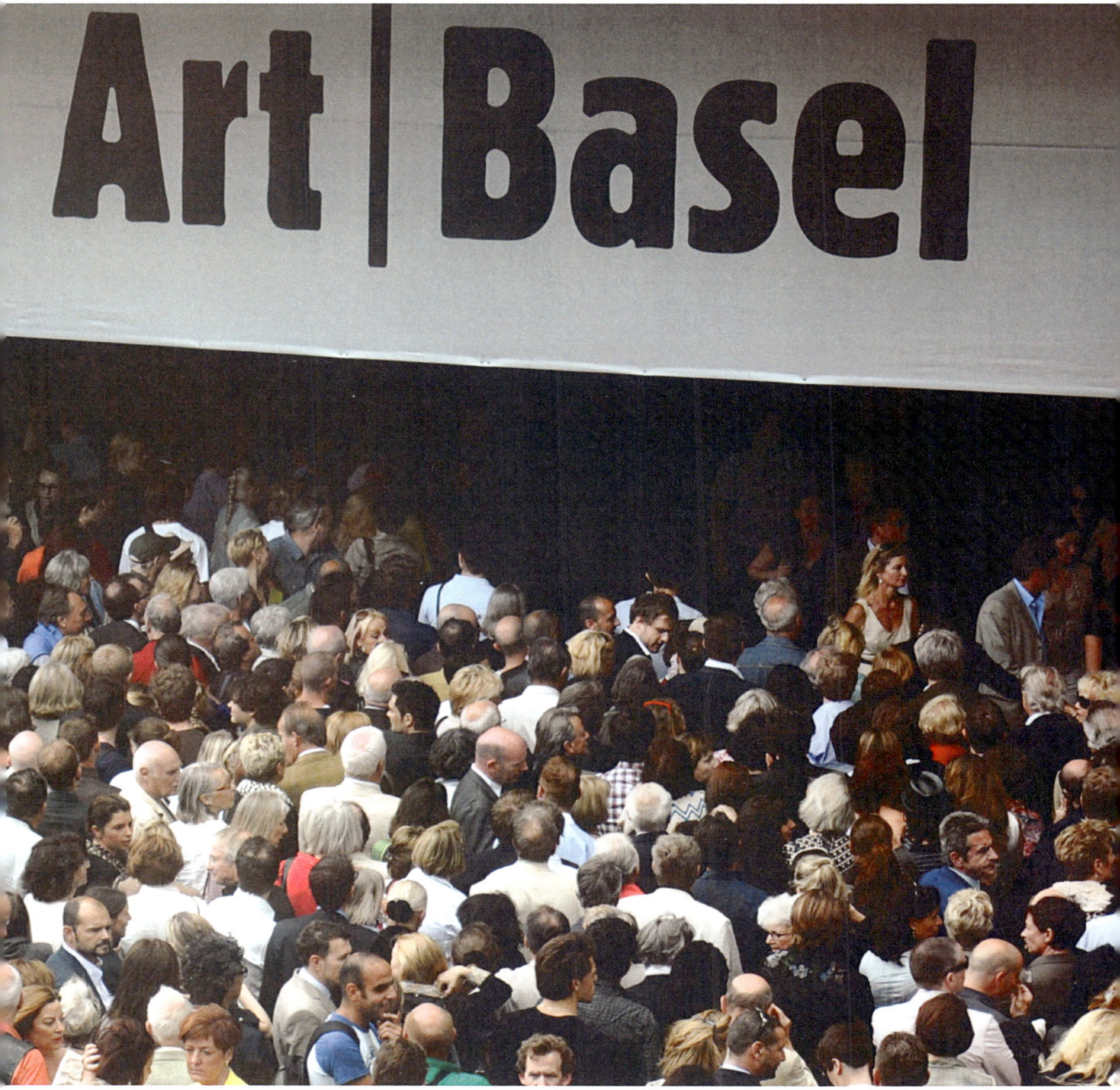

The particular difficulty of sociology comes from the fact that it teaches things that everybody knows in a way, but which they don't want to know or cannot know because the law of the system is to hide those things from them.

PIERRE BOURDIEU, Sociology in Question

It is difficult to approach the phenomenon of „one of the worldwide most important“ art fairs without being seduced by it. Anyone who turns up there becomes a player in the game. The mere intention to visit such a fair makes accomplices of us all. And there is a simple reason for this. If we had no *interest* in attending we would not be „inwardly“ involved; the brief report in the newspaper on the sale of a painting for an inconceivable sum of millions of dollars would be registered with a shake of the head and immediately forgotten after turning to the next page – as an ultimately insignificant fact. But because this is not the case, because we can contextualize the report and form an opinion about it, because we think we *know* what it means, we already lack the distance which would permit us to assess the phenomenon *as such* within an entire *logic* of the phenomena we encounter in the field of art. This impartiality of perception can only be achieved by eliminating the apparent self-evidencies of everyday understanding.

But just these self-evidencies determine the daily life of those who concern themselves with art, and they are fully *contaminated* by a discourse which is itself a part of the phenomenon. In the announcements of the fair operators, the press reports and the art criticism this discourse continuously illuminates a *front stage* which also the „most critical“ commentaries present as the *back stage*, as what „really“ happens – the money, the rich, the „society“, the „parties“, the style of dress, the demeanor, the bargaining and haggling, the power of the market and the prices. It describes processes in the indicative which are at the same time in the pejorative, without taking into account that a personal position in the field of art and the *perspective* it imposes subject this perception to a systematic „refraction“. And this perspective itself can only function on the basis of a logic which designates the field of art as a sphere in which the conflicts over a *normative right of interpretation* as the decisive stake in the game not only obscure the stake itself but with it the entire game.

For the Art Basel, the art events in New York and Miami, London and Paris, Berlin and Madrid, Hong Kong and Singapore there only exists this „view from the inside“ of the *participant,* which he regards as a „view from the outside“, as observation and not narration. But how can this problem of perspectivist bias be overcome? For here in the world of art, perhaps more than anywhere else, „facts“ say scarcely anything about their meaning and precisely the *meanings* are the decisive stake in the debates on the interpretation of the game, on the legitimacy of its presentation, mediation and appropriation. And a critical look at the standpoint from which the Art Basel as an event is seen already gives us a first impression of the logic of the happening we are dealing with.

Good News

The self-presentation of the „event“ Art Basel

The Art Basel, the „Mecca“ of the art world, encounters us as will and representation, anecdote and story-telling. The „event“ lives off its narrations. And they are all more or less „official“ and also have room for „critical“ reporting, which plays it part in the creation of *significance*. Of course the announcements of the fair operators are essentially a *façade*: the internet pages, the newsletter, the press releases, superficial commotion everywhere and deliberate exaggeration. And it would be scarcely malicious but only realistic to assume that, conversely, those responsible for the fair themselves participate much less „inwardly“ in the event Art Basel than they feel it necessary to pretend. This is simply because the event itself must be rationalized through and through in order to unfold its effects even approximately – it would be naive to believe anything else.

But what exactly is the good news? First of all it is evidently the news itself which is in the foreground. It reports on its own importance and on the importance of the event it announces. It speaks of „excellent quality“, the „entire world“, the „central meeting point“ and the crowds of collectors, museums and visitors at one of the „most important art events of the year“. But the announcement itself is a walk on a tightrope. The alleged inrush of the museums guarantees the „quality“ and the „extremely high sales levels“ bear unquestionable witness to the „business“, an essential precondition for the existence of the fair.

Gold and Incense

An art fair takes stock

Excellent quality attracts private collectors and groups of museums from all over the world and ensures extremely high sales for the galleries.

The 45th Art Basel closed its gates on Sunday, 22 June, 2014. Throughout the whole week and over the entire market the galleries reported extremely high sales levels and the Art Basel once again confirmed its position as one of the most important art events of the year and as a central meeting point of the international art world.

The Art Basel, whose lead partner is the UBS, presented 285 galleries from 34 countries across all six show sectors and showed the works of over 4,000 artists. A total of 24 galleries exhibited for the first time in Basel. These new exhibitors come from Brazil, Chile, China, Germany, France, Italy, Mexico, Spain, the USA and England.

During the six days of the fair the show attracted 92,000 visitors – 6,000 more than last year. Representatives and groups from over 70 museums worldwide took part in the fair alongside important private collectors from Europe, North and South America, including: The Art Institute Chicago; Centre Pompidou Paris & Metz; Cincinnati Art Museum; Dallas Museum of Art; Groeninge Museum, Bruges; Institute of Contemporary Arts, London; Los Angeles County Museum of Art; Louvre, Paris; Fondazione MAXXI, Rom; Museo de Arte de Lima; The Museum of Contemporary Art, Los Angeles; Museum of Modern Art, Warschau; The New Museum, New York; Palais de Tokyo, Paris; Solomon R. Guggenheim Museum, New York; Tate, London; Ullens Center for Contemporary Art, Beijing; Whitney Museum of American Art, New York; and Yuz Museum, Shanghai.

Press release Art Basel | June 2014

This performative strategy of presenting art and money as „allies", as a „natural" alliance, a relationship which elsewhere in the field of art would be regarded as a *mésalliance,* can only succeed when the „niveau" of the goods, the dealers and the buyers confirm its appropriateness. And willing witnesses can in fact be found. The galleries „were delighted with the 45th Fair", the „entire world" was in Basel, „firstclass" works of „highest quality" went to renowned museums and „important collections", the „niveau of the people" was „astounding", one encountered „a discerning clientele", „intellectual collectors", „cultivated attentiveness", a „serious public". Everything was „unbelievable" and „wonderful" – including the „strong turnover" and the „excellent sales". The wedding of „good" art and „good" money initiated here seems legitimate, a matter of course, the product of a shared cultural interest without any economic ulterior motives, of a transborder love of art.

„Good" business

Legitimations of the exchange of goods

We were delighted to place several works in museum collections. We can report consistently unbelievable sale – it was in fact our best Basel Fair ever.

Iwan Wirth, Galerie Hauser & Wirth, Zürich, London, New York

We brought contemporary masterpieces of the highest quality and placed them in important collections in Europe and the USA. The Art Basel is the place where the most important collectors come together and where first class works of art find a home.

Per Skarstedt, Skarstedt Gallery, New York, London

The fair was fantastic this year and the sales excellent.

Theresa Liang, Long March Space Gallery, Peking

Art Basel gets better every year. We had a strong turnover and were pleased to see that the whole world was in Basel for the fair.

Luisa Strina, Galeria Luisa Strina, São Paulo

It is always a special pleasure to share important works from Los Angeles and elsewhere with the discerning clientele of the Art Basel.

Kurt Mueller, David Kordansky Gallery, Los Angeles

It was amazing to see the niveau of the people who took part in the fair and bought objects this year. We sold to individuals and institutions from the USA, the United Kingdom, Spain, Russia, Germany, France, Belgium and Switzerland.

Cristobal Riestra, Galería OMR, Mexico City

We particularly appreciated the profound and cultivated attention which was present through the entire fair.

Stefania Palumbo, Galerie Supportico Lopez, Berlin

Our first participation in the Feature section of the Art Basel was an unbelievable experience. We were highly delighted to receive so much recognition from attentive, intellectual collectors and institutions at the Art Basel, who really devoted a lot of time to us.

Miriam Lozano, Galería espaivisor, Valencia

Press release Art Basel | June 2014

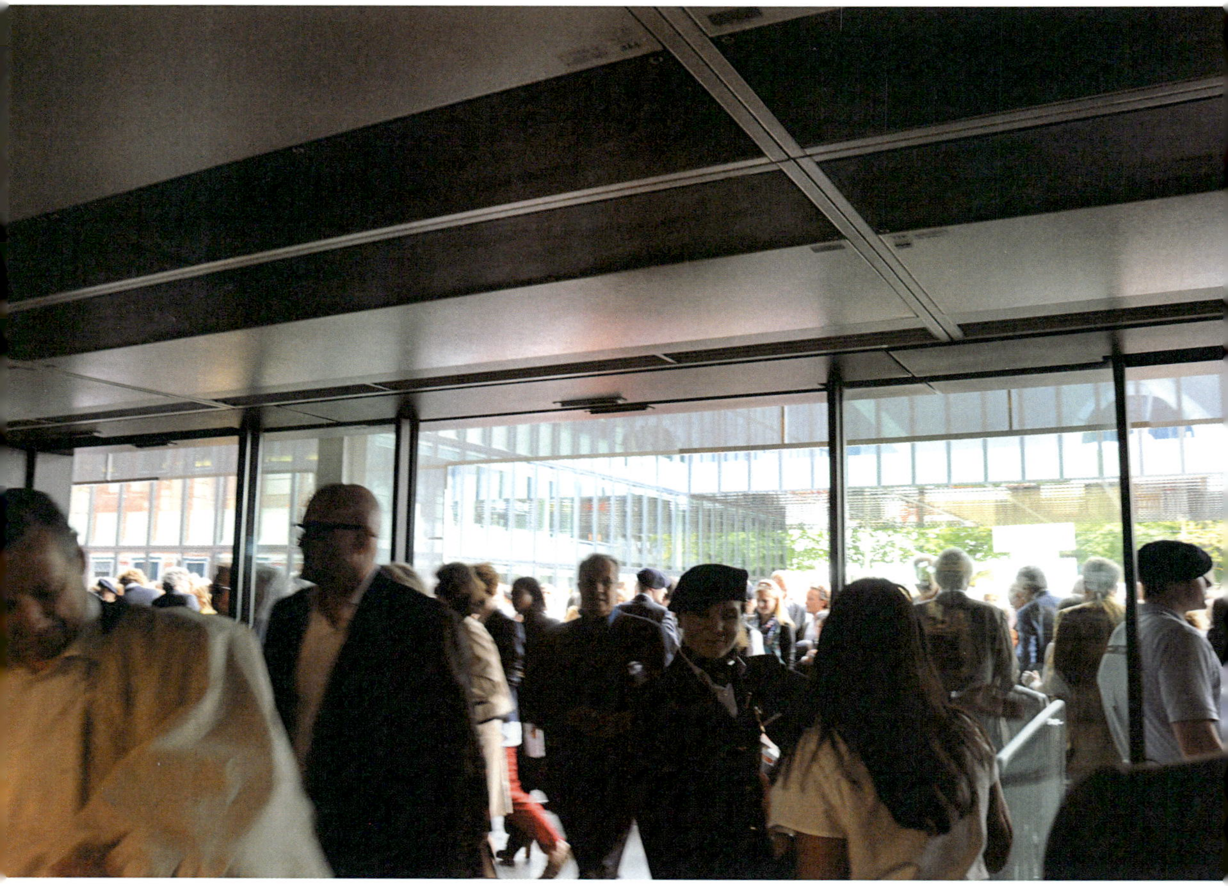

The galleries for their part emphasize the reputation of a purchasing event which, in order to be convincing, must always point to a „strong turnover“ as a criterion of its validity, whose significance, however is nonetheless characterized by an exchange of „quality“ at the „highest level“, by the social quality of the buyer and the artistic quality of the work, which should help to forget the role played by „hard cash“ in the process. Whereas the galleries, therefore, still strive to justify their activities in terms of „content“, the self-presentation of the Art Basel aims primarily to underline the quality of the „event“ *as such*. And although it necessarily talks about „caring for“ upcoming artists and accompanying their development, the *overall product* stands above all in the foreground: the „best show“, „highest quality“, „exciting“ works by „world-wide renowned“ artists, „world-wide leading“ gallerists, „world-wide reputation“, a place „where the art world meets“. And, on the margins of self-representation, the product recommends itself as one of the „Top Events of Switzerland“ from which one can always expect „excellence in art, culture, music and sport“, as products from the portfolio of the sophisticated life-style – art fair, film festival, classical music in Lucerne, jazz in Montreux, golf, skiing, horse-racing.

The „highest merit“

The Art Basel as an overall product

ABOUT ART BASEL

Art Basel stages the world's premier Modern and contemporary art shows, held annually in Basel, Miami Beach, and Hong Kong. Founded by gallerists in 1970, Art Basel has been a driving force in supporting the role that galleries play in the nurturing of artists, and the development and promotion of visual arts.

In addition to showing exciting works by world-renowned artists, Art Basel is always innovating, thus expanding its platform for new artists who represent the vanguard of the visual arts. Its world-wide reputation – earned over the last forty years – for showing work of the highest merit, and attracting the world's leading gallerists and collectors, has made Art Basel the place where the art world meets.

OUR ROLE

The dynamic relationships between art galleries, their artists, private collectors and public institutions play an essential role in today's art world, and connecting the international art community has been Art Basel's goal since its beginning.

Top Events of Switzerland

Art Basel is a member of „Top Events of Switzerland", an association comprised of eight events of the highest quality across the country – Art Basel, Festival del film Locarno, Lucerne Festival, Montreux Jazz Festival, Weltklasse Zürich, Omega European Masters, Ski World Cup Wengen and White Turf – that give visitors the opportunity to experience excellence in art, culture, music and sports.

Art Basel Website | About Us

Making the visitors fully aware of the „global range“ of the fair, praising the highest quality of the art on offer from „classical“ to „experimental“ formats and recommending the fair as a meeting place for artists and lovers of art, which one should not miss, are only marginal remarks – there is nothing more to be harvested here than the annually increasing numbers of the „casual visitors“. The true „philosophy“ of the fair is different: the

„sponsorship" of upcoming art makes way for the „partnership" with the world of the elites. The „VIP network" with its privileges, the „special welcome" and „early access to the show", the „VIP programs" and „VIP tours" calls for a subpage of its own. The „partners" are paid lavish tribute, for their „essential support" and their „fundamental acknowledgment of the arts" – and of the customers, who have a private lounge at their disposal „where collectors can meet one another away from the show floor."

The self-presentations of the Art Basel, its messages, ultimately function like the advertisements for a *luxury product,* whose quality exhausts itself more or less in the continuous assertion of its quality and in the continuous reference to its uniqueness and exquisiteness: „outstanding quality", „world's premier art show", „most prestigious of their kind". That this account has in the meantime asserted itself as the official reading of the „event" can scarcely be denied. The superlatives disseminated all over the world by the management of the fair itself have become a fixed part of the journalistic semantics, which even determines the lexical discourse – the „world-wide best and most important fair", „works of the highest quality", „exquisite paintings, sculptures, objects", „first-class galleries", a „competent public", „excellent business transactions".

The „Olympics of the Art Market"

The lexical consecration of a mercantile phenomenon

Characterized as the „Olympics of the Art Market" and „Queen of the Art Fairs", the Art Basel is regarded world-wide as the best and most important fair for art from the classical modern period to the present day.

Every year in June the biggest actors in the international art world – artists, collectors, curators, museum directors, art critics, art experts and art lovers – travel from almost all the continents to the Swiss town on the Rhine in order to see, to exchange opinions on and, above all, to buy art works of the highest quality.

At the Art Basel 2010, for example, more than 300 first class galleries from 36 countries presented select paintings, sculptures, objects, graphics, photographs, video works and installations by over 2,500 artists. There was little trace here of the after-effects of the financial crisis of 2008/09 which had also shaken the art market. A new attendance record was achieved with over 62,500 visitors, and the art dealers were very satisfied with their sales. For example, the Düsseldorf gallerist Hans Mayer, who has attended the art fair since its beginnings, rejoicingly exclaimed: „We came to the Art Basel 41 with the highest expectations, but our expectations were exceeded by far. An international, competent public enabled us to do excellent business."

Hatje Cantz Kunstlexikon | Art Basel

The emptiness of this performative semantics strikes the eye. It derives not only from the fact that precisely in this field the ascertainment of „quality" is totally dependent on shared *conventions* which can be most easily established by means of definitional monopolies – there are no material-testing institutes for art. It is also revealed, above all, in the way any kind of determination of the „event" in terms of content has receded into the background. As in business life the only thing that counts here is the „performance" *in itself,* an indisputable performance, which, by means of a scarcely disguised economic deduction, can ultimately be measured by the „unbelievable turnover". The event is what it is and what it is meant to be, in every respect „great" and „fabulous".

The critical gaze

The journalistic escort for the „marketing machinery"

Anyone who fundamentally mistrusts the releases of the Art Basel has a difficult time in the „art world". The proclaimed dominance of „quality" receives the recognition of the „critical" fraction of the art business, in spite of the absence of „uncomfortable" positions and „elements of surprise". Consensus can scarcely be avoided when „all the big names" are on the program. An approximately good contrast program with „the others" can only be offered by the Biennale in Venice or the Documenta in Kassel. They present „stand-points" which the market must first incorporate and even then only if their „format" is somehow acceptable. It is easier to adopt a critical point of view when the *social dimension* of the event, which lies behind the consensus, is revealed. The incense accompanying this scenario then suddenly dissipates, as soon as the mercantile character of the event, the smell of „money", and its social ambitions become perceptible.

The constitutive schizophrenia of a belief in art is then made manifest, which recognizes what the socially exclusive recognition of „useless" goods calls for but denies that the exclusivity of its appropriation as a *concrete social given* enjoys that universal legitimacy whose recognition graces all love of art. The tour around the fair thus becomes a kind of „test" of moral steadfastness. What, then, does this „critical" gaze see? When the knowledge of the indisputable importance of the Art Basel, of its fixed place on the annual agenda of the „art world" as part of an „obligatory program" alongside the Biennale and the Documenta, is colored by a staged narration whose manifestation as an *actual* „event" is then subjected to criticism, then this knowledge seems to describe an unquestionable fact without providing any proofs of the fact. A critical view of the fair itself then reveals the tension of belief and doubt in all its shades and colors [1].

On the one hand we have the „best fair in the world", the „world-wide most important exhibition of modern art", „in step with the times", offering the „finest" works, of a „quality" which, „beyond all questions of taste", cannot be seen together at any other place in the world, a „unique class" of works covering all sections of art. The sector *Art Unlimited* for space-consuming installations presents „stunning" works; in the 14 Rooms „often thrilling" works of art are shown, which are „difficult to sell" – this in itself a criterion of quality. This affirmative statement apodictically ratifies the *conventionalized recognition* of the art world, without asking what actually is the nature of this „quality beyond all questions of taste", which permits no doubt and affirms the absolute rightness of belief.

But on the other hand we have the commercial aspect. The fair, „in step with the times but also with the prices", produces charts listing the selling prices which are a source of amazement even among the „most hardened insiders of the art scene". And although the list of the prices realized is in the meantime widely reported in the feuilletons „because after all it interests everybody", it is always accompanied by ironical comments which reveal the underlying moral objections: „graceful euphemisms for the buying prices"; „who pays such close attention" to the prices?; „six million dollars somehow sounds modest". And the „marketing machinery" for „established" contemporary art „is running at full blast." And it is also clear to the critical gaze that people „who can afford it" invest in this art because it „functions as a social prosthesis like no other accessory". The commodity itself is mostly beyond all doubt, which is often not true of its purchasers.

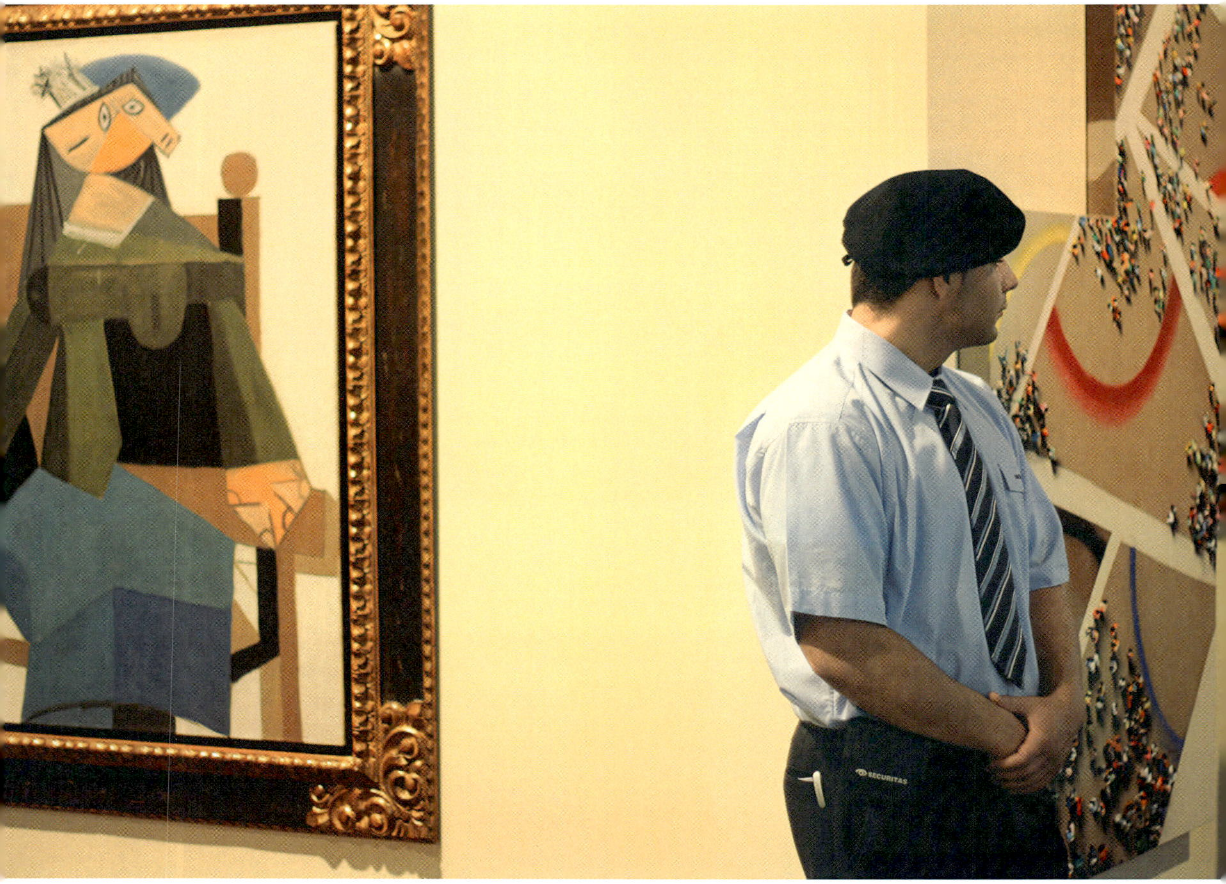
SECURITAS

Contradictions of the „refined" kind

Art and money in harmonious accord

The Art Basel is the Art Basel is the Art Basel

This fair can only surpass itself. The 45th edition of the best achievements of the art world is in step with the times – and with the prices.

In the meantime this interests everybody, even those who are only by-standers: top of the charts for prices is one of the late wig pictures of Andy Warhol, „Self-Portrait (Fright Wig)" of 1986 in pink, which the Skarstedt Gallery of New York and London reports as sold for an asking price of 35 million dollars; of course the buyer remains unnamed. The asking price, the amount proposed by the galleries and dealers on request, is the current magic word in Basel since Tuesday. How many dollars actually cross the table in the end is of course on a different piece of paper, namely the sales contract. What one hears instead are delicate euphemisms such as „north of" (followed the one or the other million) or, particularly cheeky, several millions (after all, who pays such close attention to the actual amount?).

The Art Basel is already at its zenith during the VIP previews – the fair is only open to the general public from Thursday on – at least as far as the continuously named sales contracts is concerned: Damien Hirst's medicine cabinet „Nothing is a problem for me" of 1992 was sold for just under (somehow sounds modest) six million dollars by his London house gallery White Cube; Jeff Koons' sweet steel dolphin for five million dollars by David Zwirner; Andreas Gursky's ink-jet print „Tote Hosen II" of 2013, which itself looks like a mega-chip for 500,000 dollars by Sprüth Magers; or also Georg Baselitz's big blue wooden man „Folk Thing Zero" of 2009, which had already been shown at the Berlin Gallery Contemporary Fine Arts, for 2.3 million dollars. In view of such great delightedness it is scarcely possible to say whether this 45th edition of the fair is „better" than the one in the previous year or than those of a decade ago. It can, however, be said that their presentation has achieved a certain degree of perfection both for the modern period and the established contemporary art. Just to walk around Hall 2 on the ground floor or on the first floor is a lesson on the state of the current market. It is also enjoyable; so much quality, beyond all questions of taste, is not collected for a short period of time at any other place in the world.

The marketing machinery is running at full blast. [...] Even the most hardened insiders of the art scene are amazed this year at the breath-taking asking prices for the heroes of the market (in as far as they have any information about them at all). The likelihood that these prices are also realized confirms an experience that is becoming increasingly significant. To put it pointedly: anyone who still believes that the buyers particularly of contemporary art in the high and highest price segments are seriously interested in finding a profitable investment are barking up the wrong tree. The buyers themselves probably don't even believe this. The people who can afford to invest in this kind of art – and there are a lot of them moving around the fair within a very narrow space for two or three days during the previews – do so because art, more than any other accessory, functions as a social prosthesis.

This fact by no means diminishes the attractiveness of the Art Basel, for only the very finest objects are shown. And they are at the same time presented as high-class furnishing proposals, as in the case of the New York Mnuchin Gallery, which shows a magnificent Morris Lewis „Tzadik" of 1958 hanging behind a racily shimmering early Chamberlain, the „Miss Remember Ford" of 1964, that looks good from all sides.

The unique class of the show stretches to all of its sections. This begins with the Art Unlimited, which now occupies the entire Hall 1 with 78 space-consuming positions (whereas the Statements section for up and coming artists and galleries has been reduced and relocated in Hall 2 among the other galleries). There isn't a single failure in this section – from Carl André to Hanna Darboven, from Thomas Houseago to Mathias Faldbaken and the dazzling installations of the Cameroon artist Pascale Marthine Tayou (of the Galleria Continua in San Gimignano. And then there are the 14 Rooms in Hall 2: performative works from more than four decades lie concealed behind fourteen doors, often thrilling works of art which are difficult to sell. Who outside this world-wide most important exhibition would be able to win so large a public?

Frankfurter Allgemeine Zeitung | 16. June 2014

This ambivalence permeates nearly all the journalistic commentaries with differences in the accentuation. But the perspective of this „critical“ gaze is always oriented on the „worldly“ aspect of the event, on its character as a market, on the prices, the clientele and all the accompanying perceptions. The fair is a market, event, show, spectacle, a catwalk for the „pretty people“, an event at which the spectacular flows into the vulgar. It is a warehouse designated as a luxury temple, which must thematize the social circles involved in the event, because „money“ is here perceived in its embodied form, in the visible manifestations of clothing, behavior and *habitus*. All of this brings up and refreshes fundamental aversions.

The ritual opening of the fair sets the scene: its character as a premiere, the far from „exclusive“ impression created by the admission of the VIPs, hundreds of „very, very important people“ who push and shove at the especially installed control barriers half an hour before the opening in order to be the „first choice“, then the opening of the gates by the uniformed security guards, the rush of the invited guests into the foyer, the gong and the pompous announcement „The Art Basel is now open. Enjoy the show“. The VIP art scene as such, the wedding of money and art in a closed self-celebrating „society“, the dinners, receptions and „bespoke parties“, the events and promotions, the museum and gallery dinners, the private parties in noble hotels are all an imposition for any „pure“ understanding of art. And then the hustle and bustle in the exhibition halls, interested people with plans in their hands searching for selected galleries, the continual telephoning, photographing and surfing, the ostentatious intimacy of the like-minded, people who know one another and use Christian names, the greeting rituals with kisses hugging and backslapping, the VIP lounges, the black luxury limousines of the VIP chauffeur services: the message of these „milieu studies“, even when they transport realities, in the end expresses, above all else, a glaring contrast to the „contemplative“ approach to „high“ art which remains the ultimate standard in the milieu of the „pure“ love of art.

And then the character of the fair itself: blue chips, self-proclaimed „museum pieces“ offered by the „leading“ galleries dominate the ground floor and the atrium while the younger galleries are situated on the upper floor, an arrangement indicating a conscious concentration on „marketability“. The booths are crammed full with works of art, often a colorful collage with something to meet every taste. Paintings and photography are all bundled together under the concept of „art fair art“. The requirements of market conformity and the context of commercial exploitation can be felt everywhere, whereas the ideal, the „unwieldy“ art, is moved out to the *Art Statements* and above all to the Art *Unlimited,* the area reserved for the large format installations and video projects. The major exhibits reveal the market power of the art dealers: Gagosian with Warhol, Picasso and Richard Prince, Helly Nahmad with Miró, Picasso and Calder, Zwirner with the icons of Minimalism framed by the works of Jeff Koons, Ad Reinhard, Bruce Nauman, Gerhard Richter and Sigmar Polke.

There is nothing „wrong“ about this perception; on the contrary it allows the relationships of dominance and the effects of monopoly to strike the eye. But it becomes arbitrary precisely at the point where the *names* evoke something for which concepts *beyond* everyday intellectual language are lacking. Reporting and *being able* to report on such things reveals the entire embroilment in the game, which links an ultimately marginal participation with an equally marginal distancing. Here the aversions of a „pure“ love of art are evoked, which deeply disapproves of the „prostitution“ for „money“ and its concrete manifestations and believes that the socially exclusive character of the event fundamentally harms this love.

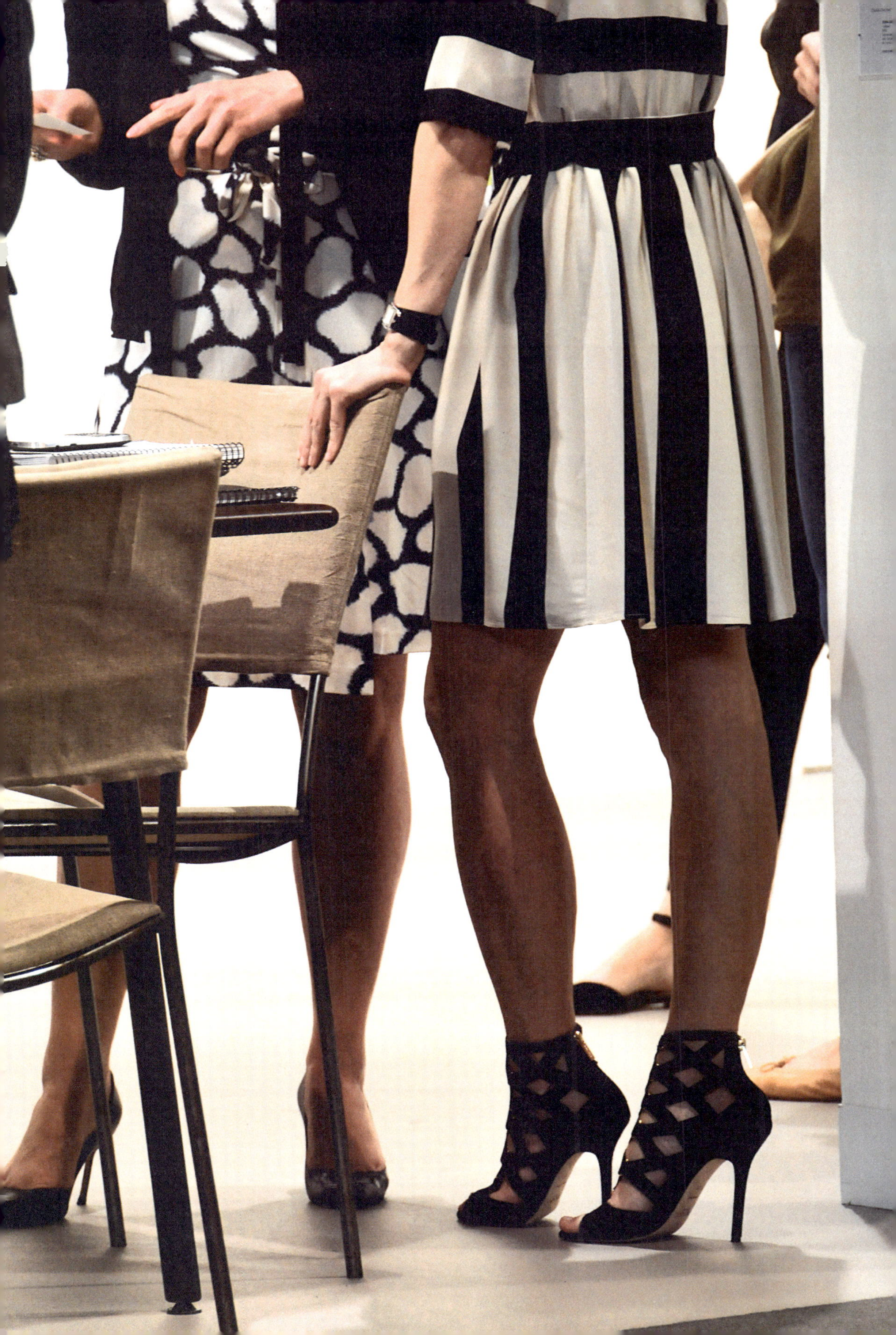

The „Money“ and the „Glamour“

Contradictions of the unrefined kind

Art Basel in Miami Beach: Art and Airconditioning

That's art? One should not put this question at all at the biggest art fair in the world at Miami Beach. First of all, because most of the works have already been sold before one has found an answer. And, secondly, because it doesn't matter in the least.

From the pedestal of his wooden sandals Gerd Harry Lübke operates a screen on a free partition wall. „We put it on the wall for you" he calls to the collector and where a David Schnell was just hanging a colorful Uwe Kowski now shines. The buyer nods and Lübke brings the next picture onto the market. Probably nobody sells more passionately than Gerd Harry Lübke, the Eigen+Art Gallerist from Leipzig; at no other stand does art as a commodity seem more physical or the sales procedure more lively, leaving the refreshing feeling that one is at a bazaar. The scene is not disturbed by the presence of a representative of the main sponsor of the fair – the Swiss bank UBS – alongside the buyer. After all, what counts at the Art Basel Miami Beach is not only art but also money. And the feeling of being a part of the scene.

Yellow light bulb in the crotch

In the „collectors' lounge" the privileged are sprawling casually on big white sofas, the carpet swallows every sound. Luxurious whispering about the party last night hovers in the air like expensive perfume. Anyone who has made it to this bright, high room is truly „in". But is nonetheless surrounded by advertising booths. Ever since art has become a status symbol for broad layers of American society, it is possible, for a few hundred thousand dollars, to become a respected collector and member of an attractive target group. Someone who has just bought a pure blue canvas four square meters in size or a felt sculpture with a yellow light bulb in its crotch will also take an interest in diamonds, islands, a private jet. But art can also be fun.

Chocolates and lolly ices

The art market is open for five hot, sticky December days in Florida. Long queues form in front of the cash-desks. This year 44,000 visitors want to see what other people have already bought, families, school classes, a surprising number of young people who are seriously interested in art and enjoy it. On Gerd Harry Lübke's screen the pictures are smaller and lower priced: lithographies of Neo Rauch for example. But nonetheless unaffordable for most of the weekend visitors.

The chocolate Santa Claus's of the US artist Paul McCarthy are less expensive. Instead of a Christmas tree Santa has an anal dildo in his hand – a 395 gram piece costs a hundred dollars; the hip-high version can be had for 6,500 dollars. You can live out your urge for possessions unchecked in the Shangart Supermarket. The Chinese artist Xu Zhen has brought an original shop from Shanghai with him. On the shelves, refrigerated counters and stalls you can find the usual range of goods to meet daily needs: condoms, biscuits, cat food. The price tags are also genuine, but there is one difference: all the packages are empty. Several times a day the gallery team has to refill the shelves because the sham packages are bought in bagfuls. An empty spirits bottle can be had for two dollars. A lolly ice with or without a stick costs a couple of cents. Cheap art, light and devoid of content. They love it.

Brush fire

The low dollar exchange rate and the real estate financial crisis have not had any serious negative effect on the art market. The Berlin gallery „Contemporary Fine Arts", for example, has just sold a large painting of the Scottish painter Peter Doig. „Cricket", as it is called, is an argument in congealed oil for buying art. The painting is less than ten years old and brightened up an apartment in an old building owned by a Berlin private collector. It had once cost 25,000 British pounds when the gallerist Nicole Hackert began going from door to door selling Doig paintings.

In the meantime the collectors have pushed the price of a Doig painting up to several millions at auctions, thus automatically increasing the insurance value of all the other Doigs, and that is the reason why the Berlin collector had to part with his painting. He simply could not meet the increased insurance fees any more. Instead the gallerist Nicole Hackert brings him the greater part of the sales return of two million euros – as a consolation for the now Doig-less apartment. Such stories circulate in the art market like brush fire.

Art at the dinner table

That is the price modern art has to pay: free and disconnected, rejecting all meaning and content, it has become the plaything of life style. Glamour, money and art melt together under the Florida sun to a single discipline. A „discussion of content scarcely takes place", Monika Sprüth of the Gallery Sprüth-Magers complains. Wrangling and jostling only happen when a celebrity turns up. Iggy Pop plays on the beach, Lou Reed shows his film, Dennis Hopper was there. For a while Paris Hilton blocks the service in the „Sultan" restaurant while the throng of photographers desperately wants to take a photo of this frighteningly delicate blonde in sunglasses with experience of prison as she bites into her sandwich. It could also be art. But nobody asks about that anyway.

Stern | 10. December 2007

The „unappetizing" aspect of this „event", which presents art, money and „glamour" together in such a concentrated form is a part of the official view of the „world-wide" most important art fair. It is a constellation which implicitly lives off its own importance to such a degree that the „shrill daughter" of the fair, the Art Basel Miami Beach, was only called to order after the champagne had all too evidently splashed around in the marketing department. The invitation *to write trash* is a part of the game and is constantly mentioned at the fair for the ears of all „critical" observers.

The purchasing side of the fair is presented by the management as a kind of *Oklahoma Land Run.* Everything has been sold out in the shortest possible time, only the best get the best works, business is „excellent", information on maximum prices is disseminated, although insiders know that the galleries inform „important" collectors in advance of their offers, that many works are reserved or even sold before the fair opens and that the original work is hardly relevant any longer. Even this truth, which is a downright imposition for the „genuine" art lover, cannot discard its anecdotal character. The same is true of the business conduct on the spot, the gatherings of directors, partners, staff and assistants, the „How much?" of possible customers, the asking prices of the galleries, the visiting cards of the buyers and potential buyers arranged on the tables, the immaculately dressed, good-looking „gallerinas", the gallerists in business-like dark suits, a selected public which makes the fair the biggest catwalk in Switzerland, because the VIPs choose their outfits especially for their appearance at the fair. All of this contradicts the customs associated with the „true" enjoyment of art and presents a scenery which is an invitation to the „well-informed" journalists to peddle trash, which can, however, scarcely avoid expressing *moral connotations.* The Vanity Fair in Basel is for its „vain" participants only a question of the right dress, but for the „art lover" it is a fundamental issue.

The fact that this development can be seen directly in the conduct of the fair is the first and final test. The Art Basel is an economic enterprise; its „partners" are present every-where; the logo of the main sponsor, the Swiss big bank UBS, is positioned over the en-trance. AXA, Davidoff, Netjets, Audemars Piguet, Absolut, Baloise Group, BMW, Ruinart, Arvi, Freeports are present, as are the partners from the media, the Financial Times, Neue Zürcher Zeitung, Basler Zeitung and Le Temps. They ensure the broad-scale media publicity without which such a big event cannot exist. The moral indignation in view of this connubium of art and money could scarcely be more total. And nonetheless, with this view, it factually and repeatedly escorts the logic of the importance of the marketing machinery.

The Rules of Art

A perspectivist agenda

It does not call for any pronounced resentment to identify the account of the fair itself and of its organizers and makers as soapbox oratory. It is a part of the „business", a part of the game. The ultimately empty assertions of the singular status and unique significance of the event, of a *collective excitement,* whose deliberate and thoroughly rationalized marketing is accompanied by marketing agencies, represent a permanent striving for self-authentication. It is all a façade, a ringing of bells at the start and end of an event conventionalized as a „High Mass", which asserts its „sacred" significance through a totally worldly baroque, the ornamentation of its „profane" significance.

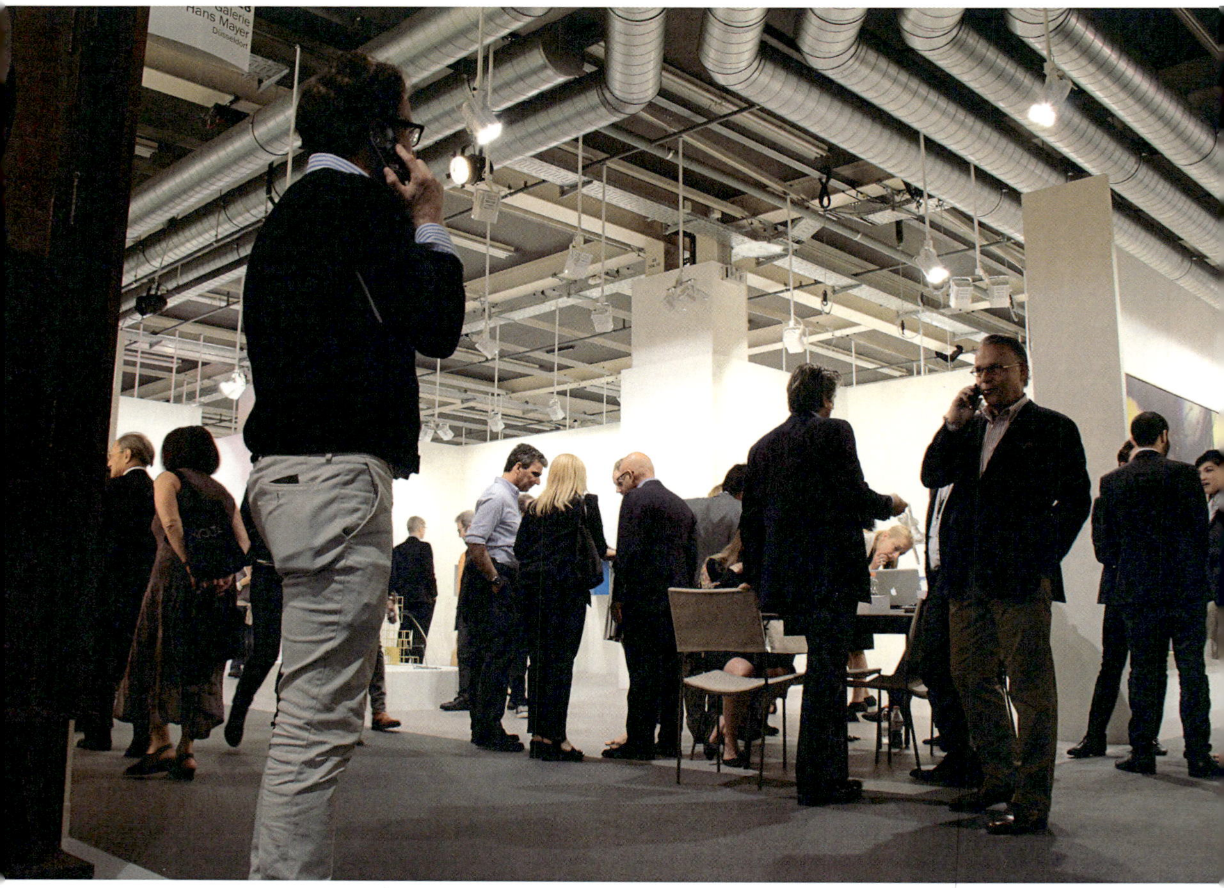
Galerie
Hans Mayer
Düsseldorf

A glance behind this façade is all the more contradictory. As soon as one approaches the Art Basel with the critical partiality of an observer who is close to the game, who is „inwardly" involved, when one listens to what he sees and above all to how he reports on it, one repeatedly encounters a similarly structured semantics. On the one hand are the „facts" which were and are created by the fair itself, in which the *representations* of the event are mixed with *self-presentations*. On the other hand, however, in the depiction of these „facts" in the feuilletons a *moral distancing* comes through, never explicit, ironically refracted, but nonetheless palpable: the *dégout*.

This „second", this critical gaze, takes a closer look, sees the reality beyond the official pronouncements. But it too only comprehends the surface of that „superficiality" which lends the event its social significance. And it is difficult to deny that this standpoint is already a part of the „official" narration. For the criticism of the event not only contributes an indispensable kind of reputation to it by making it the object of repeatedly demanded „controversial" opinions and stances. It also helps to keep alive a discourse which at the same time systematically conceals the *social preconditions* for the game, both the conditions for the possibility of participation in it and the foundations of the perspective on the game itself.

The belief in the „intrinsic value", its significance and interpretative power, which it is worth arguing over, necessarily facilitates the forgetting of these preconditions. When, therefore, the reality of the *structure of the art field,* the „rules of art", can only be articulated in *value judgments,* mostly disguised as anecdotes, story-telling and clichés, one is far from a genuine understanding of the laws to which both the enthusiasm and the disgust in the face of this event are owed [2].

For this reason the visible prejudices towards a „fair" for art, and particularly towards the Art Basel as one of the most important, and the accounts resulting from them can only be understood when they are grasped *as such*. Not the content is decisive, but the *form of the contradictions* which are elicited. They are both the expression of a systematic contraposition of „art" and „world" which pervades the entire art world and of a personal position within this strangely distant galaxy, which nonetheless draws attention in a particular way to a social universe apparently so remote from everyday life.

The Art Basel only illuminates a small segment of this „art world". But it is a segment which helps to decode its laws, its contradictions and also its upheavals not least because it lies on one of the central intersections of „art" and „world", even epitomizes them, and *represents* them in a twofold sense. And only the „third view", the view of the *perspectivity* of the judgment on this relationship, shows the way to an understanding beyond the storytelling.

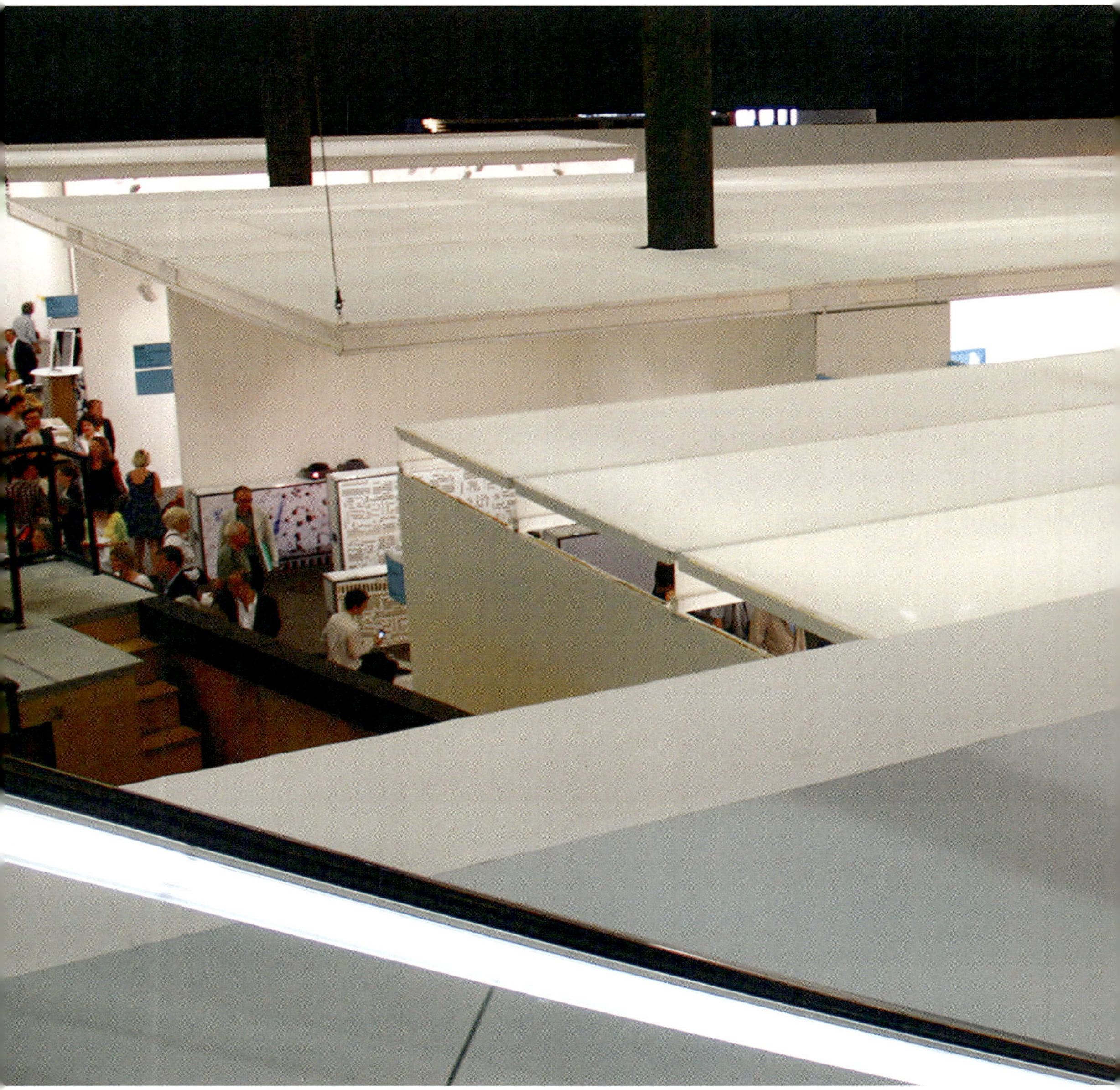

2 The Market and the Brand

Art fairs, an „Olympics“, and its athletes

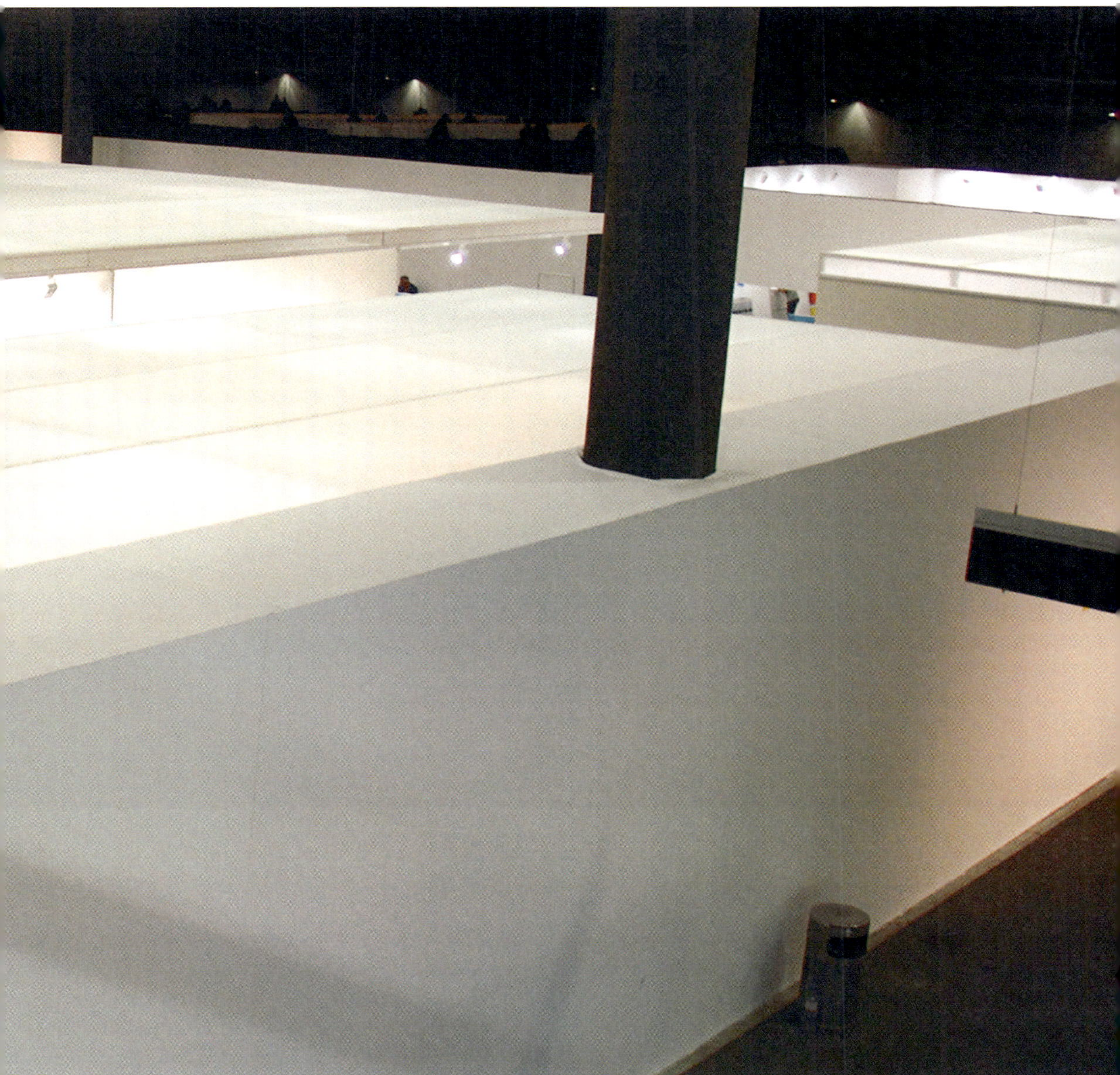

A commerce in things which are not commercial, the trade in „pure" art belongs to the class of practices where the logic of precapitalist economy survives. The challenge that they offer to all kinds of economism resides precisely in the fact that they can be achieved in practice – and not merely in representations – only at the price of a constant and collective repression of the properly „economic" interest.

PIERRE BOURDIEU, The Rules of Art

If the Art Basel is not only one of the highlights of the art world but also characterizes one of its crossroads, if it is an event which is *controversial* in the literal sense and provokes the articulation of *opposites,* this is due to a norm of the art field that is never really, never expressly articulated. This norm states that „art“ and „world“ and, above all „art“ and „money“ are quite simply incompatible and must remain so in order to maintain the powerful *nimbus* which lends a truly „sacred“ meaning to works of art in the Western world in the modern period. The „art fair“, an institution which is at least new in its historical dimensions, tangibly challenges this norm while living, nonetheless, off the prestige deriving from it. The attempt undertaken at the fair if not to „reconcile“ the fundamental opposition of „art“ and „world“ then at least to „pacify“ it for a week is in every respect an exemplary phenomenon illustrating the way an economy functions which deals with *symbolic goods*. But it also bears witness to the profound upheaval in the underlying „political“ economy of art, to the dissolution of its previous configurations. In the international art fairs the former social exclusivity of the intimate procedures governing the exchange between art and money, between atelier, gallery and bourgeoisie, is abandoned; the power of the public institutions to consecrate artistic work, the interpretative monopoly of the museums, is eroded and the new „art market“, the global fairs and auctions, enters into competition with them in regard to the evaluation of „legitimate“ art – and of its monetary price.

For exactly this reason the tensions in this relationship remain. If one asks the participating actors, fair organizers, collectors, gallerists and art dealers, their answers reveal a permanent *competition between conflicting narrations.* On the one hand the importance of the fair for the „vitality“ of the contemporary mediation of art with positive effects on art production is emphasized. On the other hand one is snowed under with critical judgments of the all too visible and tangible commercialization of art with its tendency towards „uniformization“ and „banalization“. There is widespread agreement among all the actors that attendance at this „event“ is in effect compulsory. The competitions between the narrations here yields place to competition for participation, for „accreditation“ by the galleries, for the symbolic credit it brings, for the location and size of the exhibition booth. And the VIPs compete for the best possible positions in the various VIP categories, which are a clear sign of social classification. These are the characteristic ambivalences of an art market whose attractiveness depends on the magic of the reciprocal recognition of art and its consumers and on the renegotiation of the relationships of power between them.

From the exchange to the market

Art fairs as a phenomenon of delayed modernization

Nowadays art fairs play a central role in the art market, especially in regard to contemporary art. In the course of the boom in fairs since the turn of the century they have grown into one of the most important distribution and marketing channels for art dealers and gallerists. It is no secret that this side of the art trade today already achieves more than a third of its returns at art fairs [1]. No other form of distribution offers the art-interested clientele a better opportunity to see and buy a broad range of works of art with an efficient expenditure of time and money. In view of the great attractive power and commercial success of this segment of the market numerous media reports have already proclaimed „the decade of the art fairs".

Whereas in 1970 there were only three art fairs (Cologne, Basel, Brussels) and seven in 1980 (Cologne, Basel, Brussels, Bologna, Chicago, Paris and Maastricht), the number doubled by 1990 to fourteen fairs and in the year 2000 there were more than thirty [2]. The foundation of new art fairs then increased rapidly world-wide. For the year 2012 the art market data bank Artfacts listed 216 important art fairs. At each of these fairs between 50 and 300 gallerists exhibited a total of up to 6,000 works of art.

The new institution of the art fair established itself very quickly as a periodic art market and a secondary facility for galleries and art dealers alongside their primary art business. This development is directly linked to the massive spread of the art system, to the dynamic expansion of the art market, to the significant change in the social status of contemporary art and its increasing popularization by the media and established art institutions such as museums or temporary exhibitions. Art fairs seem to follow a direct commercial logic and thus become a „symbol for the private marketing of art; they are a token of the marketing business and the marketing of art" [3].

In the meantime a three-stage system of fairs has developed with different geographical locations, ranges and perceptions, which to a certain degree reflects the development of the art market and is, now as before, dominated by galleries and art dealers from the West (USA, Europe). Whereas at the lowest level a rapidly growing number of art fairs mostly with regional, interregional and national drawing power and influence are spreading out, at the middle level a small number of fairs has crystallized which, supported by a strong anchorage at the national level, include geographically neighboring and culturally related regions and are increasingly establishing international connections. These include, above all, established fairs in Europe and North America such as the Art Cologne, Foire internationale d'art contemporain (FIAC Paris), Armory Show (New York) or the Arte Contemporaneo (ARCO Madrid). Since the beginning of the 21st century newer fairs in emerging areas of the world have joined this circle such as the Maco México Contemporaneo (Mexico City), Shanghai Contemporary Art Fair, Art Singapore, Art Dubai International Fair or the India Art Fair (New Delhi). At the peak of the relatively new institution of the art fair a handful of big events established themselves with brand names of their own alongside the renowned biennials in Venice and Kassel: the Art Basel (Basel, Miami Beach, Hong Kong), the Frieze Art Fair (London, New York) and the Tefaf (Maastricht). They recruit their potential primarily from the national diversity of the exhibitors who in turn represent the most important galleries and dealers from the countries with big national art markets.

The sustained success of these flagships among the international art fairs results from several factors. They have a personal, unmistakable profile, offer a broad spectrum of works, rely on high quality standards of the galleries, artists and works of art, conduct professional marketing and strengthen their attractiveness by offering a series of accompanying events, which additionally underline the event and happening character of the fairs. With the special help of a supporting program and public presentations such as, for example, the *Art Parcours* of the Art Basel with a curated show of installations, sculptures and performances in the old town of Basel, the big fairs also position themselves as organizers and promoters of culture, thereby ennobling the market character of the art fairs. This aspect, which is important in terms of public attention, is further underpinned by an attempt of the organizers to upgrade the art fair by means of PR work as a „temporary art exhibition". In addition they have often been the first to risk the leap into new regions of the world, as, for example, the Art Basel has done with its expansion to Miami Beach in order to establish contacts with the South American area.

The function of art fairs is thus not restricted to commercial business transactions. They also serve as a popular meeting point for the actors in the field of art such as collectors, representatives of museums, curators or art critics. In addition they offer enterprises outside the art market an attractive basis for sponsoring, co-branding and PR activities. Important art fairs are thus both a market place and a meeting point. This function as both a market and a meeting place is described by the director of the Art Basel as fol-lows: *„We are a platform for promoting art (...) there is the market place and there is the meeting place. The market place is the people selling in the halls. The meeting place is all the people who are not actually doing any commercial transactions. They are not selling and they are not buying, but what they are here to do is discover new artists, especially in the sectors where we have the younger artists like Art Positions in Miami, like Art Statements in Basel, and to discover each other, you know..."*

These „top fairs", which are regarded in the professional world and in the media as the „best" and most important of their kind evidently have an attraction for the same clientele: the most important collectors, the most respected curators, museum directors, art consultants and art critics. They all come because the others will also be there. As a result of such direct and indirect networking effects all the actors expect participation to be increasingly useful for them and in consequence a kind of monopoly position of the top fairs develops. Art fairs thus represent and reproduce a new stage in the activation and mobilization of the inner circle of the art world. The leading international art fairs in particular have in the past few years become not only „VIP meetings" but also popular „art events".

This phenomenon of „eventization", where the meeting of the art world itself becomes an important cultural and social event and the insiders have an opportunity to put them-selves on show, is relatively new and directly linked to contemporary art. It is not re-stricted to the big top fairs but can also be encountered at international biennials and „blockbuster" exhibitions. But the international art fairs, above all, provide the stage for new processes of integration of a global elite which achieves its highest degree of visibility at the intersection point of „art" and „money".

Art fairs and art markets

Secularization tendencies in dealings with holy goods

Commercial art fairs have a long tradition, although their current form of presentation only entered the scene with the rise of contemporary art in the 1960s and 1970s [4]. As elite shows for the fine arts and sales events for arts and crafts their origins can be traced back to the world exhibitions in London and Paris in the middle of the 19th century. As early as 1913 the first „Armory Exhibition" took place, an international exhibition for the art of the modern period which had a profound influence on the art world of the time and was at the same time a milestone in the development of the growing market for modern art.

The „Kunstmarkt 67" held in September 1967 in Cologne is, however, regarded as the hour of birth of art fairs focusing on contemporary art. More than 15,000 visitors attended the fair, at which 18 galleries exhibited more than 600 works of art [5]. In contrast to big exhibitions such as the first Documenta in Kassel in 1957 the works could be bought directly at the fair and the exhibits were accordingly furnished with prices.

In Basel the art dealers Ernst Beyeler, Trudl Bruckner, Balz Hilt and Herbert Cahn took up this idea of an art fair and founded the Art Basel, which took place for the first time in 1970. Ninety galleries participated in the fair, which attracted over 10,000 visitors. The organizers anticipated the weaknesses of the „Kunstmarkt 67" and implemented a concept of the fair which was from the start internationally oriented. This is one of the reasons why the Art Basel was able to establish itself so firmly and to push the competition from Cologne into the background in spite of calls for a boycott by German gallerists.

Both fairs marked the transition from discreet art dealing to staged events. As new institutions they were the starting point for an aggressive marketing of art by galleries and the private art sector. This represented a break with the hitherto customary sales transactions, which were carried out discreetly and non-publicly in the galleries and the houses of the art dealers. Of course the treatment of art as a commercial trading commodity like any other gave rise to massive criticism [6]. The organizers were repeatedly accused of bringing art to the market place.

But the positive effects, not only for art dealing, are unmistakable to this day. Art fairs serve as a platform for the galleries and are popular meeting points for the actors from the art field, who can use them to extend and to cultivate their networks. Fairs make it easier to acquire an overview of what is on offer on the art market. The temporal and spatial concentration of galleries and actors in one location facilitates the flow of supply and demand and reduces the inefficiency which can result from the geographic spread and decentralization of the market. Fairs thus strengthen the art trade as a whole – not least in the competition with the increasingly powerful auction houses and the steeply rising number of their private sales.

A further central aspect must be mentioned: participation in fairs abroad enables the galleries to leave the limited national market and to open up new markets. This „internationalization" of business practices is advantageous, above all, for the galleries which represent and have in part helped to establish artists who are in demand abroad. By participation in the fairs these artists can be directly presented and marketed on the foreign markets and must no longer be handed over to competitors or promoted by cooperation partners. However, only a small group of successful galleries profit directly from the structural change in the national markets triggered off by the international boom in fairs. These galleries have the corresponding „export" strategies and can afford to participate in an elaborate and cost-intensive fairs marathon around the globe. In view of the stagnating and in part even diminishing domestic demand in many countries the internationalization of business has become a vital requirement for artistic and commercial success, and the great majority of the galleries fail to meet the challenge and fall by the wayside.

The influence of the art fairs extends far beyond the gallery system. In particular, the event character of the fairs ensures a correspondingly wide appeal in the public sphere and among the art-interested public. Art fairs have not only helped to reduce the inhibitions about visiting galleries and to break down at least to some extent the exclusiveness of the art trade, but have also made an important contribution to the popularization of contemporary art.

In order to profit commercially from the broad public interest in contemporary art associated with the rise of pop art and promoted, above all, by the mass media, the art trade sought for suitable sales strategies and forms of communication. The art fairs quickly proved to be a suitable instrument, which led to a growing interest of the galleries in participation in the fairs and to the establishment of new fairs. Alongside the auction houses the fairs became a driving force behind the impressive growth of the (mass) market for art and, at the same time, for its visible representation. The institutionalization of the art fairs is thus also the result of an important transformation process in the art trade, which had been triggered off by the emerging upheaval of the art system in the 1960s and 1970s. This process ended with the establishment of a further distribution form for the art trade alongside the gallery system.

The radical transformation of the distributional paths and forms was accompanied by a growth in demand arising from the entry of new buyers and collectors into the market The rapid expansion of the art market, above all since the 1980s (with the exception of a brief interruption at the beginning of the 1990s) is not a singular phenomenon but the result of complex relationships in the art field. It is strongly linked to the perception of contemporary art as an object of investment and speculation.

The business policies of the auction houses have also undergone a fundamental change in the last forty years. Driven forward by the popularization of so-called pop art and other new currents in art the big international auction houses entered the business with contemporary art on a massive scale in the 1970s and attracted a group of new and partly inexperienced collectors and customers. Formerly the clientele of the auction houses had consisted for a long time of private art dealers, gallerists and a few institutional buyers. But in the 1980s they systematically opened up the segment of private customers and thus initiated a shift from wholesale to individual trading in art [7], which ultimately led to direct competition with the established gallery system. The gallery scene had also grown rapidly as a result of the increased popularity of contemporary art, but it was now confronted with a serious competitor. Above all the private art dealers active on the secondary market lost their monopoly over the buying and selling of contemporary art, but the galleries as well, which were active on both the primary and the secondary market, began to feel the growing power of the auction houses.

For the private art dealers art fairs turned out to be an effective instrument in the struggle against Christie's, Sotheby's and smaller auctioneers. The promotion of this sales platform enabled the galleries and art dealers to open up their limited classical distribution paths in which trading in art still had the character of direct negotiation and avoided the public eye. The importance of the art fair as a highly visible platform for sales and the cultivation of contacts also served to strengthen its institutional power. As early as the mid-1970s reports appear in the media which equate participation in fairs with the visibility of galleries. Those who do not participate in fairs fail to do so for artistic or financial reasons.

These developments make one point quite clear: the market has established itself in the art field. It is a market of a modern kind, which pushes the autochtonous exchange processes of the old art system further into the background, forces them into new constellations, impels their rationalization as continuous and ubiquitous forms of socialization, and thus ultimately triggers off those secularization tendencies with which the art world today is confronted. The rationalized public nature of the exchange of art into money reveals this relationship for what it is and so questions the gravitational center of an economy of symbolic goods whose existence fundamentally depended on the denial of this relationship.

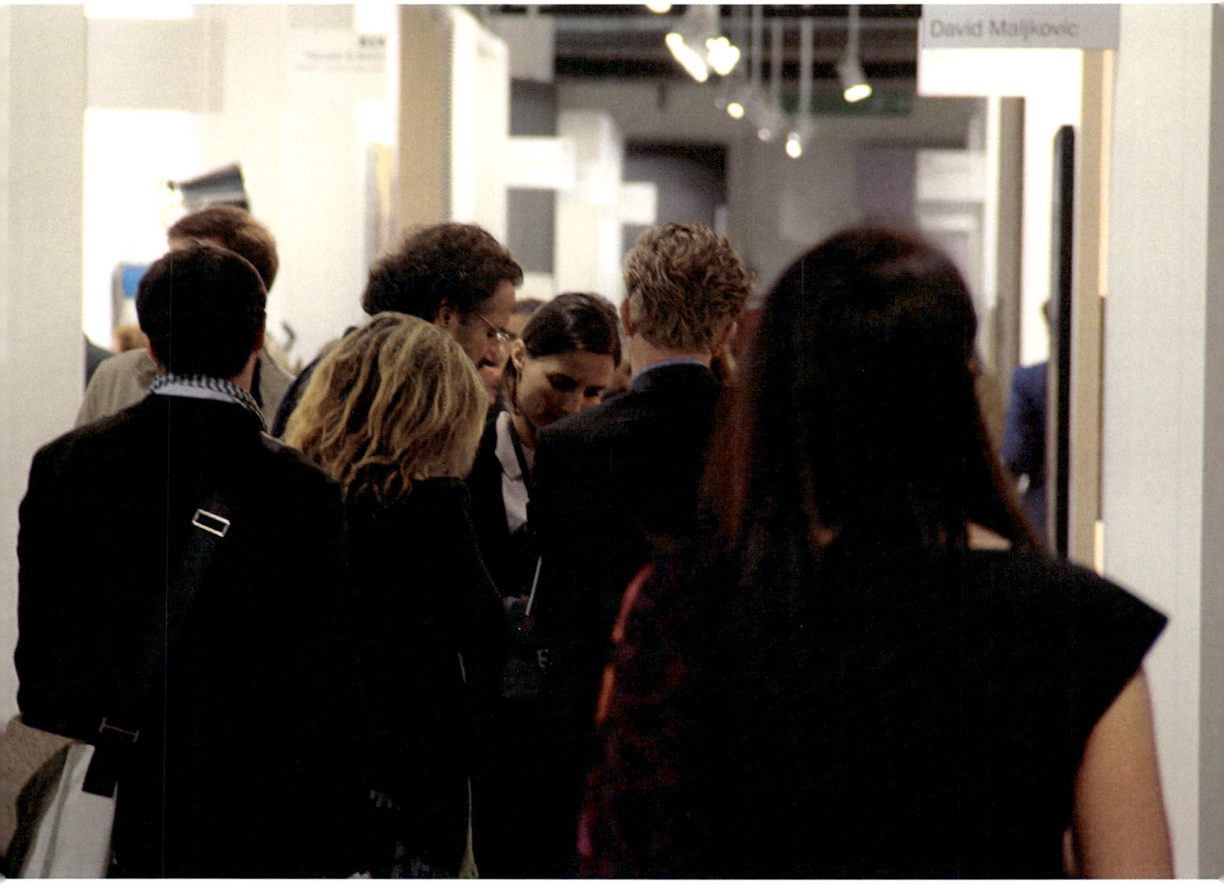
David Maljkovic

In the course of „globalization“ the art fairs are at the moment experiencing a further fundamental transformation. On the one hand the number of art fairs and similar sales and exhibition formats with mostly regional, national or local sphere of influence is grow-ing strongly, and on the other hand the three big established art fairs the Art Basel, Frieze and Tefaf are pursuing an intensive strategy of expansion and diversification. A decade ago the Art Basel established a second foothold in Miami Beach in order to cover the North and South American fields. Frieze London opened an offshoot of its fair in New York for the first time in 2012. With the growing success of the Art Basel Miami Beach the traditional Armory Show in New York lost ground and was increasingly avoided by the New York galleries. After the opening of Frieze in New York it was faced with closure. The opening of Frieze Masters parallel to Frieze London in October 2012 covered a new segment, the market for old masters and antiques, which had formerly been the preserve of the Maastricht art fair Tefaf.

Art Basel (I)

An „Olympics of the Art World“

The Art Basel, which takes place annually in June in the third largest city in Switzerland, is a fair of the superlatives. In 2014 285 galleries from 34 countries presented over 4,000 artists in an area of 30,000 square meters, and attracted 92,000 visitors, including important collectors, the representatives of 70 museums and numerous artists from all over the world [8]. The New York Times has characterized the fair as the „Olympics of the Art World".

The Art Basel not only presents itself with the self-declared claim to be the „primary show“ in the ranking of international fairs after forty years of existence but also to present the art of the 20th and 21st centuries „with a strong curatorial perspective.“ With numerous sectors and supporting programs it has succeeded in Basel in further increasing the attractiveness of the fair. As early as 1979 a platform called „New Tendencies“ was created for solo shows of less well-known artists, which was later replaced by a sector for young galleries with young artists and finally, in 1996, by *Art Statements,* at which selected young galleries present individual exhibitions with young artists at reduced stand prices – a program promoting the international recognition of young new talents. Since 2002 the Art Basel has reserved a special area, the *Art Unlimited,* for a curated exhibition of installations, large sculptures and paintings and video and performance art. In addition there are film and video presentations, rounds of talks, and, since 2010, a public *Art Parcours* in the historical neighborhood of the fair.

The attractiveness of the fair has even increased after rejected applicants came together after 1996 to organize an exhibition in the immediate neighborhood, the so-called „Liste 2000". The Liste does not, however, see itself as a protest event, but as a rehearsal stage for young galleries with the distant goal of participating in the Art Basel. In the meantime the number of satellite fairs around the Art Basel has grown to seven.

As a result of the great success of the Art Basel a North American offshoot was initiated in December 2002: the Art Basel Miami Beach. The realization of this project gave numerous galleries in Europe access to the markets in the USA and South America. In the summer of 2011 the MCH Group AG, the sponsor of the Art Basel, acquired 60% of the shares in the Asian Art Fairs Ltd, the organizer of the art fair Art Hong Kong. At the end of May 2013 the fair opened for the first time under the direction of the Art Basel.

The expansion of the Art Basel to Hong Kong was the next step in the expansion and diversification strategy of the big fairs. In analogy to the international auction houses and the big galleries the big fairs in the meantime operate like transnationally oriented enterprises. Like Sotheby's and Christie's the Art Basel and Frieze stand as big brands at the pinnacle of the art market. This branding potential makes art fairs, biennials, museums or big exhibitions important locational factors in the international competition between cultural metropolises and lends these locations the corresponding creative, fashionable and international flair.

Art Basel (II)
The way to a „global art event"

The foundation of the fair in Basel in 1970 was preceded by numerous discussions within a small group of Basel art dealers and gallerists who had to find ways of dealing with poor business, difficult customs conditions, the growing concentration of the art trade in Zurich and the developments in the neighboring countries, above all in Germany [9]. The first art fair in Cologne in 1967 and a planned fair in Stuttgart finally persuaded them to set up an art fair of their own in Basel. In contrast to their colleagues in Cologne who wanted to exhibit only „progressive" art, the Basel fair committee decided in favor of openness in regard to the number of participants, the participation of international galleries and the works to be offered at the fair. An extension involving the inclusion of antiques failed on account of the resistance of the Swiss Association of Dealers in Art and Antiques. But the opportunity to exhibit and to sell artistic positions outside the contemporary avant-garde attracted many galleries and art dealers – and precisely those who had been rejected in Cologne. At that time already the classical modern period was one of the focal points of the fair. The international contacts of the Basel art dealer Ernst Beyeler, who was at first critical about the prospects of a fair in Basel, increased the interest of galleries and collectors in Switzerland and abroad.

A hundred and ten galleries and art book publishers from ten countries participated in the first Art 70, within the context of the Basel Trade Fair. The largest contingent of exhibitors came from Germany (45), followed by Switzerland with 40 exhibitors, France with eleven, five from Italy, three from Great Britain and one from the USA. The British Marlborough Gallery, which was already internationally active at this time, had the largest booth. This already reveals the way in which economic and symbolic power are reflected in the topographical arrangement of the fair. In the following years the presence of important American gallerists such as Leo Castelli (who had also been represented in Cologne) and Sidney Janis enhanced the international reputation of the fair, which soon came to be a flagship of the parent exhibition company alongside the international trade fair for watches and jewelry. The Art Basel had already achieved its breakthrough by the middle of the 1970s; the institution of the art fair had been definitively established.

Public interest in the first Art Basel disappointed the expectations of the organizers. There were only around 10,000 visitors in comparison to around 40,000 guests at the 1970 art fair in Cologne. But the strength of the Art Basel rested above all on its concept of the „open market". As the fair was open to all art dealers as exhibitors the number of participants increased rapidly after the partially successful boycott of the Cologne fair in 1971. As early as 1973 lack of space forced the organizers to turn down the applications of numerous galleries. In the sixth year after its foundation it achieved its present size with 300 galleries. Special shows and additional supporting programs ensured good publicity and positive reporting in the media and, in consequence, increased interest in the public sphere. In this way the character of a pure sales event was concealed and the Art Basel acquired the appearance of an imposing „art show" of the 20th century. It became a „global art event", as the years-long director Sam Keller once said [10].

Processes of concentration and effects of accumulation

An „open" market, the new market forces, their branded commodities

The boom in fairs is directly associated with the rapid rise and success of the art market which, after a sudden collapse at the beginning of the 1990s, was substantially restructured and succeeded in regenerating and stabilizing itself. The subsequent strong growth in the number of art fairs led to a clear increase in the competition between the organizers who vied for the custom of well-known and potent collectors and exhibitors. This development was particularly marked in the middle segment which could not keep up with the successful „flagships" and large-scale fairs at the top end of the market. Many of the newly founded fairs soon experienced a creeping decline and were replaced after a few years by new constructions and formats. Even established fairs such as the Armory Show, Arco or Art Brussels are in the meantime undergoing a crisis and the venerable Art Chicago even had to close in 2012 after 31 years on the market.

In view of the hard competitive struggles between the fairs only those can succeed which create an unmistakable profile, attract established galleries and emanate some amount of event glamour. The strong competition of most of the fairs in the field of contemporary art also turns out to be an economic risk. For, like the Art Basel, the most successful fairs not only exhibit contemporary art but also the art of the 20th century. Other big fairs have followed the example of Basel and diversified the range of the products they have to offer. Tefaf, for example, first entered the segment of contemporary art and then extended its already broad spectrum to include the decorative art of the 20th century and works on paper. The Armory Show added a modern section and the Frieze established a parallel fair for classical and modern art, The Frieze Masters, in 2012.

The art fairs are of pre-eminent importance above all for the galleries. By participating in fairs of differing international character and prestige the galleries and art dealers can extend their geographical range beyond their regional and national terrain and achieve access to the transnational art markets. This possibility was formerly blocked by large and could only be opened up by cooperation with other galleries. As a result of the change a substantial part of the turnover of the art market today is generated at fairs.

The rise of the art fairs, which can definitely be seen as a reaction and a defensive battle against the auction houses, subjected the business models and practices of the galleries and art dealers to a radical transformation process: „Fairs now both drive the market and restructure it" [11]. As the number of fairs grew the galleries came under increasing pressure to change their business practices and to achieve increased international attention for their artists, so that they could extend the relatively small circle of their national or regional regular customers. As the important actors in the art market such as the collectors, museum directors or curators who, alongside the art market, decisively influence the „value" of art, are more likely to be encountered at fairs than in galleries, participation in the fairs becomes increasingly more important for the galleries and art dealers for more than purely economic reasons. A large part of the trade in art has long left the traditional local premises in the galleries in the direction of the market place. As many galleries also regard participation in renowned fairs as an investment in their own reputation, the pressure increases. Galleries in the middle segment, above all, find that the business has in the meantime become tough and even some of better known names have withdrawn from it.

The steady establishment of new fairs is a growing cause for concern in the gallery system. Both the marathon of venues and the economic returns are often critically questioned. The steep increase in the costs involved in attending fairs is accompanied by only a very slight or by no increase in the sales revenues. In addition, although the galleries attend fairs over a period of several years, it is not necessarily the case that they will meet old customers or acquire new ones. But because, in the premier league of the fairs, not only economic profit but also opportunities for communication and cooperation and, above all, for symbolic returns in the shape of a growth in prestige play an important role, the galleries participate in fairs even when the economic returns do not cover their costs.

These processes of concentration result at the same time in a striking uniformization of the products on offer – „fairs art" is transformed into „branded goods". The driving forces behind this development are not difficult to discern. As in the entire art market „quality" is also a key category for art fairs. In markets for symbolic goods, however, there are no precise or objective criteria for the judgment of a valuable product, in regard to either the aesthetic or the financial aspects [12]. Instead, the value of a work of art is constructed in a social process by the actors in the market. This presents the fairs with difficult tasks. In contrast to the situation in consumer or industry fairs, the quality of an art fair is primarily defined by a sometimes extremely tough selection process. Because not all the galleries which apply can be accepted as exhibitors, a selection must be made in accordance with some kind of „quality" criteria – no matter how they are determined. This is one reason why the number of art fairs is increasing so rapidly. Rejected galleries turn to other fairs, for which they are accepted, and this again persuades the organizers of fairs and their investors to found further art fairs at new locations. Art fairs cannot „grow"; they can only multiply because they increasingly marginalize the gallery system as a no longer adequate form of marketing, and so further strengthen their attractive power for gallerists and artists. These are expropriation processes undertaken by a new dominant power founded on a changed „constellation of interests".

According to this logic of „quality", the fair organizations and their selection committees or the curators they appoint are always concerned to discover those galleries which meet their high quality standards. Consequently the quality of the dealer stands at the center of the selection process and is then transferred to the artists and works they select. The juries of the international big fairs take their orientations from the „branded galleries" who impress them not only with their symbolic capital but also with their marketing power. Galleries which enjoy the highest degree of legitimacy in this segment of the art market are also sacrosanct. In their social trajectory the „branded galleries" have accumulated such a high degree of symbolic capital that the Art Basel cannot afford to refuse them permission to participate in the fair. The galleries for their part wish to participate in fairs with the highest profile and the greatest prestige. For them participation in premium fairs is a sign of quality, which brings them distinction in the field of galleries, a distinction which they must prove themselves worthy every year by presenting artists and works of art of the highest level.

As a practical consequence of this recruitment and admission procedure a tendency towards homogenization and leveling out has developed in the individual fairs, whereby the status of the galleries and their artists corresponds to the status of the fairs themselves. To put it in other words: the stronger the similarities between the status of the fairs, the status of the galleries and the status of the artists are, the more homogenous the field of the fairs, the participating galleries and the exhibited artists is [13].

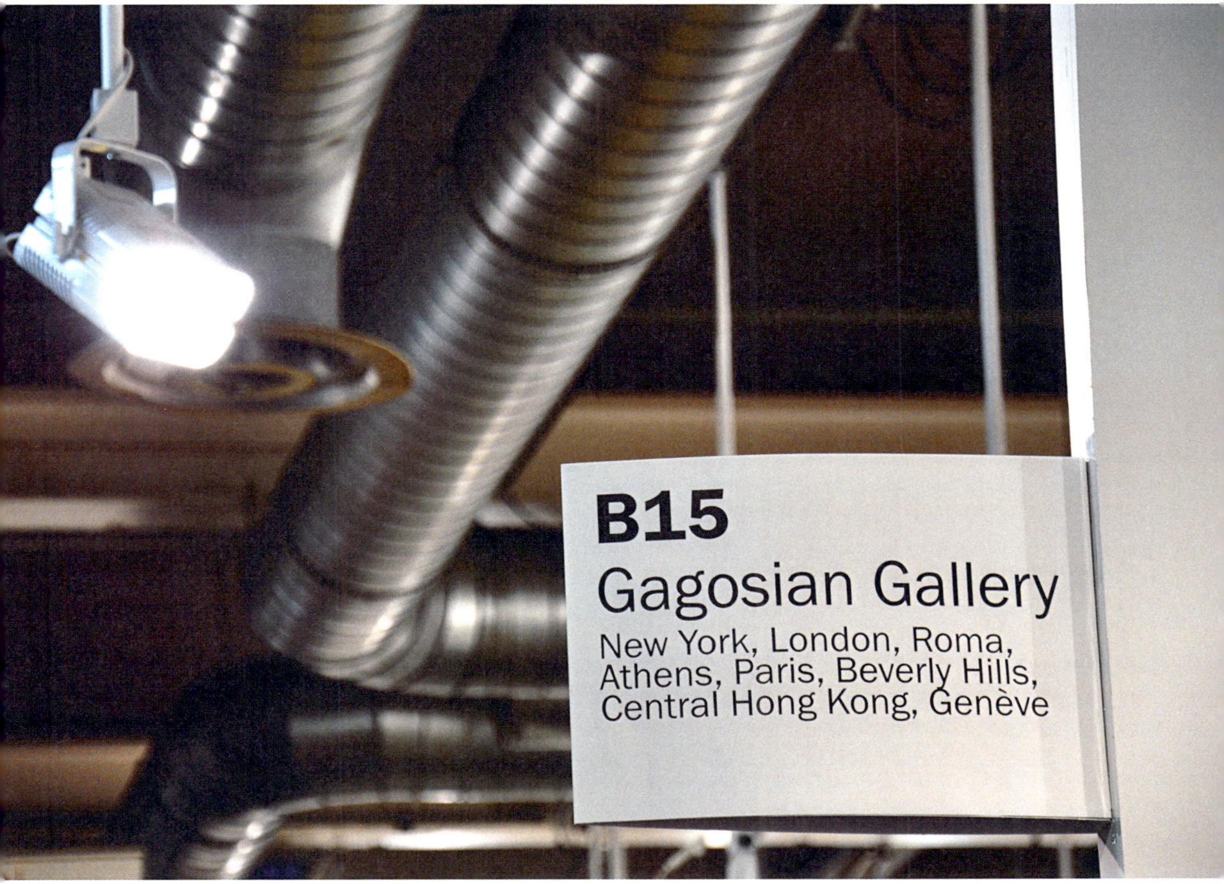
B15
Gagosian Gallery
New York, London, Roma, Athens, Paris, Beverly Hills, Central Hong Kong, Genève

The Market and its Makers
Channeling the supply at the Art Basel

Because it strongly regulates the access to its highly prestigious and highly visible „market place", the Art Basel itself has become an instance of consecration in the global struggle for symbolic recognition in the field of art. Participation in the fair guarantees „quality" and brings both symbolic and immediate economic profit. The Art Basel determines the image of the fair and its structure; it decides which galleries from which geographical and artistic backgrounds can offer their goods. At the same time the choice of the galleries determines which artistic goods are on offer. The competition for the 300 places is correspondingly fierce. Over 1,000 galleries apply every year, most of them in vain. The fact that the galleries cannot buy a place in the market but are selected reveals the special character of this market. It follows the logic of an „anti-economic economy" [14]. The galleries pay different fees for participation depending on the size of their sales booths. But whether they are admitted or not is not decided by the price they are willing to pay but by their social position in the art field and their reputation. To this extent the remark „the fair display has to be considered a way of curating" [15] is accurate. The fair does not directly reflect the global art market.

The decision as to which galleries can offer their goods for sale at one of the most important art fairs in the world and the choice of the artistic works which make up this offer lies in the hands of a small group of people. Their selection decides who can make an economic profit and has a realistic chance of participating again in the following year and who has only one, possibly squandered chance of participating. One of the members of the committee is fully aware of the power accompanying its special status: *„What we do is we start at one part of a section; so we start at 8:30, and we finish a bit before 11:00. We try to look at everything so that when we have our committee meetings we can really have a discussion, and we can say, ‚This person did a really a fantastic job. That was good.' There are some photos taken of each booth so that we can substantiate our situation. It is such a serious thing, because if a gallery, for some reason, was not wished back in a year, it is such a major thing for them."* The small circle of persons consists of two groups: firstly the staff of the fair, the Show Management, who develops the concept of the fair and specifies the „big picture", and secondly the so-called „Art Basel Committee" consisting of five or six gallerists who regularly participate in the fair. The members of this selection committee are chosen „on the basis of their integrity and expertise", according to the official statement of the Art Basel. They choose the participating galleries from a pool of applicants according to criteria which are not precisely defined. A small number of galleries decides, therefore, on which of their competitors are allowed to participate in the fair at all.

At the same time the selection criteria create the institutional framework within which the competition of the galleries for free places takes place. As the most important criterion for the selection of the gallerists the concept of „quality" is always mentioned, both in the interviews and in the „exhibition regulations" of the fair, which speaks of the „quality and dynamism of the gallery's work with the artists represented" as a decisive criterion. In the interviews the concept of quality refers predominantly to the works of art themselves. They mention the „quality of the exhibits" or the „quality, niveau and density of the artistic quality". But the galleries themselves must also meet the highest standards. A member of the Show Manage-ment goes into detail: *„Well it's clear that quality is actually... well the committee goes around regularly... It's called upon to do so; and we document it on our side. If, for example, a booth is badly arranged or presented. So that one says that there are different ways of hanging up pictures, be it in a museum or a gallery, that is to say the museum way or a free way. Or, for example, if someone only brings* *sculptures and no wall paintings so that it actually... or perhaps only one artist. That a gallery exposes itself and makes a solo show, which under certain circumstances can even be super. It can also be something that people find less interesting or perhaps even judge critically. In the case of many galleries it occurs over the years. One can tell how active a gallery is, if it has artists who really produce every year. Then there is always something new and good in the booth. If someone only attends the fair with his stocks, you notice it, don't you, after three or four years, simply that it has thinned out a bit, that new supplies are lacking."*

But an exact definition of what makes up the „quality" of a work of art is not usually given, for the „question of quality is difficult" as one art collector said in an interview. A member of the staff of the Art Basel also struggles with the concept: „It always sounds so stupid when I say it, but it's the quality that is decisive." The decisive point is that gallerists sit in the jury who enjoy a sufficiently high degree of recognition so that the other actors recognize their powers of definition. The Show Management lacks this kind of recognition. On this issue a director of the fair says: *„Well, it is always subjective by nature, it is art. There is no subjective, there is no objective, it is not, you know, this is not a marathon. You can't time it, you can't measure it, you know. So what you have to do is, you establish a selection committee. You want a selection committee which is knowledgeable, which is fair, which is well respected within the profession in the sense that people accept that these people will judge them, another people, and they set the quality, obviously, you know. We, our job is to create a process by which galleries are selected, but their job is to choose the galleries. And so the, I mean, the quality, I mean, there is another part of the job we have which is to make sure that all the galleries we want in the show are applying. You know, there is, I mean, recruitment process is the wrong way, the wrong way to say it, but I mean, I think, we, our job is to try to get, make sure that the selection pool is as deep and as strong as possible for the selection committee, because obviously they can't select a gallery that hasn't applied."*

Apart from the reference to the quality of the galleries and the exhibited works further important selection criteria do therefore come up. These include strategic considerations of the Show Management, which are hinted at in the „Exhibition Regulations". They speak of the „the competition for participation among galleries with a similar profile" on account of the „limited availability of booths". In order to achieve the goal of the „Show Management", namely a „tour d'horizon of the art world, of what is going on" the galleries must be selected in regard to both their artistic program and their regional origin. The relationship of modern to contemporary art, the covering of various epochs and styles, the regional origins of the galleries and – very important – the collectors above all play their part alongside the question of quality. Again a director states: *„So I mean, I think in the end it is the committee that sets the standard, it is not, it is not us setting the standard. I mean, the only thing we can say, our role in the selection process is to sort of things, you know, say things like strategically listen, you have really favoured the contemporary galleries over the art historical galleries, are you really sure that that makes sense, you know, is it true, because right now you have weighted the show in a way which was totally different in the past, or, saying things like, you know, it seems strange that there are only two galleries from America among these 30 galleries, is that, does that really reflect what you saw in the applications, because I think the job of the selection committee is to look at the dossiers and to measure them along quality, and our job is to stand back and give a perspective on the results and then, you know, without, we never say like you have to put this show, this gallery in the show. We have to say, listen, from a strategic perspective it is a mistake to ignore this entire continent, you know, or from a strategic perspective, you know, are you aware that you have entirely eliminated German expressionism from the show, things like that, but I mean, our job is to kind of keep the big picture and make sure that they are conscious of the implications of what they have done, but their job is to set the quality standard. In the end it is their decision, it has to be."*

This process has an effect on the postulated quality criteria. According to this logic art of high quality is primarily marketed by galleries with a high reputation. Their renown depends decisively on how present, how „visible“ and how economically successful they are. The selection of the artists presented by the gallery is in itself a proof of quality. Galleries accumulate symbolic capital which, as a reputation and a „brand“ in the field of wellknown and respected names, they transfer to the artists they represent and so equip the artists with both artistic and economic capital. This applies particularly to the upcoming newcomers who have not yet reached the Olympic heights of the top artists.

Admission Procedure

The Art Basel Committee

„The Show Management endeavors to create optimum conditions for the exhibitors and visitors at Art Basel, by prioritizing the quality and balance of galleries and artworks present at the show. In aiming to achieve these objectives, the Show Management works in close cooperation with the Art Basel Committee. This committee is composed of gallery owners regularly participating in Art Basel, who are selected on the basis of their integrity and expertise. The Art Basel Committee is reappointed on an annual basis and its membership rotates at regular intervals. It is the Art Basel Committee that decides on the admission or non-admission of an applicant at a meeting in camera. For the selection of certain sectors, the Art Basel Committee is joined by Experts. These Experts are also gallery owners selected on the basis of their integrity and their expertise in the type of art presented within the sector.

The selection decisions are taken based on the show's overall concept, considering factors such as:

- *the quality and dynamism of the gallery's overall activities;*
- *the quality and dynamism of the gallery's work with the artists represented, especially those proposed for exhibition at Art Basel;*
- *the gallery's past presentations at Art Basel and other international art shows;*
- *the specific content of the application submitted by the gallery for Art Basel;*
- *the limited availability of booths and the competition for participation among galleries with a similar profile;*
- *compliance with the conditions for admission to Art Basel as specified in the Art Basel Exhibition Regulations.*

Each gallery interested in participating must submit an application. All applications are evaluated anew each year. This means that galleries that participated the previous year must also go through the admission procedure. Every application is subjected to a thorough examination, spread over several stages, until the final results are decided after several rounds of deliberation. The Art Basel Committee takes its decisions by simple majority. The Art Basel Committee's decisions are communicated in writing. Grounds for the decisions are not given to applicants. The meetings of the Art Basel Committee are attended by the Art Basel Directors who conduct the admission procedure without the right to vote.“

Art Basel Website

The determining influence of these transfer and accumulation effects can also be seen in the art which is presented. As early as the 1970s the galleries and the art dealers mostly tended to present „established“ and „successful“ artistic positions of the classical modern period and of American post-war art such as pop art. This has not changed to the present day – the list of the artists presented at the Art Basel by the galleries reads like a „Who's Who“ of the most famous and visible names, which also crop up regularly at the other international fairs.

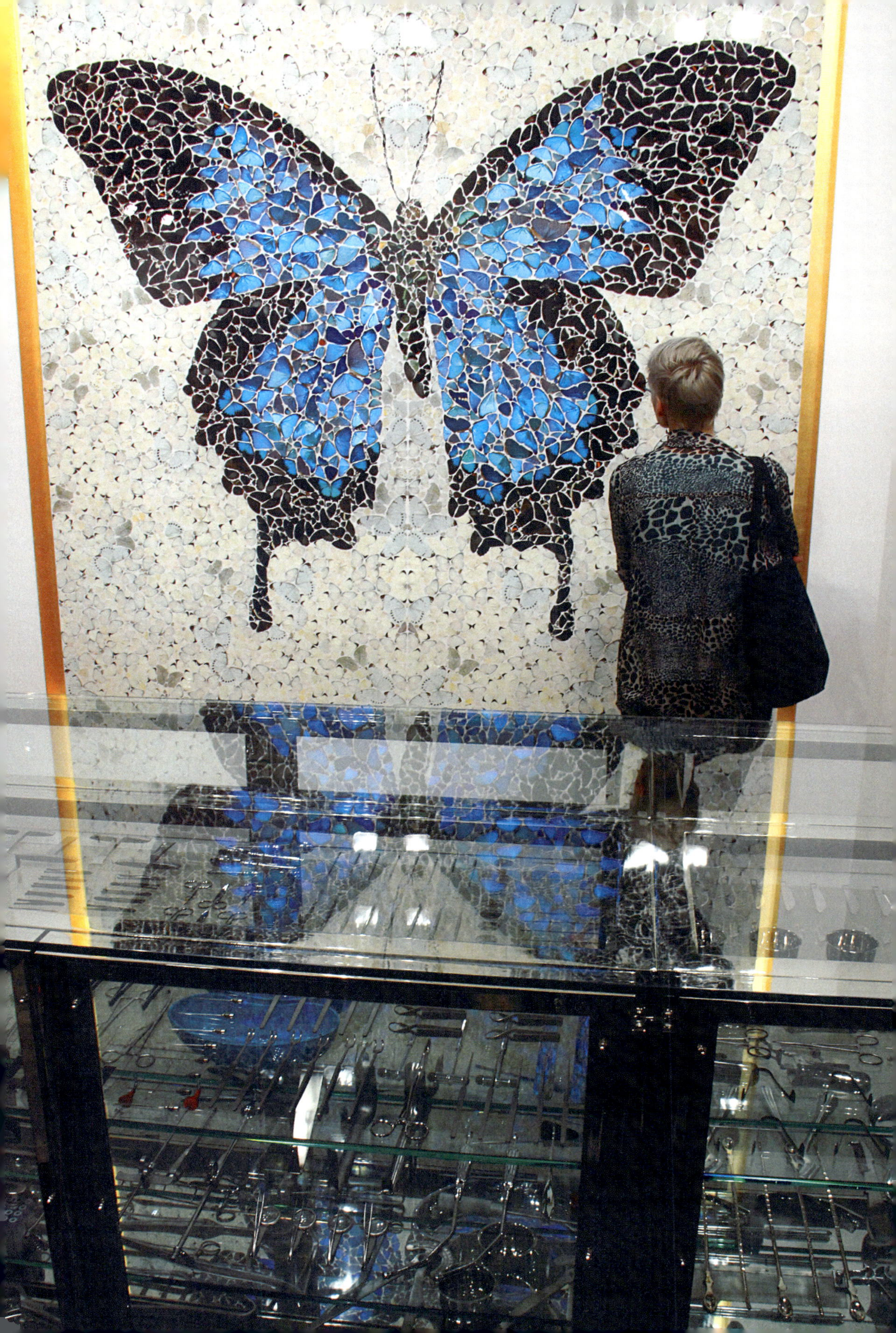

Prestigious places

The center and the periphery in symbolic space

At the Art Basel a topography of the contemporary art market is presented which is the result of the „struggle" for the „best places". The actors with the highest reputation and the greatest economic power battle over the most prestigious sites. The „space profits" [16] are reserved for the galleries with a strong capital base. Galleries in the first row profit from their exclusive position and can carry out their business in the spotlights, whereas the galleries on the periphery lie in the shadows.

This reveals a conscious spatial arrangement which points to hierarchies and structures within the fair. Not only the admission of the galleries to the fair but also their placement in the exhibition building itself is part of a symbolic economy. In contrast to the choice of the galleries, the decision on the placement of the galleries lies in the hands of a few people in the management of the fair. „It is not a democratic procedure", one of the managers said. *„And the distribution is actually done in such a way that it reflects a little bit the histories; the ground floor is more for the very established galleries, modern, which above all have modern and in the meantime also contemporary art [...] And then on the first floor there is, how should I put it, contemporary art above all and the younger galleries. A gallery that comes in for the first time has perhaps, certainly gets no more than 40 or 50 square meters. And of course not exactly there, there is a little bit of... the great thing about this hall is that it is so, it's very democratic, it's a circle, it's all the way round, it has an inner courtyard, it has daylight. And for us the privileged places are, of course, those on this round courtyard. That is where the, well that is actually the prime position. And in principle, as a young gallery, when you are admitted you simply have to work your way a little bit from the outside to the inside."*

The spatial architecture shows an ideal-typical center-periphery arrangement. The „prime positions" are on the ground floor in the Hall 2.0, in the center, around the light-flooded round courtyard. The galleries there are directly accessible from the entrance [17]. At the edge of this floor the section Feature is situated; it is curated and is regarded by upcoming galleries as the gateway to the „main show". A similar arrangement can be found on the upper floor in Hall 2.1. Instead of the sector Edition there is a sector called Statements, where galleries show solo projects of artists. Here on the peripheries young gallerists can make their first experiences at the Art Basel [18].

Gains in space and losses in time

The field of the galleries, as it is presented at the Art Basel, is hierarchically structured. Both the origins of the galleries and the number of times they have participated in the Art Basel fundamentally determine the place they occupy in both the social and the physically appropriated space. The social periphery of the field is again situated on the periphery at the fair. This is also revealed in the temporal structure of the possession of the prestigious places. Galleries which already participated in the Art Basel in the 1970s and 1980s occupy positions closer to the center. This demonstrates how unequally the starting conditions are distributed in the global competition for symbolic recognition. The symbolic profits deriving from a good position in the physically appropriated space generate profits in turn which strengthen the hierarchies or at least make it difficult to change them. A comparison of the positions of the galleries at the fairs in 2010 and 2013 makes this clear. The powers of persistence in the center of the space are very strong. The comparison shows that of the 104 galleries in Hall 2.0 (with the exception of the Features section) 56 galleries had the same place as four years earlier. Thirty six galleries moved to a different place within the hall but mostly remained close to the position they held in 2010. Only six galleries succeeded in moving from Hall 2.1 to 2.0, whereby they had already held good positions on the upper floor. A further six galleries had not participated in the fair in 2010 (although in at least one case the gallery concerned was a split-off from an already established gallery.). The periphery is left for the newcomers, who can carry out their struggles for recognition there. Very few of them manage to reach the prestigious center, and if they do, it is only after several years.

The places in the round courtyard are at the same time the end point of a trajectory which leads to the most highly legitimated places in the art field. At the Art Basel this trajectory can be physically grasped. The satellite fairs such as Liste or Scope function as exercise grounds for the creation of the necessary start-up capital for oneself and the art one represents. The Sections for young art and the galleries on the periphery of the Art Basel, which have almost reached the prestigious center, must prove that they are worthy of higher forms of consecration. A young gallerist who has managed to reach the periphery of the fair in the Statements section after several years in the Liste fair reports on the path she has taken:

Your next step would be to get into 2.0, 2.1, I assume – with the big art galleries?
Yes, but it might take a few more years. I think, generally, it is something that is very hard to get in there – maybe seven years or something to try for. It is crazy.
You have tried for seven years?
No, I haven't started to try yet, because I have done this section for three years. Now I think it could be a good time to start applying.
Oh, you haven't even applied for over there?
No, because I know you have to do this section first. You have to do your time.

The list is led by the „stars" of the art market. In June 2014, from the top ten of the current Artist Ranking of the Artfacts data bank 27 galleries at the Art Basel exhibited works of Andy Warhol, 24 works by Picasso, 17 Lawrence Weiner, 16 Sol LeWitt, 14 Gerhard Richter, 11 John Baldessari, Cindy Sherman and Ed Rusha, nine Bruce Nauman and eight Joseph Beuys. In 2013 a total of 98 galleries and art dealers, that is to say around a third of exhibitors, brought works to Basel by artists who were placed among the top twenty of the rankings – and up to seven artists were presented per gallery.

The predominant strategies here are oriented on economic success. Goods fresh from the atelier, and not seldom produced out of commercial calculation, stand alongside the works of international art „stars" and are offered for sale in a market-conform manner. The works are predominantly meant to meet the aesthetic taste of a broad circle of buyers, who primarily wish to decorate the walls of their homes with the works they have purchased. This tendency towards conformity has been described as „art fair art": format, content and form are more or less clearly adapted to meet the expectations of the customers, „these works (...) are moderate in size, which makes them easy to transport and fit into fair's booth, and are in tune with dominant market trends" [19]. In addition, the best works are selected for the fair. The gallerist Rudolf Zwirner remarks: „Back in the days, we used to hold back pictures for openings. Now they are being held back for the fairs" [20].

The actors in the field have also registered the fact that art fairs, in contrast to curated art exhibitions, are more and more oriented on the market. An important collector from Switzerland explains that in his opinion the art business has split in two, into *„an art curator's, Documenta and Biennial art and an art which is market-oriented. I wouldn't say that these artists only work for the market, but they are prominently present in the market, in the big collections and in the museums with established art. I wouldn't say that these artists only work for the market, but they are the market and the others are marginal to the market."* For him the Art Basel links the two poles, *„but of course it is closer to the market. Two-dimensional art, the glossy surface, dominates there. It is just the opposite with other forms of art, installations, experimental things, multimedia, which actually have a hard time on the market. It is difficult for them in regard to the medium, because they cannot be integrated into the house of the average collector. But it is also art created according to different rules, it's not just the medium."*

The curator of a renowned art museum in Switzerland describes the exclusion of art forms which do not fit in with the customary presentation format of art fairs: *„The conditions in fairs exclude ninety per cent of the art. One cannot show land art, and performative art only under difficult conditions. The fair demands certain forms."* But when the satisfaction of individual taste by the production of easily consumable art shifts into the foreground at the expense of the debate on the nature of art, and the shape of the works and the brand names of their „creators" become more important that the contents and statements of the work, then the parallels to the entertainment industry become unmistakable. As a result art whose consumption and reception is not so easy is pushed to the margins, although it continues to make an important „autonomous" contribution to art discourse.

A Swiss gallerist describes this impression as follows: *„As the second oldest fair in Europe, the Art Basel, this old instance, has succeeded in becoming a world brand in the last fif-teen years, in becoming the most important fair for the art of a century. With Miami and now with Hong Kong it has developed a global strategy and from a perspective specific to the fair it is a center of profit. That's how the fairs are structured, how they*

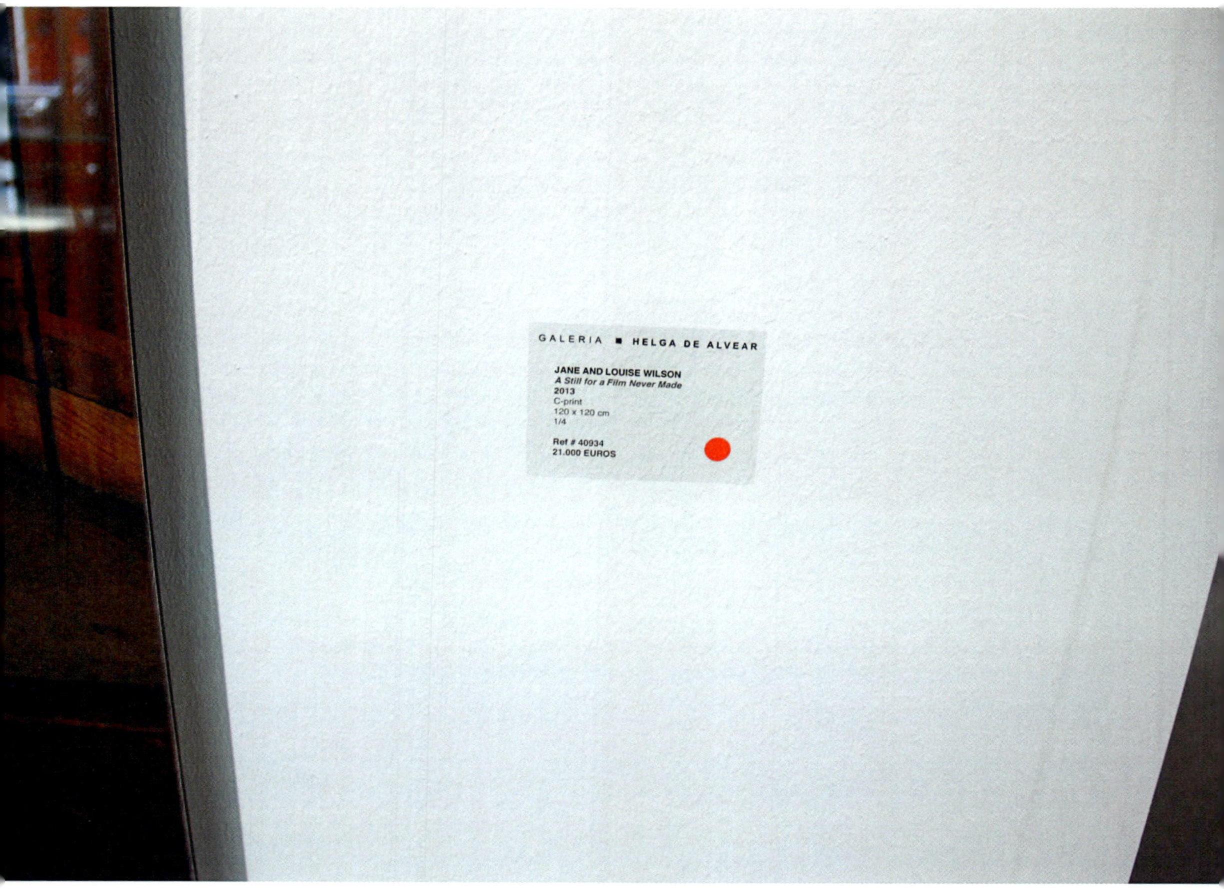
GALERIA ■ HELGA DE ALVEAR
JANE AND LOUISE WILSON
A Still for a Film Never Made
2013
C-print
120 x 120 cm
1/4
Ref # 40934
21.000 EUROS

must be understood. Of course there are certain risks, that's clear. It's always the same. It's like Gucci and Prada. People go shopping in Madrid, Zurich and New York. They always go to the same shops; they can find Gucci and Prada in all three towns. But perhaps they simply lack the information that in Madrid, for example, there is a wonderful leather industry run by young designers. They don't know that there are really cool shops in New York and they don't know that in Zurich there are institutions which produce the best Swiss ladies fashion. But they don't happen to be in the Bahnhofsstraße, and that's the way it is with the fair in Basel. Do you know what I mean? It's up to the fair in Basel to find the right mix so that it will still be really understood globally. Otherwise it can be negative; otherwise they're just shopping malls that look alike."

Fairs, towns, lifestyles

The arrival of art within the international world of goods

„I think Art Basel is, without doubt, the leader in its field in terms of contemporary art fairs, and the standard is really extremely high – just in terms of the professionalism of the whole show, how it's put together and presented. And that professionalism and that precision and Swiss organization taken out of Switzerland to Miami coupled with the different lifestyle that Miami presents was hugely successful and a very seductive mix of the Miami Basel mix. I think the same will be true of Hong Kong. And I think it's a very interesting business plan that Basel has got – very different from Frieze. You know Frieze is playing the safe centres. Basel has really taken art to different territories, where there isn't – and the public will follow, as has happened, the public will, from all over the world, come to these events. And the cities are very interesting cities. I think it's a really smart business model. It's probably Brazil next, I guess."

Gallerist, London, Hong Kong, São Paulo

„Well I mean at the end of the day, the Art Basel is the bluest of the blue chips. I mean it is really a certain iconization of the best galleries and it brings momentum and energy in this very strong international mix of people together, and so I view it as very very very important in terms of repute, in terms of energy, in terms of culture, in terms of ideas, in terms of just the web of curation, artists and collectors and museum groups and art groups linking everyone together and creating this incredibly virtuous cycle impulse of energy, so I think it is just extraordinary what it does for the city of Miami, what it does for the city of Basel and I think it is very very important for the art world."

Gallerist, Zurich and London

„There are two nice jokes about this which went round the Art Basel last year. The one was about two Russian oligarchs who go to New York to do some shopping. The one says: ‚Look at this, I've bought this tie for 5,000 euros' or maybe 5,000 dollars. ‚Are you stupid. You could have gone round the corner. The same tie costs 10,000 there.' Well. Where art is no longer perceived, where art is cheap it was also bad."

Collector, Hamburg

The obvious department store or „shopping mall" character of many art fairs also points to a cultural change in the acquisition of art in which the buyers increasingly turn out to be „consumers". Presence at a market acclaimed for the opportunity it provides for consumption, which finds its most visible expression in the art world at fairs and auctions, pushes art further into the category of desirable luxury goods and „life-style" objects.

The „own“ and the „other“

At the intersection between the hostile worlds of art and money

The evaluations and comments of the galleries participating in the Art Basel are predominantly positive. The extraordinary quality of the fair is repeatedly emphasized. Conversely, some of the actors, who have more distance to the art market, react with reserve towards the Art Basel and the institution of the art fair, which in their eyes cannot deny its market character. They express a resistance to the art market as they feel that it threatens the autonomy of art and stands in contrast to the traditional collection, exhibition and presentation methods of the public museums. The director of an important Swiss art museum puts it as follows: *„It is certainly the most renowned international fair. It is well organized. It attempts to formulate an aspiration and attempts to provide platforms with the Art Unlimited, where one can show bigger works, and Statements, where young artists are exhibited. I think there are many phenomena in it, which attempt to optimize the possibilities for presentation within the medium of a fair. That is clear. But one must simply always be aware that it is a fair, a sales place... An exhibition is one thing, a fair is another."*

This frequently expressed view is confirmed by the curator of an Austrian exhibition hall. *„I really enjoy going to fairs, but they are not exhibitions; they are market places ... The fair is a fair and a market and not an exhibition and the Art Basel and the art fairs are not idealistic affairs. They are markets; they are only concerned with money. We know that, and that's what's so disgusting and makes it so strenuous. Of course those people go there who have money and regard art as an object of prestige or a commodity to invest in."*

The differences between fairs and exhibitions lies not only in the different formats and forms of presentation of art but also in the exploitation relationships and the omnipotent presence of the media, which such large-scale events inevitably trigger off. As part of the „art industry" the fair becomes „the place most hostile to art on earth". Fairs have nothing to do with the meaning and content of exhibitions, as the Swiss museum director further explains: *„Where things are up for sale that's big in the media, whereas a good exhibition in Appenzell or Glarus has the greatest difficulty in being noticed by the media. But the art fair in Basel is covered by the media, although it is the place most hostile to art on earth. After all artists have demands in regard to the presentation of their works. They can act them out in an exhibition hall, a museum or a gallery, but not at a fair."*

The character of the „sales fair" and the resultant forms of presentation stand at the center of the criticism. Whereas an intensive debate on artistic positions is possible in exhibitions or at biennials, at fairs these customary forms of reception are prevented by the funfair atmosphere surrounding them.

„It's intolerable. Well these fairs are fundamentally, most of them are intolerable." This is the way the director of one of the most important entrepreneurial collections describes the situation. *„Well really, this entire system...One feels truly sorry for the artists. Because a piece is hanging up somewhere or other fully, fully decontextualized and you think to yourself... after all that's not what it's all about; it's all about selling the piece. I only ask myself sometimes, how can it be sold if it's shown like that, but there it is."*

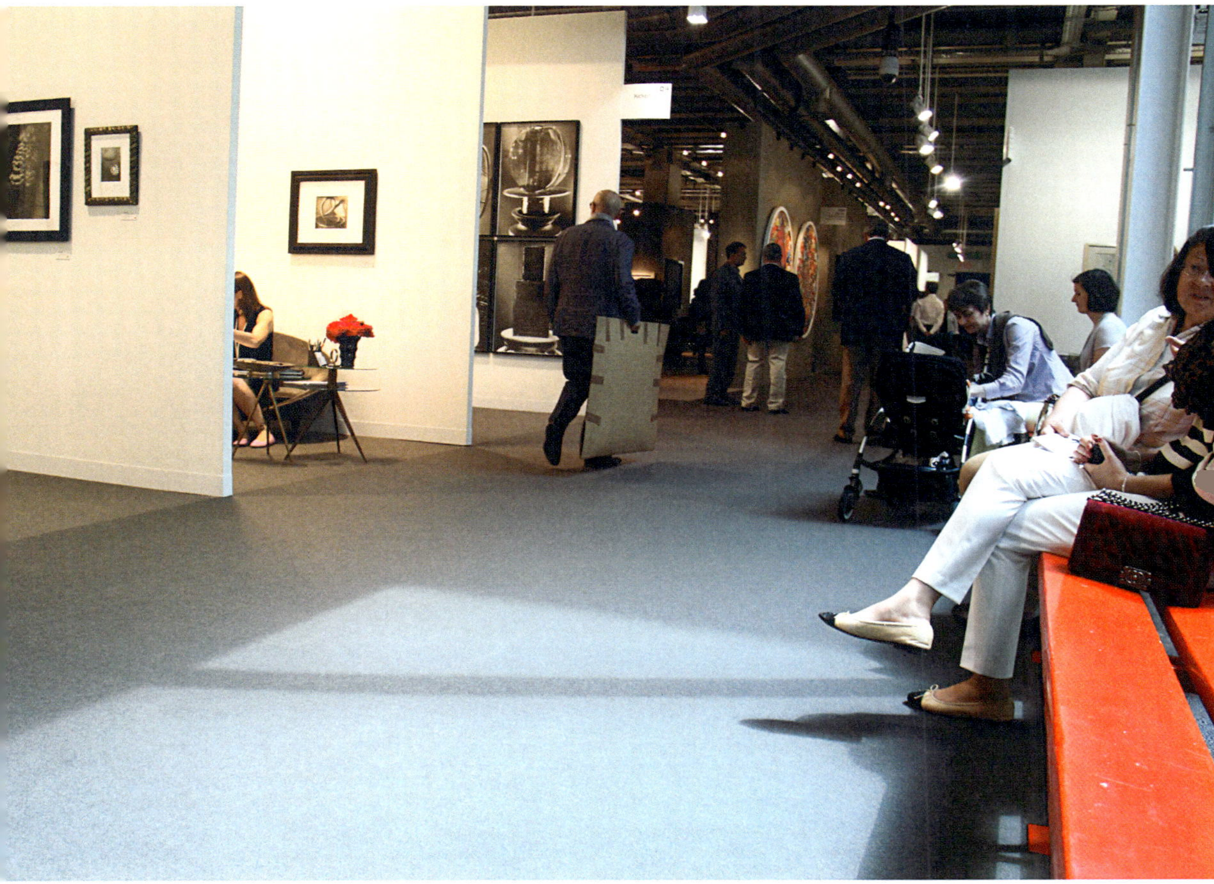

Alien worlds

The Art Basel between autonomous and heteronomous art

Both the social and the physical topography of the Art Basel point to divisions within the art field. The two competing principles of hierarchization within the field have an effect on the fair in terms of spatial boundaries and „cluster formations". The „subfield of large-scale production", which is clearly dedicated to commercial success, stands opposed, ideal-typically, to the „subfield of limited production" in which art eludes more or less the direct relationships of exploitation – in reversing the fundamental principles of an „economic" economy [21].

The „subfield of large-scale production" lies at the center of the fair. The „commercial" galleries occupy the lower floor of the Art Basel, Hall 2.0. They present the works of artists with the greatest prestige and the highest sales. An exception are the galleries of the *Editions* section, which offer editions of top artists and are situated on the upper floor, in Hall 2.1. The „commercially" more peripheral galleries, however, are located on the upper floor, in Hall 2.1. They represent „documenta artists", who must be assigned to the more autonomous pole of the art field [22].

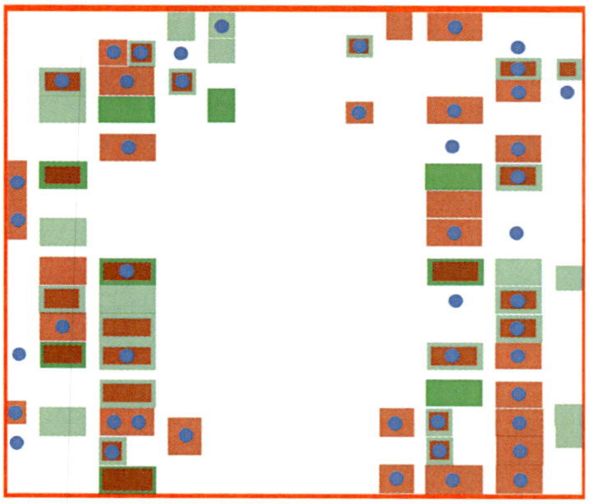

Hall 2.0

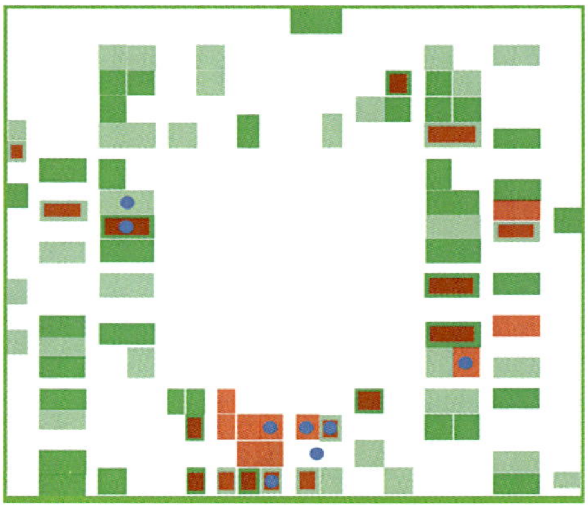

Hall 2.1

The galleries presenting the twenty top-selling artists world-wide in 2012 are marked with a blue dot. Galleries with artists who were among the twenty highest ranked artists in the Artfacts ranking of 2012 (only three of them were among the top sellers) are marked in red. Galleries offering artists who were represented at the Documenta 13 in Kassel are marked in green.

This contrast between market and sales oriented mass production on the one hand and „limited" production on the other corresponds with the strategic use of the space by the actors. When asked which galleries he visited first in order to make purchases a financially strong collector-gallerist answered: *„On the ground floor on the right, so to speak where the big, established galleries are located, generally on the ground floor. I actually take a close look at the ground floor. And the upper floor, I go round it once. And again that shows a little bit where my focal points lie."*

Since the success of pop art on the market art criticism has sometimes reacted vehemently to the degeneration of works of art into commercial products and goods and has seen the end of the avant-garde looming on the horizon [23]. This phenomenon is by no means unknown. The vulgarity of the art market has been pilloried at regular intervals in the periods of economic boom since the beginning of the 20th century. What is new is the really explosive growth in the demand for contemporary art. And this has been accompanied by a massive change in the attitudes towards art as a „product".

But is it really so difficult to understand these changed attitudes? If one takes into account how quickly the power of the market changed the foundations of our society and its traditional practices in the not too distant past, and continues to do so, if one takes into account how much participation in the market seems to promise above all *social* returns, which, however, can only be realized after the complete establishment of the new regime, then the attractive power of the progressive market socialization in art as well does not come as a surprise. The fairs for art, the factual presence of a genuine „market" for symbolic goods, whose acquisition half a century earlier was not only economically but also socially strictly limited, opens up „rational" opportunities for the symbolic shaping of existence for a very small social group which is struggling for social recognition.

The accompanying ambivalences are, however, just as intelligible, if one considers the specific economy of the „art world". That in a sphere which is almost apodictically removed from the profane „world" the purely *physical* impression of the fair, the *social dimension* of the cult, is enough to give rise to feelings of *moral* imposition. We are here in the sphere of that modern religion of art which can only serve bourgeois self-elevation when its social character is denied. The „peddlers" on the global art market are thoroughly aware of this embarrassing situation; they are figures involved in the rationalization of the art trade, just as they are „victims" of the demystification of a product which has become a commodity. And this is also true of the old established „collectors", the artists, the critics, the entire world of art. All of this, the fair, the market, the brands, the *rationalization* of a world which could afford the apparent irrationality of an illustration of its existence, places a question mark against a social configuration which a few decades ago had a decisive influence on the world and the value of art.

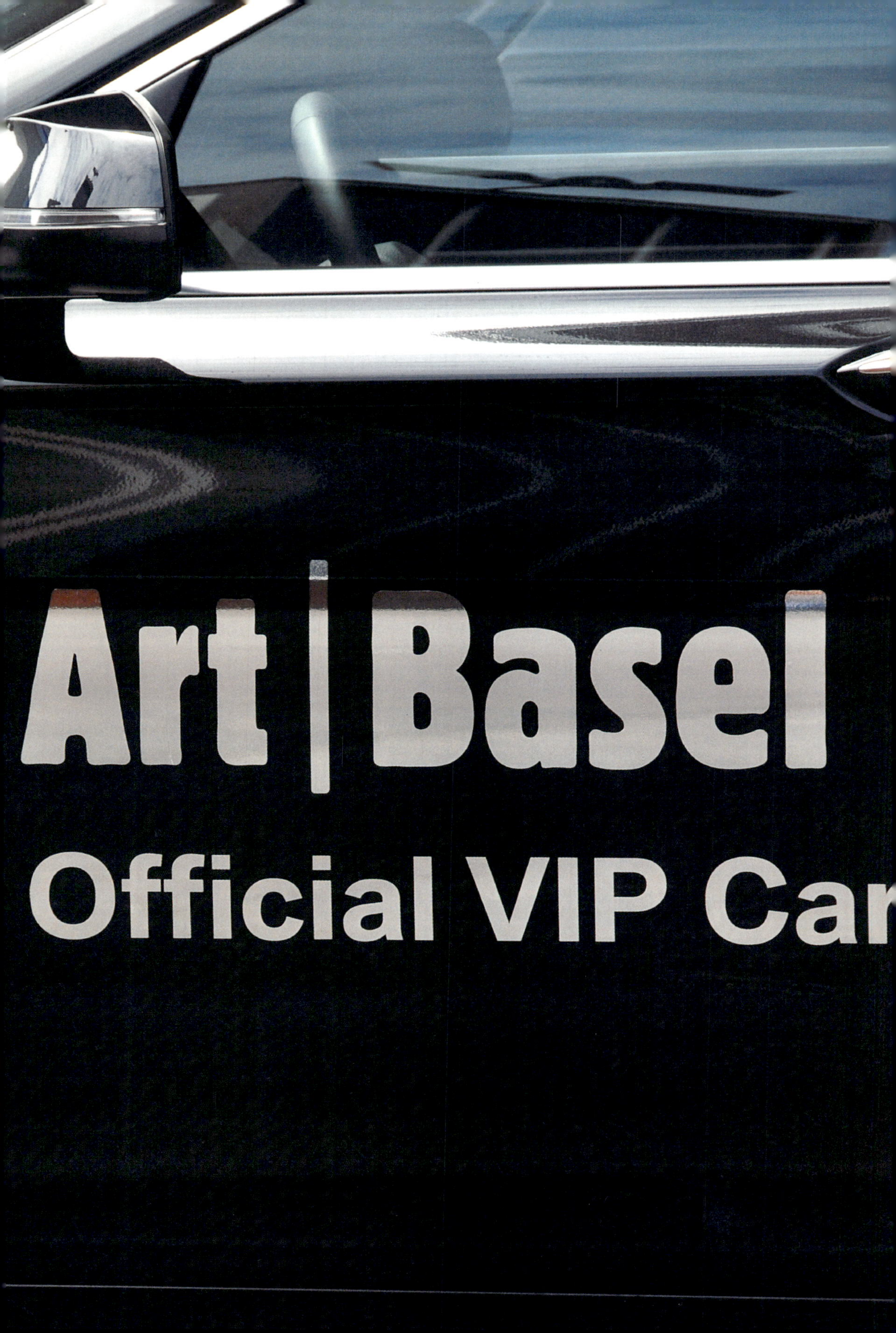
Art | Basel
Official VIP Car

A safe bank

A digression on the symbolic returns of modern art ...

There is no better place for the observer of the event „art fair" to encounter the symbiosis of art and capital than the entrance to the Art Basel, where the logo of UBS – the main sponsor of the fair – is flaunted alongside the fair's own logo. But although this alliance of the art fair and the big bank seems so obvious at first sight, the strategies employed by the global finance institute in the field of art are nonetheless diverse.

What motivates the UBS to enter these fields so remote from the economy? And what does it do there? What profit does a world-wide operating financial institute hope to make from its commitment to the Art Basel? It is clear that the operators of the fair have an obvious interest in a regular flow of money, even though the connection with the UBS could well be seen as a *mésalliance* with a dubious side to it for the self-understanding of the actors in the art field who participate in the fair. One can, moreover, assume that this problem does not arise in the same way for the Formula One races, which are also sponsored by the UBS.

The logo and the symbol of the bank put their stamp on the public image of the fair, but that is not all. The bank is also present inside; it has reserved a special enclosed sector within the exclusive VIP lounge for itself and its hand-picked clientele, and it is by no means enough to possess a VIP card in order to be granted entrance to it. The main sponsor has in any case a clear say in the distribution of the VIP quotas and it would be idle to ask about the selection criteria that are applied. Of course this privilege is accorded to the wealthiest of its financially powerful high segment clients. And it is not by chance that we find in the VIP lounge a very special concentration of topclass art collectors who are not only hosted in a princely fashion by „their" bank but are also provided with a wide range of service offers. But what does the relationship of the UBS to the world of art exactly look like?

The art of „art banking"

First of all it can be seen that in its self-presentations this bank explicitly presents its complex involvement with the „art world" as a global strategy. Among the official „departments concerned with art" of the bank we find „Sponsorship", with an emphasis on the Art Basel, the „Arts Forum" in cooperation with Guggenheim, the „Arts Competence Center", the „Art Collection" and a cultural foundation. The activities united under this umbrella show the specific alliance of the financial institute in different lights in each case even though they all closely interlock. The UBS sponsors institutions in the field by means of financial support for events at different places in the world with an interesting mixture of generous patronage and interest-guided marketing by means of public self-presentation. In addition the bank buys works of art at all of its locations and now possesses a collection of around 32,000 objects. This in-house art can be found in all of its branches, in offices, firms, foyers and meeting rooms, subtly and hierarchically distributed according to the importance of the locations and their global rank – „blue chips" in the head offices of the big cities, local artists in the provinces.

The „Arts Collection" of the UBS is officially subdivided into the categories premium, advanced, developing, emerging and decorative prints. The number of works counted among the „premium artists" is calculated to be 3,000, and here one is speaking of the „most renowned names in the art world". The selective curating of the bank's own collection takes place according to geographical and economic-geographical points of view and is repeated within each seat of the bank in accordance with the given social topography – the most important works are to be found on the executive floors. In the words of the bank itself: *„The development of the collection supports the overall UBS strategy and visual identity and meets the needs of the real estate department, furnishing offices worldwide. Client-facing areas house a display of art linked by a cohesive theme wherever possible, reflecting the international reach of UBS. Most significant client areas display most significant works of art. Staff offices and working environments ideally feature displays of large edition decorative prints by recognized contemporary artists"* [24].

The special form of the bank's love of art seems to feed on a variety of motives and strategies. As is shown by the interviews with the representatives of the bank from the departments concerned with art, the exhibition of the art collection primarily serves the purpose of self-presentation. One is not just a financial institute; one pursues more than merely economic goals of profit maximization and the growth of revenues; one does not think only in economic categories and beyond the calculability of the actual core business one has an appreciation of the finer things in life, something which cannot at all be harmonized with the public image of the UBS. How did this bank come to acquire art treasures which, according to the assessments of diverse experts, make up one of the most important collections of modern and contemporary art?

When we take a closer look, the picture of a passion for such priceless goods which has long accompanied the business of the bank fades. We discover that the family silver was not acquired by tireless, passionate collecting of these goods over generations, but mainly through the incorporation in the year 2000 of the investment bank PaineWebber, whose chairman was an art collector „of the old school". In its self-presentation, therefore, the bank is evidently adorning itself with borrowed plumes, whereas, in the three decades before its sudden career as an institutional collector of top-class art, it had been mainly active in the numismatics market, where the elective affinity of art and money is all too evident. In order to cultivate its newly gained access to legitimate world-famous art, the UBS appointed an advisor, a former director of a renowned auction hall, and thus publicly celebrated the seemingly exotic love match of money and art. In the self-presentation of the bank the corresponding pretentions run as follows: „Hundreds of companies collect art – but only a few make an art of collecting". And these elitist claims in the sphere of art did in fact find recognition: in 2007 the magazine *Euromoney* awarded the UBS the accolade „Best Art Banking".

The financial institute had, therefore, purposefully and successfully invested *new money* in legitimate cultural capital and ennobled itself at a single stroke. This happened precisely at a time when the UBS began to shed its image as a traditional and venerable Swiss enterprise, whose employees regarded themselves as „private civil servants", to blossom into a global player on the late capitalist finance market and to enter the US-American capital market on a large scale. Here the bank commended itself to super-rich investors not only with the merits of Swissness – banking secrecy, tax advantages, discretion – but also with a life-style marketing tailored to meet the wishes of this demanding clientele, in which art and capital were mentioned in one breath. One of the highlights of this self-staging strategy was the opportunity to present itself as a generous patron at the center for the consecration of contemporary art, the New York MoMA, in 2005. The bank donated to it „blue chips" from its still young stock of works of art, which were then shown with high visibility to the discerning New York public.

The splendor and the misery of global art banking

If one takes literally the bon mot attributed to Andy Warhol that good business is the best art then the development of the so-called art banking from the 1990s on is a truly ideal-typical reflection of this cynical view of the social world. The art of doing business with art, the institutionalization and professionalization of dealing with art as capital has been promoted not least by the UBS. It was not by chance that the decision, in the late 1990s, of one of the in the meantime most important art fairs, the Art Basel, to collaborate with a bank in the process of joining the global leaders of the financial world, fell at a time in which the fair was preparing to establish a foothold on the American continent. And it is not surprising that the UBS then became the main sponsor of the fair not only in its home country but also in its new location at Miami Beach.

The new policy of this bank in the process of transformation into a global finance institution corresponds to a surprising degree with the philosophy of the global „elite" which the Art Basel itself used to promote itself at the latest since the turn of the century – no less than the best. First came a brutal restructuring of the labor force with several massive waves of dismissals, euphemistically termed as „releasing" employees, and this in an enterprise which had hitherto been proud of its paternalistic stakeholder culture. Then, following American models, a radical shareholder doctrine was devised along with an elaborate bonus system which ensured handsome gratuities for its top managers in return for the acquisition of wealthy new clients, especially in the USA [25]. At the same time this fundamental reconstruction also led to a departure from the hitherto dominant logic behind the recruitment of its leadership. From now on managerial staff was recruited internationally under the label „diversity"; English was now spoken in the „executive floors", and the habitus of this new urban elite, freed from the ethical ballast of the now transformed traditional enterprise, harmonized perfectly with the new structures and strategies of the UBS – and as the brand name of a new corporate identity contemporary art has since become the symbol of a total break with the past, of a radical orientation towards the future, of a philosophy of permanent revolution, of a so-called „change management". And the best authentification for this „contemporaneity", this revolutionary modernism, seemed indeed to lie in a liaison with the global leaders in the market for contemporary art.

The shift of interest from the faithful smaller and medium-sized investors it had hitherto taken care of to wealthy major clients fits perfectly into this picture.

Exactly this high-end segment of the bank's clients overlaps to a large extent with the art collectors of the VIP category to whom the Art Basel offered privileged access conditions – ultimately this was the desired target group. It is in the meantime a well-known fact that the acquisition of clients, particularly at the Art Basel Miami Beach, was often pursued with methods on the margins of legality which have attracted the attention of the Swiss and US-American legal authorities [26]. One of the main actors for the UBS on the American finance market described the deliberate entrepreneurial in-strumentalization of commitment to art in court as follows: „*Mr. Birkenfeld testified that UBS not only authorized and paid for the business trips to the United States, but also provided the Swiss bankers with tickets and funds to go to events attended by wealthy U.S. individuals, so that they could solicit new business for the bank in Switzerland. He said that UBS sponsored U.S. events likely to attract wealthy clients, such as the Art Basel Art Fair in Miami; for example, the Subcommittee found that at least five UBS client advisors travelled to the United States for trips coinciding with the Art Basel Art Fair, an annual UBS-sponsored event held in early December in Miami Beach since 2002. The data shows that over the years several UBS Swiss client advisors were in Miami during the art show, including three in 2007. On the customs forms completed over the years by UBS-travellers prior to landing at Miami International airport, only one client advisor stated that the purpose of the trip was for business, while five described the visit as for pleasure. These client advisors' trips, however, coincided closely with the dates of the Art Basel event, including an invitation-only private showing. Despite these prohibitions, it appears that Swiss bankers in the United States servicing U.S. clients routinely undertook actions that contravened the UBS restrictions. Mr. Birkenfeld described, for example, an art festival sponsored by UBS in Miami each year, which he attended with other Swiss bankers for the express purpose of soliciting new accounts. ‚We went to these events. We went to dinners, we went to art exhibitions, we went to private homes as private bankers, knowingly by management that they were paying for our hotel, paying for our airfare, paying us our salary, and getting us tickets to the UBS VIP tent to drink champagne with clients'"* [27].

This admission shows how far business with art was incorporated as a matter of course into the entrepreneurial strategy in the period of neoliberal radicalization of the finance economy and only plunged into a profound crisis with the bank crisis itself, a crisis which, quite apart from its legal dimensions, also involved a crisis of reputation. In this dramatic phase the bank decided to withdraw from the art business. It closed its department for „art management" in Basel, in which at the time 14 experts actively advised the superrich, art-collecting clients of the bank throughout the world; it dismissed the curator of the in-house gallery in Midtown Manhattan in 2009, and it abandoned the label „art banking". Only the sponsoring of the Art Basel remained unchanged. The bank continued to value it highly as an aspect of its image management and corporate identity.

In these times of crisis the bank instead considered giving up its art collection, whose value was assessed at several hundred million dollars, in order to plug the holes caused by the financial crisis. Was it „love of art" which led to the abandonment of this idea? The decision was more likely guided by the realization that selling the family silver would contribute even further to the public image of an ailing financial institution. And so the UBS remains today the proud owner of the art collection as its figurehead.

This is, however, not a unique case. The strategy of instrumentalizing art for branding purposes and the public demonstration of patronage and trustworthiness outside the field of „commerce" is typical of the symbiosis of money and art which has characterized the art collecting of many banks and insurance companies in the last two to three decades.

Of course the apparently altruistic expenditure of economic resources also yields a return even though it cannot be entered into the balance sheets down to the last penny. What do these returns consist of for a financial institution? Although the incalculability of the currently booming art market is not a particularly prominent factor in view of the experience made by the UBS in the crisis with its overall high-risk operating model, this in itself cannot provide a sufficient motivation for commitment to the art world. What counts is probably the strategic importance of using adornment with art for branding purposes and public self-presentation. Especially in a time in which the banking business as such is becoming more and more virtual and intransparent self-presentation through art can offer a compensatory backdrop and serve as a visiting card.

But art is, above all, used to good purpose in order to establish affinities with demanding clients who themselves often collect art works and to use the liking for art as a communicative topic and a symbolic framework for the conclusion of business transactions. Embedding business in a cultivated background and a cultured ambience seems to fulfill an important function for the success of agreements and contracts. The official mission statement declares: *„The contemporary works of art in the UBS Art Collection are part of our corporate identity and contribute to a rewarding client experience in UBS locations, to a motivating work environment and to a positive public image of UBS. The UBS Art Collection creates a positive atmosphere for UBS employees; art encourages to think creatively. It also serves as a point of discussion between clients and their UBS relationship managers; art connects with the public"* [28].

The presence of art is seen as a means of furthering creative and motivated work, as a stimulating and trust-building factor which one can always refer back to in discussions with discerning clients. From this standpoint art creates an ambience in which the crude calculations of finance economy are shown in a civilized light beyond the logic of „business is business" for the cultivated customer. It seems, therefore, that art, in spite of its antieconomic claims, does indeed rhyme with capital and can be effectively used in its centers of control, not least in order to generate social trustworthiness and creditability. And what could be more valuable for a bank than creditability in times when the financial world is undergoing a profound crisis of confidence?

In the round of sponsors

… and the model for milking them with their consent

The economic added value of apparently altruistic expenditure, the truly ostentatious squandering of material resources for art and its social framework, can scarcely be explained more outspokenly than in the statements of the person responsible for sponsors at the Art Basel. He clearly sketches the special character and status of a business model in which the investment of large sums of money in an art event is praised as economically profitable marketing. And the fact that he does it in such an outright way permits the conclusion that in the enterprise „art fair" there seem to be no ethical thresholds worth mentioning when mediating between art and money.

What is the specific nature of this business model? Simply put, the Art Basel offers enterprises a platform on which customers can be found whose profile is tailor-made for the purchase of the company's own high-segment products and services. The population brought together here with the help of the catalyst „interest in art" and the selection criterion „art collecting" represents, both in terms of its shared economic, social and cultural properties and of its specific habitus and life style, a latent social milieu which only needs a binding agent („love of art"), a meeting point (Basel, Miami Beach, Hong Kong) and a point in time (art fair) to manifest itself.

The Art Basel provides the choreography and the stage for this production with clear stage directions. The etiquette it lays down for this both cultivated and profitable event includes the rule: „Business" is not simply „business"; one does not get down to the hard tacks without further ado. It is rather the finer things in the world of art which bring people together, provide the topics of conversation and create an atmosphere of spiritual kinship and so lay the foundations and the legitimation for the initiation of apparently secondary forms of exchange related to the business interest of the parties concerned. These remain latently and decently in the background until the requirements of etiquette have been fulfilled.

As under the rules of *savoir-vivre* of upper class social events, the socially sophisticated and the business aspects are clearly separated and staggered over time; first the reception with cultivated rituals, evening music and festive dinners, then the retreat of the „businessmen" to the „smoking room" where one gets down to the actual business. The cultural supporting program and the cultivated dinners play the part of a community-building overture and with the help of small talk create the foundation of trust needed for the subsequent initiation of business relationships. A cultural pattern of courtly etiquette taken over from the aristocracy and cultivated and kept alive in a variety of ways by the bourgeoisie during the last two centuries is also effectively celebrated at the wedding of art and money at the Art Basel.

„My work here has two dimensions, one of which is concerned with sponsoring. Every show of the Art Basel has partners, who contribute to it financially. In return they profit from a value transfer at the level of the brand because one links them with our name, because they are given a privileged place within the fair, because they can regale their customers there and especially on account of the privileged access to the show etc. And they profit from the opportunity to build up new

business relationships. Our VIPs include people of niveau, collectors, people from the art world, economic leaders or entrepreneurs who come to the fair to show their passion for art. We have a fascinating and valuable clientele for companies such as UBS, Cartier, Netjets. All of them are companies which are well positioned in regard to luxury or have an interest in encountering a specific, very wealthy and cultivated clientele.

So we sell them this access for hard cash and in return they can associate their names with ours. That is the essence of our sponsorship. There are many business negotiations for every contract and every relationship that is established; we fulfill obligations, provide catalogs, advertising space, presence on our internet pages, all of these things. That is an important dimension because they have a substantial share in the turnover achieved at the fair and, what is more, when Cartier comes, it brings its customers with it.

There are, of course, many different kinds of people under the VIPs and collectors. And it is true that we are very careful in choosing our sponsors. We don't want companies we bring together with such people to be totally commercial in their conduct. Netjets is a company which sells shares in jets. That starts at a minimum of 500,000 US dollars, for which one can fly around the world. But every time a hiring fee per flying hour has to be paid etc. In the end the cost can amount to two million dollars a year and one has to be able to afford that. But the people at Netjets have been trained as engineers, the salesmen as well, and they haven't the slightest idea about what happens in the art world. So when we introduce them to this milieu they are completely lost and we then come to their help. We help them to translate what they actually want to do, so that they can make contact with the VIPs. But what really matters in the end, and we have now realized this, is that as sponsors of the event they enjoy automatic credit, what I call a ‚hard share' in English. Emotionally a transfer takes place – one is grateful. When the UBS invests a lot of money in the love of art, the art collectors and the philanthropists appreciate the UBS. And so the people from UBS do not have to walk up to a collector and say: ‚Well I sell real estate mortgages. Are you interested?' That would be a catastrophe!

So one undertakes the journey together, shares experiences, supports cultural activities. That is also the approach of BMW. Everyone knows what kind of cars BMW produces. What it now wishes for is to position itself sustainably in the art world simply by financing cultural initiatives. And that is enough to win new customers as a target group. But that has to happen in a very sensitive way. Otherwise, if the approach is purely commercial, it's a catastrophe. And that's true for us as well, as the experience we provide would then be a miserable experience. I see no reason for an art collector to come to the Art Basel, to spend money, to fall in love with or to buy a work of art, and to profit from a place where one can relax, and then be pestered by somebody who wants to sell a boat or an apartment. That's just not on!

It is a matter of translating cultures and worlds, because the UBS is a financial world. They have a special culture and in their commercial approach they are actually quite aggressive. We are there to mediate so that they can get into conversation with these people. We are valuable for them in this situation because we know the milieu very well, or at least that's the way it is perceived.

Interview with the *Head of Sponsorship* of the Art Basel

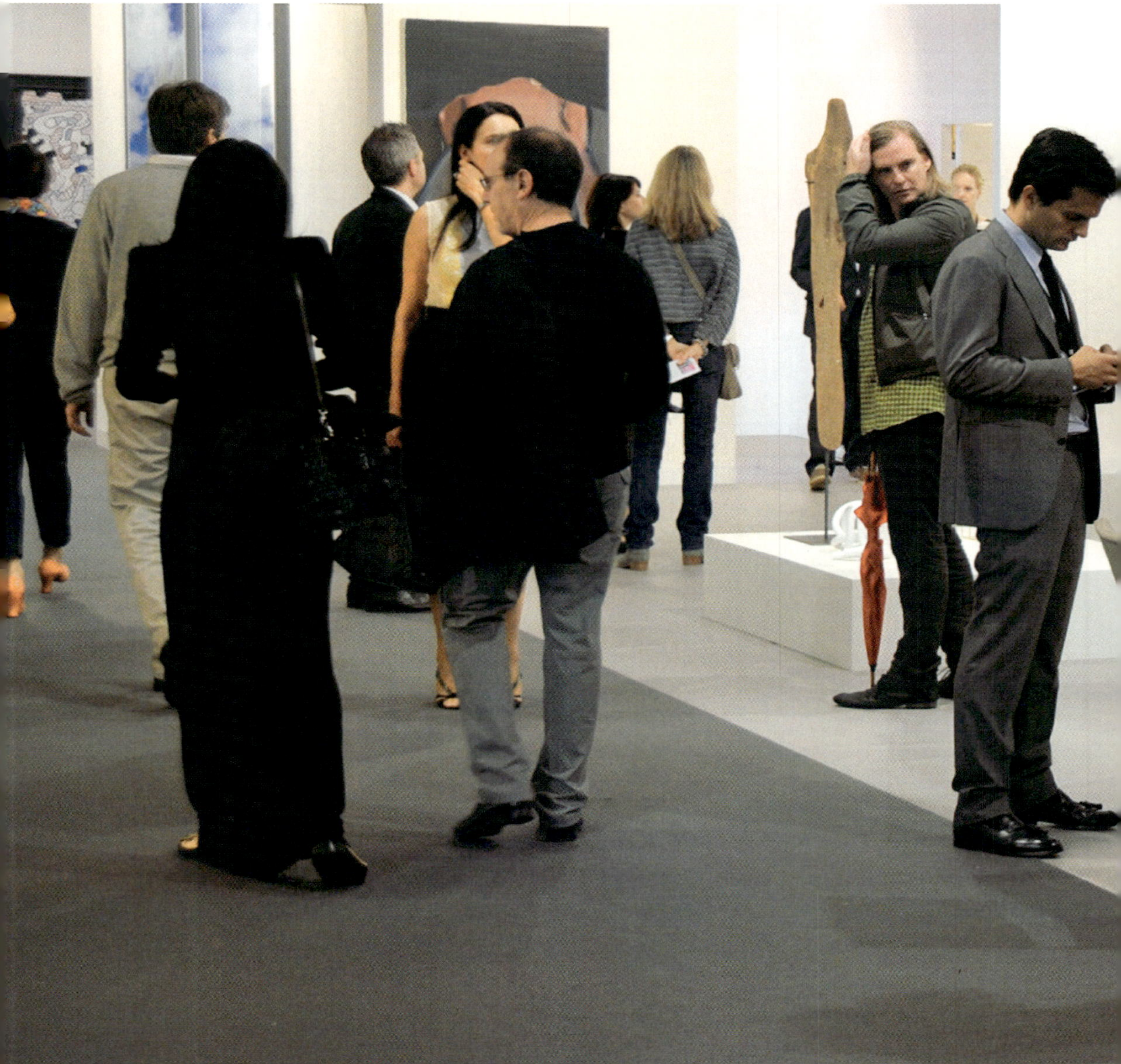

3 Liaisons dangereuses

The galleries and the trade fair

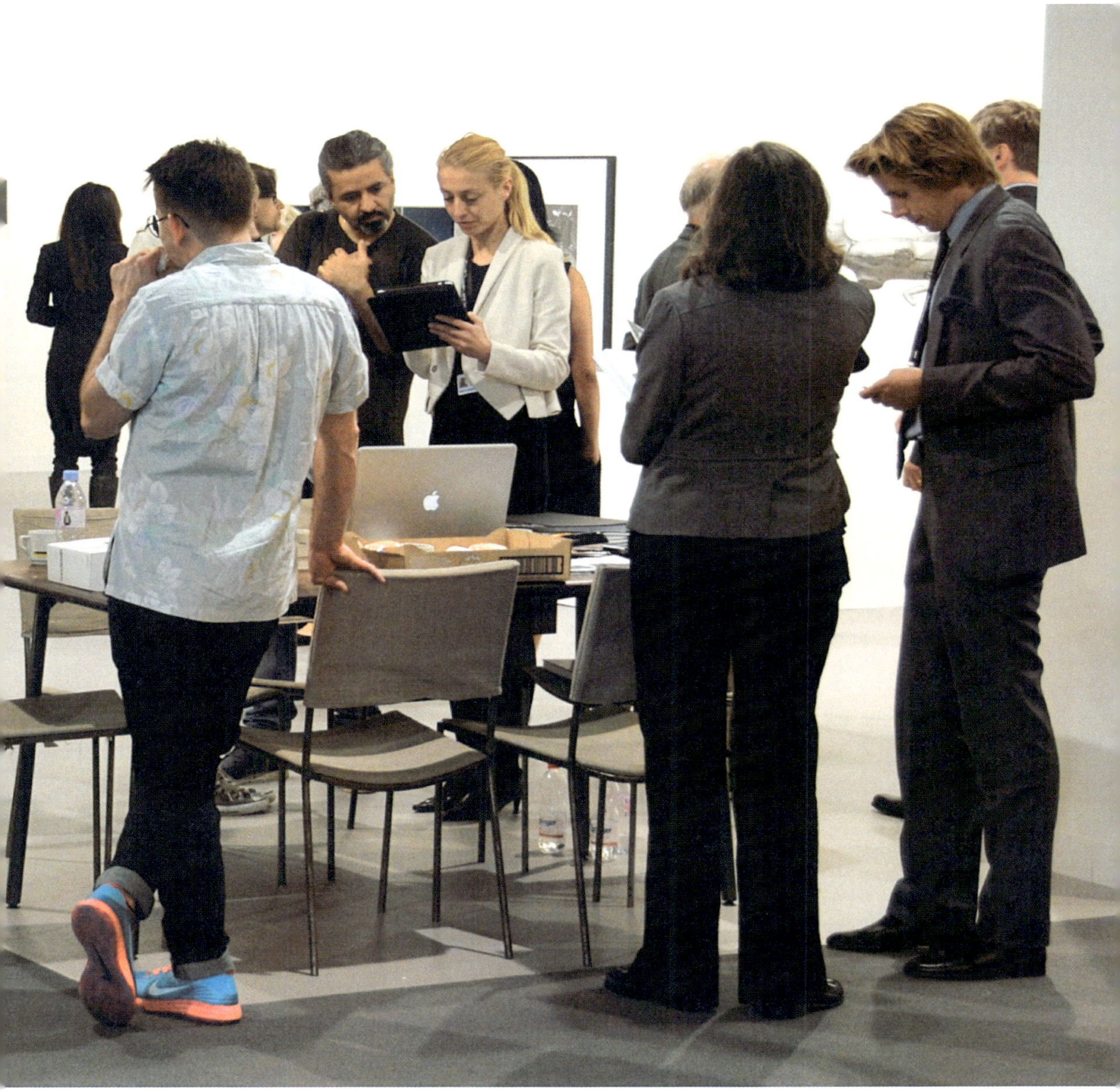

The „economic“ enterprise denied by the art dealer or the publisher, in which art and business are conjugated, cannot succeed, even „economically“, if it is not governed by a practical mastery of the laws of the functioning of the field and of its specific requirements.

PIERRE BOURDIEU, The Rules of Art

The museum, a consecrated building presenting objects withheld from private appropriation and predisposed by economic neutralization to undergo the „neutralization“ defining the „pure“ gaze, is opposed to the commercial art gallery, which, like other luxury emporia („boutiques“, antique shops etc.) offers objects which may be contemplated but also bought, just as the „pure“ aesthetic dispositions of the dominated fractions of the dominant class, especially teachers, who are strongly overrepresented in museums, are opposed to those of the *happy few* in the dominant fractions who have the means of materially appropriating works of art. The whole relation to the work of art is changed when the painting, the statue, the Chinese vase, or the piece of antique furniture belongs to the world of objects available for appropriation, thus taking its place in the series of luxury goods one possesses and enjoys without needing to prove the delight they give and the taste they illustrate.

PIERRE BOURDIEU, Distinction

„My God, here we go again. In view of the steadily increasing number of annual fair events the market is turning more and more into a travelling circus. Curators, collectors and dealers are showing the first signs of exhaustion." This reaction of the Art World in 2007 to the rapid boom in art fairs comes from the pen of the former art journalist Mark Spiegler, who is now the director of the Art Basel [1]. For professional gallerists and art dealers in particular these sales events have acquired an eminently increased significance in the last two decades and have in the meantime become one of the most important distribution and marketing channels. As periodic art markets they present a new kind of institutionalization, which has provided the galleries and dealers with a second mainstay alongside their primary business operations. Without the income from the sales at art fairs many art dealers would be facing financial ruin. At the same time quite a few gallerists complain about the substantial financial, personal and organizational expense involved in the participation in the ever-growing number of events on the international art fairs circuit. How is this phenomenon to be interpreted and what conclusions can be drawn from it about the present-day relationship between „art" and „money"?

Even though in the context of the „art world" the terminology may seem strange and even though it must run against the grain especially for the decisive protagonists, there can be no disputing the fact that in this development we are dealing with processes which would be described elsewhere as rationalization. The emergence of a market with its condensation of exchange processes, its thorough spatial and temporal structuralization, the increasing dependency of the exchange partners on this market and its economic and morphological constraints and the increasingly strong subjection of the market activities to commercial calculations are all unmistakable indications of rationalization tendencies in the practice of exchanging goods, which could until quite recently be understood as a purely „personal" affair. The more or less strong *compulsion to participate* in this market itself confirms this perception. The fact that these processes have in the meantime acquired a new and quite evident quality in a world which has always reacted to such tendencies towards a „secularization" of its practice with deep suspicion helps us to understand the enormous tensions we encounter at the Art Basel. And the gallerists as „mediators" of art are at the center of these tectonic shifts in the relationship between „art" and „world", in which a fundamental antagonism remains perceptible in spite of all attempts to rationalize its ethical implications. This antagonism is profound, profound enough at all events to see the continuing influence of the unchallenged power of a game which may never question its own rules. Even the most commercial „arrangements" pretend to serve a cause which ultimately remains beyond the grasp of the world of „money".

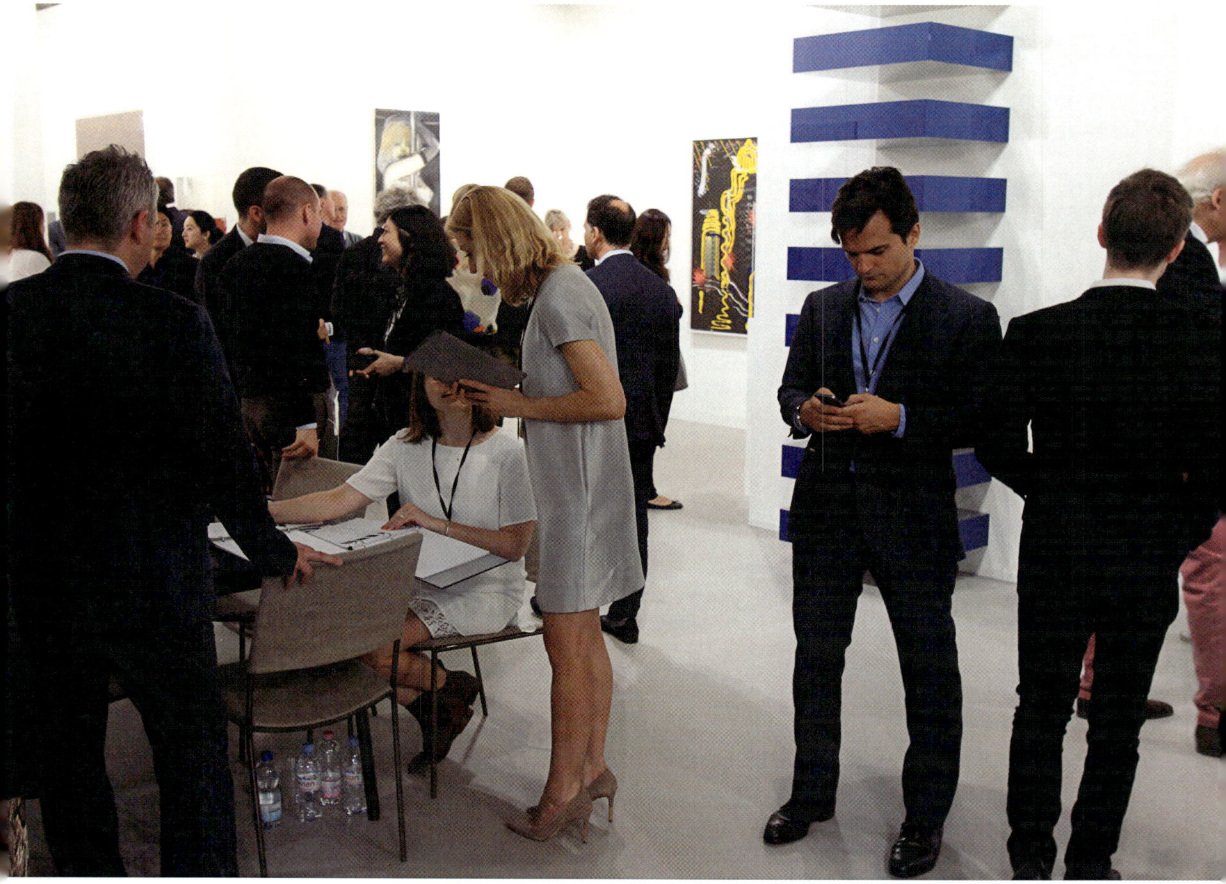

A necessary evil

Galleries, fairs and the transformation of the art market

As the mediators between art producers and art consumers the gallerists occupy an important position not only in the art market but also in the art system as a whole. They function as „gate keepers“ [2], who decide which new works of art and styles should come to the notice of the public. Or, to put it another way, they separate the wheat from the chaff. As exhibition forums especially for contemporary art they above all help young artists to win public attention, which they would otherwise scarcely receive, as they lack reputation and cannot be found in museums. Artists' careers would be unthinkable without galleries. And, conversely, the reputation of the galleries stands and falls with the artists they represent. In brief: the galleries have the central task of organizing the dissemination of works of art. They provide a structure which is accepted by all the other actors in the art field.

In order to carry out a sale the works of art must be presented in the right environment. This takes place primarily on the traditional premises, in gallery rooms, but also in back offices, gallery floors and private rooms, in which particularly discreet business matters can be transacted. The so-called „white cube“ [3] has asserted itself as the most appropriate form of presentation for contemporary art. It is an exhibition hall with a light-colored floor and white walls, whose prototype was already in use in the 1920s, and it serves to add an additional aesthetic moment to dealings with art. As an „ideal space“ it protects art from all disturbing influences.

The gallery system with its traditional premises and extensive „showrooms“ continues to fulfill an important classical function in the field of art. Apart from commercial dealings it offers a complex of services for the mediation of art ranging from the public presentation of art to expertise and consultancy activities and the creation of discussion forums for art. For just this reason many gallerists do not see their profession as trade in art, but as a cultural activity. They are promoters of art for whom commercial motives do not stand in the foreground [4].

Whereas at the beginning of this century art fairs were predominantly restricted to the European art sphere, where they rapidly established a monopoly, they are today subject to world-wide competition. Alongside the old art fairs in Basel, Cologne, Maastricht, Paris or Madrid new fairs have mushroomed everywhere in metropolises around the globe. Particularly for the established and successful galleries in Europe and the USA this development has been a kind of wake-up call. Instead of doing business almost exclusively in the developed national markets as in the past, many art dealers saw the need to turn to the growing foreign markets in order to ensure future success. The popularization of the fine arts abroad created a new stratum of art lovers with spending power who gave a strong impetus to the art market as a whole. Whereas ten years ago the top galleries only attended two or three fairs, they now go to more than a dozen. The rapidly increasing flock of international collectors has also become more mobile and in the meantime jets from one fair to the next around the world.

But in spite of the continuous hype about fairs one should not overlook the fact that only a modest, albeit increasing part of the art market is subject to internationalization. The predominant part of the galleries and their artists continue to depend on the domestic demand at the national art markets, where, in contrast to the international markets with „top quality art“ for „top prices“, business is not exactly booming.

The ambivalent relationship of the galleries and the art dealers to the art fairs must be understood against this background. If one asks the gallerists participating in the Art Basel about the economic value of the art fair for their art business, the answers are unequivocal. Sales during the Art Basel are of central importance for their annual sales; a great part of their income is achieved at the fairs.

These results largely coincide with the picture painted in the press releases, which are gladly taken up by the media. They speak of „excellent results" and „strong sales at all levels of the market throughout the entire week" [5]. *„We can report consistently unbelievable sale – it was in fact our best Basel Fair ever"* states Iwan Wirth of the Galerie Hauser & Wirth about the 45th edition of the fair in 2014. Larry Gagosian speaks of „significant and steady sales each day" and Theresa Liang of the Long March Space gallery in Beijing records that sales have been „excellent" [6].

Hardly one of the established galleries can now afford not to attend regional or international fairs. About one third of the annual turnover is achieved at them. They are the most important source of sales in private art trade after the sales in the local galleries (50 %). Private sales account for only 7 per cent of the returns, and 5 per cent each derive from auctions and online platforms [7].

According to this picture everything would seem to have turned out for the best in the relationship between the institutions of the gallery and the art fair in the contemporary art market. But is the expressly proclaimed „decade of the art fair" which is supposed to have superseded the „decade of the biennials" in fact a kind of consistent and harmonic further development of the forms of art mediation traditionally cultivated by the galleries? Or does the label „gallery" conceal a broad range of highly heterogeneous economic and social realities and practices which show the relationship to the institution of the art fair in different lights and with clearly divergent nuances? And did not one of the founding fathers of the Art Basel, the art dealer Ernst Beyeler, clearly express his unease about this kind of art market? „I don't have such a good opinion of art fairs; there's something ‚leveling' about them. And I'm not particularly interested in them because I was satisfied with the gallery and our charisma", this old hand in the art trade had already declared on the occasion of the founding of this „mother of all art fairs". Heinz Berggruen, another old hand in the art trade has even categorically refused to take part in art fairs in spite of many invitations.

The participation in fairs has advantages and disadvantages. At art fairs new relationships can be established and new customers won; the gallerists forge new links to the collectors and vice versa. In addition the fairs offer an opportunity for more profound cooperation and the creation of networks with other gallerists and collectors and it is possible to win an overall picture of the market for a relatively low expenditure of time. But regular attendance at such fairs also involves increasing costs and the continuous pressure to bring fresh goods on to the market and to present them at the fair. In addition business at the local gallery is often neglected because the necessary staff and the capacity are lacking. The evaluations diverge accordingly. Whereas some gallerists and art dealers see the growing number of art fairs as a positive development in the art market, others regard it as „a necessary evil" [8].

In fact the expressions of opinion, the reports on the experiences made and the diagnoses of the gallerists and art dealers we interviewed reveal a highly differentiated and at the same time contradictory picture. A small Swiss gallerist indicates how ambivalent participation in the fair is from his point of view. He presents a picture of the new constraints with which the „traditional“ forms of art trading are confronted and a picture of a revolution in the „values“ they had invoked: *„In my view the Art Basel today is a platform for the trade in art; art itself is no longer mediated there. Today just the big names are there; it wasn't like that in the past. But this is a development one can readily understand, because a booth at the Art Basel costs a lot of money. You can't go there at all with a normal artist. You have to be able to ask at least 30,000 to 100,000 Swiss francs for a painting when you're there. That is a selection mechanism. The art trade functions in accordance with the principle of investment.“*

And the consequences of a hypertrophy of the fairs are painted in the darkest colors, being regarded as a sign of cultural decline: *„Well, I'm not so sure if galleries will even survive. My thoughts go along the lines that there are many art fairs nowadays and that these fairs are of course the death of all galleries. I believe that the traditional gallery will not survive. I'm not talking about the next five or ten years, but long-term. Nowadays there's an art fair in almost every town, but the quality is questionable at many fairs, apart from Basel. They simply have to sell what they have in their booths and of course the quality then suffers. People are in any case accustomed to going to department stores and shopping malls, and fairs fit into this picture. It's a completely different culture. In the past you went to specialist shops, for example if you wanted to buy a good suit. They aren't surviving either. People sometimes buy expensive things and then again cheap things. I don't want to judge that at all. But the tendency is in the direction of the big market. For me it's the same with art fairs; the kind of consumption is similar. The small specialist shops which stood for good quality have now disappeared. It's exactly the same with the galleries.“*

The sweeping prophecy of a „dying out“ of the galleries is, however, qualified by restricting it to the „culture“ of „art mediation“, which serves as a „non-commercial“ cloak for trade in art. *„As I said, the galleries will die out; I'm convinced of that. Some will survive and those are the one's which pursue art as a business. There will always be trade in art and that's the reason why these galleries will continue to exist. But in order to go to the fairs these galleries need local premises somewhere. I could now say that instead of bearing the costs for my gallery I'll simply go to a fair with my artists three times a year. I've always been at this fair since it began. I was here in the 70s and have followed it permanently. That's why I can see the change that has taken place.“*

This critical assessment of the long-term effects of the institution of the art fair is particularly sharply formulated, but it can be found again in similar form in many conversations with gallerists and other actors in the art world. It amounts to an assertion that the enormous commercial success of this institution and its pronounced marketability are associated with strong monopolization effects. They undermine the traditional, spatially fixed gallery system and the intensive and enduring relationships between the galleries and their „regular customers“, who make up a more or less stable and locally rooted circle. If gallerists can generate as much revenue at a fair in a few days as in their local premises in several months in spite of the intensive cultivation of the customers and visitors at the local level, then it is more than understandable that their business priori-ties shift in the direction of an increased participation in fairs.

The boom in fairs „cannibalizes“ the gallery sales at the local level. The sales at gallery exhibitions have clearly declined, as gallerists repeatedly report. They also complain that the collectors in particular are now willing to travel long distances to fairs but seldom visit the galleries. This has a negative impact on the returns generated in the gallery.

Upswing and turnaround
The gallery system under the banner of commercialization

The 20th century is in the meantime regarded as the „golden" century of the art trade [9]. In the course of the „commercialization" of art the professions of the art dealer and the gallerist not only experienced an undreamed-of economic and cultural upswing but were also subjected to the extensive changes in a rapidly expanding art market, which can most fittingly be described with the terms continuity and contraction. Whereas the majority of the galleries continue, primarily out of a passion or „love of art", to offer unknown artists a public platform and sell their works, for which no other market for further sale exists, at relatively low prices, at the other pole a surveyable number of top galleries and art dealers has crystallized out, which, together with the auction houses, in the meantime dominates the top segment of the market for modern and contemporary art [10]. As central figures in the boom in the art market gallerists like Gagosian, Zwirner, Jopling or Glimcher have long become the quintessence of institutionalized market power.

World-wide 375,000 art dealers and galleries are registered who deal in the fine and decorative arts and antiques. One of the reasons for this number is that the concept of the gallery as a private undertaking includes many different forms of art trading [11]. The quality and the professionality of the galleries varies widely, as is well-known in the art world. The spectrum ranges from the international „branded galleries" to part-time businesses run as a hobby. The core of this highly fragmented group is, however, formed by around 5,000 to 6,000 galleries which, together with the auction houses, generated about half of the world-wide returns on sales in the art and antiques trade in 2013, amounting to a total of nearly 50 billion euros [12]. A mere four per cent had a turnover of over 25 million euros, six per cent achieved between 10 and 25 million euros, 37 per cent lay between 500,000 and 2 million euros and 34 per cent remained under 500,000 euros [13].

For a long time the art dealers and galleries dominated the art market. From the end of the 1980s on, however, a clear shift can be recorded in favor of the auction houses, which have strongly professionalized their business activities and have thus not only become an important competitor in the secondary market but have also penetrated the traditional domains of the art trade and of gallery business, the private sales and the primary market. In contrast to the auction houses, which are active in various sectors of the art market, the art dealers and galleries have experienced a process of differentiation and specialization according to genres, segments and price levels. Their competitive advantages over the auction houses continue to lie in their high level of expertise, their unrestricted control over prices and the waiving of a commission from the buyer. In addition they can guarantee complete confidentiality in regard to all the details of the sales.

The shift in the balance of power in the art market over the last thirty years has also changed the foundations of the system of supply and demand. Many art dealers and gallerists have had to adapt their business models to the changed framework conditions. The old maxim of the art market „buy cheap, sell dear" has long ceased to suffice. This has led art dealers and galleries to work harder than before towards finding art of good quality for their potential buyers, placing it at an appropriate price on a highly competitive market and accompanying it with valuable services and know-how. Whereas some of them have concentrated on a broader „mass market" for wealthy buyers interested in the mainstream of art production, others have turned to the various „niche markets" which are founded on distinguished connoisseurship and proven expertise. The commercialization of the art market and the development in general of a market as such has led to an unmistakable segregation of the supply, the exchange processes and their participants and, together with the field of art trade, and of artistic production.

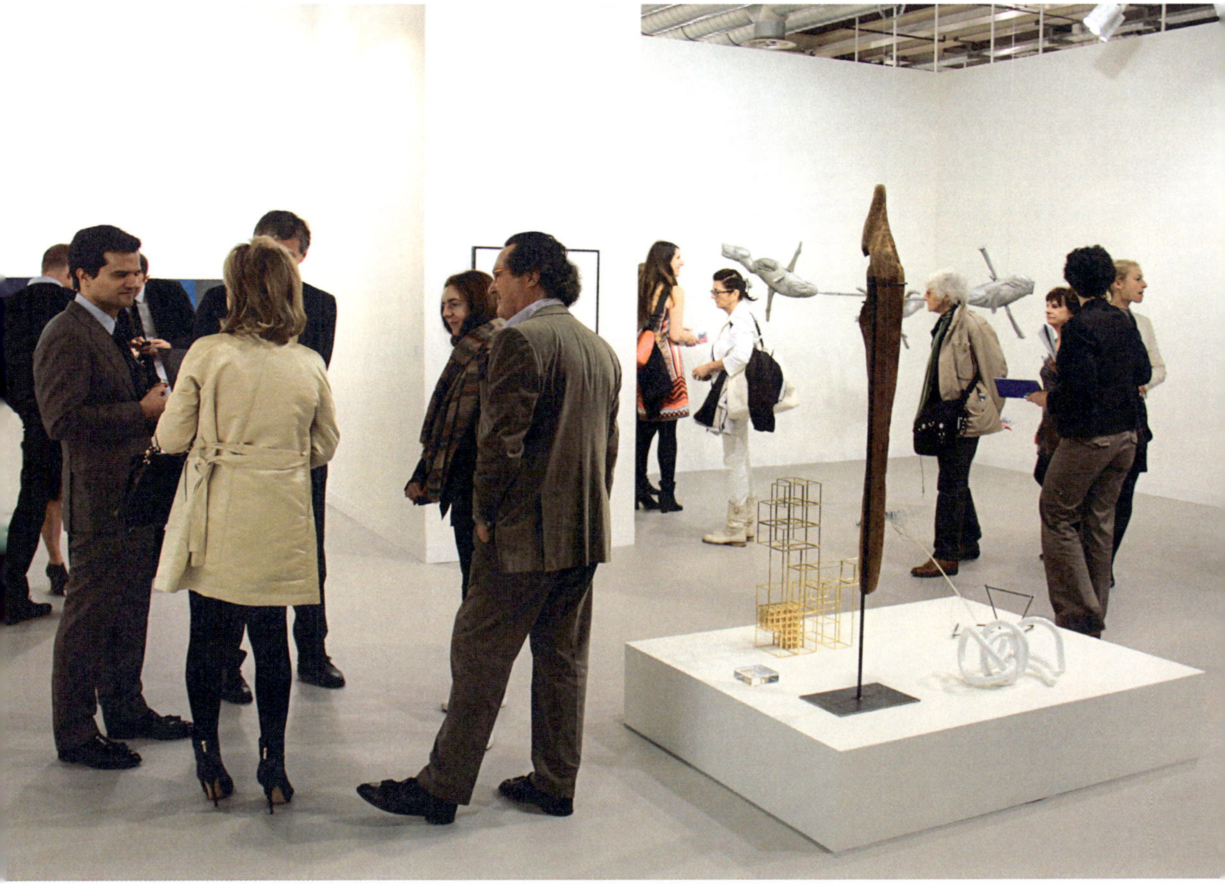

This finding, which is confirmed by other studies [14], is characteristic of the steady decline in the numbers of drop-in customers in the art shops operated by the galleries since the 60s and 70s, when it was still the „in-thing" for the culturally interested upper classes to participate regularly in happenings, vernissages and events in galleries or to wander around art and antique shops or flea markets at the weekend. If one leaves aside the „mega spaces" of the big international galleries, which resemble modern art halls, and the new forms of art events such as the gallery weekends many towns in the meantime organize, the interest in visiting galleries seems to have declined noticeably. As the art critic Jerry Saltz says, gallery activities only play a subordinate role nowadays [15].

As the drop-in customers no longer buy spontaneously above a certain quality and price level, the number of dealers has increased who only sell at fairs because they can expect to find their regular customers there anyway. Consequently many gallerists no longer feel the need to maintain a permanent visible and central presence [16]. For those galleries which are not admitted to the big fairs problems can quickly arise, if only a few collectors and occasional buyers come into the galleries. Some close down their businesses, others fall back on local or small regional fairs or continue their work as private dealers without a „showroom". But the practice of exhibiting is precisely the most important and visible aspect of classical gallery work and distinguishes it from classical art dealing, which can do without such public platforms [17]. Of course this institutional sclerotization has an effect on a further central task of the classical gallery activities: the „discovery", promotion, representation and mediation of the up and coming young artists and the new contemporary styles in art. Without this „visibilization of art", which is expressed not only in the gallery exhibitions but also in their documentation in the form of catalogues and reporting in the media, the modern galleries lose one of their central functions within the institutional structure of the „art world".

The previous core of the gallery system, the local show room as the center of gravity and cultivated socio-cultural ambience for the local world of art, begins to lose its significance. The galleries become depots in which the ground staff work to put together the scarcely dried materials produced under high pressure in the ateliers for the next show at various fairs that come up in increasingly short periods of time. In other words, there is a geographical concentration of the world-wide market activities in a limited number of occasional „big markets" at the expense of the „retail trade", an ousting out process which one of our dialogue partners compared with the disappearance of the „small corner shop".

This critical forecast of a development towards a flexible and globally fluctuating art trade without galleries is linked to a critique of the economic exclusivity accompanying this concentration. Works of art which undertake journeys around the world must justify such an investment; they must be placed within a high price segment. For this reason there is often criticism that young art in particular is clearly underrepresented at fairs, as the majority of gallerists rely on recognized and successful artists who are already well established on the art market and can guarantee cost-covering sales successes. Because the business must yield a profit many galleries and collectors prefer to rely in any case on art which involves little financial risk rather than to represent new and unknown artistic positions. Artists whose prices have not developed in an upward direction over the years, who are not in the category of the so-called „hot artists", are in the course of time ignored by the art market. „Normal" artists – by which the dialogue partners presumably meant the predominant majority of artists without a big name, ranking and reputation – represented by small local galleries fall by the wayside.

This development describes a process which has become unavoidable. Once the market with its authoritarian directives and existential constraints takes control of those traditional exchange procedures which create the value of the exchanged objects in a social act of reciprocal „approval" there can be no escape except at the price of insignificance. And the resultant accelerated and increasingly rigorous division of the art field, the drifting apart of „high brow art", the art of the market and „autonomous art", the art intended to be „provocative", is in full swing.

Boom & Boomerang

The competition of art fairs is growing

For gallerists attendance at fairs has become a decisive element in their business. The capital deriving from visibility multiplies in the market places of art. Absence from them increasingly results in economic and symbolic losses.

The analysis of the galleries represented at the fair in Basel in 2012 reveals an ambivalent state of affairs. On average the galleries offered their works for sale at five art fairs in 2012. There were, however, substantial differences between the galleries. Seven per cent attended only the Art Basel, whereby the majority of the galleries came from Switzerland. About one third attended at most three fairs and just under a half used five or more fairs as platforms for their products. A top segment comprising four per cent of the galleries were present at ten to fifteen fairs in 2012. In this distribution the size of the galleries played an important role. The frequency of attendance was significantly greater among the big galleries, here defined by the number of their subsidiary branches, which thus increased their visibility and chances on the market.

The boom in art fairs is accompanied by severe pressure to attend them. The galleries with exhibits at the Art Basel in 2012 together attended a further seventy art fairs in Europe, North America, South America and Asia. More than half of them were at the Art Basel in Miami Beach and a third in each case at the Frieze Art Fair in New York, the FIAC in Paris and the Frieze London. A quarter of the galleries had a booth at the Hong Kong International Art Fair. Hong Kong, a market from the emerging BRIC states, has asserted its position against classical strongholds such as Cologne, Berlin or Madrid.

The many newly established fairs are an indication of the „fair hype" which has been glaringly apparent since the beginning of this century. Out of seventy art fairs only twenty took place for the first time before 2000 and only five before 1980. Almost fifty fairs were established after 2000, including fourteen established after 2010. The new fairs of the last few years were not only set up in places peripheral to the art world such as Abu Dhabi, Dallas, Rio de Janeiro, Singapore or Tel Aviv, but also in central locations such as Cologne, London or New York. From this we can deduce an expansion of the art world to hitherto unexploited areas, which operates in accordance with a logic of „market socialization". On the other hand, in the centers of the art world an intensively competitive situation arises between the fair operators for the favor of the gallerists, collectors and the media which report on the fairs.

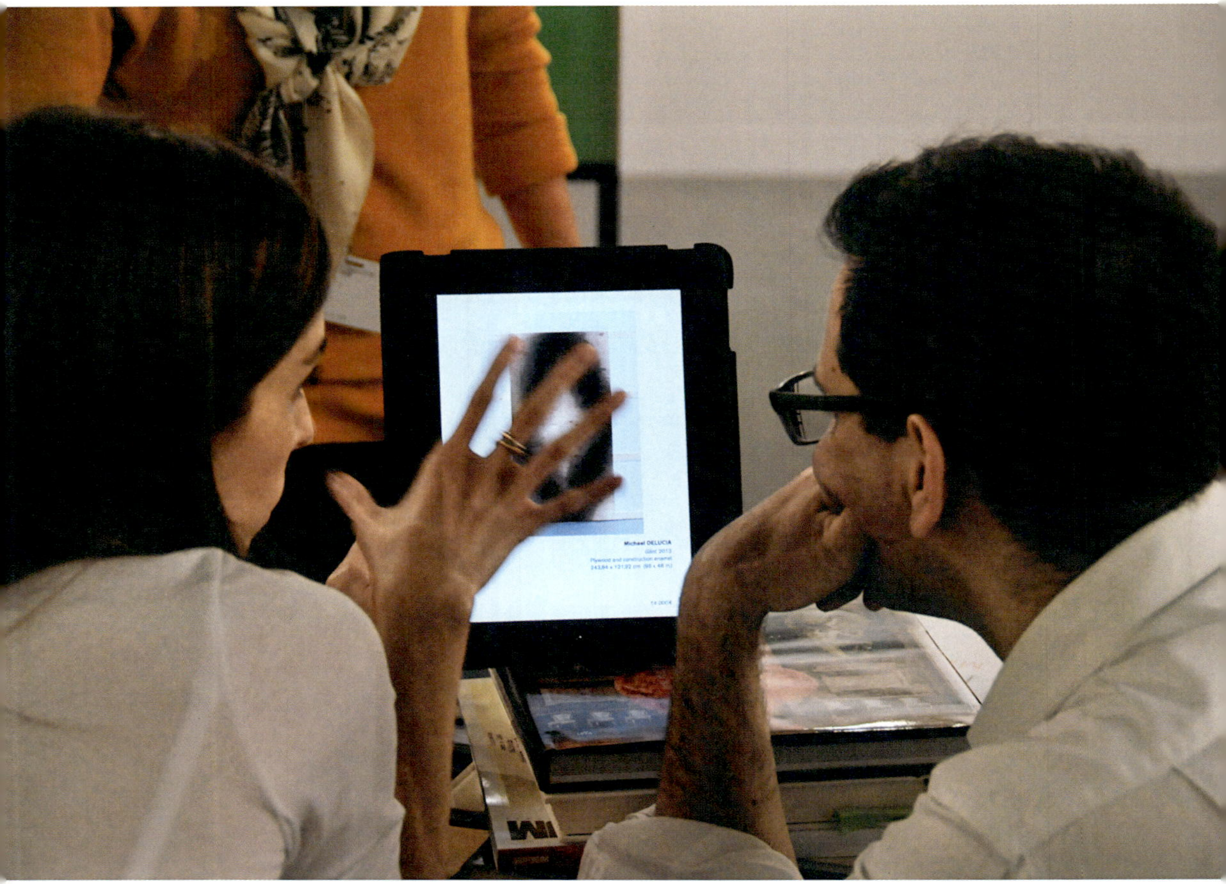
Michael DELUCIA

Double binds
The new contradictions of art trade

The polemically pointed account of the gradual decline of the traditional cultural institution of the art gallery may at first sight look like a nostalgic idealization of the supposedly „good old times" of an intact institution of the educated upper class. But it must be taken seriously as an aspect of an often thematized problem, the „economization" of the art trade. In this case we are dealing with a variant of the progressive „market socialization" in the shape of a weakening and marginalization of the gallery as an institution dedicated to dealing in art on the primary market, which is not exclusively profit oriented. Conversely institutions such as pure art dealing and art fairs, which more and more blatantly pursue commercial goals, are growing stronger.

The particular „cunning of history" lies in the fact that the representatives of the institution gallery themselves developed, out of economic interest, the fatal strategy of participation in a business model which undermined their own existence and degraded them primarily to the status of potential sellers at art fairs. This dynamics of progressive commercialization is characterized by the concentration of marketing opportunities among the „big players", the financially powerful „branded galleries", and by a shift in the distribution of symbolic capital in the field of art at the expense of the galleries which are active on the primary market. They are receding increasingly to the backstage of the public presentation of art, whereas the big international galleries attract more and more capital in the shape of attention and visibility. At the same time a shift in the existing forms of the „division of labor" between the galleries active on the primary market and the art dealers who are primarily active on the secondary market seems to be manifesting itself. Whereas the former continue to invest time, effort and financial resources in building up young artists, the actual „harvest" is brought in by the powerful actors on the market: the transnationally operating big galleries and the auction houses.

A renowned art dealer and highly committed member of the Swiss Art Trade Association sums up the discomfiture of many of his colleagues, who on the one hand complain about the loss of buyers in their galleries and on the other hand feel that they are overtaxed by the fairs circuit. At the end stands the question whether it is worthwhile maintaining a visible presence in a local art gallery: *„Some of the dealers are also groaning. One can have very interesting and widely differing talks with the participants at the fair. They say again and again: I have to be here; it's very important for the cultivation of contacts; I meet new people here. But at the same time they also say: I can't carry on with this circuit, attending yet another fair and yet another one. A friend of mine who was in Maastricht a few years ago and then stopped going said: I've been going to it for many years, but now I don't need it anymore. But he only stopped for a year. The next year he was there again. And that really says a lot. Once you're a part of it it's very difficult to stop. Because, of course, many customers then come and ask: ‚What's up. You weren't at Maastricht; aren't you doing well?' So it's difficult to make a step backwards, so to speak. And then of course there's always the much discussed model of the gallery business. Many firms afford one; but many also say: ‚It's absurd really; no one comes into my gallery from the street, looks at a painting on the wall and says: I'll buy it. Business is no longer done like that.' Many ask themselves whether they should keep a gallery open at all. But many carry on nevertheless. Of course it is also a question of the example one sets if one suddenly closes a gallery."*

Hustle and bustle

The galleries and the fairs marathon

Here is a list of the art fairs in 2012 attended by galleries which were also present at the Art Basel. Although this cumulative survey cannot give us a picture of the fairs calendar of individual art dealers, it does show the overall extent of the commercial demands made on the gallery system and the enormous frequency of the contemporary fairs, which practically fill the entire year without exceptions, apart from the most important holidays in the Western cultural sphere, Christmas and Easter.

12.01. – 15.01.	*Art Stage Singapore*	17.05. – 20.05.	*Hong Kong International Art Fair*
12.01. – 16.01.	*photo l.a.*	18.05. – 22.05.	*ArteBA*
18.01. – 22.01.	*London Art Fair*	23.05. – 26.05.	*SWAB Barcelona Contemporary Art Fair*
19.01. – 22.01.	*Art Los Angeles Contemporary*	31.05. – 02.06.	*Loop – The Video Art Fair*
25.01. – 29.01.	*India Art Fair*	14.06. – 17.06.	*Art Basel*
26.01. – 30.01.	*Arte Fiera – Bologna Fiere*	13.07. – 15.07.	*Art Bodensee*
09.02. – 12.02.	*Art Rotterdam*	31.08. – 16.09.	*Art-O-Rama*
15.02. – 19.02.	*ARCOmadrid*	07.09. – 09.09.	*SH Contemporary*
16.02. – 20.02.	*Art Wynwood*	12.09. – 16.09.	*ArtRio*
17.02. – 19.02.	*MARKET*	13.09. – 16.09.	*abc art berlin contemporary*
07.03. – 11.03.	*The ADAA Art Show*	13.09. – 16.09.	*Berliner Liste*
08.03. – 11.03.	*The Armory Show*	13.09. – 17.09.	*KIAF Korea International Art Fair*
08.03. – 11.03.	*Moving Image*	14.09. – 16.09.	*Art Copenhagen*
16.03. – 25.03.	*TEFAF*	19.09. – 23.09.	*Unseen Photo Fair*
21.03. – 24.03.	*Art Dubai*	20.09. – 22.09.	*Expo Chicago*
22.03. – 25.03.	*Art Revolution Taipei*	20.09. – 23.09.	*Viennafair*
08.03. – 11.03.	*Art KARLSRUHE*	10.10. – 14.10.	*Pavilion of Art & Design London*
29.03. – 01.04.	*Art Paris Art Fair*	11.10. – 14.10.	*Frieze London*
29.03. – 01.04.	*Drawing Now Paris*	11.10. – 14.10.	*Frieze Masters*
29.03. – 01.04.	*The AIPAD Photography Show*	11.10. – 14.10.	*Sunday*
30.03. – 01.04.	*Art Fair Tokyo*	18.10. – 21.10.	*FIAC*
12.04. – 15.04.	*CIGE*	18.10. – 22.10.	*Artbo Bogotá International Art Fair*
13.04. – 15.04.	*Dallas Art Fair*	18.10. – 22.10.	*Art Verona*
18.04. – 22.04.	*Art Cologne*	01.11. – 04.11.	*IFPDA*
18.04. – 22.04.	*Nada Cologne*	07.11. – 10.11.	*Abu Dhabi Art*
18.04. – 22.04.	*Zona Maco Mexico*	08.11. – 11.11.	*Art Market Budapest*
19.04. – 22.04.	*Art Brussels*	08.11. – 11.11.	*Kunst Zürich*
25.04. – 29.04.	*Artgenève*	09.11. – 11.11.	*Artissima*
29.04. – 02.05.	*Art Beijing*	15.11. – 18.11.	*Paris Photo*
04.05. – 06.05.	*MIA Milan Image Art Fair*	21.11. – 25.11.	*Cologne Fine Art*
04.05. – 07.05.	*Frieze Art Fair New York*	23.11. – 26.11.	*ST-ART*
04.05. – 07.05.	*The NADA Art Fair New York*	05.12. – 09.12.	*Art Miami*
09.05. – 13.05.	*Art Austria*	05.12. – 09.12.	*Ink Art Fair*
10.05. – 13.05.	*SP Arte*	06.12. – 09.12.	*The NADA Art Fair Miami*
15.05. – 19.05.	*Fresh Paint Contemporary Art Fair*		

How are we to understand the dilemma depicted here? Many gallerists participate actively in the growth of the fairs although they feel that they cannot stand the strain of this „travelling circus". Whereas some of them believe they can even do without it, others question the sense of their presence in their own galleries. However, both options are problematic. On the one hand the economic potency of a gallerist who freely decides not to participate in the big international art fairs is questioned. On the other, the gallerist who decides to close his local premises is open to the accusation that he is neglecting his proper work in the gallery for purely commercial reasons. It is a dilemma that reveals the constitutive contradictoriness of a market which lives off an anti-economic gesture, off the suppression of the economic sphere in all its aspects, an attitude without which „art" cannot be what it will and must be. And the contradictoriness becomes more and more apparent as the economic power, the opportunities and constraints of the market, themselves become increasingly visible.

Other actors in the field of art present a similarly contradictory picture. If the world of art just happens to work in this way and no other, then why not simply burn the bridges to the primary market behind one and ultimately submit to the logic of the increasingly predominant „new regime"? This is an existential question for gallerists who are often more or less strongly disoriented by the distortions and shifts in the traditional structures and roles of this field. The ambivalent attitudes of the galleries towards the art fairs described here is also expressed in a conversation with an important Zurich gallerist. On the one hand the returns on participation: *„Well, it's like the World Economic Forum in Davos. When I go to a big art fair and take the time as a collector, gallerist or whatever in order to be there, then I can meet with gallerists, artists and exhibitors: in the context of the conferences that take place, at presentations, excursions in the surrounding area, the pre-pre-vernissages, the VIP vernissages – all of it before the public crosses the carpet. I can then discover certain trends and use networks in this sense... I can swap artists and so on. And of course this kind of thing also costs money in the end, because the entire transport and the possibilities..."*

But on the other hand the financial burdens: *„That makes up a huge part of the expenses. A small booth at the Art Basel costs 50,000 Swiss francs. And then I have to be there personally. The transport and so on. I would have to sell for practically 600,000 or 700,000 francs for it to be worthwhile. Or I can book it under promotion costs, if I have the money, as a confirmation of quality."*

And finally the „quality" of supply: *„Well, when you go to the Art Basel and walk around for three hours or a day and your mind is... where is it? I don't know exactly. In principle it's enough to look at the ground floor in the main building... Then you look at the catalog and see that the same names always come up again and again. You see only the names of known people, of the dead, the known and the very well known. In the end, if you consider the big galleries you only find names that are already known. Then there is of course a hall with unknown people and so on. For a curator it makes good sense to go to such an international fair because he can see everything on one big pile. Again the Davos theme. One looks..., one can perhaps sometimes buy the one or the other object."*

The assessment of the owner of a French agency for art consultancy and of a gallery, who is himself at the fair, sounds similarly ambivalent. In answer to the question as to how he sees the fair in Basel he answers: *„Of course it remains a must. But one must add that this kind of fair cuts the ground from under the feet of the galleries thanks to the media hype they profit from and above all to their capacity to bring together for a definite time* *the non plus ultra of art, selected according to the most demanding criteria. Most of the galleries concentrate their annual turnover on these few days. Formerly the collectors went to the galleries they were interested in. But today the concentration enabled by these fairs provides a hitherto unknown and easy accessibility."*

Here too one has the impression that the gallerists are in a kind of double-bind relationship to the institution of the art fair. Although they frankly recognize the great significance of the fairs for the contemporary art market they also see the effort and the cost involved in attendance. The Zurich gallerist takes the analogy to the Davos World Economic Forum as an occasion to emphasize the way the „art world" celebrates its annual rendezvous at the Art Basel. Anyone who wishes to participate must turn up. For the gallerists and art dealers the Art Basel is a first class seal of approval and brings prestige for the gallery itself and for the artists it represents. To meet the high costs for renting the booths, the transport, insurance and board and lodging for its staff the galleries must be in a position to offset the costs through high sales and profit margins. Participation in five fairs can involve costs of up to 300,000 British pounds and more. The costs for a big booth of 80qm at the Tefaf in Maastricht including transport, upkeep, board and lodging can quickly amount to 80,000 euros [18]. At the Art Basel 42 in the year 2011 the participants paid 590 Swiss francs per square meter for the booths and at the Art Basel in the year 2014 this had already risen to 690 francs [19].

As a result many dealers and gallerists have somewhat reduced the number of their participations and applications for fairs in the last few years, not least because of the high costs and the lack of tangible results at some of these events. In addition, the profits realized at the fairs must often be reinvested in renewed activities and promotion work at further fairs [20]. Small galleries with a turnover of under a million euros can scarcely afford the participation at such fairs, as very little is left over after subtracting the continued expenses for the local gallery, attendance at the fair and the fees for artists. Furthermore, the substantial personal strain should not be underestimated. As a consequence of attendance at the fairs the gallerists are away from their premises for weeks, must undertake extensive preparatory and follow-up work in the connection with the fairs, and cultivate their contacts intensively. Presence in the local gallery almost becomes a side-line [21].

A gallerist from Berlin gives us an insight into his pragmatic arrangements, whereby service for the love of art seems to be a beneficiary of a flourishing business at fairs. In this double function he reminds one of Stephenson's „Dr Jekyll and Mr Hyde": *„Of course we have to make sales in order to cover the costs of the fairs. And there are fairs where we have a really good turnover. But we also do a lot of business after the fairs. You meet collectors there who are interested in something but don't want to buy immediately. If you add all that then it works out about right. But the direct sales are less; maybe 30, maybe 40 per cent."* But it is not only this argument that makes participation necessary. It is also the „customer tie" that counts: *„Yes, clearly, that's true. There is an international fairs' circus. The galleries travel; they are invited; the collectors are invited and travel with them. They get their golden or black VIP card and travel around the world. So you actually see mostly the same faces at every fair."* But just this former „core business" of the local galleries, standing for an hour with people in front of a picture and discussing it with them. mediating art, fades away: *„That still happens, but then you are talking about customers who buy a picture for 3,000 euros and pay for it in three installments. They exist and we cultivate them. After all we need the so-called secondary market in order to prepare our young program for the market in a unique quality."*

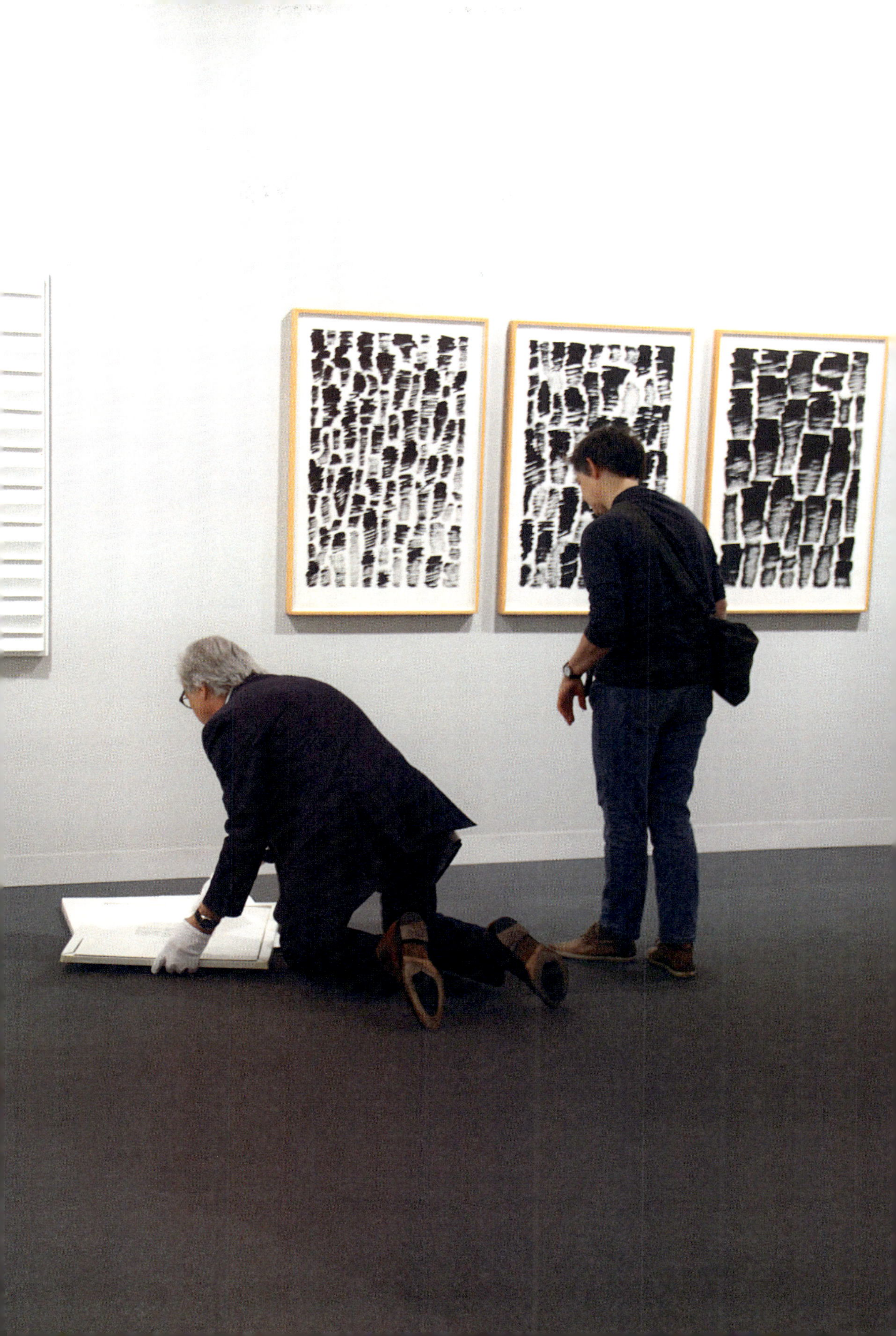

Active participation in the „fairs' circus" with its evidently less edifying aspects is justified here by the „good cause" in the shape of a cross-subsidization: the promotion of young artists and a „young program". It sounds like Robin Hood romanticism, when one takes the money from where it lies with the right hand of the businessman and passes it on with the left hand of the art promoter to those who are far removed from the business of the fairs and do not even possess the means or the possibility of being corrupted by it.

Whereas some of the galleries supposedly use and need their commercial success at fairs in order to promote young artists, it is difficult if not even impossible for many galleries with an ambitious program to make the leap to the Art Basel. The already mentioned costs are one barrier associated with attendance at the fair, as a Zurich gallerist reports: *„The good galleries have grown with their artists. It is above all always a criterion of quality whether a gallery is at Basel or not. But it has always been incredibly difficult just to get in. And the financial expenditure is also enormous. Many galleries simply can't afford it, although it would be good from the point of view of the artists and the program."*

From the perspective of the management of the Art Basel the ambivalent relationship between the gallery system and the activities at the fair looks different, as one of the directors says. The art world is, in his view, a gateway to the world, which brings a hitherto inaccessible international clientele into the local „white cubes". *„A gallerist does not come to a fair to meet the same collectors they are already selling to. They come also to meet new collectors, new museum directors, new curators, new critics. And I think, you know, each of these groups uses the show in a different way. The artists come to make contacts, maybe they are looking for a new gallery and they want to see where they think they might fit. The collectors come to buy obviously, but also to make new contacts. The gallerists come to sell and make new contacts. The museum curators come potentially to strike deals with galleries to support their shows, you know, or to look for artists that they can exhibit. The museum directors come often to reinforce relationships with their board, but in the same way to arrange loans and that kind of thing. You know, but I think what is interesting to everyone is, what is Art Basel, what is a show at this level. A show at this level provides a tour d'horizon of the art world, of what is going on. It is really, it is ideally all the best galleries showing all the best artists, all the best works that they have available, and so in what would take you, I mean, it would take you a month and a half to visit all these galleries and get some sense, of what is going on. And here, working intensely, you can do it in a day and a half. Now obviously it is not the same to see a stand as to see a gallery, or as to see a museum show, and we are very conscious of that and we never pretend otherwise, but our hope is that people will discover a new gallery, discover a new artist, and then go to the gallery itself, and then see the artist shows and museum exhibitions."* Here the fair is not just an inescapable contact exchange but also a kind of concentrated propedeutics for the contemporary understanding of art.

From the unmistakably apologetic perspective of the organizers of the fair the charisma of the Art Basel as an event extends into the local areas, extends into the traditional gallery business sphere: *„We say always that for us the impact is not two weeks a year, it should be fifty-two weeks a year, you know, for instance, people often ask us what do you think about the Gallery Weekend Berlin, the event which is – yes, okay, I see you are familiar with it – and people try to position it as something which is competitive with us, and we say, no, this is absolutely wrong, for us it is great. It means, it gives an opportunity for people who have discovered these galleries in Basel or in Miami Beach to go and see* *them in situ, because in the end, and this is why I travel to so many galleries, you know, when I am travelling, an artist doesn't choose a gallery for their booths and their fairs, he chooses it for the gallery itself. It is important to understand the physical spaces that the galleries have chosen, the neighborhoods they have chosen, the cities they have chosen. And so that is, I guess, that is the relationship that we see."*

Here the art fair as a „success story" is presented as a harmonious alliance with the core tasks of the galleries in the field of art. It is the appropriate modern hub of the art world, which, in the shortest possible time, offers a *tour d'horizon* of all the noteworthy and legitimate artistic goods available world-wide. Nonetheless, even the renowned international association of art dealers, the Confédération Internationale des Négociants en Œvres d'Art (CINOA) in the meantime issues warnings about the disadvantages of the hype at the international fairs: *„Yet there is a downside to art fairs. The competitive frenzy and compressed timeframe do not encourage quiet contemplation. Dealers may not have as much time to chat as they would in their own galleries. Art fair booths are comparatively small, and though dealers put enormous effort into their installations, a booth cannot match the breadth or depth of a gallery exhibition. At a gallery, a collector can usually see many more examples of an artist's work and get more information before making an acquisition. Though art fairs have their place, collectors should make a point of also visiting galleries"* [22]. This statement clearly reveals the difficulty gallerists and art dealers are faced with in finding a balance between „art business" and „money business".

It is not for nothing that the factor of „acceleration" is attributed a key role in presentday social change in the diagnoses of the modern social sciences [23]. That tendency is also evident in the art world, the epitome of inner-worldly asceticism and the experience of contemplative transcendence. One cannot afford to wander for weeks on end around the art galleries of the world when the entire spectrum can be surveyed at one place. There is no discussion of the fact that the traditional visits to galleries have come to be seen as too time-intensive only as a result of the acceleration in consumption made possible by the art fair. And the hope that a quick, time-saving trip through the global world of art will be followed by a leisurely period in which the stressed citizen of the art world can rediscover the charms of the local art scene and make up for the „lost time" is doomed to disappointment.

Here again we are confronted by one of the many contradictions, or even paradoxes, of the contemporary art world. The manifold dynamics of its increasing „economization" also has a determining impact on the structuring of time in everyday life. The idea that the practices of art consumption can be optimized according to a philosophy of „time is money" is diametrically opposed to the stylish celebration of an enjoyment of art which forgets time and the world and to the corresponding habitus of the art lover.

The fact that a good part of the traditional aura of art mediation has been lost, in regard to both the gallerists and the collectors, is put in a nutshell by an intimate connoisseur of the art market, who has observed at close quarters the development of the art fairs in Cologne and Basel since their beginnings: *„Yes, the fairs have become essential for the gallerists. I believe there are many gallerists who make 90 per cent of their sales at the fairs. That's the reason why the fairs have become so essential for the gallerists. Anyone who can't participate doesn't get a share in the cake. And that's also dangerous. But as there are so many fairs which offer the collectors everything in a concentrated form, they of course have said: I can't manage to see so much all at once anywhere else. I would have to run around the galleries for weeks. On the other hand, let's be honest:*

the fairs are an intolerably chaotic mess. Everyone has his rabbit hutch. Where is the order? Where are the formative powers? A good gallerist doesn't just sell for his artist; he also tries to position him. He tries to find the right museums. He has to act strategically... But I don't think that in art you can just hang up a picture somewhere on checkered wallpaper. There's a need for a moment of contemplation at some point. After all you can't read Tolstoy's ‚War and Peace' at Zurich Main Station. You don't find the time and leisure. To reach a deeper understanding you really need time for contemplation. And how do you find that at these annual funfairs?"

But anyone who is directly involved in the international business of trading in art and exhibits at the Art Basel tends instead to follow the doctrine of the conciliation of the two worlds as it is propagated by the fair itself. A New York gallerist who has attended the Art Basel for years sees the issue as follows: *„I think that fairs have now got to be, I mean at the beginning, obviously, I think fairs have taken a different role. I think at the beginning, twenty years or thirty years ago, an art fair was something completely different than it is today. I think that people would bring the work that they hadn't sold, and they would put it up. It would be another chance of selling the work. Now artists are actually producing the work for the fairs, because the fairs have become almost like satellite points for the galleries. I feel that, if you had spoken to me about four or five years ago about an art fair, I would be very angry about it, because I felt that there was no longer a dialogue in the gallery anymore, no longer people saw shows, and they were really just buying for their... It was like literally with a shopping cart, going around and popping things in. I think because the market has relaxed, now people are much more discerning, and all of that... I guess you are talking about the new collectors that don't really know anything. They have all kind of disappeared really. You just have got the more interesting collectors, who really are interested, and do want to know more. So, they are both coming to the fairs, but we have definitely found that actually quite often, we will open a dialogue at the fair, but we will actually finish at the gallery. It is just a platform in which to start conversations sometimes. It does bring them to the gallery, which is really where they need to be."*

Here the ideal picture of a fruitful symbiosis between the art fair and the gallery system beneficial to both sides, as drawn by one of the directors of the Art Basel, tends to be confirmed – but in a way which nonetheless permits us to see that the „genuine" way of understanding art must ultimately be mediated in the gallery.

Actors who occupy a more or less peripheral position in the art field, who are located in the economically and symbolically dominated regions of the world, often have little reason to quarrel with this last remainder of „conviction" coming from galleries which have been long established at the center of the art world. These peripheral actors see the presence at the international fairs as an incomparable opportunity.

The significance of the fair as a platform for communication between the various actors in the art world and for the exchange of information cannot be underestimated, especially for galleries from the emergent regions of the world. They can conclude business with actors on the market so to speak in the center of the European-American art world, which would otherwise be prevented by the great geographical distances between the parties. And the contacts and business partnerships based on reciprocal interest can be stabilized beyond the temporal and spatial limits of the fair.

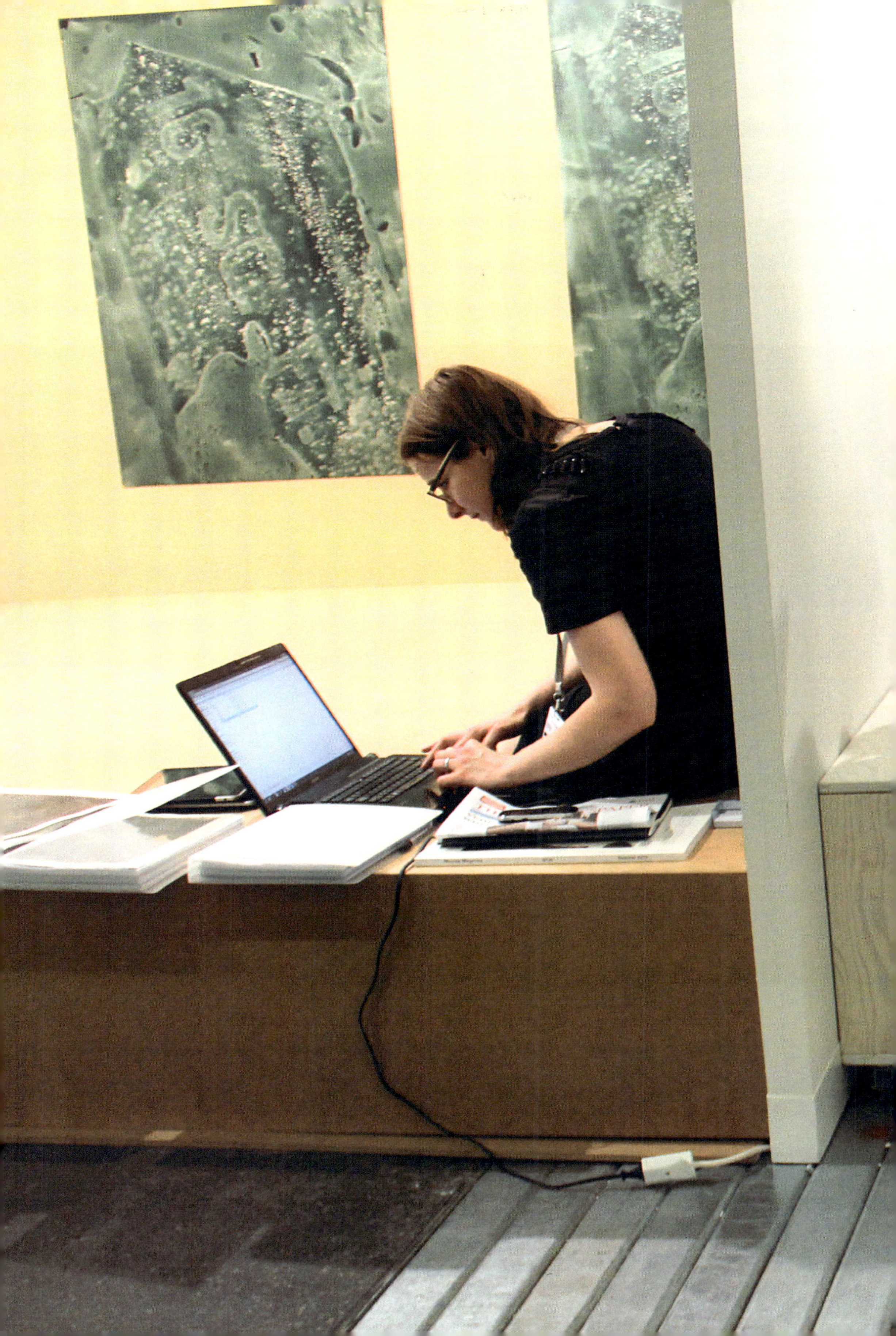

A Globalized Art World?

The Center and the Periphery as exemplified by the Art Basel

In the last decade there has been frequent talk of a globalization of the art market, of the ascent of China and other „emerging markets" into the higher circles of the older art centers in Western Europe and the United States of America. If we take a closer look at the developments, however, a differentiated picture emerges. This is true, first of all, of the structures of the art trade. The boom in art fairs has indeed led to a clear expansion of their operations. For example, the galleries represented at the Art Basel in 2012 participated in the same year in a total of 69 different fairs. Nonetheless, apart from a few events in Asia, the Near East and South America, the fairs continue to be concentrated in Europe and the United States. In particular, the most important fairs take place in western cities, in New York, London, Paris, Miami, Cologne and Basel. An exception, even before the takeover by the Art Basel, was the art fair in Hong Kong.

The greater part of the galleries which participate in the Art Basel also comes from these Western centers. In the year 2014 63 per cent had their head office in Europe (180 out of 286), 28 per cent came from the USA (80 out of 286) and only one in ten of the galleries at the fair came from outside „the West". The center of the art world is the USA, where a quarter of the galleries have their head offices. At 19 per cent (53 galleries) Germany alone can claim to enjoy a similar status.

The dominance of the West has not changed essentially during the history of the Art Basel, although an increasing geographical inclusion of galleries from a number of other countries is making itself noticeable. Nonetheless, the percentage share of Europe and North America has not declined substantially. In the founding year, 1970, galleries from ten countries participated, whereby only one of the 96 came from outside Europe – namely from New York. In 1975 galleries from 21 countries participated, and the number rose in 1984 to 26. Towards the end of the 2000s a further expansion occurred. In 2010 36 states were represented and in 2014 the number went up to 33 [24].

Above all North America, and especially the USA, built up its presence at the fair. Asia was represented at the fair in the 1970s by Israel, Iran and Japan. Further Asian galleries came from China (1988) and South Korea (1994). Around the year 2010 new galleries from India, Thailand and the United Arab Emirates entered the field. The development in South America was similar. As early as the 1970s galleries from Brazil and Venezuela offered works for sale at the Art Basel, and Argentina and Columbia joined them in the course of the 1990s. Africa continues to play only a marginal role in the art field; apart from galleries located in South Africa, no dealer from any African country has been represented in Basel. The same is true of Oceania; only single galleries from Australia and New Zealand have participated in the fair.

The art field concentrated in Basel has therefore expanded geographically, above all since 2010, and has extended its range further into Asia. But if one takes a closer look at the „fine differences" a rather different picture emerges. In spite of the geographical expansion, the center with it prestigious sites continues to be occupied by the West. The places around the round courtyard on the ground floor at the Art Basel, the „prime positions", are the exclusive reserve of galleries from North America and Europe. More than half the galleries there come from the USA and 44 per cent have their head offices in New York. Other countries with galleries in „prime positions" are Switzerland (24 %), Germany (16 %), Great Britain (8 %) and Belgium (4 %). In the „second row" on the ground floor, with a single exception from South Korea, the galleries represented come exclusively from Europe and North America, with the majority in this position coming from Europe. The *Feature* section on the ground floor also reveals the predominance of the West; apart from two galleries from Brazil the first row is occupied exclusively by galleries from Europe and South America. Only in the second row and in the sections *Feature* and *Statements* galleries from Asia and one gallery from Africa can be found.

This pronounced concentration of galleries corresponds to the „heart" of the international art market, which – in spite of all the talk circulating among art critics about the „globalized", „flat" and „cosmopolitan" art world – continues to beat in the USA and Western Europe. The „new face" of an internationalized art market has not made its appearance. The Art Basel, like other top fairs, continues to be dominated by Western art dealers [25].

Galleries at the Art Basel and their fair locations in 2012

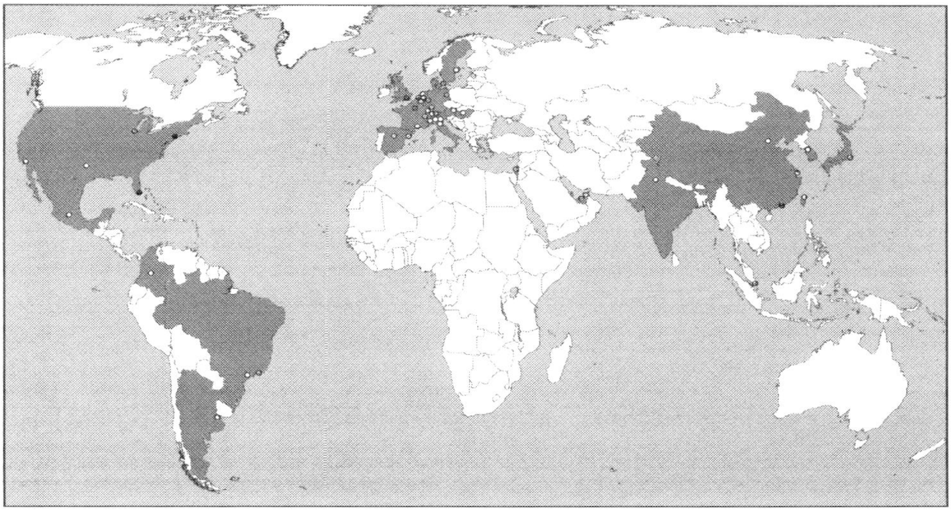

Whereas the „gatekeepers" of the art world in the shape of the most important galleries continue to come from the West, the origin of the artists reveals a growing diversification. Between 2005 and 2010 substantially more works of art by young artists from South America, Africa and Asia were on offer. At the Documenta in 2012 the share of Asian artists was almost 20 per cent. But again, if one examines the origin of the artists who have the greatest symbolical capital in the art field, a different picture is revealed, namely a very clear concentration of the „most important" artists in a few countries of origin. Although, according to the Kunstkompass [26], the 100 most important artists in the year 2014 came from 25 countries, two-thirds were from Europe and almost 30 per cent from the USA. Only six Asian names and one African are to be found on the list.

A substantial „global" shift is therefore not recognizable. The share of artists in the ranking who do not come from North America or Europe is under ten per cent and is scarcely higher than it was in the early 1970s [27]. If one takes into account that the majority of the artists from the non-Western world either live or have studied in the West the „spatial inclusivity of the art field" [28] becomes even more pronounced than the figures on countries of origin suggest: „It should be underlined that, although globalization is supposed to rule the contemporary art world today, national concentration is extremely strong and the West is clearly dominant when it comes to the most visible artists on the international art scene", and „the weight of the nationality factor is nevertheless clearly perceptible" [29]. The predominant opposition between a „center", a „semi-periphery" and a „periphery" in the world art market continues to exist. The USA and – with qualifications – Germany are at the „center", Great Britain, France, Italy or Switzerland are on the „semi-periphery" and the rest are on the „periphery".

A development towards transnationalization or „globalization" can at best be recognized at the top of the hierarchically structured art market, where a clientele of wealthy buyers from the USA, Europe and recently also from the „emerging markets" acquire and collect contemporary art, which is produced by a small circle of internationally renowned or „trendy" artists and marketed by transnationally operating galleries and auction houses. However, a great part of the art market still remains inside national and cultural boundaries; artists, their galleries and buyers very largely belong to the same cultural circle and have the same nationality. This weak inclusivity can be traced back, above all, to the strongly hierarchical structure of the field [30]. Young galleries, their artists and their first buyers, in particular, are embedded in local conditions, relationships and networks, which, precisely on account of the uncertain artistic and commercial assessments of the value of works of art, are strongly determined by relationships of trust and mutual support [31].

A gallerist from Mexico, who was also admitted to the Art Basel Miami Beach, speaks similarly: *„I think that our role in the art fairs, and the reason why we are in, you know, in the main art fairs is because of what we present. If I was to start representing big names like all the big galleries do, there would be, there wouldn't be any, I mean, why would they accept me, I mean, I would not be interesting and I would not, I mean, I would be competing with them and they don't really need that. The thing is that we do represent young contemporary artists from Mexico as well as other artists that we feel that have, you know, something to bring into our discourse. We have one or two new artists, but, I mean, we all tend, I mean, it is, our group of artists is stable, that is what you represent. I cannot, I mean, I do not have any infinite number of artists. I work, in order to work well, we are a small gallery, we don't have branches anywhere, we work with the staff, I mean, all in all with the workers and everything we are about twelve people at the gallery. So we don't really have the capacity of working for a lot of artists, in order to work well and to follow all, you know, all good means and, and so we have a group of perhaps 15 artists who are actively working. There are always some artists with, with whom we work, but they are slower at producing and they are, they are good artists, but they are, you just have to take different care of them. But the very, the very active artists are about 15 and we tend to bring... Of course, the art fairs have in a way changed the dynamics, because the artists have to produce for the art fairs. And sometimes it is very toiling for them, you know, it is, some artists do not want to show works at art fairs before they have been shown at proper shows, you know, at the gallery or elsewhere. And, and so they have to work for the shows and they also have to work for the art fairs, because the art fairs are important. It is a window to the world, especially for us in Mexico. I mean, not that many come to Mexico. It was the first year we were at Basel, there was a big discussion for the second year among the committee about us being up to the standards of the art fair, because we are not, you know, part of that big scene, you know, big New York, European, German kind of gallery or Swiss kind of gallery. And, and we had to defend ourselves, you know, why we thought our point of view was as valid."*

Perhaps the degree of „conviction" is more pronounced here because it can help to close a disproportional legitimacy gap in the field of art which arises when one is promoting „young" and „good" art from remote regions of the world. Here too a glance through the „window to the world" reveals the immense pressure exercised by the international fairs' business on the „actual" work of the galleries; the smaller and more remote they are the greater the pressure. For this reason it seems as if an overwhelming gratitude predominates here, a thankfulness for the mere opportunity to attract international – and that means Western – attention.

The particular interest in big international art fairs expressed here is not, however, restricted to galleries from the so-called „threshold countries". Galleries from Europe and the USA which are not located in the established art metropolises but in more marginal or rural areas see in participation in the Art Basel a means of moving closer to the center of the art market and the art world. A fair like the Art Basel is after all the best publicity a gallery can have. The achievement of a similar degree of public attention and awareness outside the participation in the fair would call for very substantial efforts and expenditure. The interest of the media is also visibly greater at fairs than at gallery exhibitions, which largely pass unnoticed.

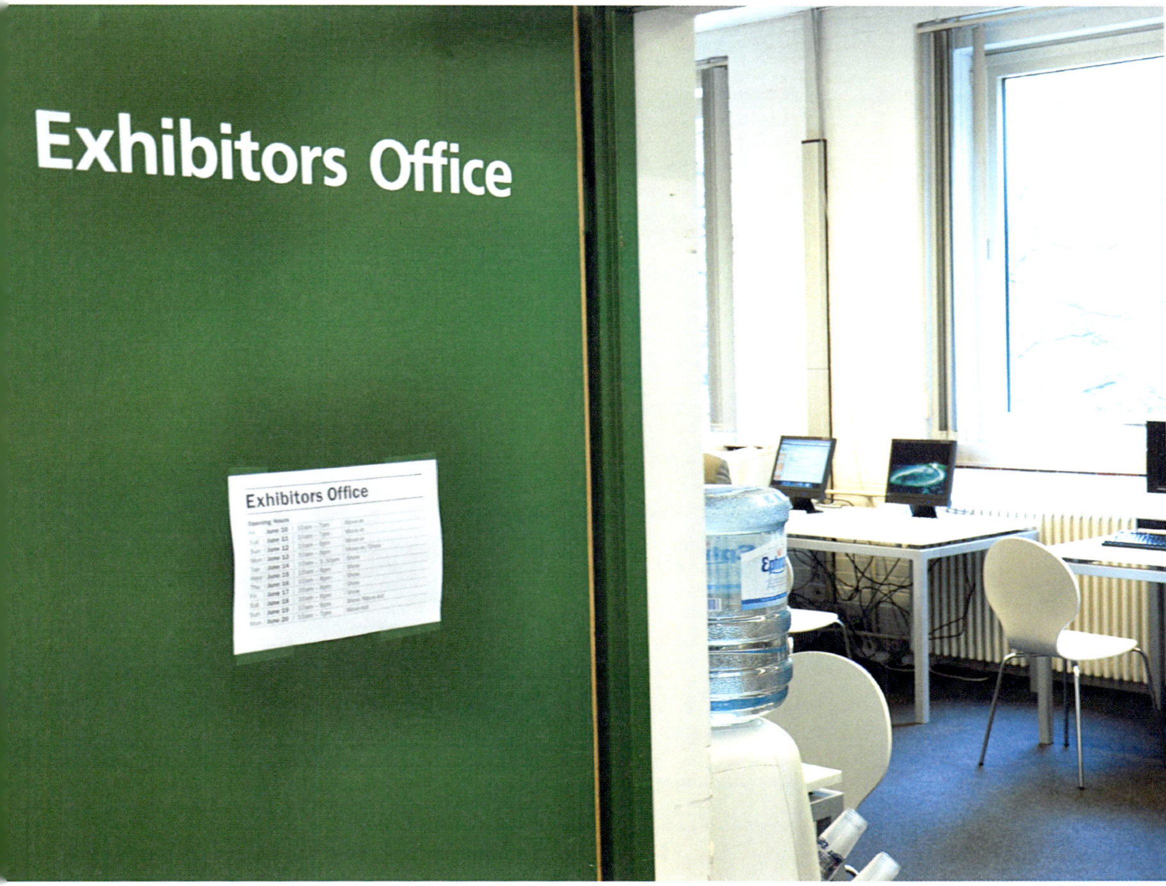
Exhibitors Office
Exhibitors Office

Booth Fees

The art fair as the scene of suspended contradictions

A survey undertaken among the gallerists present at the Art Basel provides interesting references to the different aspects of the relationship between the fairs and the galleries. It is not only possible to acquire a clear picture of the frequently recognizable and to the present day *constitutive tension* in the art trade between „art" and „capital". Among the gallerists it bears thoroughly realistic, pragmatic and even openly „commercial" characteristics, but only up to a certain point beyond which the foundations of their „calling" would be challenged. It is, in addition, exactly this tension which manifests itself as a kind of *suspended contradiction* at and about the fair: The behavior revealed in the answers of the gallerists creates the impression that in a place that is visited on account of its short term „business" and long term „business-promoting" promise „art" and „money" have virtually nothing to do with one another. The „schizophrenia" of this constellation, in which one half, the „universal" half of the profession, wants to have nothing to do with the other half, the „banal" half, appears as a kind of *invisible booth fee* which is paid over and beyond the visible hard cash entrance fee.

The constraints of the establishment

Among the exhibitors at the Art Basel no trace can be found in *practice* of the sometimes problematic nature of the relationship between the fairs and the gallerists in regard to the „actual" task of the gallerists, the „mediation" of art. For them participation in art fairs is a part of their business. A quarter of the gallerists interviewed attend five and more fairs every year and the great majority go at least to the „blockbusters", the Art Basel and the Art Basel Miami Beach, and the direct competitors Frieze in London and New York and often also to the FIAC in Paris and other renowned locations. For all of the interviewees the art fairs are „very important" or „important".

Only five per cent of the gallerists at the world-wide most important fair, the Art Basel, were newcomers; more than half had been there more than ten times. They thus make up a global establishment of art dealers, whose attendance at the fairs subjects them, however, to a variety of constraints. For the attendance at the fairs is not only „very important" for clearly business reasons, namely the *buying* of art with all its specific preconditions, the personal „contact with new clients" and the „presence of the major customers", whose buying power is frankly named as the decisive characteristic of the Art Basel. Attendance is also important because participation in itself brings the galleries symbolic gains which guarantee a profitable rate of exchange in a field which depends existentially on returns from „belief". For practically all of the interviewees the „quality of the exhibiting galleries" is, more than all the other advantages of the Art Basel, a confirmation of their own quality – and of their marketability.

A modest but promising „refraction" of the purely commercial aspect of the fair can be perceived in the reference to the „quality of the exhibits" and the „connoisseurship of the clients" and in the almost necessarily negative response of the majority to the „worldly" aspects of the fair – only one in ten of the galleries interviewed regarded the „events" and „parties" accompanying the fair as „very important" and only one in fourteen the favorable tax conditions. But it remains, above all, clear how far the potential supply corresponds to the potential *demand.* The fact that all of the galleries interviewed wanted to apply for booths at the next fair in Basel, three quarters for Miami Beach and half for Art Basel Hong Kong again reveals the constraints of the establishment. And the fact that three quarters of the galleries made the *choice of the exhibits* at the various fairs dependent on the cultural environment and the buying public confirms that the „mediation of art" they envisage is commercial and not content-oriented in character. The clear line taken for the program in Basel follows the mutually agreed conventionalized claims of both buyers and sellers, without any precise definition of the „quality" of the goods offered for sale: „best possible works", „important works", „very strong pieces", „major ‚museum-like' pieces, „international established artists" – only the best of the best for „international clients". At Miami Beach the accent is differently placed, with an emphasis primarily on US-American and especially on Latin-American art and a choice of artistically less subtle descriptions such as „"colorful" or „colorful/big". And the selection for Hong Kong is designed to meet the needs of „Asian clients" and the „Asian market", is to be less „conceptual", but „traditional and ‚brand name'" and should present „nothing delicate or intricate". The establishment at the international fairs is far removed from any „conceptional" mediation of art even in the simple sense of the word.

The existential nature of the *pacification of the conflict* between „art" and „commerce" is finally revealed when we juxtapose the answers to two questions dealing with the overall judgment on the Art Basel and the assessment of its artistic profile. On the one hand the general impressions are predominantly positive to enthusiastic – „solid as always", „good", „very good", „excellent", „great", „fantastic", „as usual the best", „best art fair in the world" – and only isolated voices range from a critical to a withering judgment of the fair as „conservative, declining, bad quality for emerging artists". On the other hand, for two-thirds of the galleries interviewed, the Art Basel is „market-conform and commercial" and „in step with the times", which only few galleries find „surprising". In view of the more or less clear awareness of its *commercial function* the artistic demands made on the fair are reduced to the conventional image of the „important work".

A secret self-portrait

However, the other side of the picture can at least be surmised. Even though the answers in the survey on typical activities regarded as „very important" show that „representation" and „positioning" lie close together („maintenance of an international network", „representation of established artists", „cooperation with museums", „presence at art fairs"), the entry „increasing the gallery's annual turnover", which was ticked without embarrassment by two thirds of the interviewees, had only the same value as the classical paternalistic formula „building up and promoting young artists on the market". The galleries own understanding of their work, namely the „discovery" and „mediation" of art, here regains its traditional place.

And the criteria named for the success of an artist are also equally „classical": „very important" for reputation are, above all else, the way into the museums, in the meantime also the acceptance of works in a well-known private collection, but also „solo exhibitions", in other words high *visibility in legitimate institutions* of artistic consecration in contrast to the „rankings in Art Price", which are evidently frowned upon. In regard to material „output" a similar pattern is revealed: as is only realistic „strong sales" remain a very important criterion for almost half the galleries; „good prices at art fairs" and „good prices at auctions" are treated with more reserve, being named by only one in five of the interviewees; and the answers to an open question repeatedly speak, in an almost obligatory fashion, of the „quality of the work".

The attitude of the gallerists to „virtual" art fairs on the internet can be regarded as a kind of litmus test, as it represents potential competition not only for the galleries and on-site fairs but also for the *traditional kind of art mediation* in general. The galleries we interviewed took part in virtual markets only in isolated cases and could seldom even imagine doing so. „Maybe" is the most positive answer given; otherwise there are many „no's" and an indignant „silly, never, ever". For the conventional art trade of the galleries the challenge of the „virtual art fair" is evidently not only entrepreneurial but also „ethical". The opinions on virtual art fairs are very predominantly negative and are supported by arguments similar to those which emphasize the personal contact with the client and the „material nature" of the „experience" of art: „no personal connections, clients don't see the artworks in reality", „discussion is also important, a direct contact with collectors to understand what they like", „we believe a personal face to face relationship with a client is more important", „the collector wants to see the piece", or, yet more simple, „artworks need to be seen".

In the classical gallery business the economic act of purchasing, the acquisition of a symbolic good for money, is systematically concealed behind a „personal relationship". This *intimacy of the purchasing process* in the galleries permits us to recognize the tendential „blemish of the art fair". Almost two thirds of the galleries interviewed stated that many of their „regular customers" did not go to such fairs precisely because their „market character" was so disturbing. These collectors could not bear the „hustle and bustle" and the „throngs of people", behaved in a „very private" way, but are „interested", „knowledgeable" and „serious" – an implicit but telling judgment of the gallerists on the seriousness of art fairs and their public.

Although, therefore, the relationship between fairs and galleries is subject to constraints which reflect not only different relationships of power but also *a new regime of art mediation,* this constellation nonetheless remains double-edged. Even in the establishment of the art trade the „trade" itself emits the „unholy" smell of the exchange of money in the temple of art.

A gallerist from central Switzerland emphasizes how important the fair is for the attention and the reputation he acquires through presence at the fair. *„We have been at the fair since 1992 and often applied for attendance before that. We applied three times before we got in. Then as now the Art Basel was an important advertising window. So that, for example, all the German Swiss notice that we exist. In the first few years, but even today as well, the Art Basel was a kind of poster for us in order to say: ‚Hey we exist as well!' Sure, you sell at the Art Basel too. But it is also important, particularly when you work together closely with artists over a period of years, to present yourself to a broad public, to say: ‚Hey, if you want an X or a Y then you have to come to us'. That is really the main message, and it works as well. For me personally it's also a network. You get to know collectors.The same people are there every year. It's a ritual. You know one another. I know more or less what we spoke about the last time. A year later, maybe, an E-mail comes: At the Art Basel you had this one or that one, or, do you have something like this or that. These contacts are very important, and if you are at the Art Basel there is no discussion about whether your gallery is good and serious or not. It's simply clear, independently of the program: You belong to an elite.*

The notion that participation in the Art Basel resembles the „award of a knighthood", which makes the gallerist or art dealer a member of an honorable and noble „elite" of his profession, can, however, be deceptive. The fairs were always mainly successful in the top segment of the market. But at the top end of the market, the desires of the buyers, and above all of the strongly growing group of „trend collectors", is directed towards renowned and well-established artists and works or highly demanded „hot" young artists, who seem to be on the verge of making an international breakthrough. Consequently, the „lack of supply" of market fresh goods is one of the greatest dangers for these „high end fairs" [32].

The pressure on artistic production resulting from the permanent presence of art fairs is enormous. In order to give artists the necessary time to create mature new works exhibitions are usually held in galleries only every one-and-a-half to two years. But if gallerists have to attend art fairs every two to three months that necessarily requires the artists to increase their production to meet the demand. A London gallerist states: *„I think the thing about the artists, the whole art world, is the idea of rarity – like something is a special thing to look at. If you are sort of all over the place all the time, I don't think it is very... I don't know. Also that thing of asking your artist for new work for fairs all the time is really boring."*

In this respect massive changes have indeed taken place. Always having to produce something new for the most important fairs blatantly contradicts the old philosophy of artistic „development": *„You have to bring something that nobody has ever seen before. It is really boring for them, I think. It is great to make money, but if you are just sitting in your studio – unless you are an artist that doesn't use handmade techniques and maybe who makes works that are in editions, photography and that stuff. I just don't see how it can be interesting to be feeding. If you have more than one gallery, it is already hard enough to feed each gallery for Basel. So then it would like Basel, Hong Kong, Dubai, Miami, London. When do you get to do an interesting exhibition? That is like out of the question."*

This mostly often leads to uniform and repetitive works which not seldom bring the artists a short term market success, but run counter to the long-term planning of the artists' careers. „A significant part of the artist's production is now dedicated to one of the many art fairs his dealers are frequenting [...] These works, referred to bluntly as art fair art, are moderate in size, which makes them easy to transport and fit into a fair's booth, and are in tune with dominant market trends" [33]. Whereas in the 1990s „controversial" and „unwieldy" art works were still shown, a trend has developed in the meantime towards „pleasing" art oriented on the collective taste of the buying public and above all of the collectors, which amounts to nothing more than the stringing together of blocks of works of those artists who are, above all, hyped up in the media.

This process of mainstreaming and „marketability" accompanying the success of the art fairs shapes, aside from the canon of art history, a sort of „parallel" canon tailored at the fairs, where, in contrast to the so-called „biennial art", a conservative taste oriented on tried and trusted art predominates. This tendency towards conformity in taste is in turn reinforced by the economic constraints of participation in fairs. For many gallerists it is scarcely worthwhile, on account of the costs, to take works from the lower and middle price segments with them on their journeys. Visibility is accorded to those who have already achieved visibility. The increasing orientation of art production on the demands of the market is only one aspect of the process of progressive „economization" that systematically questions the autonomy of creative work, as it is demanded and proclaimed by the classical artistic ethos of l'art pour l'art, and is a decisive source of the charisma of artistic production.

This questioning is ubiquitous and can even be traced among the „successful" actors in the „art world" to whom the market is well disposed. One can only understand the enormous „demands" made upon the protagonists of art mediation, of the galleries and gallerists, who formerly presented themselves as *social institutions* and *social figures,* when one sees them as part of a configuration which had been able to impose its powers of interpretation for more than half a century because the processes of the reciprocal economic and symbolic attribution of value were practically *withdrawn from the market.* The „moral" demand can be recognized everywhere and the „material" demand is quite evident, but the two can only stand out clearly in a market which more or less radically ignores the social basis of its denial. The galleries stand in the middle of this process. The compulsion to participate struggles „inwardly" with *credo* and „calling", while the sphere of the mediation of art and money splits further and further apart.

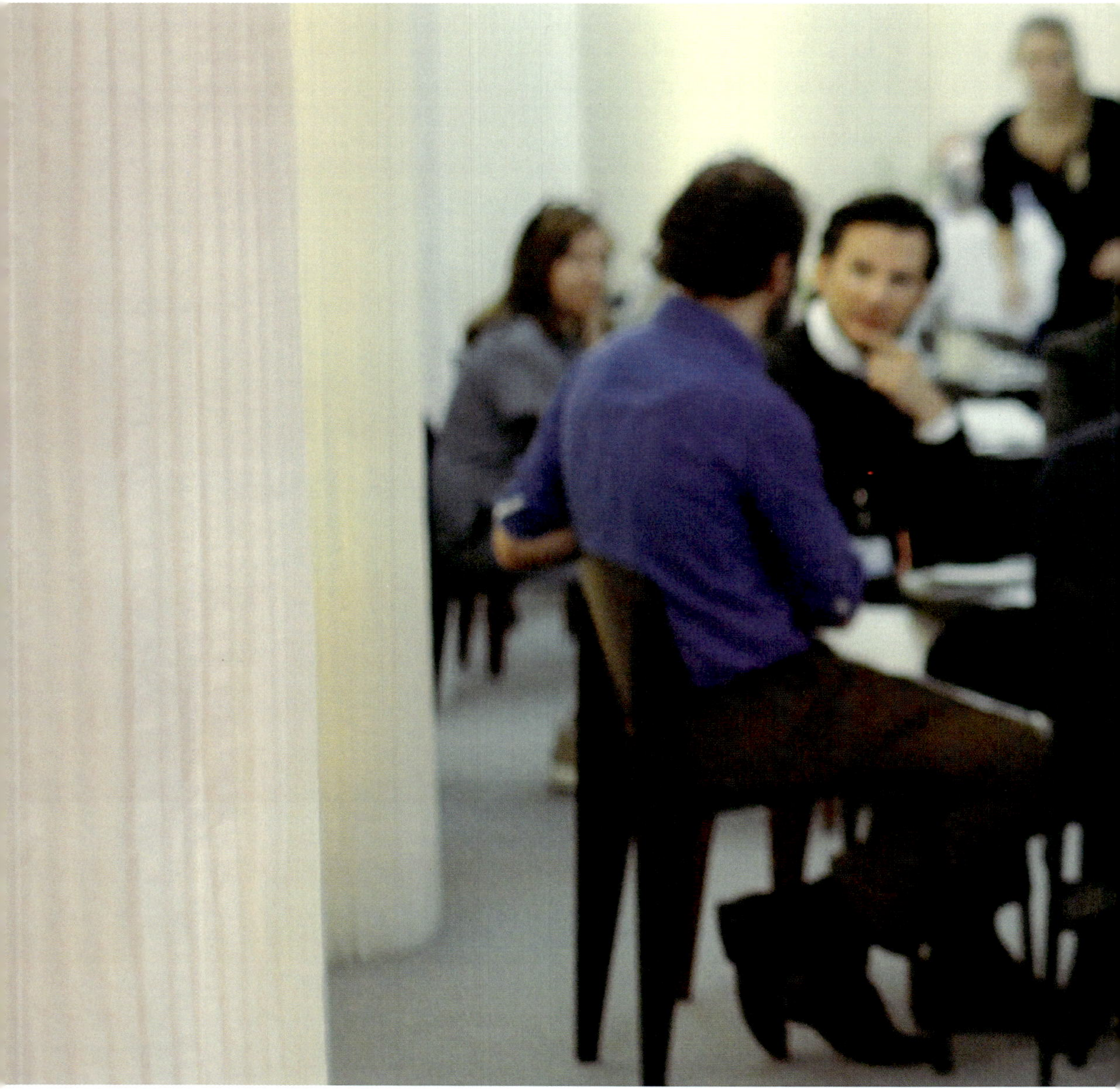

4 An Art of Distinction

Collecting – On the appropriation of immaterial goods

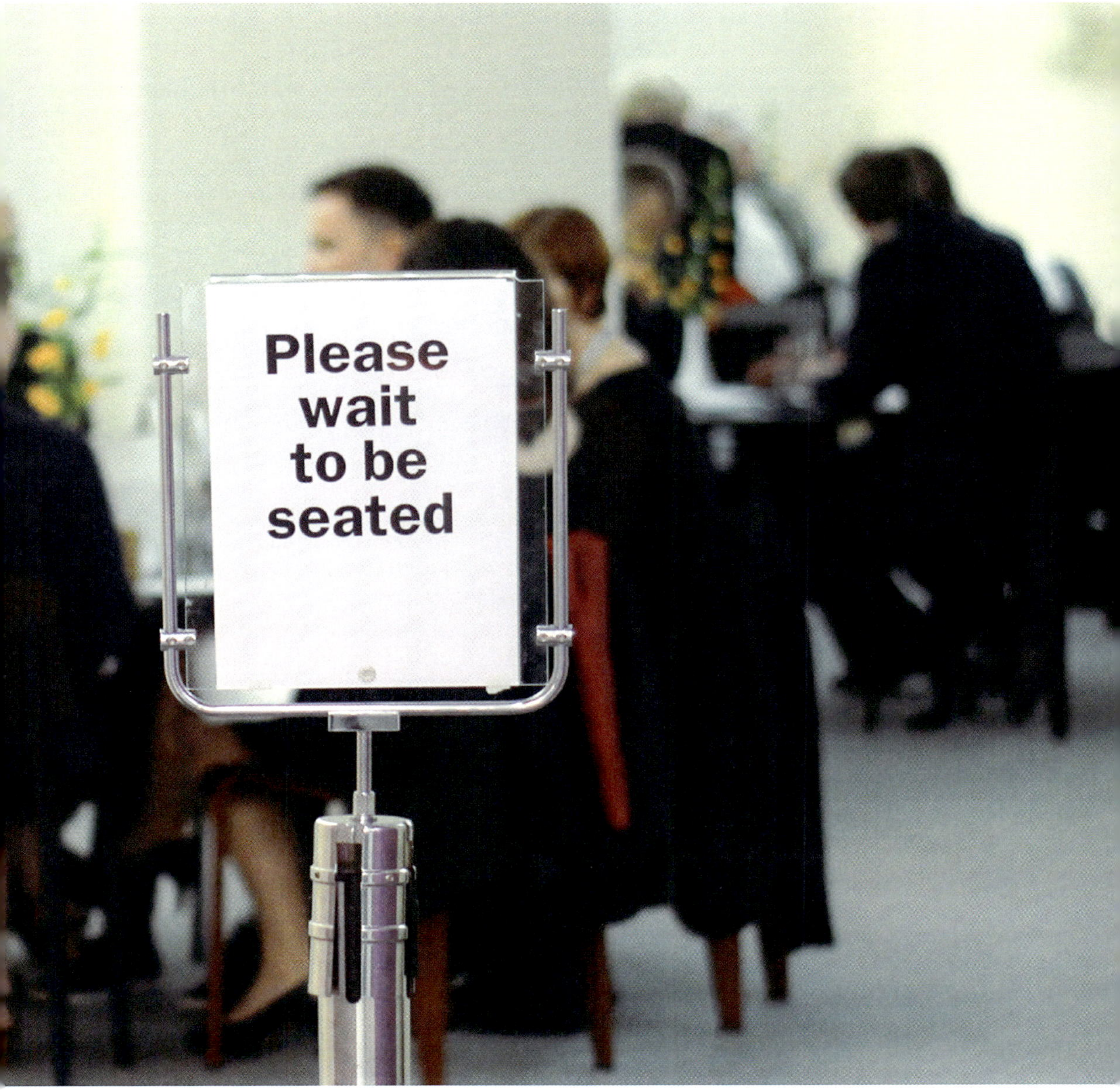

What is at stake is indeed „personality", i.e., the quality of the person, which is affirmed in the capacity to appropriate an object of quality. The objects endowed with the greatest distinctive power are those which most clearly attest the quality of the appropriation, and therefore the quality of their owner, because their possession requires time and capacities which requiring a long investment of time, like pictorial or musical culture cannot be acquired in haste or by proxy, and which therefore appear as the surest indications of the quality of the person. This explains the importance which the pursuit of distinction attaches to all those activities which, like artistic consumption, demand pure, pointless expenditure, especially of the rarest and most precious thing of all – particularly for those whose market value gives them least of it to waste – namely time, time devoted to consumption or time devoted to cultural acquisition which adequate consumption presupposes.

PIERRE BOURDIEU, Distinction

Of all the conversion techniques designed to create and accumulate symbolic capital, the purchase of works of art, objectified evidence of „personal taste", is the one which is the closest to the most irreproachable and inimitable form of accumulation, that is, the internalization of distinctive signs and symbols of power in the form of natural „distinction", personal „authority" or „culture". The exclusive appropriation of priceless works is not without analogy to the ostentatious destruction of wealth, the Irreproachable exhibition of wealth which it permits is, simultaneously, a challenge thrown down to all those who cannot dissociate their „being" from their „having" and attain disinterestedness, the supreme affirmation of personal excellence.

PIERRE BOURDIEU, Distinction

From a historical standpoint the „collecting“ of „art“ is an entirely modern phenomenon, at least when one considers the specific manifestations of the two concepts. It is modern, even though the evolvement of the wealth of nations after the end of the Middle Ages was already accompanied by a blossoming of the „arts“. In the great courtly society of the „world empires“, in hegemonial 16th century Spain, later in France, in the Age of Absolutism, precious objects and curiosities from all over the world were collected and kept in „cabinets“ by the incomparably rich and powerful – yet at the time of the Renaissance the splendor of the Vatican collections was already exemplary. But the acquisition of goods whose possession underlined the status of the owner simply because they were „precious“, and only rarely on account of their material properties, rarely but then increasingly on account of the „artistry“ involved in their creation, scarcely permits a comparison even here with the modern acquisition of art.

The economic aspect, the relationship to the social position of the owner, the social preconditions enabling „collecting“, the *ostentatious display* of these preconditions, must all be denied nowadays, at least formally. Modern collecting is not motivated by the material „preciousness“ but by the *singular* and hence necessarily „expensive“ nature of the objects collected, and for this reason it is at one and the same time both a *denial* and a *confirmation* of the social prestige which permits their acquisition. The collection of „art“ today acquires its particular significance through the ability to take possession of *immaterial* goods, goods which it is worth „showing“, „exhibiting“ publicly and celebrating. The gold and the ultramarine in the pictures of the Renaissance, their direct reference to the social position of the owner, have disappeared, the „artistry“ degraded to „craftsmanship“. Modern art and its legitimacy, in contrast, live from the collective recognition of an *immaterial* value, whose material acquisition, the acquisition of this special attribute, is only open to the few „special“ people.

But this precisely describes the tension inscribed in modern art collecting, and it is all the more problematic the more the material and the immaterial „value“ of art diverge. The explosive development of prices on the contemporary art market harms not only the nimbus of modern art, lent to it by the historical opposition of art and „world“, art and money, as the guarantee of art's extraordinary significance, but also casts a garish light on the exchange of money for social reputation which had hitherto occurred within the framework of intimate social relationships. The spotlights with which the objects of desire are illuminated at the Art Basel not only show a painting; they also give an impression of the entirely profane conditions enabling its possession.

On the Glory of Wastefulness

The distinguishing mark of art

Of all the luxury goods works of art are the purest form of uselessness, of „purposeless" expenditure, of economic „wastefulness" in its socially most distinctive shape. Access to them requires substantial material and cultural resources, means which are extremely unequally distributed in society and in their combination have become the privilege of a tiny minority. Originally the collection of art was a part of „elegant life", of the savoirvivre of a tradition-conscious social elite, of the nobility and the upper bourgeoisie, which surrounded itself with works of art as a matter of course, without needing to pursue a conscious practice of self-glorification. Its love of art manifested itself as an apparently spontaneous expression of a cultivated life style. The owner of a French art consultancy agency, himself an art-lover, nostalgically recalls: *„I have been sensitive to art since my childhood. My grandfather was a collector, but in the sense of the word at that time. One did not speak of collectors but of art lovers; the term collector was pejorative, like for example a stamp collector. The art lover was a man with a vision, who lived with his objects. He had his own point of view, be it about his paintings, his furniture or his tapestries, etc. The view of art was not simply oriented on a discipline; it encompassed a much wider perspective; one could say the ‚fine arts'. He was an art lover with a beautiful collection, but he regarded it as a life style."*

In the age of an unchallenged social elite art was an expression of the art of living, of the ability to make one's own life a „total work of art", a sign of true noblesse. The possession of a work of art was not only an indication of economic wealth but also of „good taste" and in the *consciousness* of this class it was detached from its material and social preconditions. For just this reason there was something *normative* about this manner of seeing art. A „genuine" collector – an expression used again and again in the conversations at the Art Basel – is „cultivated". „Anyone who wishes to buy culture should himself possess culture", as a big art collector from Switzerland put it. But precisely this equation opens up the possibilities for the fulfillment of social pretensions. Anyone who „buys" art can hope to acquire the insignia of „cultivatedness" in return for his money; thanks to their collectively attributed authority symbolical goods, above all works of art, bestow social recognition on their owners. But what is the basis for this specific power of art?

Works of art are singular goods whose uniqueness is intended in their genesis, in the act of their creation, and the quality distinguishing them from all other goods can be appropriated by the buyer as an emblematic sign of his own social rank. By means of a magical transfer the *singularity* of such symbolic goods, their extraordinary nature, congeals into a „personal" quality, into a source of charismatic aura and social distinction. One of the collectors interviewed puts this relationship in a nutshell: *„I believe that in a society that is so extremely differentiated as ours is art has a quality that has become rather rare, namely to present in a sensual, vivid and tangible way a value which can moreover easily be exhibited in a social process, which enables someone to enter into social interaction with others. And you can after all see that such exhibition collections are also the terrain for certain social events: receptions, parties, aperitif parties and the like. The social em-bedding of these exhibition collections and their use as indicators of social differentiation is of course quite evident."*

The distinguishing feature of art, the originary quality and function of its language, whose meaning can only be mediated through the distinguishing power of its bearer, is elevated in the collection of art to a very special art of distinction – here the singularity of each of the collected pieces of art is raised to a higher power by the reciprocal references and reinforcements and their accumulated charisma as part of an incomparable complete work of art, of a unique ensemble of singular elements. But this is not everything. The collecting of art evidently gives rise to an increase in the „waste" of material resources for the purpose of acquiring symbolic goods, which even lose their practical „marginal utility" as beautifying props for cultivated living, because they are kept in archives and depots or stored in private museums away from the everyday life of the owner – again and again the interviewed collectors complain that one scarcely finds an opportunity to look at the works, that some almost vanish into oblivion.

For this reason the concept of „art collecting" cannot be so readily taken for granted as might seem at first sight. When does collecting begin? At what number of works of art, at what frequency of acquisition, for what motives and intentions and under what cognitive and aesthetic preconditions of the buyer? The collectors interviewed at the Art Basel already revealed an ambivalent and sometimes even hostile attitude towards the concept itself, frequently preferring the title „art lover". Here the material nature of the process of *accumulating* art as property already bears a stain.

But, conversely, this seems to be its „purest" feature. For when the transition from buying single works of art for mainly decorative purposes within the interior of one's home to „collecting" is concretized in the self-perception of the actors, when the space for hanging up or exhibiting paintings is no longer sufficient even though one has several places of residence, when storage space is needed in order to stow away further purchases, then the dividing line evidently lies at the point where even the purely visual „utility value" of the work of art can no longer be realized and the only value is left for these works of art turned into „collectors' objects" is – apart from their exchange value on the market – the meaning attributed to them by their owners. By the suspension of any further practical utility value the significance of the collector's item is yet again inflated, and it is removed a step further away from the „everyday".

The essential aspect of art collecting is revealed, however, in its objects. If the activity of collecting „in itself" has features which are still thoroughly petit-bourgeois, „smallminded", almost childish, describing no more than the *piling up of things,* the material appropriation of the „world" in accordance with one's own standards, anticipating empowerment over it, then the „special" nature of the items collected, including the activity as such, takes a *qualitative* turn wherever the suspended utility value of the objects resulting from all kinds of collecting, *their withdrawal from everyday life,* is already inherent in the act of their production – seashells and stones lack this *aneconomc intentionality* as do postage stamps and model railways. It is a question of the *social legitimacy* of the objects themselves, inseparably attached to the „non-everyday nature" of their creation and use on account of the enormous nimbus of art, which our society, not least for this reason, attributes to them. But the fact that the award of social significance to a practice of collecting „useless" items, of economic *wastefulness,* can only develop in a context of „non-everyday" economic possibilities tells us something about an increase in a social privilege which, conversely, only „art" can turn into a „personal" privilege.

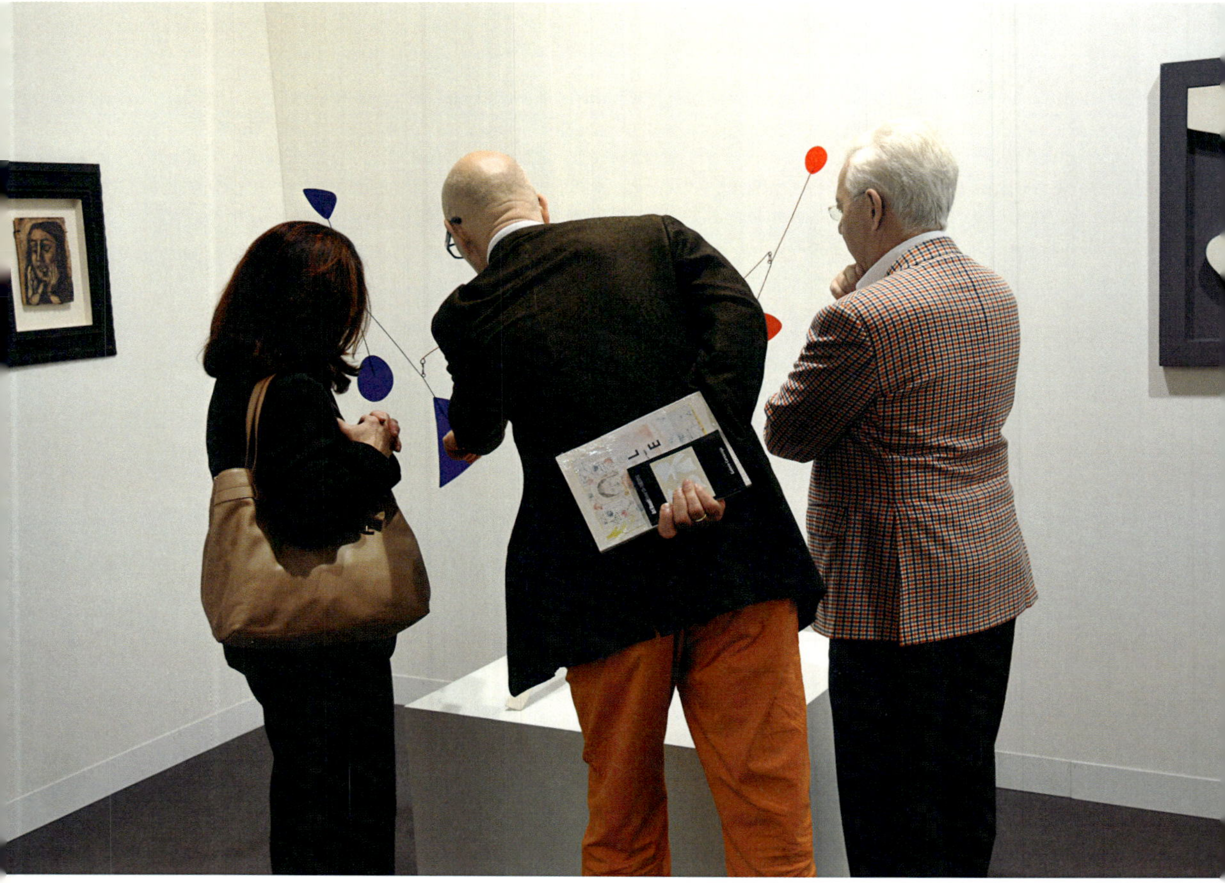

The Art Basel as a Meeting Point

A *Missa Solemnis* of the global collectors' world

The various actors of the art world meet on the stage of the Art Basel at a level of social representativeness, demographic density and public visibility scarcely achieved anywhere else in the world. This is particularly true of the art collectors, who play an undisputed major role in this event of art lovers, whereas the actual heroes of this epos, the artists, on the whole prefer to avoid appearing at the event at all. *„You always see the same famous artists who come up to Art Basel but there are also artists you will never see because they hate it. I mean, compare an art booth at Art Basel, a sales booth, to a good gallery or a museum show. There is no comparison"*, an art consultant said in a conversation. At this point already it becomes clear how far the „consumers" of art have in the meantime outstripped the producers and taken up center stage in the art world, a point which a collector at the Art Basel in Hong Kong makes in all clarity: „We are the true artists". And whereas the artists interviewed did indeed express a definite discomfiture if not disgust when talking about the Art Basel, the judgment of the collectors ranged from positive to enthusiastic: „the best", „the highest quality", „incomparable", „a must".

And this is so although Basel, a small, sedate town in Switzerland, can scarcely compete otherwise with the world metropolises of the art market such as New York, London or Paris. The American collectors, in particular, intimated that this location scarcely corresponded to their expectations on high-class travel befitting their status and they would not even have been able to locate it geographically if they had not been forced to discover it in order to undertake the pilgrimage to this high mass of art piety. *„You know, Basel is not the most happening town you have ever been to. It could be the dullest place I have ever been. You live there? You are not going to parties, you are not going to clubs. The mentality is different there. They are concerned about taxes, you know, we don't have those kinds of things here, we don't, you know, we are kind of blissfully ignorant about it."* But if one nevertheless exchanges the comforts of one's New York domicile for the staidness of provincial Switzerland, there must be a good reason. A pilgrim to Mecca does not have tourism or culinary delights at the top of his list of expectations.

And good reasons do indeed exist. On the one hand the extraordinary spatial and temporal density of what is on offer: *„Precisely at a fair like the Art Basel one can see art that one cannot see in this magnitude anywhere else on earth, not even in a museum"*, a renowned Swiss collector said. And a German colleague was of the opinion that *„the Art Basel is unbelievably important because one can inform oneself in the shortest possible time about the newest currents. It is also quite important because the entire art complex is packaged together in a few square meters".* Instead of having to fly half way around the world to a gallery in New York, another in Paris or a third in London to find the missing items needed to complete a collection, a collector can find here, concentrated in time and space, a representative range of everything that the top segment of the art market has to offer at the moment.

Then there is the „incomparable quality" and the „high class" nature of the galleries and the artists. The three hundred first choice galleries which offer their art treasures to the collectors are accredited by a strict, if not always transparent, selection procedure and furnished with an aura of the highest creditworthiness; and the artists with classical or prestigious names are the „most valuable" in the ranking lists of the art world, which in the meantime offer the buyers orientation. Even Biennale art is represented.

Collecting Art

On the genesis of a bourgeois cultural pattern

The concept of the *collectionneur*, of the „art collector", is of relatively recent origin and only asserted itself in official usage in the pioneering country of modernism and its aesthetics, in France during the epoch of the July monarchy (1830-1848), that is to say at the time of the genesis of an autonomous art field outside the patronage and control of religious or secular powers [1]. This does not come as a surprise as the art collector is a key figure in the game of art, who seems indispensable alongside the artist and the gallerist for a market of symbolic goods. His demand for this good first generates the market, nourishes it with economic capital, which here changes its form and significance.

The idea of the »maison-musée«, a bourgeois-elitist ideal, in which an early form of the private museum enters into competition with the public museums [2], accompanies the rise of the bourgeoisie and its emancipation from the aristocracy and its symbolic dominance. Art collecting developed in an epoch with the slogan „Enrichissez-vous" to a fashionable cultural pattern of the new establishment, as an aspect of its „elegant life", illustrated, for example, by the art auctions which took place regularly in Paris from the 1860s onwards. According to contemporary observers a stage is erected here on which representatives of the »monde«, ministers, theater people, millionaire financiers, entrepreneurs and ladies of high society can present themselves [3]. From this time on the private museums of the well-known art collectors are cataloged in the same way as public museums and achieve a comparable visibility and legitimacy. The increasing social significance and public recognition of this practice is expressed not least in the assumption that we are concerned here with a noble mission in the service of eternal and universal values, with art patronage in the noblest aristocratic spirit.

It is interesting to note, however, that the symbolic conflict about „true" and „false" collecting, legitimate and illegitimate practice, genuine and pretended love of art, already begins in this early phase of art collecting. As early as 1840 the „collectionneur pur-sang", the thoroughbred collector, is distinguished from two types of „false" collectors, the „fashionable collector" and the „dealer collector". The latter seems repellent because he acquires and resells art out of greed for profit, whereas the former is accused of superficial collecting out of vanity and an obsession for reputation. Again and again in these early discourses on art collecting the connection between this practice, upward social mobility and the search for symbolic means of expressing the desired status is emphasized.

It is characteristic of the manifest struggles over status and classification in this emerging field of art collecting that at very early stage the criterion of the length of membership of the field becomes the key to social distinction. In accordance with their social nature the collectors of aristocratic origin demonstrate their superiority in the competition with the rising bourgeois class, who, in their passion for collecting distance themselves from the pattern of the back-ward-looking, patrimonial art collecting of the nobility, but nonetheless stubbornly pursue their strategy of ennoblement by adopting the practice of the noble squandering and expendi-ture of economic goods as a means of acquiring the symbolic insignia of social distinction.

For this rising social class modern art provides an arsenal of symbolic weapons, in which, following the centuries-long established aristocratic mode of legitimating worldly privileges by demonstrating extraordinary qualities in the form of generous wastefulness, it finds the means to distinguish itself as an elite, but at the same time to distance itself from the elite of the traditional *Ancien Régime*. If, according to Rimbaud, the slogan of the „modern age" is „Il faut être radicalement moderne", then the terrain of art as a site of permanent symbolic revolutions is the ideal treasure chest for outfitting the new ruling class on the stage of bourgeois life.

Thanks to the emergence of relationships of trust between collectors and gallerists it is, in addition, possible to „optimize" attendance at the fair in many respects and to enjoy valuable services. A Swiss collector: *„Of course when one has gallerists one knows and they say ‚I've got something worth looking at', especially when they're gallerists from abroad, then that's practical. There are gallerists and galleries that work traditionally, that translate, say to you as a collector ‚Listen, I've now got, at the Art, I've got ten new works by this artist here. Are you coming to look at them?', people who offer a service, specifically to the collector. I've just got a case from a gallery in America who say, yes we have, I've already bought from them, and they say they now have such and such things they can send. They happen to be at the Art Basel at the moment and could show it to you live, physically."*

Finally, the place where the world of art blossoms briefly for a week provides collectors from all over the world with the best framework conditions: favorable tax conditions, an infrastructure for the long-term discreet storage of the works of art purchased in the open depots of the Swiss airports, an image of „Swissness", the virtues of security, reliability and solidity. And because the Biennale in Venice every two years, also a „must" for the collector who is a man of the world, is an invitation for a stopover, the date of the fair is also well-chosen.

But this is only one aspect of the attraction of the event. Just as important are communication and information – the possibility of social communitization. Not straight away at the inrush of the VIPs on the opening day. This is more like the situation at a clearance sale when the bargain hunters use their elbows and the entire weight of their bodies to win the best starting position in front of the gates of the fair. In Back for Blood Tom Wolfe has described the storming of the Art Basel at Miami Beach by a horde of art-loving multi-millionaires. *„Two hundred or so restless souls, most of them middle-aged men, were squirming like maggots fifteen minutes before Miami Art Basel's moment of money and male combat. They all had an urge... All theirs! See it! Like it! Buy it!"* The description of an art consultant on the occasion of the Art Basel in 2013 has a similar ring: *„Oh, it is not a VIP feeling. You get five thousand people who try to push each other. It is more like a football stadium. And people lose their manners if they ever had manners. They lose their manners. And that is rather strange."*

But afterwards. Then, without any intention to buy, the opportunity is taken to meet acquaintances from all over the world in the shortest possible time and to exchange views with them: „It is a very private world", a Dutch collector says, emphasizing that for this reason „word of mouth" is regarded as the best visiting card here. As at other, less noble collectors' fairs informal communication with other art lovers in the corridors, coffee shops and lounges is a central aspect of the cultural pattern of „collecting". This also includes the invitations to dinners and receptions, vernissages and parties, with the obligatory repertoire of a successful immersion in this milieu of the global world of art. From the perspective of the collectors interviewed the Art Basel is an excellent market for the exchange of information, at which all the big names in the field, all the opinion leaders and *taste makers* are present. And if you wish to be visible as a member of this elite world, to see yourself in your role as an art lover, you simply just can't miss it.

The significance of this art fair as a stage for the self-presentation of an increasingly consolidated global economic-cultural elite cannot be under-estimated. It provides an opportunity for active communitization, for a cooperative friendly exchange, for regular renewal of acquaintanceships, just as one knows it from the annual meetings of big family clans. The head of a corporate collection describes this function of the fair as follows: *„What clearly counts is the networking. Fairs are extremely important for networking because the people who are there take the time, they want to acquire new collectors and of course the buying is also, well, you can buy things there, you go there for both, but in our case it is quite clearly for the networking or so that you can say once again ‚Hello, how are you?' and so you can say that at the preview of the Art Basel, that there I practically don't look at art at all. You walk around, see someone, talk for ten minutes, then you meet someone you possibly haven't seen for over two years. That's what counts. I first take a look at the art on the next day."*

One of the decisive moments in the encounters of the self-celebrating collectors' community in Basel lies, last but not least, in the concentration of all possible forms of social resources of an economic and symbolic kind, which permits one to see this event as a kind of „cultural Davos", as an annual meeting of international capital in all its aggregate states and manifestations. Participation in the event in itself already promises returns in the cultivation and accumulation of high-class social capital, whose significance goes far beyond the mutual love of art and involves tangible economic interests in the shape of initiated or consolidated business relationships, in which the sponsors represented at the fair also play an important role – in analogy to the two faces of the art gallery, where the front stage, the White Cube, seems to be totally devoted to art as an end in itself, and the business and monetary aspects are removed to a backstage, to offices which are not accessible to the public. These business activities at the Art Basel do not take place in the booths dedicated to „pure" art, but in the VIP Lounge or the even more exclusive „Collectors' Lounge" of the UBS. The opportunity to „diversify" these business talks at the dinners in the town in the evenings is also a part of the „all-inclusive package" of the Art Basel.

An Exclusive Passion

Social Rationalities of the Irrational

At first sight, particularly when it is nourished by the medial presentation for a broader public, the world of the art collector seems to be highly homogenous and closed. The essential precondition for membership, the admission ticket for this exclusive circle is quite simply the availability of the necessary wealth, of substantial „purchasing power" – the spectacular reports on record prices for works of art at auctions and art fairs, which are again and again surpassed, regularly call this to mind. Big collections can only be had for this price. Someone who flies into Switzerland on a private airplane from the USA, Brazil, South-East Asia or the Emirates for the opening day of the Art Basel, is picked up at the airport by a limousine with chauffeur and taken to the fair, relaxes in the VIP Lounge and contributes to the annual assessment of the Art Basel as a great financial success is part of a small planetary elite and participates in the aura intended for it.

„The art world is very small". This is the characterization of her milieu by a well-known Zurich art collector. Her American „colleague" estimated that this exclusive circle amounted to about several hundred persons world-wide in the 1980s; thirty years later this rare species had, in his opinion, increased at least tenfold. But even on this estimate the world of the collectors would still be overseeable and exclusive enough.

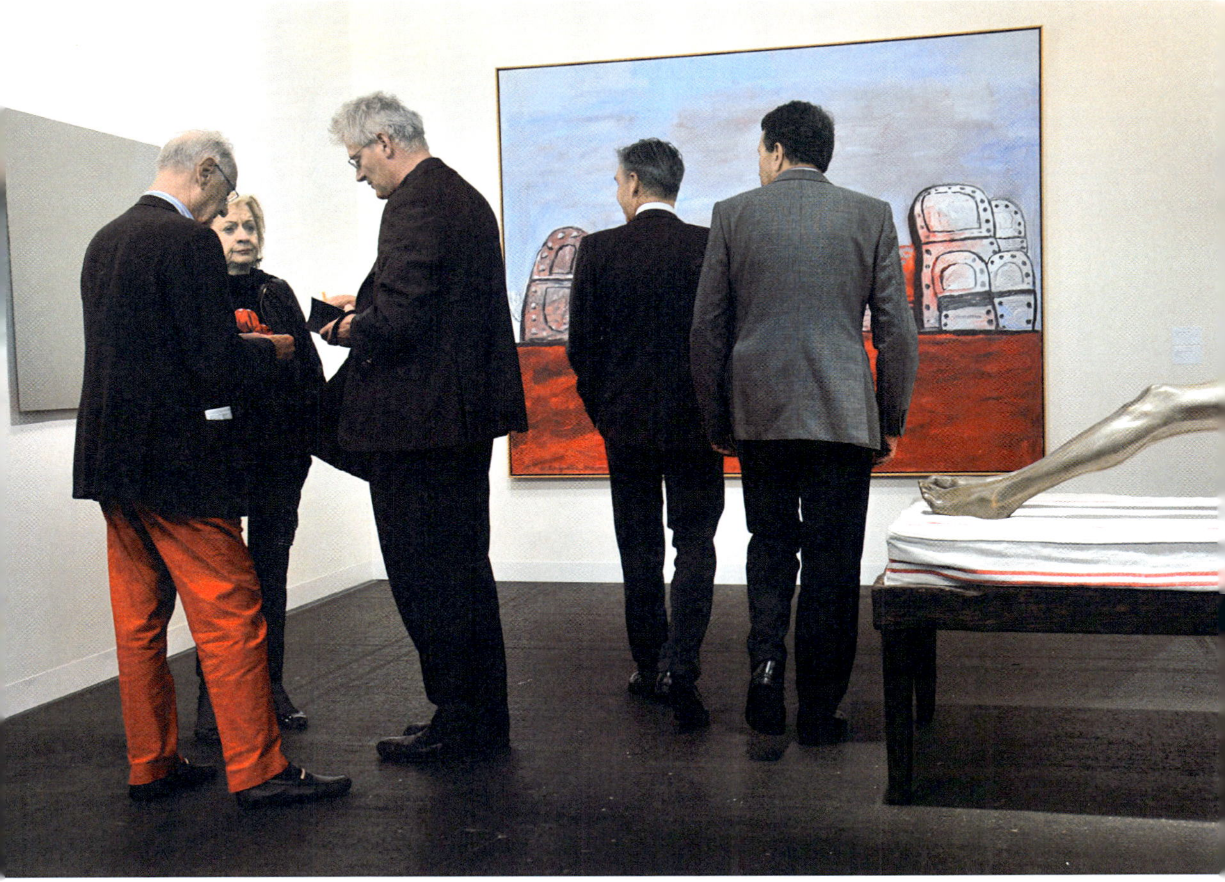

The making of VIPs

The Basel Classification Machine

How much the participation in the international „collectors' community", a conceptual construction that not only suggests exclusiveness but also „community spirit", a shared passion, a shared belief, how much this participation is subject not only to „social" but also to „business" demands is revealed by the ordination of the VIPs for this event. Who decides, according to what criteria, on which of the many candidates for VIP tickets for this event are worthy to receive one? Who plays, according to what rules and principles, the role of the gatekeeper in the process of selection in accordance with three different, hierarchically ordered classes of VIPs? And who draws the dividing line between them and the „mass public" who are only admitted to the fair from the third day on?

The socially highly selective access to the event in Basel is regulated first and foremost by a business model of the fair management, an organized classification machine which assigns a certified status to the visitors from all over the world by issuing VIP identity cards, thereby attesting to a kind of class membership. Until 2012 the gallerists were given a certain quota of VIP cards and could then decide which of their collectors would be accorded the privilege of VIP status. But the Art Basel management board has now taken the matter into its own hands. It uses lists of proposals submitted by the galleries, makes its own choice and then invites the chosen addressees anonymously, without any reference to the galleries which proposed them. For the collectors interviewed and for other groups of visitors to the Art Basel, being among those chosen in the VIP classes 1, 2 or only in 3 seems to be an extremely dramatic indicator of standing, which provides direct information on personal status in the art world, recognition and reputation, visibility and legitimacy. In numerous interviews collectors expressed unconcealed annoyance, anger and feelings of personal offense because they were not awarded a place on the Mount Olympus of the first category, but were only admitted to the fair in the second or third group, or, in extreme cases, were not given VIP status at all and had to join the mass public admitted only on the third day of the event.

An art consultant reports that he had begun lobbying at an early stage in order to acquire a First Choice VIP card for himself and the art collector he was looking after. Because he could attest to substantial purchases by this collector during the year he was placed on the VIP list of several galleries, and the sum of these recommendations led the Art Basel to grant him this privilege. Others dug deeply into their pockets in their need, in order to be admitted at least to the Art Vernissage on a 300 Swiss francs ticket, or to persuade visitors with a VIP card who were unaccompanied to take them in tow and so – regardless of the humiliation involved – to become a part of this hand-picked elite of the art world.

No matter what the classification criteria in the preceding processes of selection looked like, they led to a clear and visible social selection and segregation between different status positions, whose logic was elucidated as follows by one of the managers of the Art Basel: *„It is, I mean, it is somewhat subjective... but I mean, we do have a system when someone approaches us for a VIP card, we send them a form, depending on whether they are a museum curator, a private collector, or an art advisor, and we ask questions like which galleries are you working with closely, which artists are you collecting, which museum boards do you belong to, if they are a private collector, you know. And then we check those back with the galleries that they say they are working with, so you get a sense, is this someone who is working, is this a major collector, is this is minor collector, is this someone who bought one piece. So, you know, we do a lot of research, obviously the people who, you know, we have people on staff and on retainer whose job it is to know which collectors are moving, are moving things".* The power to set something „in motion" in the art world, the possibility to translate financial into definitional power here evidently takes first place.

And a great deal of effort is in fact put into this selection procedure. *„I mean, it is always a difficult thing in the sense that there is a lot of ebb and flow with collectors. A lot of collectors start really* *strong and then they lose steam and then maybe they come back, you know, things like divorces and financial crises or financial successes can change people's level of collecting, and this is why we reevaluate every year everybody on that list in the same way that we re-evaluate every year all the galleries in the fair. You know, we are very conscious of the volatility of this world."*

An effort designed to identify the „top population": *„And so, again it is not an absolute thing. It is not, you know, like for instance, there are banks that have VIP areas or VIP events and they say, well, you have to have X number of dollars under management in order to qualify for this event, you know. It is not that simple, because we don't know how much people are spending, we have to do it in a, in a less, in a less subjective sort of way, but, I mean, the goal is always to make sure that the people who are at the highest level of collecting are treated like VIPs. And at the same time we have two levels of VIPs, because there are also people who are not quite there, but are still VIPs, and if the halls were infinite we could just put all the VIPs in the halls, but because they are not, we have to really figure out a way that when a VIP, you know, if you have the top of a VIP moment, then that is also the top of a VIP."*

This practice of channeled access to the fair in the shape of a gradually opening funnel and the granting of privileged access for collectors was not, incidentally, criticized as such by any of our interview partners, whether they were collectors, gallerists, curators or consultants. All of them found it appropriate to reserve the first two days of the fair for the VIPs. Criticism occurred when someone personally felt that the classification was unjust in his or her case. A Dutch visitor, for example, complained that he had not had the honor to be reckoned among the first group of VIPs although he was one of the most important art collectors back home and invested considerable sums of money in art every year. Others seemed flabbergasted when, for the first time in 2013, they were not granted a VIP card „without any reasons or explanations being given".

From the perspective of those affected by it the classification machinery of the Art Basel seems to resemble a lottery for placement on a reputation market. Of course the market regulation undertaken by the management of the fair for the exclusive collectors' days also serves the purpose of excluding unwelcome guests, as is reported by one member of staff of the Art Basel: *„Yes, well, I mean, of course there are favorite collectors. They are the ones who are really clever and build up really great collections and approach things in a very intellectual and serious manner. And also build up artists. And above all don't resell their art. Because the collectors one doesn't like so much are precisely those finance..., are often, not always, but often people who speculate with art and then go to auctions. And that's not good for the artists and the market of these artists. And it's not good for the gallerists either, because they don't get anything out of it. And that's why it's not good for the development of the market. And it's also unfair towards the gallerist and the artist. That's why we support the format of the gallery and would never support the format of the auction with our platform. And don't want to give them a platform and do everything so that they can't spread out here and make use of us. These are the most unpleasant collectors".*

This makes it clear that those responsible for the art fair are concerned to enforce certain rules of the art world and the principles of good practice, rules which attempt to translate the „sheer" pressure of „money" into „more civilized", „more cultivated" forms of art acquisition – a strategy essential for the survival of the fair's reputation. This form of organized exclusiveness with its hierarchies structured according to the differing importance and legitimacy of the visitors has a direct counterpart in the classification conflicts within the collectors' community in regard to the drawing of boundary lines between the so-called „genuine" and the „false" lovers of art („Incidentally, the true collectors have always been a minority", a French collector says), between „connoisseurs" and „philistines", between the „impassioned" and the „investment-oriented" actors in the art world. If one has the various species of the art milieu described by its inhabitants one quickly realizes how deep the social divisions are in this supposedly so closed community of collectors united in their love of art. „Collecting" itself is a terrain full of conflict, in which the *normative* weaponry, the conventionalized „propriety" of the ways of acquiring art, plays a decisive part.

But the sparing use of the label „collector" obscures the fact that world-wide there are probably several hundred thousand contemporaries who regularly buy works of art and see and describe themselves as art collectors. The very fact that the majority of the interviewed members of this elite do not, however, include them in the collectors' community is itself a meaningful sign of the symbolic relationships of power, the closures and exclusions in the field of art collecting. The term „collector" seems to be tacitly reserved as a kind of title of nobility for a small group of chosen lovers and connoisseurs, an intimate circle of initiates. Just as only a tiny minority of contemporary artists succeed in stepping out of the shadows of insignificance and acquiring broad public attention, so too the world of collectors resembles an iceberg, whose tip above the water majestically towers over the huge inert mass beneath the surface.

However, the privileged pecuniary endowment of this exclusive circle is only one side, the „profane" side, of art collecting. Apart from the necessary economic capital as a downright banal and basic precondition for the cultivated practice of collection in this region of the art field there is another resource regarded as even more essential, the possession of cultural capital in the form of aesthetic and intellectual competencies and dispositions – an ability to „read", „understand" and „appreciate" art. But the fact that this ability, an essential ingredient of „genuine" collecting, of legitimate practice, itself lives off the social conditions enabling its acquisition and recognition is nevertheless subject to a systematic pledge of secrecy. The reinterpretation of the privilege as a personal talent is also one of the basic preconditions of the game. The big collectors we interviewed „just have it in their blood", as the founder of a German private museum explained. It is something, as a well-known Swiss collector believed, „that you simply cannot learn". And a further collector states: *„I believe it is innate. Perhaps it needs an awakening, a kind of formative experience, and afterwards it calls for a sense of adventure, but not everybody has it."* This naturalistic vision of a love of art firmly anchored in the DNA is often concretized in the image of collecting as an „addiction" or a „drug".

And the inspiring effect of childhood upbringing when one „just happened to be surrounded by these things" and „grew up like that" appears to be purified of all social connotations: in the unsuspicious context of family socialization, at visits to museums („I was dragged along"), in conversations with adults over dinner („My parents often spoke about art"), through art on the walls of the parents' house, art in everyday life (*„My father had pictures at home above all. He had developed a passion. And the pleasant thing about it was, I believe, that he didn't do it so systematically according to some dry standards. It was a pure affair of the heart. He was just fond of aesthetics and it was simply a part of his everyday life."*) The love of art was acquired and ingrained by these heirs to cultural capital in these ways, gradually becoming a kind of second nature and later providing the foundation for their self-confidence in dealing with art, for the competencies which cannot be acquired anywhere near as naturally, as matter-of-factly, by means of formal education.

But this is not all. Precisely in regard to such cases socially exclusive passion is not everything. The practice of collecting requires further investments, time above all, for reading, acquiring knowledge in order to „cultivate a certain way of seeing", *life-long learning* („One must keep on studying all the time", „I read the specialist literature for at least two hours every day") – the refinement of the aesthetic sense calls for a certain competence in art history and turns into real work.

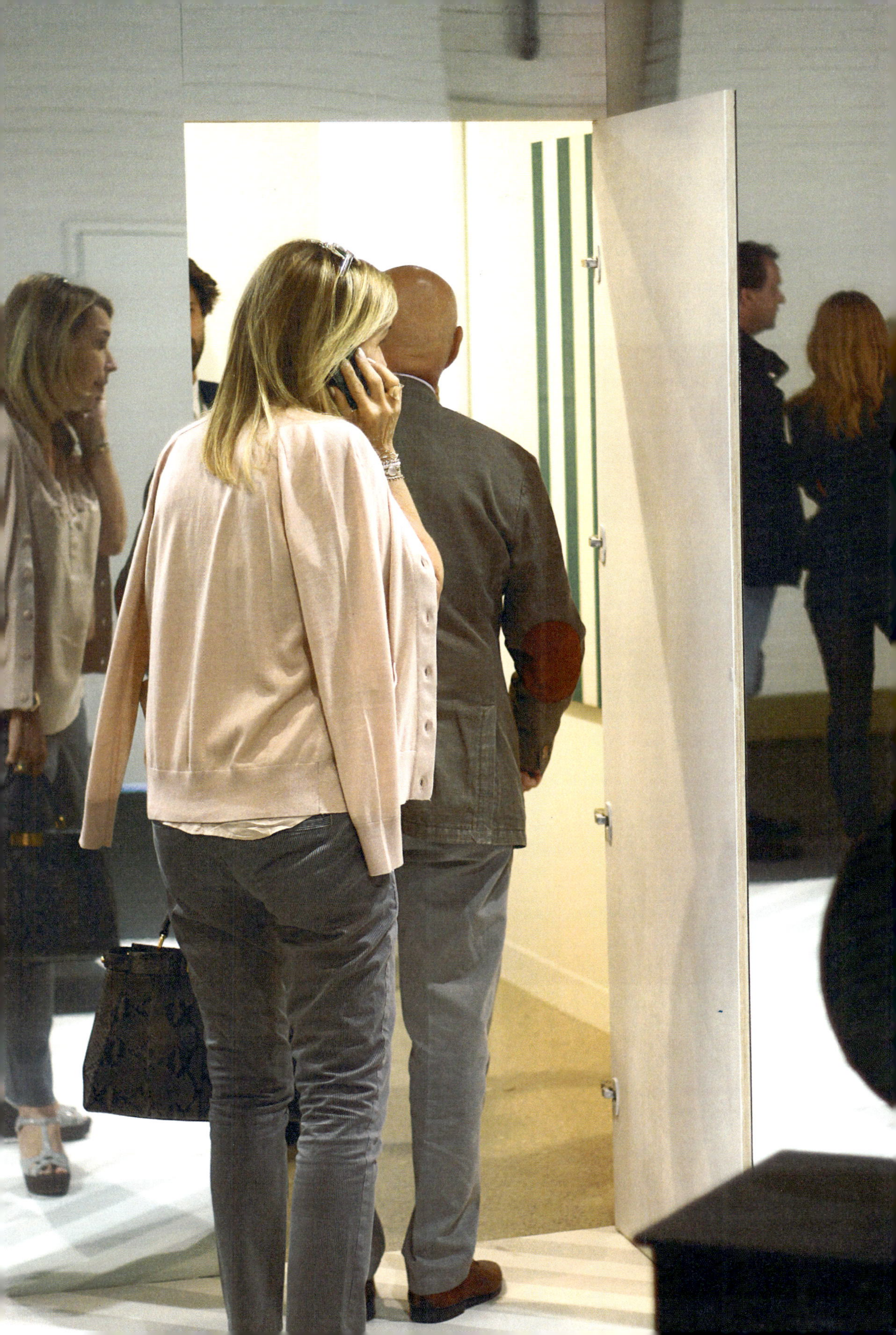

At the Top

The background and art interests of the most important collectors

The US-American art periodical ARTnews publishes annually a list of the 200 most important art collectors, „The ARTnews 200 Top Collectors" [4]. This alphabetical list is not based on the evaluation of data but on an unspecified number of interviews with art dealers, collectors, museum directors, curators and art consultants. It represents, therefore, a subjective assessment of the symbolical capital of the „mega-collectors" and is at the same time a performative instrument. Anyone found on this list is one of the most important actors in the art world and will be listened to because of this prominent position.

The art collecting of the „super-collectors" is mostly practiced by couples (90 out of 200). Men who collect on their own are represented 86 times on the list, whereby „on their own" does not mean that they are not supported by curators and art consultants. Female art collectors are clearly in the minority; there are only 18 women in the illustrious circle of the most important collectors. Six families are also listed, who collect collectively, as brothers and sisters or across the generations.

As in the case of artists and galleries, the origin of the „mega-collectors" reveals the dominance of North America. More than half of the persons, couples and groups named live there, 99 of them in the USA. One third of the top collectors comes from Europe, whereby the „classical" and economically significant art countries Germany, Switzerland and Great Britain are each represented by more than ten collectors. Asia with 16 and South America with six collectors are the home of only a small per centage of the „super-collectors" [5]. In comparison to 2010 a slight increase in Asian collectors is revealed. The well-known results of auctions in China indicate, however, that the list of top collectors could well be subject to Western „reservations" as it is put together by a US-American periodical, which here takes on the role of a „symbolic banker" and evidently attributes greater significance to Western collectors than is actually due to them globally, at least from a financial point of view.

The sources of the economic capital that collectors invest in art illustrates the structural changes of the last 40 years. Only seven representatives of the liberal professions (lawyers, doctors, psychologists) can be found on the list, and the manufacturing industry is represented by only around ten per cent. The finance branch is dominant: 38 collectors earn their money in asset management, bank services and hedge funds. The capital of every fifth collector comes from various investments. Another important source of income is provided by real estate and properties (31). Further business fields of the collectors are the media and PR, retail and wholesale trade (15), IT and technology (13), fashion and design, and energy and raw materials (12). 16 collectors finance their passion for collecting from their inheritance – among them almost 40 per cent of the women who collect alone.

The great majority of the „mega-collectors" collects contemporary art (85%), that is to say art of the period after the Second World War. 87 out of 200 collect exclusively contemporary art. Almost half also collect modern art, six of them exclusively. Other periods of art are collected only by a minority, for example art of the 19th century by 28, old masters by 22 and ethnographic art, for example pre-Columbian or Coptic art, by 16 collectors. There are a few isolated examples of the collection of furniture (5), design items (4), antiquities (3), coins and weapons (1).

More important than these facts for the state of the art world is probably the simple circumstance that this list compiled by the ARTnews exists at all. For such a pseudo-objectivization of art events not only reveals the beginnings of a new personality cult concerning the *consumers* of art, which a short time ago would have been absolutely inconceivable. It also makes it clear how massively the field of art has in the meantime gained a performative reflexivity, which is gradually cutting the ground from under the feet of the *operating conditions* for the entire „old", „traditional", „intimate" socially enclosed configuration of art acquisition. The ranking of art lovers is a practice which also indicates the end of the practice of a purely *social* attribution of legitimacy.

At the same time the collectors are often supported by professionals, employ curators or entire teams of consultants, who are not seldom flown in to meetings, sometimes even from abroad, several times a year, in order to prepare important decisions on the extension of the collection with the relevant expertise. And attendance at art fairs is also an investment in one's own passion for collecting, as it enables the initiation, renewal and maintenance of relationships, exchange of knowledge on the newest trends, acquisition of important information and documentation of personal presence.

But it is also understandable that there are clear gradations in the „exclusiveness" of this passion. In a socially so massively differentiated practice such as the collection of art and the enormous symbolic returns that can be generated by it, conflict over the determination of the „right" kind of collecting becomes inevitable. And if one applies the standard of the „purity" of the *interest,* the differences in motivation already tell us a lot. For when a good part of the collectors interviewed talk about an art crazy parental house, about the influence of friends and acquaintances, sometimes about the experience of conversion, about a passion for art arising from „love at first sight" or awakened „all of a sudden" by a particular work of art, then the „urge to collect" as such, which would classify the collection of art simply as a particularly noble variant of a socially widespread activity, is clearly the least noble variant of the collection of art – a practice which is fully self-sufficient. An American collector provides a good example: *„I have been collecting art for thirty-three years now. I started when I was twenty-two years old. And I started by, I worked in an art gallery that sold bad art, art that matches your sofa. And I grew intrigued, but like somebody like you who is interested in subcultures, I grew intrigued with the idea of what was the difference between bad art and good art. And I began to learn about it when, didn't buy anything at that point, just continued to sell the bad art, a decorator, you know. And then I bought my first piece of art at twenty-two. I bought approximately a thousand works of art in the last thirty-three years. And I was drawn to it, I think, because I was always a collector. When I was a young boy, I collected pennies, I collected stamps, I collected bottle caps, I collected baseball cards. So there is just a natural, you know, kind of outgrow that, when you are a boy, but there was a natural tendency to want to continue to do it. And I think from an emotional standpoint the collecting, you know, if you have three of anything, you have a collection, but also collecting brings a sense of order to a world that, that people are looking for order in the world. And I think, for me collecting gives me, allows me to pretend I am achieving that order. I think this is the best way to say it."*

Others speak about their „hunting instinct" which urges them on when they collect art, or compare themselves with a „truffle pig" searching for hidden treasures, or they speak of the joy of discovery when they find a missing piece for their own collection, of the satisfaction deriving from having a good nose or eye for investing in the right artist at the right time. But here too one fully realizes how „profane" these motivations are in the normative coordinate system of collecting. For in the same breathe the „love of art" for its own sake is always emphasized. Love of art as a passion manifests itself in the self-presentation of the collectors interviewed as an indisputable basic feature of their existence and personality, in spite of all the „gaffes". The mere question about the reasons for this enchanted self-portrayal is already regarded by most as an impertinence. Some of the interviewees place an „intellectual" interest in contemporary art in the foreground, speak of the role of the artist as a „prophet", see contemporary art as a seismograph of present-day social dynamics, wish to feel that they have their „fingers on the pulse of time" with it.

The „Club“ of Collectors
Similarities and differences

A classification of the collectors is difficult. The group seems to be too heterogeneous and confusingly unclear, and the concept of the collector itself is not uncontroversial. The spectrum of the types of collector is huge, ranging from the so-called „trend collectors“ to the non-conformists and intellectual enlighteners. Some of them follow the ever-changing fashions, others devote themselves to a genre, a style, an epoch or even to individual artists, whereas others again collect only the art of their own country or prefer a mixture of artefacts, styles, epochs and regions of the world.

Alongside the collections of public authorities in museums or art galleries a broad system of private collections has arisen, which have in the meantime largely established themselves as institutions. These include, above all, the big corporate collections such as the corporate collections of the UBS, of the Deutsche Bank, of the Alliance concern or JP Morgan Stanley, of Microsoft and IBM in the USA. A further type is provided by the private collections on private premises or in specially built private museums, such as, for example, the collections of Mera and Don Rubell, Charles Saatchi, Reinhold Würth or Frieder Burda. In addition there are cooperative undertakings in the form of public private partnerships between private collections and public art facilities such as the Sammlung Ludwig or the Sammlung Marx. There are, furthermore, a large number of well-known and unknown collectors whose collections are not shown in public and who only occasionally and selectively make individual works available for exhibitions or as loans to museums.

The collectors‘ club also differs in the way the individual collections are organized. Whereas the corporate collections of the big companies and concerns are mostly led by art experts and more or less systematically arranged, the private collectors adopt a variety of approaches. In all cases, of course, the subjective dimension of the collecting and personal decisions are in the foreground. But some of them are advised by „art consultants“ or former museum directors on the acquisition and development of their collections. And others, in turn, place their trust more or less in a house gallery from which they seek support and buy almost all their works. Most of the private collectors, however, rely on their personal intuition and individual taste. But collector personalities who meticulously appropriate a scientific knowledge of art and proceed according to criteria like those of the museums tend to be the exception.

The problematic nature of the categorization of the private collector is shown by examples such as the so-called „super-collectors“ with respectable collections who do not come under the categories of the financial aristocracy, the newly-rich or the speculators, for example, the numerous gallerists who have built up powerful art collections of their own or, finally, the artist Damien Hirst, who has opened his own museum.

The scientific literature presents widely differing typologies of private collectors and collections. In a French study of the 1960s [6] they are divided up into the collections of „big millionaires“, bourgeois collections, „professorial“ collections of discoverers, snobs and speculators. In a follow-up study a distinction is made between „notables“, „big billionaires“, the „newly rich“, „speculators“ and „cultivated young people“ [7]. Other studies name five motivational situations: „responsibility for the preservation of art“, „joy in discovering artists and art“, „relationship to artists“, „investment“ and „family tradition“ [8]. In spite of these widely differing impulses one aspect is, however, quite evident: the unquestioned and unquestionable significance our society attributes to art, its „magical“ attractive power – a collective mania from which the „speculators“ also know how to profit.

Others speak of transcendental experiences, of the expression of „the eternal" or of a means of preserving the traces of collective history, others again of self-realization beyond professional and entrepreneurial everyday life with its impersonal economic constraints – all of these nuances of the motivational basis are, regardless of their importance for the „inner morality" of the collectors and their normative verdicts, only specific variations of a profession of faith, a profession which seems to proclaim the power of art, but above all else the power of the collector himself, who can take personal possession of that art.

It is not, therefore, surprising that in the self-presentations of the interviewees there was no talk of „vulgar" motives for collecting art, of investments, speculation or striving for prestige, and if they did come up, it was only in regard to the „usual suspects" from the circle of „New Money" – here lie the external, the normative boundaries of personal self-understanding. But nor do the manifold subjective motives for collecting art, which are indicative of a pronouncedly polytheistic devotedness to art, speak in favour of a tolerant co-existence of differing „tastes" under the cloak of the „love of art" as a common denominator. Quite the contrary.

Trench warfare

The subtle distinctions in the art of collecting

If one listens to the stories of the collectors about their paths to art, the notion of a closed circle of equals and like-minded people, with a similar social background and membership, similar artistic preferences and a similar „attitude" towards art quickly dissipates into thin air. Instead one is confronted with a highly differentiated social category in which the *dispute over legitimacy,* the definition of the „right" way of collecting leaves deep traces. One is supposedly playing the same game in the same league, but in reality one is continually confronted with the drawing of more or less subtle boundaries. As long as the collection of art was the affair of a relatively overseeable and socially closed circle of family dynasties from the nobility and the haute bourgeoisie there was no need for any barricades worth mentioning against illegitimate pretenders. But in times of massive socio-structural upheaval and high social mobility, with the rise of new large fortunes and their access to the insignia of cultural and symbolic legitimacy, demarcation discourses have become part of the standard repertoire of the „establishment" [9].

During the VIP days at the Art Basel the dominant class still sticks to its own kind. But fractions become visible which differ from, and wish to be seen as different from each other in regard to the scope and composition of their economic and cultural resources and to the length of their membership of the social elite. These socio-structural differences form the background to those symbolic struggles carried out over the definition of the „true" and the „false" art lover; the social „trajectory" into the heights of the dominant class determines the social perception of legitimate membership in it.

And it is inevitably manifested in the *habitus* of the actors and their practices, which their environment can identify and classify – the „heir" with his early socialized feeling for the „subtle distinctions" always has a home advantage in this social game. He plays it in a „natural" and relaxed manner, whereas the parvenu always comes up against the limits of his cultural „assets"; his attempts to achieve distinction seem to be „labored" and pretentious and his all-too-obvious eagerness exposes him as an upstart [10]. For in

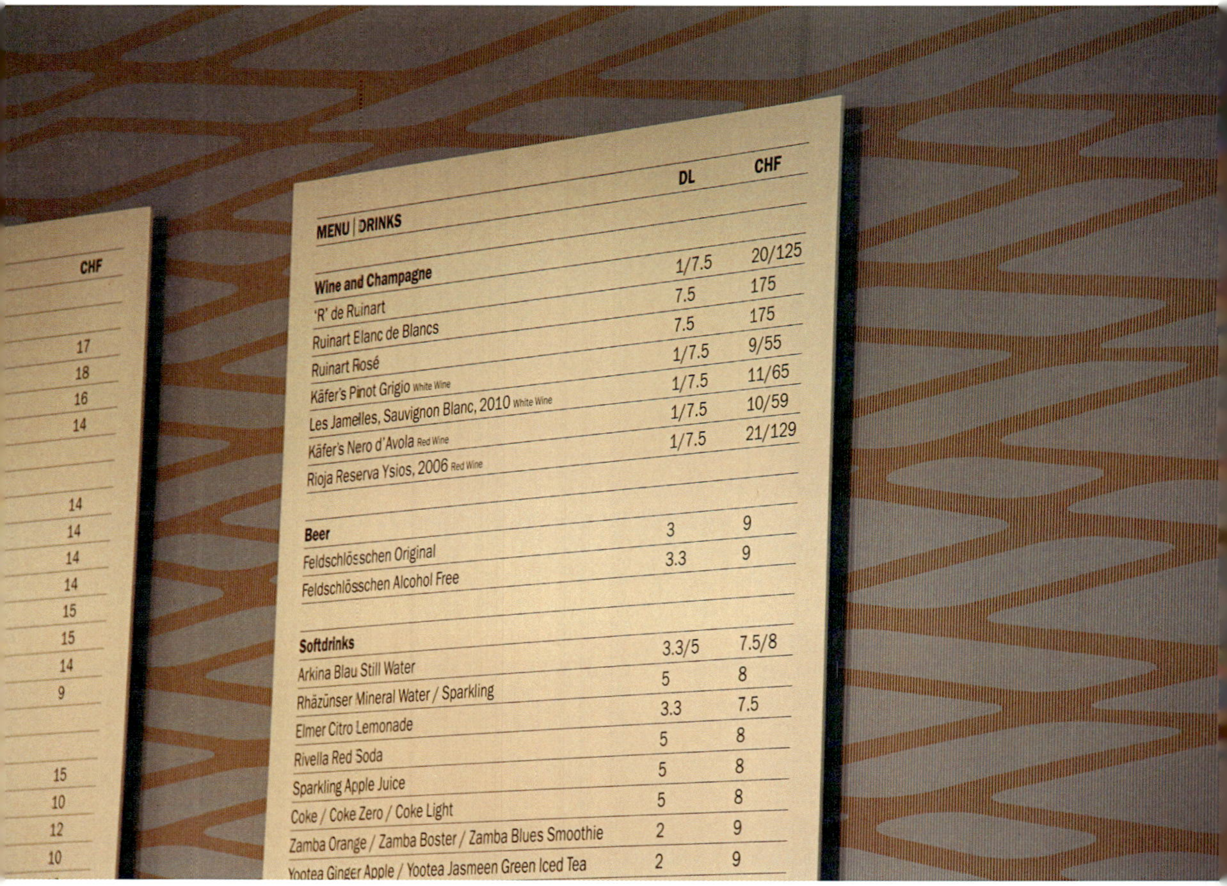
CHF
17
18
16
14
14
14
14
14
15
15
14
9
15
10
12
10
DL
CHF
MENU | DRINKS
Wine and Champagne
'R' de Ruinart 1/7.5 20/125
Ruinart Blanc de Blancs 7.5 175
Ruinart Rosé 7.5 175
Käfer's Pinot Grigio White Wine 1/7.5 9/55
Les Jamelles, Sauvignon Blanc, 2010 White Wine 1/7.5 11/65
Käfer's Nero d'Avola Red Wine 1/7.5 10/59
Rioja Reserva Ysios, 2006 Red Wine 1/7.5 21/129
Beer
Feldschlösschen Original 3 9
Feldschlösschen Alcohol Free 3.3 9
Softdrinks
Arkina Blau Still Water 3.3/5 7.5/8
Rhäzünser Mineral Water / Sparkling 5 8
Elmer Citro Lemonade 3.3 7.5
Rivella Red Soda 5 8
Sparkling Apple Juice 5 8
Coke / Coke Zero / Coke Light 5 8
Zamba Orange / Zamba Boster / Zamba Blues Smoothie 2 9
Yootea Ginger Apple / Yootea Jasmeen Green Iced Tea 2 9

the end it is not the collection of art as such which lends social distinction but the way in which one collects. Collecting „with style", „true" connoisseurship and „genuine" passion require more than material wealth; true manners protect against mannerism, true education against laborious cramming, self-confidence against conformity. If the difference between collectors was only gradual along the scale of the capital invested in the work of art or even the size of the collection, and not essentially attached to the idea of differing cultural legitimation, a quantitative and not a *qualitative* issue, it would be scarcely possible to understand why the conflict on the boundaries between the „right" and the „wrong" practice of collecting is fought out so bitterly.

As the saying goes, there is no accounting for taste, and nonetheless the arguments on the nature of true art, of authentic artistic taste and legitimate love of art, are endless. But these debates are not just „hair-splitting" discussions on the „sex of angels". They have a profound social significance – what is at issue is no less than the legitimacy of the appropriation and use of „art" as a symbolic good and participation in the establishment of a particular definition of „genuine" art. The collector at the Art Basel provides a model illustration of this logic of qualification and classification. *„There are a few, they are the truly committed collectors, who collect out of passion, who totally commit themselves. Then there are the pseudo-collectors who collect for social reasons. They are not really committed. But it is the ‚in' thing to do. And then there are the investors who collect. They buy to earn money."* Deciding on the category in which the Swiss art-lover sees himself calls for no further research. The picture he paints of the collectors' world is a simple one: genuine collectors with a true love of art as a small elite on this side, a prestige-hungry or a money-grubbing majority on the other.

His American „colleague", also one of the most important collectors in his country, has a completely different view of it all, not basing his judgment on the aesthetic-normative standards of quality of the European intellectual, but on quantitative standards: *„I think of the collecting world like an onion. You know, there is this core of, this super hard core of collectors, people that have ninety per cent of their work in storage. And in Miami we have a significant number of those kinds of collectors, but what has been interesting is that then you have the next layer of people who, maybe they buy ten or fifteen things a year, that is a whole lot of art and in ten years, they have a hundred works. That is a lot. And then you have in the next group, they may buy five things a year and will travel to two art fairs. And then you have the next group, in Miami at least, who, so you know what, art fair is here, I am going to go buy something. And they might buy one or two things a year. So they are very, it is really about the intensity level of what you are doing in the art world, where you are willing to pay a lot of money to maintain a space for your collection, you know. It is really about the degrees of how consumed you are"*

Among the two dozen art collectors interviewed at the Art Basel one encounters the heirs of collector dynasties which in part reach back to the Ancien Régime, or at least can claim to have shown a long-lasting true love of art or good taste in art over several generations. They come from an upper-class, if not even aristocratic background and are genteelly reserved in talking about their own practice as a collector. In dealings with this type it is possible to feel the staying power and the broad vision in regard to art, its history and its manifestations. The legitimate inheritance of taste in art, often handed down over several generations like a material patrimony, here lends the contact with art an inimitable lightness; it is spontaneous, effortless, the expression of deeply internalized aesthetic dispositions, which have become second nature to its inheritors.

Buying works and creating value

The new market power of the collectors

Collecting art is „in". Particularly private individuals who acquire contemporary art on a larger scale nowadays enjoy attention in the public sphere which they would never receive without this fine and exclusive „hobby". The media in particular, ranging from the specialist journals to the feuilletons and the boulevard press, are particularly fond of taking up stories again and again about art-minded collectors as a positive image of the idealistic „consuming citizen" [11]. Collecting art is not only a part of the life-style of the rich and super-rich clients who underpin their privileged position in the social hierarchy with the help of works of art and other luxury goods. The world of the „celebrities" has also long discovered art as a life-style and status symbol. Consciously or subconsciously, they all promise themselves a gain in social prestige from the possession of art.

According to the generally accepted idea art is bought and collected first and foremost out of a „love of art" and „passion". But even if this is possibly still the predominant motive, the „love of art" is losing its importance among collectors. As early as the 1980s it was ascertained in interviews with collectors that a spontaneous association with the „love of art" as a motive for collecting had notably declined in comparison with twenty years before [12]. Financial motives had of course existed earlier, but in their concentration they are a relatively new phenomenon. In the age of finance capital art as an alternative to other classes of investment has moved into the focus of actors from the financial sector and of both institutional and private investors [13]. As a result billions have flown into the art market and have driven the prices to dizzy heights, above all for the „blue chips" which are safe and stable in value.

The circle of collectors has grown greatly in recent years. The main reason is the rapid increase of wealth in the hands of a small minority. The number of wealthy people, of the so-called *High Net Worth Individuals* has in the meantime increased world-wide to over 12 million [14]. In 2013 32 million millionaires were registered, 42 per cent of them in the USA alone. At least 600,000 of this group are reckoned among the middle-sized to big art collectors [15]. They are today regarded as powerful investors in the art market. This also marks a qualitative turn in the art market, in which the economic success of the artist moves increasingly into the foreground. As a result the market is further split up into a „premium" segment in which, above all, the big auction houses and mega-galleries are active, and which promises a potential for value appreciation, and a broad mass segment in which buying as an investment seldom pays off – unless the actors have sufficient power over the market to „discover" so-called „young" artists, to build them up and to establish them accordingly on the market.

The power of money, concentrated in the hands of wealthy private collectors, does not fail to have an effect on the art scene. There has been a shift in the classical division of tasks among galleries, museums and art criticism. Today private collectors play a dominant part. The museums, financially weakened by budget reductions and cost-cutting policies, can often no longer afford to buy new works and are moving increasingly into the background of the art market. Art criticism has lost its leading role in the complex process of recognizing and establishing artists to curators and the organizers of exhibitions.

Instead, the power of definition rests more and more upon the private collectors. It is not just that the galleries voluntarily provide what the art market dominated by the collectors' desires. Through presence in big private collections, which are primarily determined by individual preferences and seldom do justice to art-historical criteria, the careers of artists can be promoted and their position in the art market, with a time delay, even in the art-historical process of canonization can be legitimized. The frequently encountered reference in the art world to presence in a private collection („collected by") increases the value of an artist, as the „brand" of the collector as a taste-maker and institution brings a symbolic gain.

There is no ostentation, no straining after effect; the legitimacy of the membership of the elite accumulated over generations seems to give them older rights than all the other groups in their claim to be true lovers of art, true connoisseurs; and it is a right on which one need not insist, but can build. These representatives of „old money" and a mature culture have a highly developed awareness of tradition, do not relegate „classical" art to the lumber room of history, but honor the collecting spirit of their ancestors and the „ancestral gallery" they have successively expanded even when they do not share their ancestors' taste – „selling" would in any case be out of the question in view of such a marked family ethos. This distinctively sovereign attitude in dealing with matters of art at the same time permits an „unconventional" approach to epochs, genres and styles; here we find collections which combine contemporary art („but please no Warhol or anything like that") with bronze sculptures of the Renaissance and religious art of the Middle Ages to form a „virtuosically" composed ensemble. *„Putting individual works of art together is for me a form of art and hence worthy of preservation. It is possible that one has a cabi-net of wonders in one room and Italian painting in another – the way one combines them is for me a form of art."*

Collectors from the haute bourgeoisie also reveal such a „noblesse" of understatement when talking about their love of art, and they often also come from collector families. A well-known Swiss collector: *„I come from a collector family and what then matters, of course, is the quality of what one possesses. I can only say that in my personal case we have works ranging from old masters up to contemporary art; and, before my time, my husband, who also came from a collector family, so two collector families met, and that was, of course, ideal".* She then goes on to say that she cultivates a distinctly unconventional syncretic collecting style which is also understood by artists. Impressive namedropping follows. A German big collector also says of himself that he is „a pioneer in this kind of combined collecting of old and new and that has become the spirit of the times right now." Another claims he has sufficient competence not only to do without the expert advice of „professionals"; he says of himself: „I am rather in a position where I advise others on the acquisition of art." A further collector speaks of himself as a „passionate all-round connoisseur" who takes decisions in seconds and distances himself as a „dynamic collector" from the „boring" conventional collectors.

Incidentally it becomes clear at this point to what extent some collectors claim that they participate directly in the „creation" of art, not only discover it, but really „curate" it in such a way that what is „essential" about every piece is first made manifest by the interplay of all the pieces. Thus the collector more and more frequently becomes an element in the chain of consecration in the production of „art", transferring his own symbolic capital to the work of art. This process finds its ultimate confirmation when a private collection molded by the individual taste of the collector is converted into a public institution and so makes „art history". This is a form of boundary dissolution which more and more strongly encroaches upon the present-day field of art.

A second group of collectors can be identified as self-made men, representatives of the capitalism of the post-war period, whose careers often ran parallel to the emergence of „contemporary art" and whose path to art was not primarily determined by family heritage but by „secondary socialization". This group, which is strongly represented among the collectors, has a particularly radical „contemporary" orientation and often develops its passion in a mixed form involving both private and corporate collecting. When the boundary between „business is business" and „art is art" is unclearly drawn kind of „accountability" in the collection of art often shines through. One of the most important private collectors in Europe: *„I would regard myself as a combination. On the one hand as a genuine collector, because I like these works of art. But that is only natural. Of course the businessman in me also always plays a part. To give an example: if I had five works of art, all the same price, and I had to choose which I would take, and I liked all of them, then it's only logical that I would buy the one with the highest potential for value appreciation. There are certainly other scientifically oriented collectors who think along aesthetic lines, who are humanists and have possibly inherited a huge fortune and have never built up a fortune on their own. Where a few millions don't really matter."* The relationship between entrepreneurial marketing and the love of art is also sometimes undisguisedly revealed in this context. A German big businessman with an art collection which is admired world-wide relates, for example, that he also collects *„in order to document the fact that the firm is not meaninglessly focused and fanaticized simply to make profits and increase revenue. But that we are also receptive for the beautiful side of life. And of course that includes the fine arts"* [16].

Alongside these representatives of the business world there is a group of „qualified" decision-takers, a product of the educational explosion of the 1960s and 1970s and the collective social advancement of an entire generation, active in top positions in the economy or in the liberal professions. Here, as in the case of the „heirs", one often finds a tendency towards „idiosyncratic" collecting and emphasis on „one's own signature" as a „curator" in contrast to the „conventional" collector. The owner of one of the three largest private museums in the German-speaking countries says: *„There are very rigorous, yes, even almost small-minded collections. If, for example, a collector only collects items from the 60s, then that's his scene, that's his home ground, and he doesn't have to reproach himself for collecting in a superficial, untalented or non-professional way. But I have always picked out certain nuclei and then said that the collection can be further developed after my time and then the individual focal points will come together of their own accord. A quite typical example of how I collect: there are really big names in there, from A to B and so on, but also quite young, unknown artists. And that has led to a won-derful kaleidoscope, so this exhibition is really fantastic".*

Finally the younger, also „qualified" representatives of financial capital, of the new wealth of the old world, whose presence is increasingly felt, much to the chagrin of the collectors of the „old school". In the often highly emotional portrayals of the representatives of the „true love of art" they are painted as money-hungry speculators who, in the guise of art lovers, wish to profit twice over. A representative of the haute bourgeoisie, himself an „enthusiastic" collector: *„I observe two motives. The one motive is the usual motive, to make money with art. And the second motive is to run a business which is also associated with social prestige... to have art, to deal with art is fashionable, it opens up access to certain social circles and so on. These, then, are the two motives and you can come across them everywhere, if you go to the Art or anywhere else."* A further dialogue partner on the motives of the new money: *„In view of the rather uncertain economic situation today a lot of people are in fact investing in art – leaving out for the moment the top, let's just say, the most expensive things. Because people say: What should I do then? Bonds bring no interest, shares are volatile, gold too expensive, no interest on money, so real estate or art are an absolute alternative. And then I say: It's better to look at the stuff on the wall than to own shares that may be worth nothing more at all in two or three years time."*

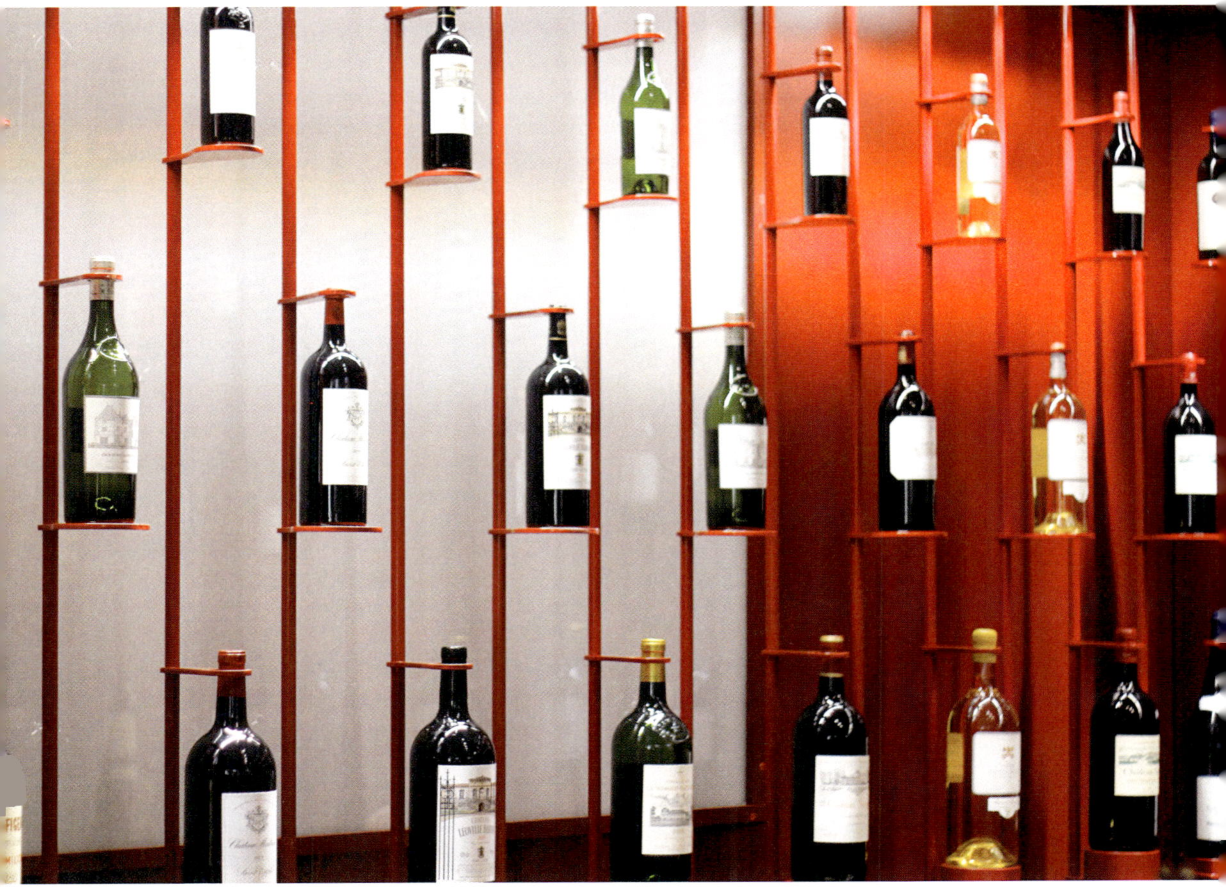

The art consultant of a bank argues along the same lines: *„On the one hand, then, people have now realized that the traditional bank products bring little or no interest. So why not invest in art for once. But invest intelligently. Nothing short-term. That's what we are now experiencing more often. I have just had two cases of people who had had nothing to do with art up to now, who have now decided that they want to invest a percentage of the assets in it. And of course there are a lot of people nowadays, perhaps also younger clients, who have discovered this. Maybe they have heard from others: ‚Why don't you buy art? Why haven't you been invited to the Gunter Sachs Preview in Zurich? You'd meet other people there.' And so on. It's both."*

But the art market seems to hold a further, quite specific fascination for the „Wolves of Wall Street", the artists of finance capital. An art consultant reports on his clients: *„But it is a bit strange. I think there is no economic scholar that has ever really... A lot of people have tried to describe the art market but it is a bit like art itself, they try to, whatever, the art market likes a certain amount of mystique and mystery. It is important. Especially, it is one of the main attractions for big clients. I mean, if you have people who made their own fortune that are able to buy on this fair, if they are self-made men for example, they pretend to know a lot of the world. They have made a fortune, so they have succeeded in something in life, and from a psychological point of view, you often see that these people have got a kind of impression that because they once succeeded in something, they have knowledge about a lot which is not true but it is a feeling they have. But in the art world, all this feeling is immediately gone because they feel insecure. And insecurity is, in a way, it is part of the reason why they are there. They cannot grasp it. It is interesting. It is also, for example, even somebody who is extremely rich. He comes here and he wants a painting and it is for sale, because you can still buy it, you are at the opening, you have the first ten minutes, you go to the gallery, you see this painting and it is under 10,000 euros, then you want to buy it and they say: ‚No. We are not going to sell it to you because we don't know you.' For somebody who is very rich and is surrounded by people who say ‚Yes' and only ‚Yes' to him, it is very, very frustrating, strange, ungraspable."*

The rules of the market reach their limits here, in a market of symbolic goods with its own rules, and for the representatives of the new capital, who have been spoiled by success, the experience that the art market follows a logic which is concealed from the usual logic of the market is an additional incentive to invest in this game against all the rules of reason.

The Extension of the Battlefield

New money in search of symbolic returns

The „big" money and the „new" money are certainly among the biggest challenges for the traditional „collectors' community". It is not just that the financial dimensions of the possibility to collect art shift – works which the established „elite" could hitherto take into their possession are suddenly beyond the reach of their financial resources. But precisely those mechanisms of *sublimation,* of the ennoblement of personal wealth, which permit the conversion of hard cash into cultivated taste and the social point in time of its acquisition into the personified quality of its „owner", have become economically obsolete. The battle for the appropriation of „art" is a battle between factions of the ruling class, a battle for social legitimation as such.

Contemporary art for the wall

From a questionnaire among collectors

The typical average collector is male, aged between 50 and 70, university educated and self-employed. This, at least, is the result of an international survey carried out by the art insurance company AXA Art in which almost 1000 collectors participated in 2013 [17]. According to the survey 76 per cent of the collectors interviewed were male, 84 per cent were university graduates and 46 per cent entrepreneurs or self-employed. More than half (57%) were over fifty and only 16 per cent under forty.

According to the study collectors acquire, above all, what can be hung opun the wall. In the scale of popularity painting dominates at 89 per cent, followed by works on paper at 63 per cent and sculptures at 60 per cent. Photography, for a long time an illegitimate genre not acknowledged as art, is nonetheless collected by 60 per cent of the interviewees. In contrast installations and video art are not much appreciated as collectors' objects. They were part of the collection of only 14 per cent of the interviewees. The comparison with other classical collectors' objects is interesting. 29 per cent also collect furniture and design, 15 per cent jewelry and watches and 7 per cent wine.

If one compares the collector's categories with one another two tendencies are, according to the study, striking. The overwhelming majority (82%) today collect contemporary art, whereas the classical modern period with only 39 per cent no longer enjoys great appreciation. Who collects which genres is, however, strongly dependent on age – for example 94 per cent of the under-40s collect contemporary art, whereas the share among the over-60s is only 68 per cent.

The shifts in the art market are also reflected in the purchasing of art. Even though galleries remain the most important locations for purchasing art for 75 per cent of the interviewees, art fair and internet offers nonetheless find greater resonance. 95 per cent of collectors attend art fairs, mostly only as sources of information, but 39 per cent also buy works of art at them. 95 per cent also use internet platforms as a source of information and 34 per cent have in fact already used an internet portal to buy art. At 59 per cent, auctions are also very popular among art collectors. Moreover, the „informal" art market should not be underestimated: 63 per cent of the collectors state that they buy art directly from the artists and, in addition, 39 per cent make use of private contacts when buying art.

The study also sheds light on the different motives of the collectors for buying. Only one third of the collections are relatively small and have a value under 100,000 US dollars. Every tenth colletion is worth more than a million dollars. Here, however, secretiveness prevails, with a third of the collectors interviewed refusing to give any information. Two thirds of the collectors interviewed do not collect systematically, but let themselves be guided by their „instinct" when buying art. They buy what they happen to like. Other collecting criteria such as quality, content or value potential are found more seldom. Only in every fourth collection does the content of the works play a part. One collection in twenty is, however, planned by a curator.

The study identifies four, different collector types by means of a multivariate data analysis. The „art aficionados", who make up 37 per cent of the sample, collect primarily out of passion. The „traditionalists" (16%) continue the family tradition. These two groups correspond most closely to the classical ideal type of collector who lets himself be guided by the „love of art". The third group, which has only developed recently according to the study, stands for a new kind of collecting. For the „investors", who at 24 per cent make up almost a quarter of the collectors interviewed, the investment value and the diversification of their assets portfolio play the dominant role as a core motive, but art is also important for them as a status symbol. In striking contrast to the other types the „investors" have mostly only been collecting for a few years and have concentrated their activities above all on high-quality and rare objects with a potential for appreciated value. They also take the advice of art consultants to a disproportionate degree. The last type, the „hybrid" collectors, collect for a wide variety of motives and cannot, therefore, be assigned to any group.

The all-pervasive stigmatization of the newcomer, the „upstart", the „uncultivated", this „hedge fund community", „new money", „reputation hunters" permits no doubt: „There are people who collect or call themselves collectors because that's the social thing to do, so to speak so that one can see oneself as having made it socially". The lack of understanding of art among these „collectors" in inverted commas is continually pointed out, ironically and often sarcastically: people „who buy with their ears", „philistines", who „as one says in English, tend to be *socially insecure people,* who prefer to buy what can be recognized on the wall. It's a bit saddening if that is the main goal of collecting." The Swiss collector from an old family dynasty: *„With unserious, with not so important collectors, who simply buy art because it is good form, a status symbol, who think that in their offices they must... Or, for example, those fund managers who buy paintings for unbelievably high prices."* The legitimate guardians of the holy grail of art put a simple insight into a nutshell here. Because the possession of works of art is not only regarded as a sign of the wealth but also of the good taste of its owners, this alone can provide the basis for the claim to social legitimation – and the „blessing of early birth", the *inheritance* of legitimacy, the patrimony of previous generations, is systematically misappropriated.

Among the representatives of a new bourgeoisie of post-war capitalism we also find another category of collectors, the „new money" of the non-European countries, the „old" newly rich, economically extremely powerful, but equipped with a cultural habitus which only partly does justice to the civilizational claims to distinction of the European elite. Until the triumphal march of „contemporary art" set in the 1960s this category included the frequently caricatured type of the US American entrepreneur.

Although today in „Old Europe" one would scarcely mock about cultural divergencies in view of the existing dominance of the US market, they still exist on both sides of the Atlantic in a clearly visible form in the eyes of the collectors interviewed. An American collector is disconcerted by the privatistic affectation of the European collectors' scene: *„There is not, you know, private collectors there, just only recently started opening their home to people like me who have been opening my home to them for years, you know. The mentality is different there"* [18]. The owner of a renowned auction house puts the European view of the American collectors' scene in a nutshell: *„In America they were all super-rich people. All big industrialists who had no past, no nobility, no hundreds-of-years-long tradition; they were then still collecting their history."*

The discrepancy between the Western core culture of art collecting and its social habitus and the appearance of the representatives of *new money* from the Chinese sphere is probably even more distinct. A collector who is regarded as one of the best experts on the Chinese art scene: *„The collector I regard as the biggest collector in Asia didn't even know what art is six years ago. Within six years he has spent hundreds of millions. The behavior is different than here. And it's precisely the new money that behaves differently."* Again and again the Western collectors point, with attitudes ranging from amusement to smugness, to the prestige motives of the rising new rich from the emerging countries. The art expert from a family dynasty going back five centuries: *„Just to come back to the collector groups we have in both China and Russia. These really big Russian collectors are, of course, somehow a bit like pariahs as well. That's why they buy these huge yachts, play a bit like James Bond, buy a football club and all that kind of thing. They have to surround themselves with social prestige. And to find prestige in our bourgeois society, at least in the West and earlier in Russia as well, it was usual, if you wanted to display prestige in society, that you had to have achieved something. If you wanted to get a doctor's* *firm you had to accomplish something, otherwise you wouldn't be the boss. There is virtually only one single factor through which you can buy social prestige without having to work for it and that is collecting art."*

Others, on the other hand, emphasize that genuine taste in art can be awakened gradually in an investor: *„They are also very ambitious; in the course of time they don't just want to buy the brand. They buy for investment reasons, because it's been drilled into them that it's a good investment. But then they want to be different. Slowly they reach a point where they don't want to have the same collection as another multimillionaire." And a French colleague: „Some of them begin with a purely financial attitude, become involved in the game and then are gripped by it and begin to reflect on the composition of their collection."* The mysteries of culture also „know their catechumens, their initiates, their holy men" [19], and the borders between the established and the pretenders are fluid – and only a question of time.

Numerus clausus

Social borders on the market of singular goods

„Well that's the way it is nowadays, that coveted works of art are not bought, they are allocated. You have to be part of the system in which you can get an allocation. And that's why certain prices occur at auctions. People buy at them who don't have an allocation. And then they battle with each other at the auction", an established Swiss collector relates. Whereas the typical market is the most impersonal relationship of practical life into which humans can enter with one another, as the great sociologist Max Weber had taught a hundred years ago, in the art market the *standing of the buyer* is of the greatest significance. And it is so in many regards, from financial solvency to credit-worthiness of the client to the expertise and trustworthiness of the gallerist and the motive of the client for buying and what he does with the works of art he has bought; if, for example, there is a danger for the gallerist and the artist that they will see a newly purchased work offered for sale at an auction at a clearly higher price or, even worse, that no taker is found, which creates the risk of a clear loss of reputation on the market. Many collectors proudly report on a very long-lasting personal relationship of trust with their gallerist and emphasize that they only buy from him even though it might be more expensive. If one considers the high volatility of the contemporary art market it is easy to understand the importance attached to a long-lasting personal relationship between the offerer and the buyer. Under the special conditions of trading in singular goods ano-nymity is a risk for both sides.

At the same time it seems to be the case that the person of the collector together with the symbolic and social capital attached to him, that is to say his „reputation" and public visibility, itself becomes a central factor in the assessment of the value attributed to the purchased item – a renowned collector who adds a newly acquired work of art to his highly regarded, high quality collection himself becomes an important element in the chain of consecration which defines the value of a work of art in social terms; his reputation radiates out to the piece he has acquired. It is, therefore, thoroughly plausible when collectors report that the reselling value of a work of art increases simply because it has wandered through the hands or on to the walls of a reputed collector and that for this reason many gallerists proceed strategically when dealing with a potential buyer of a work and give priority to a well-known and well-reputed member of the collectors' community even if the proceeds of the sale are lower rather than choosing to sell to an anonymous interested party. Whereas traditionally public museums enjoy primacy in the consecration of works of art the function of serving as an instance of consecration is now more and more frequently accorded to the private museums and collections which are growing in number and are often financially better situated. The reaction to this *shift in the relationships of power* in the field of art ranges from skeptical to highly critical.

If all the collectors interviewed in the context of the Art Basel adopt the standpoint that love of art is the only legitimate access to it, what then motivates the defensive attitude towards a new group of collectors? The symbolic battles being fought out with such vehemence on the field of art and the often undisguised resentment of the collectors interviewed are not least due to the fact that the absolute number of those who are financially in a position to acquire works of art is growing strongly, thus undermining the *exclusiveness* of the practice and at the same time diminishing *its distinctive marginal utility* on account of its lack of „style".

„Many a little makes a mickle"

The „rank and file" at the Art Basel

One last social group at the Art Basel also has a right to existence, even though it is not visible on the VIP days – it consists of the collectors whose wallets do not match their love of art. When the doors of the Art Basel open after the VIP days the halls fill up, whereas many gallerists, who can now scarcely reckon with prestigious clients and notable sales, abandon their booths to their employees. What counts in this situation, however, is not only business but the fair as a social event. A scenario like this needs the public, the „spectator", the simple lover of art, if there are to be reports every year of umpteen thousands of visitors, of records of attendance and attention.

From the point of view of the communications officer of the Art Basel it is also necessary to think of the art lovers who follow the VIPs and to take care of the small collectors. *„Well, firstly, it is of course the case that it is also in some way or other a fair for the public. That's why tours are arranged for people who know nothing about art. Of course one also somehow has just a little bit of an educational interest. And then one can also say ‚many a little makes a mickle'. Some dentist or other from outside Basel might come along, and these people are not uninter-esting for the gallerists as well."* And so the Art Basel unites everyone beyond all class boundaries – everyone is welcome to communion at the High Mass of the art world.

And in fact the highly-priced art which dominates the Art Basel makes up only a negligibly small but all the more visible part of the total number of works offered for sale at the art fairs of the world, whose average price at auctions and gallery sales is probably only a little higher than 3,000 euros. The owner of a big auction house: *„The layer of society which holds the galleries above water world-wide is the classical educated middle-class. You and me. That's what they live off."*

The interviewed VIP collectors also emphasize again and again that it is possible to put together „quite a nice collection" with slight financial means. And a big collector reports on an association of Swiss collectors which shows that it has a heart for less wealthy art lovers: *„Occasionally we accept, we want to accept nice young people. That happens. After all someone dies from time to time. We want to keep it relatively small; it shouldn't become huge. So we sometimes accept younger, interested art-loving young people. But we examine very closely what kind of background they come from, what their motives are and how they approach it all. We have just accepted someone, a young man of 34, who has some means of buying art, not a lot, but he is very committed."*

Within the materially and immaterially privileged classes a permanent battle takes place over the legitimate disposal of those symbolic goods which themselves lend social legitimacy, and the field of art seems in many respects predestined for the carrying out of such symbolic battles. For it is not primarily the possession of objects of art as materialized cultural capital which defines the „genuine" collector – with profane and sometimes even dubious wealth at his disposal anyone at all can acquire these cultural trophies. On the contrary, the precondition for the legitimate acquisition of a work of art and even more so for „genuine" collecting is a specific attitude towards art and the *manners of its use* deriving from that attitude. A person who lacks sufficient legitimacy for dealing with consecrated goods desecrates them, deprives them of their enchanted quality, their magic, holds only an empty shell in his hands, but not the extraordinary power.

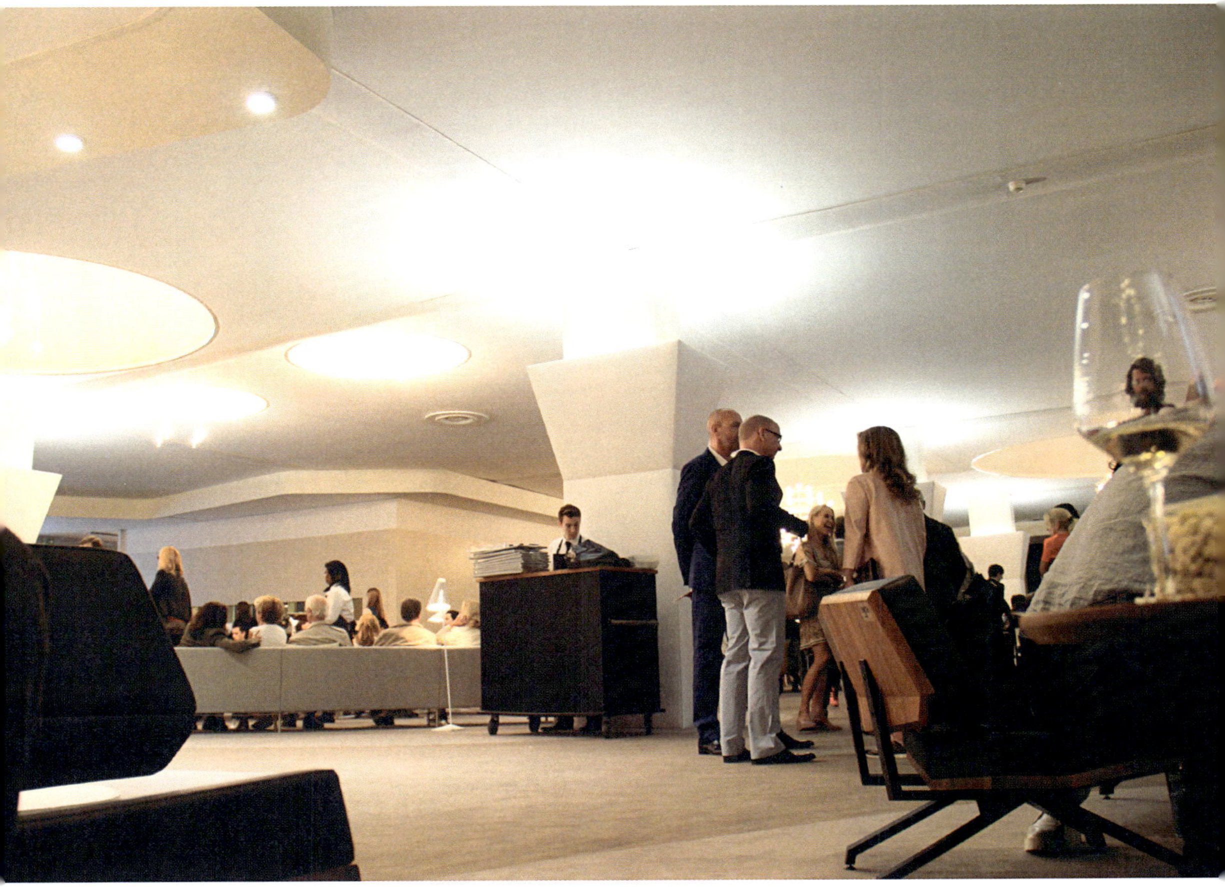

On Discomfiture in Art

The dissolution of a traditional configuration

If we review the interviews with the collectors at the Art Basel, the overall picture is thoroughly ambiguous; doubt and discomfiture about the art scene on the one hand, but insistence on one's own highly personal love of art on the other. Reference is made again and again to the massive upheavals in the art world which are dated to the last decade of the past century and the early „noughties". A German big collector, one voice among many: *„It has become a business in its own right. I believe the boom is connected with these socio-economic factors. It has very little to do with the quality of art in a different sense as it might perhaps be discussed among experts or art critics or intellectuals. I believe that essentially the concern is not for profundity but for renown. If an artist is renowned then he is also interesting for this circle and you can even see how certain actors in this field of art are in a position, thanks to their skill and marketing and other measures, to increase the renown of certain artists and so to increase their value."*

In many of the dialogues it is reported that in the context of these fundamental changes in the art field *business practices* have also undergone a substantial change. The criticism of a conduct that is becoming increasingly common in the time-honored world of the gallerists reveals a strong discontent particularly among the collectors of the „old school" who are increasingly less inclined to attend such occasions. An art consultant from the Netherlands who accompanies an entire group of art collectors to the fair year for year: *„It is a kind of strange ten years that we have all seen, we have had a crisis, but we have also had enormous wealth just before the crisis. And I see a lot of collectors who started around 2000, 2001, 2002, who started that period, they are disappointed. They want to move on to another world. I talked, last week I talked to a famous Belgian and he said ‚It is not fun anymore. If I look at a piece of art in a show and I stand longer than three minutes in front of this painting the gallery will come up to me, they know you because you are a big collector, so they know you, and say: Hey, do you like it? It is 20,000, but I can get you for 10,000'. And he is like: ‚I am not even interested. I want to understand why the artist painted this'. And he says: ‚Then I came home after a trip of two days and FedEx has sent me this thing of books on the artist. I don't even know how they know my home address'."*

Or the assessment of a no less renowned collector with a private museum, which is marked by a certain degree of self-pity and resentment: *„When I was once again invited at the last Art Basel to one of those fulminating dinners, I was suddenly sitting in the tenth row at the back and had to make conversation with some idiot or other. Well, I stood up after the dessert and simply left. I just don't feel like going any more. But the logic is clear. The tables at the front are occupied by people from Kazakhstan and God knows where else and hedge fund managers and madmen who are willing to pay one or two million for a single work."*

The judgment of an art consultant of a Swiss bank on the development of art fairs is also sobering: *„Yes, as I've said, they're a debatable issue, these fairs. This is something that in recent years – you know this as well as I do – something that has acquired a new dimension in recent years. Since art has become a part of the entertainment industry fairs and auctions have taken on proportions which one must enjoy with a certain, yes, with a certain degree of reserve. But nonetheless there's no escaping it. And I can't escape it either. Sometimes you have to work together with auction houses. And you have, and* *everyone who doesn't work there has, certain reservations towards these new phenomena. And the art fairs as well. In the meantime there are, well, one could go to an art fair somewhere every week. It's all a bit overvalued. It's become a social game, all the art, the entire art scene. And that's why we have to offer it to our customers as well. There are some to whom it means nothing and others who like going to the fair but definitely not to the opening, because they don't want to see all those people, all the hustle and bustle. And we, when we go to the fair, we do that as well, also with a certain degree of criticism. So we like going. We do a tour but I point out the advantages and disadvantages of such an event. When we are at a booth I sometimes say ‚Look, they work together with these and these other people'. And ‚The three pictures you see here, I'm looking at them for about the twenty-fifth time'. Or: ‚That picture was bought only last week at Sotheby's and I don't understand why it should cost fifty per cent more in the meantime'. This is just as an example. So we do point out all the aspects of this kind of art fair. And so it's quite alright to go as long as one says that. Because that happens to be the reality. And we don't want to withhold it from our customers."*

The discomfiture of the „classical" collector in regard to the contemporary art world is evident. He is a figure whose *fictional* aspect seems so pronounced exactly because it already always contains all the normative connotations which it is sufficient to refer to in order to awaken a collectively cultivated self-understanding of one's own personality. For it is not the discomfiture of individuals but of an entire generation – and of an entire *social configuration*. No matter how different the motivational impulse, the collecting practice, the relationship to art, and dealings with it may be – differences which even here within the notorious „collectors' community" leave enough room for differentiation, for more or less subtle hierarchizations of „legitimate" collecting. The „movements on the market" of the last two decades question precisely what was apparently an indivisible part of it – time, money and an „unpretentious passion" to spend both lavishly on immaterial goods. With the explosion of prices for art – indubitably a direct consequence of the new political-economic relations of power after the radical departure from the *welfare state* with its at least superficially defused blatancy of class antagonisms – the entire constellation is rendered obsolete. Quickly accumulated wealth and its swift conversion into art, the *art of the market*, substantially devalues not only the symbolic possibilities for investment of the „old money"; it also destroys the aura formerly surrounding the tacit understanding that the transformation of profane money into social recognition as a personal merit can be achieved through „art".

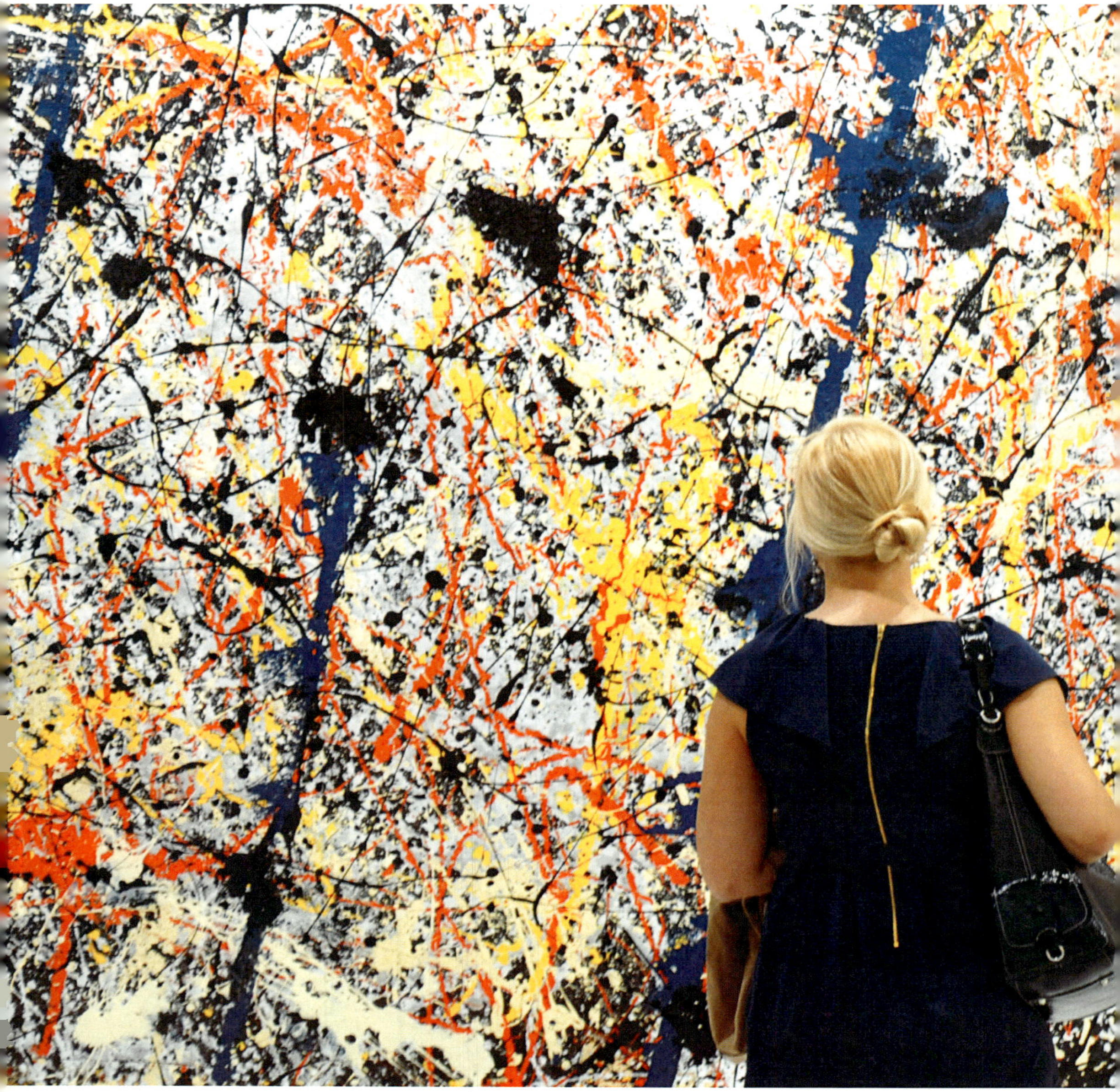

5 Commitments and commodities

The cult of art and its public

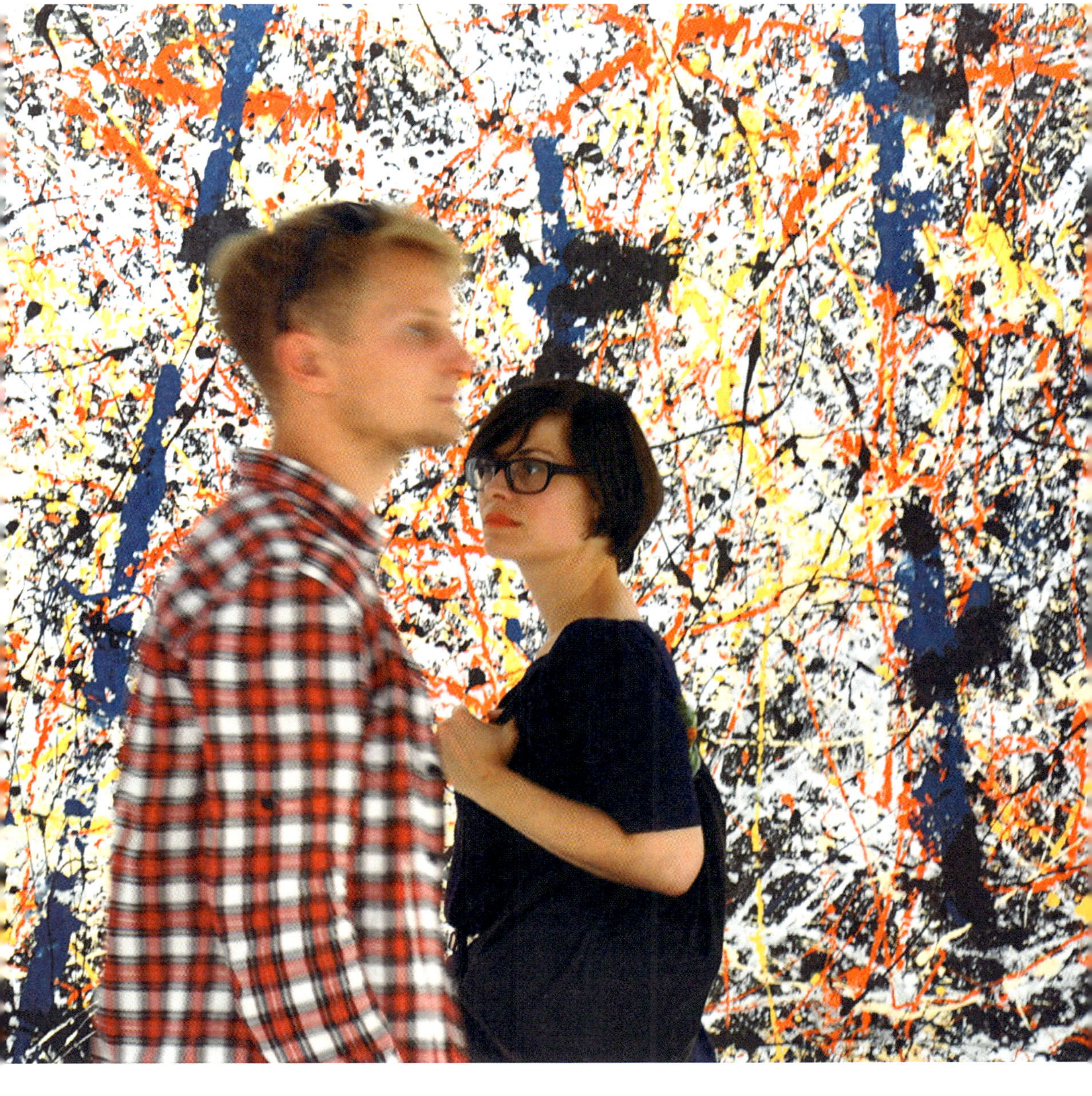

A vague awareness of the arbitrary nature of admiration for works of art haunts the experience of aesthetic pleasure. The history of individual or collective taste is sufficient to refute any belief that objects as complicated as works of learned culture, produced according to rules of construction developed in the course of a relatively autonomous history, should be capable of creating natural preferences by their own power.

PIERRE BOURDIEU, The Love of Art

For culture to fulfil its function of enchantment, it is necessary and sufficient that the social and historical conditions which make possible both the complete possession of culture – a second nature where society recognizes human excellence and which is experienced as a natural privilege – and cultural dispossession, a state of ‚nature' in danger of appearing as if it is part of the nature of the people condemned to it, should remain unnoticed.

PIERRE BOURDIEU, The Love of Art

Why do people come to the Art Basel? Of course there is a simple answer to this question, obvious as always when confessions of faith are evoked – it is the art itself by which the visitors are „moved", the stream of visitors is set in motion. But social reality is seldom so simple. When the many all do the same their motivations can nonetheless be quite diverse. If the sermon is important to the churchgoer is he following a habit or a community constraint, is the Sunday event, the „feast" decisive, or is it the conversations after mass with all their social preconditions and effects and the claim to reputation they involve, or is it the „business" which is possible within this context? There is no simple answer. And it becomes even more difficult as soon as the character of such an event, which is situated in both the world of values and the world of purposes, presents itself so clearly in all its ambiguity – a „fair" for goods believed to have no place in the world which registers the pennies and farthings in its account books, a fair for art must necessarily present the „true" love of art with greater challenges than a visit to a museum, the traditional practice for the „enjoyment of art" in general.

But the reality is different; it reckons up differently. Just as the commodity character of what is offered at the fair is dissipated because we are not dealing with „worldly" goods, with tractors or camper vans, kitchen appliances or garden tools, so too are the pretensions of the „public" sustained by a quite specific *belief* which, in spite of all the possible differences in motivation and social background of a nonetheless highly homogenous „community", creates an all-determining *feeling*, a feeling of participation in „extraordinary" and not primarily „worldly" events, in things which are not of this world. This impression imposes itself if one suppresses the experience of the unprejudiced observer, his images of huge crowds, of ordinary „business" in favor of an „experience" about which the visitor often speaks as if he were talking about a pilgrimage. These *affective* achievements are certainly among the most amazing phenomena to be observed at one of the most significant fairs for art in the world. Much more than at any other consumer fair the imperative of *immaterial* interest, of interest in its own right, rules here. The individual, personal *inner* participation in an event requires, like the object of its desire, the shedding of all collective character, refuses to see the „public" as such and nonetheless remains a part of it – while the entire production conveys, like the chorus of antiquity, the ritual significance of the play.

The lonely crowd

Experiences of art as „person“ and „public“

Art fairs are remarkable constructions. If one classifies this business model according to the business nomenclature they belong to the sphere of consumer fairs, of an offer of „business to the consumer“. But who are the „consumers“ in this case and what is the nature of their „consumption“ when, in contrast to specialist fairs for bicycles, household goods or information technology, only a vanishingly small number of the visitors can act as consumers? In scarcely any other fair is there such a blatant discrepancy between „looking“ and buying, between a *visual* and the possibility of a *material* appropriation – for by far the cheapest works at the Art Basel the equivalent of the price of a small car has to be paid and at most five out of a thousand visitors buy one of the works of art offered for sale.

And nonetheless this fundamental dichotomy, which makes the entire *class-specific* dimension of the relationship to art so tangible, seems to dissolve in that special aura that is not only claimed by the works offered for sale but is also accorded to them almost unconditionally. Just next door, at the „Baselworld“, a fair for watches and jewelry that is no less important „world-wide“, many more visitors come to marvel at the „exhibits“, which scarcely any of them are either ready or able to buy. This is a fair involving „business to business“, where the *voyeuristic visual pleasure* is understood as what it is, as a delight in looking into the shop windows of luxury which requires no further legitimation, and is fully aware of its class-specific possibilities and hence also of its status as a provider of visual pleasure for a crowd of extra-territorials, for the ordinary „public“. But here, at the Art Basel, the „guests“ are not willing to accept the *commodity character of* the works on offer or their place in the portfolio of luxury goods, or to thematize the *impossibility of possessing* them or the resultant *role as onlookers.* The public at the Art Basel defines itself almost exclusively in terms of a non-negotiable personal property – its „love of art“.

But what is „personal“ about this inclination, what is „individual“, what is shared in common and what is remarkable beyond the shared belief in the uniqueness of this „personal“ relationship to art. If one asks the visitors to the fair a striking profile is very quickly revealed – the image of a „class society“ of art for which the class society itself provides the foundations. Only a person who believes against all experience in the universality of aesthetic language can find it surprising that this „individuality“ is massively colored by the educational level of each of the „lovers“ who can be encountered at such fairs. The „common people“ are not present at all. It is in effect a purely „academic“ event; most of the visitors are university graduates or students on their way to graduation. If one takes into account the very close relationship in our societies between the acquisition of education and social status, this is a clear indication of the *class character* of these inclinations which are felt to be „personal“.

And it also becomes clear to what a great extent a society which is in this respect more or less „closed“ not only raises itself above the „masses“ but itself also reveals systematic *internal* distinctions between the laymen, who are scarcely able to build up a certain distance to the „art world“, and the professionals, who know the business, and the „scene“ – a world of its own in which, nonetheless, the closeness to or distance from the magnetic pole of the art business leaves unmistakable traces.

The Public at the Art Basel – A „Preview“

Streams of visitors to the art fairs are as old as the fairs themselves. The first Art Basel in 1970 already reported over 15,000 visitors; in the meantime there are more than 90,000 paying guests. But the profile of this public remains vague and the media reports gladly deal in detail with the „rich and beautiful", less often with the „big collectors" and virtually never with the „rank and file". However, two surveys of the visitors at the fairs in Basel and Miami Beach with almost three hundred participants give an impression of the character of this public.

It is doubtless significant that for various, above all organizational, reasons this survey could not be based on a random sample; instead the population of the participants was determined by a more or less strong process of self-selection. The resulting segment is already so highly specified in regard to its characteristics that the genuine „rank and file", the art enthusiastic „onlookers" could apparently at first sight only be depicted to a limited degree – a good forty per cent of the interviewees had participated in an „exclusive" preview. But, on the one hand, even the „customary" guests have a profile whose social characteristics are strikingly similar to what has been observed for decades among museum visitors. On the other hand, precisely this segment is well-suited to reveal *internal* differences, the „fine distinctions" which permeate the public of the „elect", of those selectively invoked by this survey.

The most striking feature of this profile, on taking a closer look, is certainly the educational background of the interviewees. Four out of five of the participants in the survey had an academic qualification, and one in seven had at least attended a college or was still studying – the „common" people are virtually unrepresented. The age structure is similarly relevant. Almost half of the visitors were under forty, a quarter under thirty and only one in eight over sixty – like visits to museums, art fairs tend to be „young" events. This educated, young affinity to culture is also typically more feminine than at other kinds of fairs. Among those interviewed women are slightly in the majority. And, another point which also leaves us unsurprised, the majority of the public comes from urban centers, is metropolitan in character [1].

Young, well-educated, mostly urban: these signs of privilege – or of the chance to claim it later – are, however, unevenly distributed, differently accentuated, even in this population. A sifting of the professions recorded in the survey clearly reveals relationships with the art field. There are even „genuine" artists on the list, alongside gallerists, collectors, curators, museum directors, art historians and a further circle of „artistically creative" professionals, architects, designers, photographers, actors, writers or mediators of culture, publishers, booksellers, art teachers. Two thirds of those interviewed overall, and even four fifths of those at Miami Beach, stated that they were concerned „professionally" with art, even when in the open entries occasionally only „art lover" was noted, this in itself being an indication of the tendency towards self-aggrandizement which often goes along with the „love of art". However, a third of the interviewees comes from the almost classical clientele of art appreciation, the liberal professions, the business bourgeoisie, lawyers and doctors, entrepreneurs bankers and real estate agents.

It can readily be assumed that a decisive dividing line exists here between the „professionals" and the „laymen", not only in regard to the *knowledge of art,* which has become more and more specific in the „post-modern" period with its scarcely manageable amount of „material" but also to the specific *attitudes,* the cultural practices, the entire self-understanding. The distinction between the participants in the previews and the rest of the clientele must be no less decisive, as it reflects a clear *two-class society* – four out of five interviewees at the previews were „professionals", whereas only half the „artistic" professions were allowed to attend these „exclusive" events. And only a quarter of the „laymen" reported on such preferential treatment. The fact that the percentage share of these privileged persons was *in reality* very much lower than in the surveys give an impression of the massive social hierarchization of the structure of the entire event.

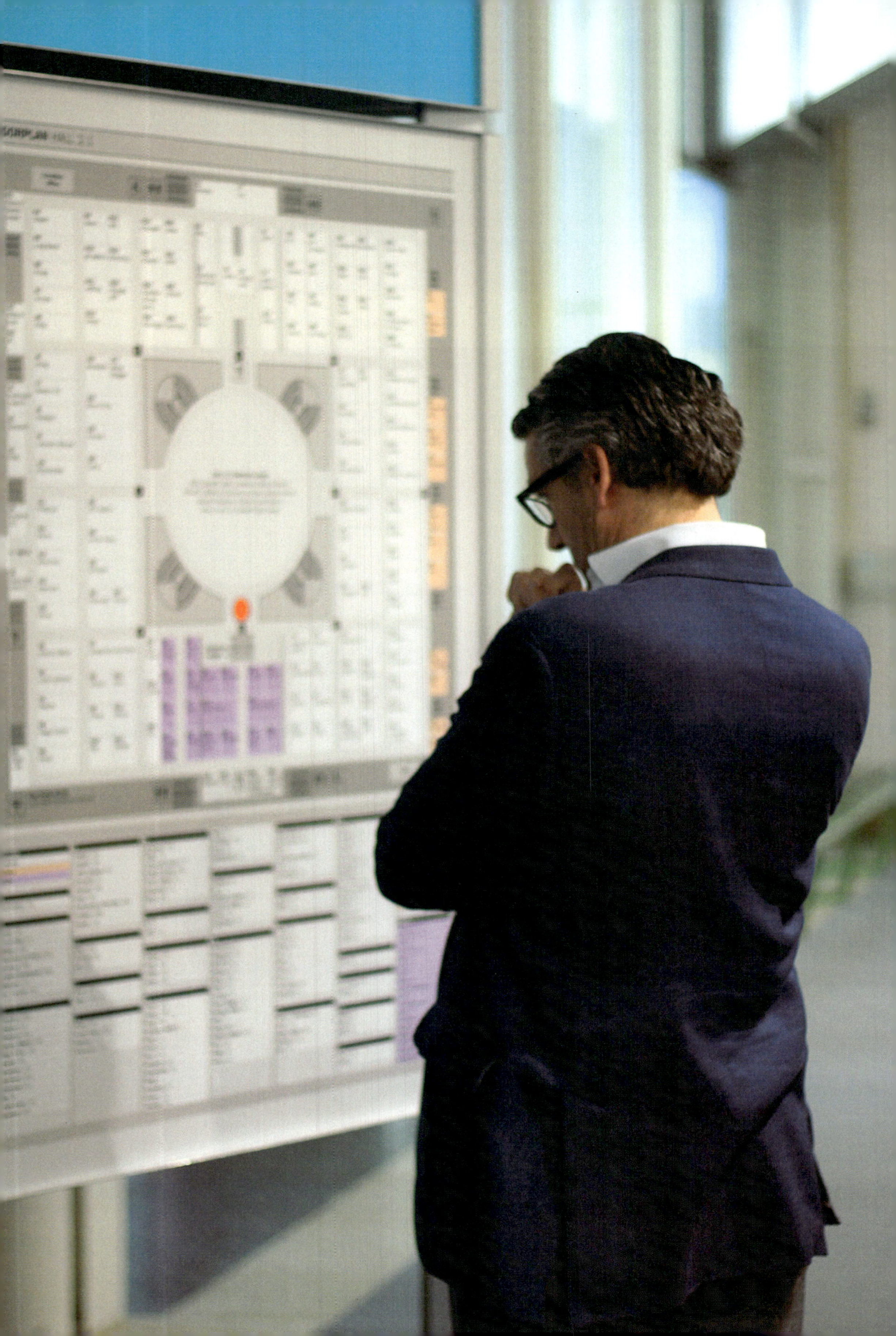

On the one hand we see the genuine *professionals,* the participants in the previews and not the public: those who are themselves actors, the gallerists, art consultants, curators, critics, the „important" people and their conversations, the „art world" in its personified form – no matter how diverse the nuances in this more or less exclusive society can be, or how different the social circles and their significance are. It is quite evident that even here blatant differences exist, made tangible in the separate VIP areas for the „important" and the „very important" personalities.

Then, in the same environment, the „opposite" side, the actual *customers,* mainly the private collectors, well-funded „amateurs", but also the „professional" representatives of public and private museums and foundations. Here too there evidently exists a scale registering the social, economic and cultural significance of the clients in each particular case; *status differences* exist which are already „approximately" approved by the management of the fair in its classification of the VIP quotas.

But within these classes further finer distinctions are certainly articulated not institutionally but practically, which correspond precisely to the degree of the closedness of the social circles, of the *social interaction.* And this in turn at the same time reveals that the *actual* proceedings, namely the exchange of money and art, are in the final analysis only of secondary significance. Status differences, the difference between economic power and artistic competence, are always involved, whose practical dissolution in a „business deal" must always involve a compromise between subjection to the primacy of economics and an open or subtle *pedagogics* of the „adepts".

On the other hand we have the „ground floor" of this art world, the many professionals or „semi"-professionals, washed up by its enormous charismatic undertow, a group *deficient in status,* unknown artists who cast an eye on this penthouse of the world, at the same time fascinated and disappointed, „inspired" and disgusted, the „free" art consultants, assistants in galleries, with or without the ambition to be accepted in this world, graphic artists, designers and architects. In this group the belief in an inviolable „spirit" of art is more or less strongly pronounced depending on the closeness to the „business dealings" and the biographical status. It is certainly at its strongest where the outsiders and the „young" meet. They lack the social detachment in which enjoyment and business can be brought together without irritation, „enthusiasm" is socially tempered and the „spiritual" side of art is little more than an empty phrase.

And finally the genuine *public,* the „laymen", doctors, judges, lawyers, administrative officers, teachers, banking experts, engineers, software specialists, booksellers and, not least, the students, all of them split between the more „bourgeois" and the more „modern" taste in art, between young and old, a heterogeneous throng of visitors, united by a class privilege, but differing in its overall *disposition,* so that the „love of art" can be differently chosen and differing relationships with it fostered. The „spirit" seems to be even less tarnished by the „business" aspect here, but nonetheless such an antagonism is pervasive even within this population of „spectators", contrasting an only partly informed „enjoyment" of art with the unconditional love of it. The difference between the subaltern or self-styled professionals and the „occasional customers" reappears among the outsiders of the art world as an opposition between „bourgeois" interest in art and enthusiasm for the „new" love of art, without permitting the different *social* generations of taste in art to express doubt in each case about their very own love of art [2].

No matter how unifying this privileged and privileging love seems to be, the public at the Art Basel is anything but united. A class society exists, which rigorously separates the actual „actors“ of the art world from the „amateurs“, a striking dichotomy which not only reflects the degree of participation in this world but at the same time also the differences in social status. Enjoyment and business come together in only a small sector of the fair, physically separated from the rest and socially in a class of its own. They legitimate one another reciprocally – dealing in art turns out to be not an economic but a *social* occurrence, which is always conscious of its character in spite of all the clichés about love. The apparently „pure“ but „naive“ and economically impotent love is to be found „down below“, among the genuine „public“, which, last not least, is a spectator of its own veneration of art and celebrates its own no less rigorously divisive class privilege.

And this public moves as a public in concentric circles, in orbits at different distances from the central star of the art world bundled together in this „event“. The VIP contingents in the forecourt of this event, this highly stylized „Holy of Holies“, who represent a class society of their own, graded by the organizers of the fair themselves according to financial, „intellectual“ or medial significance, do not see themselves as a „public“ but as individual „actors“ in this theatrical performance.

But where the possibility of this kind of participation rapidly disappears, the factual distance from the actual occurrences is transformed into a lack of distance such as can only be developed by a „genuine“ public. Participation in a collective event which is worthy of being celebrated as such not only negates the distance in regard to the social realization of the event but also in regard to the objects to whose adoration this event is apparently devoted, although what is actually involved is nothing but *social* self-adoration.

For the idea that here the „person“, the individual motivation, feels itself ennobled by a collective force, a „collective spiritual state“, as Marcel Mauss puts it, which verifies the magic powers of the event, the *magic* of the place, would not for this reason contradict the realization that these motivations have very little that is individual about them. The belief in the individuality of one's own inclinations is not personal but *ubiquitous* and the inclinations themselves are not personal but *conventional,* as they feed on the canon of art history and contemporary art on the way to its canonization. But the mantra of the „person“ does not stand in any experienced contradiction to the fetishism of the artist's name, because it is the *class character* of this relationship to art which first makes the naming of such „unique persons“ at all possible and because the „public“ does not present itself as such, when outside the uncultivated „masses“ are going about their daily business.

In spite of all the differences that exist between the lovers of art, their status in the art world and their role as „actors“ or „spectators“, differences which can be pronounced or trivial, experienced or repressed, it is always the *social privilege* whose worship unites the participants, a privilege which both enables and demands of the „lay person“ that he should attend a fair on modern art on a normal working day. This point suffices in order to explain the enormous, self-elevating force of a circumstance, which can, however, only be made public as a „personal“ inclination without any social preconditions, if it is to have its full social effect. The „love of art“ is a social privilege which in turn brings social privilege.

Insiders and Outsiders, Professionals and Amateurs

The fine differences in the appropriation of art

The surveys among the visitors to the Art Basel clearly show how differently the love of art can turn out, different in the form and intensity of its practices, in the nature and „direction" of taste, in the entire attitude towards modern art and its legitimacy – all of this, moreover, narrowly related to social status differences. This already begins with the degree of „internationality" of the guests, itself a strong indicator of the prominent role of social position. But although the fair continually emphasizes its international flair, in this highly specific section of the visitors only one fifth of the guests in Basel come from countries other than Switzerland and Germany, and a third come from Basel, Bern and Zurich. The same applies to Miami Beach where a third also comes directly from Miami, the majority from Florida, only one in six from New York, and only one in five from outside the USA. If one excludes the community of the representatives of the media, a genuinely *transcontinental* internationality practically exists at these fairs only on the *business side* in supply and demand, among the sellers and their potential clients.

Now we turn to the history and practice of attendance at the fair. Here too there is a similar picture of selective access which manifests itself so tangibly at the gates to the fair. „Newcomers" are the exception on the exclusive days, above all the „amateurs"; the potential customers turn out to be regular guests, not only in regard to the frequency of their attendance at fairs in the past but also to the intensity of the visit – only a vanishing minority of the „normal" guests, particularly the „laymen" among them, had already been to the fair five times or more in contrast to one third of the VIP public; four out of five of the amateurs among the „occasional customers" were able or wanted to spend more than one day at the fair; in contrast the professionals without VIP status stayed longer, and the guests at the previews and their „agents" maintained a massive presence.

But what does the visit specifically look like? Everything indicates that here quite different attitudes towards the event do in fact exist, that the *intentions* are almost radically different, as is the social, economic, cultural, the practical context. It is otherwise scarcely possible to explain the lack of decision with which the amateurs attend the fair, half of them simply allowing the fair to „make an impression" on them, without consulting the catalogue or show guide and without specific intentions even in regard to visiting particular sectors, whereas the potential customers, in contrast to the „outsiders", consciously plan to look at particular works. Here *purchasing* interests shine through, matching the more or less clear *business* interests of the „exclusive" professionals. And their statements on purchasing behavior confirm precisely this relationship. The customers come almost exclusively from the group of VIP amateurs and even when the professionals apparently more frequently regard the question about their purchasing interests as indiscrete or „vulgar", without it being possible to ascertain whether they have acquired works or not, there can be no doubt as to who can report, with a pride not necessarily regarded as subtle in this world, on the material appropriation of art, which is virtually only possible in this segment. And thus the social character of the „love of art" takes on a particularly incisive form at this very point. The „lonely", the museum-like approach to the visit, as it tends to be encountered among the outsiders, recedes almost entirely into the background in the case of the „exclusive" amateurs in favor of a *common celebration of personal presence* at this event; partner, family, friends and acquaintances surround the financially strong laymen; it is a *social event* which frames the economic event, lending it a symbolic character which serves to obliterate this social aspect.

This pronounced *profanity* of the visit to a world of sacral objects, whose strongly social embeddedness is also witnessed by the „ordinary" layman, finally takes on a downright banal form among the VIP public, when one goes through the various reasons for this visit. The intention to gain an overview of contemporary art or to discover new artists, the *intrinsic* moment, is clearly lacking among the potential buyers, whereas the participation in an important „cultural event" and the enjoyment of a „special atmosphere" rockets upwards. It reminds one of a bourgeois evening at the opera. The *social event* is in the foreground; making contacts and inspecting possible purchases, activities which are virtually meaningless for the outsider at a greater distance from the art world, play a prominent part here, as is only fitting for a cultural supporting program for bigger business dealings.

The radical difference to „true", „disinterested" love of art can also be seen in the lack of sovereignty in dealing with the content of art, a *lack of distance* born of the only short-coming of this clientele, its deficient knowledge of art. The mere fact that the works of classical modern and contemporary art presented at the fair are much more frequently perceived as being „totally" representative in this group, whereas the genuine profes-sionals in the VIP contingent are predominantly skeptical, is a first indication of a *structural naivety* of those amateurs who as potential buyers are almost constrained to be convinced of the artistic significance of the event.

The judgment of the trends represented at the fair also makes it fully clear that this undistanced enthusiasm is particularly predominant among this clientele – negatively connoted descriptions of such trends achieve the lowest values, positive descriptions, on the other hand, the highest approval rates. The „commercial" character of the offer in the sales situation alone is very clearly emphasized. This is probably not only a concession to the opinions which are in the mean time commonly expressed in the media but also the concrete experience of the customer. Here the response matches that of the professionals who participate in such deals – only here, as a result of direct practical experience, is something resembling healthy realism evident.

The *overall judgment* of the fair also makes it clear that the substantial enthusiasm of the VIP amateurs reflects neither the „exclusive" understanding of art among the professional participants nor the more content-oriented inclinations of the „creative" people who have no access to the insider scene of the art world, and least of all perhaps the disappointed expectations of the „common" art lover, who in this question is just as reserved as the decisive actors on the art market, although certainly for reasons other than those of content. This is not least because differences of social context always lie behind the love of art of laymen and because here *differences in social status* play a part. In the one case these differences make themselves felt as a specific incompetence of both a general and a personal kind and in the other case they set in motion a „service" which attempts to achieve a business-enabling balance between economic potency and the lack of specific competence at an enormous pedagogical-curative expense. If one observes how massive the participation in the environment of the Art Basel is among the „exclusive" segment of the visitors – participation in the supporting program, attendance at other art fairs, „satellites" of the big event, at the museums nearby – and if one knows that the „competent nurturing" of *social status* is an essential factor in this situation, then the difference to the capacity of the laymen for enthusiasm becomes truly intelligible. Frequent attendance at art fairs and the important biennials is also an indicator of a *social privilege* which covers up the *lack of specific legitimacy* for the acquisition of art.

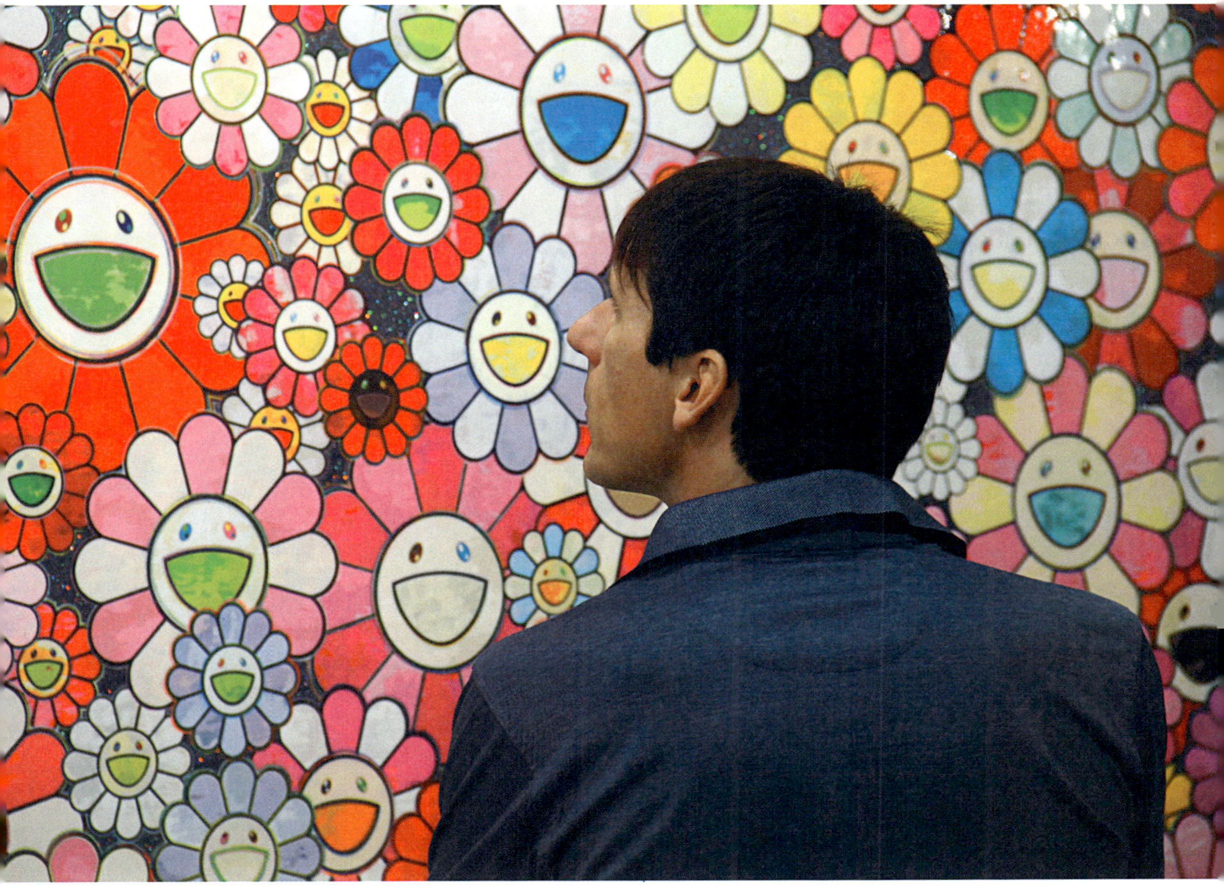

Attendance at the fair, taste in art and cultural practice

	Professionals Previews	Amateurs Previews	Professionals Public Days	Amateurs Public Days
Attendance days				
1 day	23	37	55	80
2 days	30	26	18	12
3 days	25	17	18	4
4 or 5 days	22	20	9	4
Attendance history Art Basel				
never before	15	8	29	35
twice	7	14	13	14
five times	12	11	12	4
up to ten times	26	22	16	6
Kind of attendance				
alone	28	11	38	33
with partner	20	35	19	15
with family	7	14	10	14
with friends / acquaintances	28	30	20	32
with an organized group	0	0	4	0
with art experts	5	3	1	1
with business partners	3	5	7	3
with clients	9	3	1	1
Attendance aids				
without a plan	24	57	34	50
Attendance intentions				
certain sectors	69	42	47	40
certain artists / works	45	43	30	28
Works of art bought				
no statement	19	4	15	8
yes	4	39	0	3
Most important reasons for attending				
art historical overview	23	19	23	17
contemporary overview	79	60	77	72
important cultural event	35	54	35	44
discover new artists	76	46	68	62
enjoy special atmosphere	39	70	45	58
follow interesting debates	16	11	10	9
make/renew contacts	57	46	35	15
view interesting purchases	31	43	21	13
Representativeness modern art				
perfect	27	44	35	28
to some extent	65	47	52	63
Representativeness contemporary art				
perfect	27	42	28	31
to some extent	65	47	61	64
Trends represented				
fully up to date	59	57	48	40
conventional	31	22	26	27
ephemeral	21	16	13	17
surprising	11	19	14	8
forward-looking	25	24	18	12
critical-reflective	1	14	13	21
repetitive	23	24	23	27
commercial	51	49	44	40
Overall judgment of the fair				
enthusiastic	36	60	46	38
impressed	56	35	51	53
disappointed	7	3	4	7

Attendance at the fair, taste in art and cultural practice | continuation

	Professionals Previews	Amateurs Previews	Professionals Public Days	Amateurs Public Days
Cultural activities during the fair				
participation in the supporting program	51	50	41	14
attendance at other fairs	90	70	68	33
visits to museums	58	57	33	29
Cultural activities outside the fair				
attendance at other art fairs	75	81	50	39
attendance at biennials	78	61	46	35
Venice biennial	68	60	30	26
documenta Kassel	32	20	18	17
Interest in art by epochs				
premodern art	24	23	32	33
modern art	61	51	69	63
post-war & contemporary art	87	78	69	68
Reading of art periodicals				
yes	88	55	73	34
Purchase of original works of art				
yes	87	83	67	47
private	72	76	58	44
professional	25	8	14	3
Love of art / influences				
family	42	66	45	49
friends	5	10	9	17
colleagues	7	7	8	5
work	9	0	5	2
personal experience	36	10	33	27
Love of art / other genres				
yes	84	76	82	76
literature	62	66	59	66
lyrical poetry	24	23	33	23
classical music	39	46	53	46
opera	30	49	35	37
ballett	44	26	32	26
theater	49	66	54	46
jazz	29	23	42	33
popular music	56	49	49	43
film	64	80	69	64
Preconditions for experience of art				
spontaneous pleasure	41	60	41	57
previous art historical knowledge	35	23	22	23
sensitivity and personality	56	54	59	53
early acquired familiarity with art	36	14	28	24
good taste	12	23	15	20
quality of the art itself	59	60	46	47
Relationship to one's own works of art				
familiarity and reciprocity	44	31	33	41
beautiful sight in beautiful home	15	31	18	33
good long-term investment	12	23	19	14
appreciation of the work as such	74	63	60	50
Relationship of quality and art market				
good art always wins through	22	40	18	18
art world determines the value of art	33	27	47	53
art world helps good art to success	44	33	35	29

Source: Surveys among visitors to the Art Basel and Art Basel Miami Beach | 280 participants | Percentages rounded off.

The *interested naivety* of the VIP amateurs is revealed everywhere. If one looks at the artistic preferences in terms of a rough division into epochs, one discovers, on the one hand, characteristics of the *fashion follower* – there is virtually no interest in pre-modern art and even the classical modern period is clearly rated lower in a comparison with other segments of the public. The potential buyers follow the genuine professional, who here achieve the highest values, in their interest in contemporary art, whereas more „classical" inclinations strongly oriented on the existing canon tend to be found among the „outsiders". On the other hand this naivety, which strives to follow the „taste of the times", has a thoroughly „rational" aspect, if one simply considers the range of the offers in the field of contemporary art. For the *private acquisition* of art takes first place among this clientele. Purchases are also made in the outer circles of the art world, less often and certainly not in the higher price categories: small works, graphic works, nothing that could be had at the fair. But in the inner circle of the amateurs the *purchasing interest* beats everything else. In regard to taste, in which the „clients" can occasionally even be classified as „critical/reflective" in their judgment of what is offered at the Art Basel – a judgment from which the genuine professionals are far removed –, the financially strong amateurs turn into „apprentices" who are dependent on the intellectual competence of the „master"; but as regards *acquisition* they are the masters of the procedure.

There are in fact decisive differences among the „public" in regard to taste in art, above all between the professionals and the amateurs. The fact that the laymen proceed less purposively at the fair, do not visit certain galleries or wish to see certain artists or works, is already a reference to the differences in *specific competence* and when one takes a closer look at the area of artistic interests, one sees not only that this area is much more narrowly staked out among the amateurs, less widely spread, but also that it is much more conventionally tailored. Whereas the professionals at the previews almost always mention only artists who practically never come up in the canonical discourse, with the exception of a few big names, Doug Aitken, Dan Flavin, Richard Serra, Sol Lewitt, the „exclusive" amateurs at the fair are drawn towards works of „Basquiat, Rothko, Warhol, Pollock", or towards the even more classical works of „De Chirico, Picasso, Dubuffet" or quite simply towards „expressionism". And it is scarcely any different on the visitors days in regard to the laymen, who are interested in „Chagall, Picasso", „Andy Warhol, Gerhard Richter", „Bacon, Basquiat, Soulages", or „old classical artists", „expressionists, impressionists". Here a *conventionalism* is revealed which is oriented mostly on well-known names and canonized movements.

The *power of the canon* itself becomes all the more impressive when one takes the gen-eral artistic preferences into account. Then a strongly unifying taste asserts itself throughout the entire „public", in the case of the „old masters" for Da Vinci, Raffael, Michelangelo, Botticelli, Caravaggio, Rembrandt, Velazquez, Vermeer, and the interest in the modern period is also very „classical" in its preference for Van Gogh, Gauguin, Monet, Cézanne, Kandinsky, Klee, Picasso; in post-war art Pollock, De Kooning, Rothko, Rauschenberg, Johns, Lichtenstein, Warhol are beyond all doubt, and the hit list of established contemporary art with Baldessari, Basquiat, Bourgeois, Hockney, Kiefer, Nauman, Polke, Serra, Richter, Twombly, Viola, or the more recent „mainstream", Hirst, Koons and Ai Weiwei, Abramović, Barney, Cattelan, Eliásson, Kapoor, Murakami, Gursky, Struth and Wall confirms the extremely *levelling character* of the art business as it is shown at the fair. Even among the „genuine" professionals the names from outside the world of global interests which are accorded a place in the portfolio of their personal taste in art are growing fewer.

Of course the fair has its apparent „dissidents". They distance themselves from the „hustle and bustle" of the event, criticize the manifestations of „commerce" and the accompanying public, the conventionality of what is on offer, the high prices for the works, everything which contradicts the inclinations of the „pure" love of art, the evident involvement of art in the „world"; the professional insiders more often and more sovereignly than all the amateurs, with a skepticism also born of practical experience and specific competence – the selection of items is „predictable", „always the same", and there is talk of „kitsch". But this anti-economic dissidence is also in a certain fashion highly conformist and fulfils the conventions of the artistic sphere. For as soon as the prices for the artistic products, widely regarded throughout the entire public as „excessive", are no longer thematized, as soon as this anti-economic reflex subsides, and the market value as the *criterion for the quality* of art is questioned, and as soon as the core of autonomistic self-understanding is touched, the judgment becomes less certain. Among the professionals there are substantial concessions; the privileged amateurs are more reserved, but massively approving, as a kind of „populist" indignation about the violation of the „purity requirements", among the laymen in the „ordinary" public. The sensitivity towards the power of money in the universe of art depends on one's own position in this world, but anyhow in all cases the *illusion* may not be destroyed.

The market value of art – Judgment of the visitors

	Professionals Previews	Amateurs Previews	Professionals Public Days	Amateurs Public Days
Market value as criterion of quality				
completely / rather correct	63	56	63	73
completely / rather false	37	44	37	27
Reasons for price increases in art				
increased quality	7	5	11	3
more people interested in art	37	38	33	31
more educated people	15	11	13	9
more buyers among the new rich	67	60	51	62
demand from the emerging countries	63	30	39	40
investment and speculation	51	51	52	54
Prices for art at the Art Basel				
often too low	0	0	1	0
on the whole appropriate	19	12	14	15
partly /totally exaggerated	81	88	85	85

Source: Surveys among visitors to the Art Basel and Art Basel Miami Beach | 280 participants | Percentages rounded off.

Even when the visitors scarcely relate the recent price increases for works of art to im-proved quality, no less unanimously see „investment and speculation" as a significant influencing factor, quite rightly register the role of a new group of buyers, particularly among the professionals, and the increased demand from the *emerging countries,* it is nonetheless clear how stubbornly the belief in an interest in art *without any social preconditions* is maintained. On the one hand the existence of more people interested in art is seen as a factor which could be responsible for price increases, but on the other hand an increased level of education is largely dismissed. This striking discrepancy again reveals how much the indisputable relationship between „love of art" and *social privilege* calls for denial, so that the *idealization* of art, which contributes to personal idealization, can be maintained.

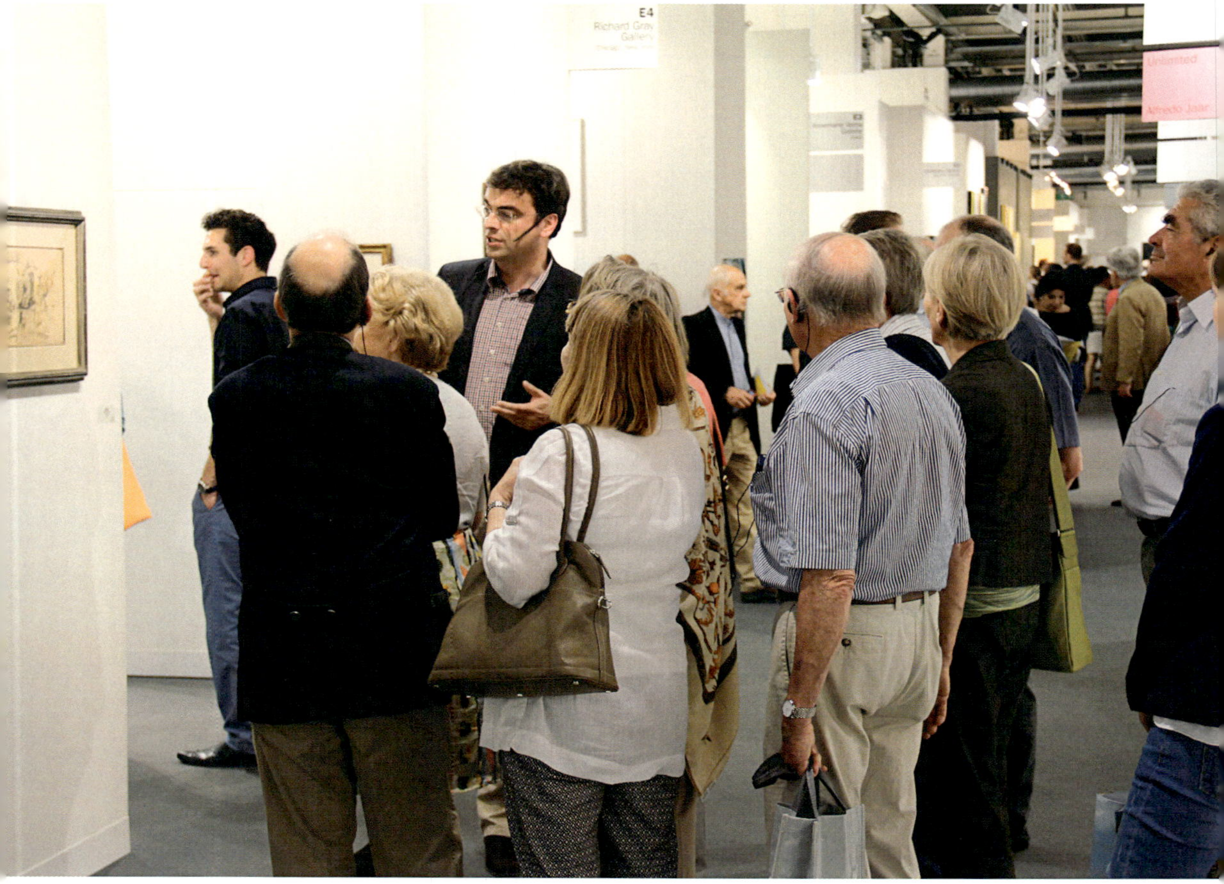
E4
Gallery

The Sacred in the Profane

„Art" and „world" as borderline and borderline experience

It is this logic of „desecularization", historically inscribed in the genetic code of the modern field of art, which the public, in spite of all existing differences, again and again articulates. And at the same time, precisely in the manner of this articulation, it reveals an „attitude" towards art which is not only socially constituted but also indicates a *characteristic position* in this field with which all of these differences are associated. Insiders and outsiders, professionals and amateurs, the entire hierarchizations even within these „ideal types" – hierarchizations not least in regard to the *legitimacy of participation* in this field – are determined by implicit and explicit polarities, the contraposition of „genuine" connoisseurship, laborious study of art and naive enthusiasm, of the capacity for the material possession of art and an ascetic, purely ideal appropriation out of necessity, of conventional and avant-gardist taste: everywhere the battle over the legitimacy of this relationship to art shines through and the *social constitution* of what is unquestioningly regarded as „sacred" in art is pushed into the background, because the struggle makes use of art's own categories. It is exactly these struggles to which „art" quite decisively owes its unifying and binding character and the belief in its „worth in its own right".

That the „love of art" can be jealous about a market which puts the objects of its adoration up for sale depicts a strange circumstance. At fairs for watches and jewelry the state of mind is certainly different, and different again in sales events for information technology, camping vans, anglers' needs and household goods. The innumerable gradations of the possibilities for the acquisition of goods and the accompanying perception of social differences, of the fascination emanating from luxury goods or technical innovations, of considerations of utility, of social „constraint" in ever-changing combinations and degrees cannot be compared with the feelings released at an art fair like the Art Basel. A watch for 50,000 dollars or a yacht for millions reveal a *class gap,* can fuel resentment, but in the end they are no more than *commodities* furnished with a social seal, whose symbolic pretensions can clearly be recognized as class pretensions. At an art fair the „museum quality" of the objects for sale is frequently invoked, the claim that they are worthy of a place in a museum, where an *exchange of commodities* is impossible and what is universal in our society is preserved. But as soon as the material realization of this universal property is put up for sale, powerful, mostly impotent feelings, of contradiction, disgust and disappointment, are evoked.

But not everywhere and not to the same degree in everyone. The irrevocable „love of art" is a variable feeling, depending on one's position in social space, in the field of art, and it is all the more unconditional the more one attempts to disguise the *social* character of that position. If one takes a look at the dimensions of the cultural and artistic inclinations of the public this becomes clear once again. On the one hand the „history", the initiation of this love, is most often declared to be a „family" affair in the entire population of visitors. Its social aspect, the *social inheritance,* disappears behind the generational inheritance. But here already differences are recognizable. The „exclusive" dilettantes achieve the highest values, emphasizing an inheritance divested of its class character, whereas the professionals emphasize their „own experience", the *personal* moment – the former thus refers to a legitimacy based on social exclusiveness, the latter to a *specific* legitimacy. And the portfolio of cultural interests is *similarly* differentiated. Attendance at the opera and theatre, the classical bourgeois social events with primarily social characteristics, meetings of the bourgeois „milieu", is particularly prominent among the privileged amateurs in comparison to the other visitors, pointing to the aspect of shared *entertainment,* as does the massive consumption of films which are not in the „art house" category. At events offering a more *ascetic* kind of cultural enjoyment, readings of lyrical poetry or classical music, the „subaltern" professionals tend to be well represented, and this is also the case with jazz, the typical medium of „intellectual" interest. The special preference for ballet performances among those who feel called to culture on the preview days indicates a kind of intermediate position. Such gradations in the continuum between social and „personal", sophisticated and ascetic, in a relatively homogeneous population permit the recognition of the status accorded to the enjoyment of art, to art itself, in the practical life context and its emotional household.

Enthusiasm, fun and good weather

VIPs in the ecstasy of the carefree enjoyment of art

The dilettantism of the laymen on the preview days is almost unbrokenly visible. Although some of the interviewees occasionally regret the lack of the „unconventional", the unrestrained *enthusiasm* stands in the foreground; it is mostly of a simple and artless kind. An administrative officer from Miami presents himself as more assiduous, but the lack of distance runs through all the entries. The *event character* of the fair is also omnipresent, the fun, the meetings with „old friends", the weather – the carefree enjoyment of art.

Great show, Statements not really good quality, Unlimited without a young highlight
(banker, Basel, 36 years old)

Not a lot of new ideas in contemporary art. A good overview of the market for modern art
(lawyer, Basel, 49 years old)

Better than last year but still too conservative (marketing consultant, Miami, 46 years old)

Very good fair (industrialist, Veracruz, 36 years old)

Excellent (pensioned lawyer, San Francisco, 73 years old)

Great (doctor, Santa Barbara, 60 years old)

Great (banker, Oklahoma, 66 years old)

Great and fun (real estate manager, Paris, 52 years old)

Great, informative and fun (engineer, New York, 60 years old)

Marvellous! (real estate agent, Berlin, 36 years old)

I always look forward to the experience and seeing new works and old friends
(pensioned US federal official, Seattle, no age indicated)

It's an important fair! With good quality in a nice setting while winter in Europe
(real estate developer, Brussels, 43 years old)

I found ABMB 2011 to be profoundly appealing. The obvious care and thoughtfulness that went into the selections gave visitors a remarkable sensory experience. Much of the work was exciting, sometimes demanding, and I was rewarded with new appreciation (administrative officer, Miami, 60 years old)

It is evident how divisive this attitude towards art among the visitors is in spite of all the things they have in common. In the answers to the question of the preconditions for the „right" experience of art, „sensibility and personality", the „classical" highly personalized unconditional „competence", is consistently named as a quite essential condition for the enjoyment of art, but the dilettantism of the laymen votes even more strongly for „spontaneous liking", quite differently from the genuine „professionals", who much more frequently emphasize the prior knowledge of art history and a familiarity with art acquired early in life, the *educated intellect* as opposed to the smug trust in one's own powers of judgment. And it is this self-empowerment which makes the totally *contradictory nature* of the personality cult associated with the experience of art so clear. Among the „exclusive" amateurs, who mostly point to their „family" as the background to their enthusiasm for art, the „early acquired familiarity" with art as a measure of their experience of art is lost – the reference to the *social predicate* that one comes from a family which is enthusiastic about art has done its work and enables a *personal taste* which no longer wishes to be confronted with its social origins.

From sovereign to critical

The „insider" and the „professional" view

For the insiders of the art business, the professionals on the preview days, the fair presumably does not give rise to even the slightest of „inner" challenges. The detachment in dealing with the market character is again and again clearly revealed, the lack of „surprises", the conventionalism, is named but not judged; all of this scarcely affects the status of the fair. Criticism tends to come more from the camp of the com-mentators, but even in their case it seems detached, an ascertainment and less an objection. The show is the way it is and is perceived as the international standard for a supply of items which tends to be in conformity with the market. For this reason the „place in the sun" of a Parisian gallerist at Miami Beach is both: the recognition of the significance of the event and an ironic distancing through the reference to the good weather.

A fair assessment of contemporary market interests but lacking risk and spontaneity (curator, Chicago, 65 years old)

It stands as the most important purely commercial „art" fair in the world where glamour and glitter is confounded with concept (curator, Basel, 52 years old)

Art as entertainment and a coming together for the international moneyed aristocracy (journalist, Stuttgart, 58 years old)

Many artists in Venice were not represented at AB. Most of the AB galleries offered conventional brand name art (art journalist, Salzburg, 34 years old)

A rather boring event this time, which wanted to play safe in order to achieve high prices (architect, art reporter, Zurich, 31 years old)

A good place in the sun (gallerist, Paris, 50 years old)

For this reason it can no longer be regarded as contradictory that this taste seems to follow almost naively the ideology of a quality of the works which „speaks for itself", that it believes that good art will always win through, that it not seldom and quite frankly characterizes its purpose as being a decorative object „in a beautiful home" and also as a good long-term investment. On the contrary it confirms the unblinking social self-empowerment of the dilettante, who values what has to be valued, acquires it in order to be able to do with it as he likes and necessarily perceives precisely this relationship as a unique expression of his „personality". The „sacred", transformed in such a *conventional* way, enters into a completely unirritated and at the same time socially highly distinctive association with the profane uses to which it is put.

There is very little irritation, therefore, among the „insiders" who mediate art, who „on account of their profession" have to support the ideology of artistic „quality" and for this reason are the group which, far more than all the others, see the art market as helping „good" art to be successful. Here too, at a completely different level of specific competence and from a totally different position, a *reconciliation* of the sacred and the profane takes place.

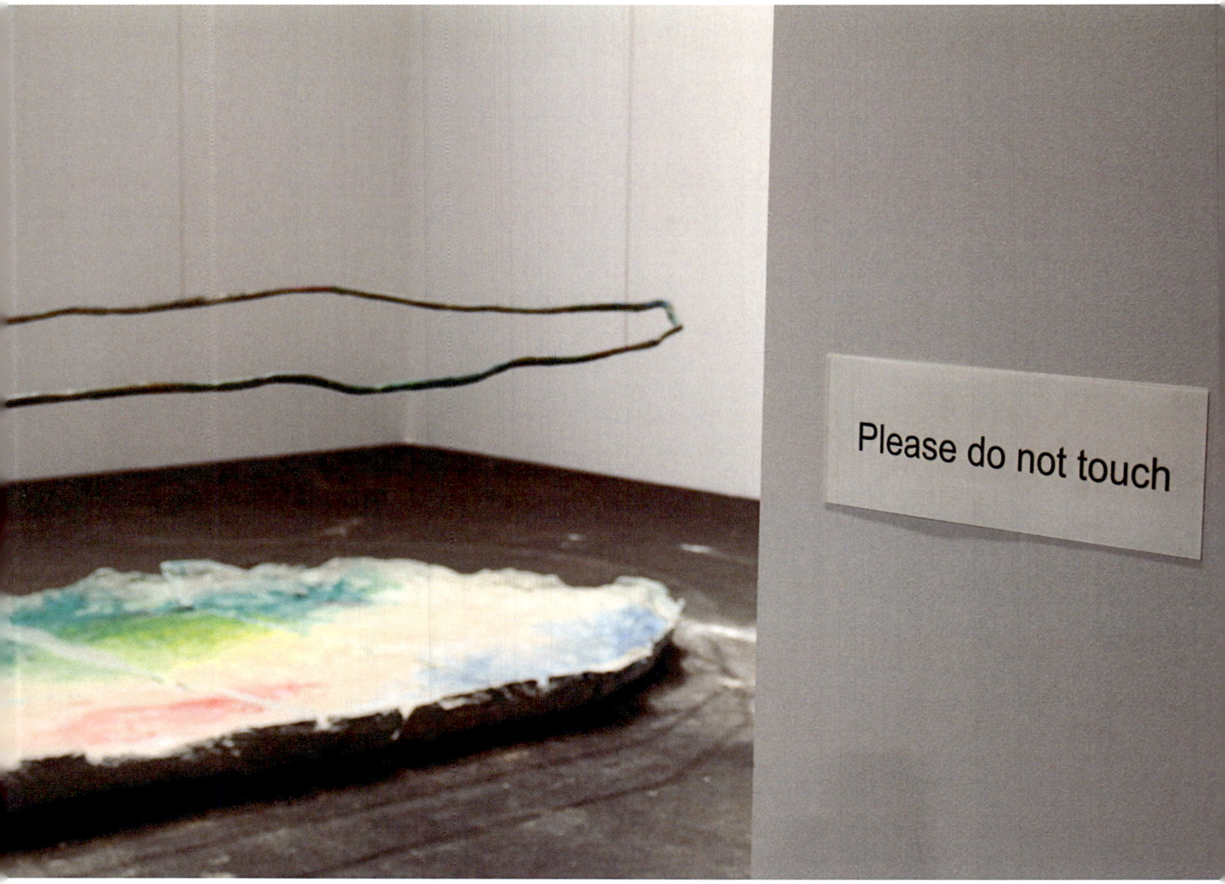
Please do not touch

The irritation is, however, pronounced among the „outsiders", both professional and amateur. It is an indication of a „more inward" and in a different way more naive belief and consequently of a more profound disappointment. For this group „good" art by no means makes its way unchallenged. Its value, its place in history is instead determined by the art world, by „the world".

Quality meets commerce – without „surprises"

The margins of the art business between devotion and detachment

On the public days the artistic professions are faced with probably their greatest challenge. Although the fair is also recognized here too as a kind of „benchmark", the conventionality, the lack of „surprises", of anything „new", the uniformity, are much more clearly and frequently criticized, along with the obvious „commercialism", the masses of people and the „vulgarity". But the criterion of the „quality" of the art is less questioned here than anywhere else, the *illusion of the intrinsic significance* of the expression of an art which distances itself from the profane is maintained, and the dedication to the „sacred" in art is all the greater.

It is like any other art fair I have visited (artist, Berlin, 43 years old)

Same as other years in terms of the art shown (artist, Miami, 65 years old)

Important cultural event. Conversations had the most educational value. I find that the fair itself is often overwhelming as the crowds of people increase. It is sometimes difficult to enjoy/appreciate the work (development coordinator in a museum, Alabama, 34 years old)

Had fun. Saw some nice things. But despite being overwhelming, due to the masses of people, the sensory overload, and the whirlwind of events, it was somewhat underwhelming in terms of seeing new, exciting material that makes you think
(business development agent in auction house, Houston, 39 years old)

It was fine, it's always ok. I always hope to see something different on the major fair circuit (which for me remains Art Basel Miami, Armory, Art Basel, Frieze) and feel that there is a lot of repetition among them (publicist, New York, 29 years old)

High-class fair which fulfils its purpose, little that is new but nevertheless pleasure in looking at the works (journalist, Berlin, 40 years old)

Too commercial, too few surprises (photographer, Freiburg, 48 years old)

Good quality but few surprises (art consultant, Paris, 28 years old)

Lovely works, a lot of variety, but everything is moved and impulsed by money – art is supposed to be activated by questions and self-reflection and I see lots of dollar signs involved
(artist, Buenos Aires, 23 years old)

A gathering of snobs (typographer, Basel, 23 years old)

A lot of short-lived kitsch, some works of high artistic quality
(art student, gallery employee, Basel, 22 years old)

It is a very complex situation. How much „profanity" art can tolerate, how much „vulgarity", how conventional, how decorative, how „ready-made" it can be, to whom it should be sold, all of this is up for negotiation at the fair, mostly tacitly, but also not so seldom quite explicitly. There is a cease-fire which no small part of the professionals involved in the „business dealings" conclude with the „profane" side because *economic constraint* calls for it – in spite of reservations about a certain clientele, who in their style of dress alone often reveal a lack of „decency" and in their habits and habitus disclose the specific, both intellectual and social, dilettantism of hard cash, in spite of the satisfaction of occasionally encountering „seriously" interested people – „old" collectors, museum directors, curators – and in spite of the art critics and journalists who go along with the game but then ironically and sarcastically comment on this major event with all its conventionalism, self-presentation and illustrations of money fighting for social respect. And then there are their „customers", also heterogeneous but perhaps the least afflicted with scruples, the „secular" centre of the event, for them a *social happening,* like a visit to the opera, whose profanity in the perceptions of the others here is seldom felt; on the contrary it is a „special occasion" embedded in the special occasions of an elevated life-style to which, among others, the acquisition of „cultural goods" belongs – the „taste" and the „enjoyment", both inseparably linked and combined with an awareness of social significance perceived as „personal" significance, does not share the intellectual reservations that wish to turn this special but nonetheless entirely *worldly* event into a normative event, a question of belief. But more or less consciously this „taste" perceives its own inability to decide this question for itself and brings a sacrifice instead on the altar of the „universal" goods.

Unique, exciting, nice and interesting

The „public" and the ambivalence of the love of art

The „laymen" on the public days reveal perhaps most clearly of all the entire spectrum of sovereignty, assiduousness, enthusiasm, irritation, undistanced admiration („unique", „fantastic"), distanced recognition („liked it", „nice"), among the „sorcerers' apprentices", the students of art, ostentatious sovereignty („agreeable thought-provoking impulses", „no surprises"), assiduous interest without specific competence („interesting to get to know something new"), lack of understanding in view of the – for laymen – „provocative" side of the exhibits („when the wish to shock is in the foreground"), the hermetic language of art („very difficult to analyze", „should not be considered as art") and finally the market character („Bratwurst and Raclette, and far too expensive into the bargain") – here the relationship between specific incompetence and social background is highly differentiated.

I love it! (software engineer, Miami, 51 years old)

Fantastic, wide-ranging (bookseller, Zurich, 34 years old)

Unique (assistant manager, Geneva, 47 years old)

Sensational! (lawyer, Zurich, 44 years old)

Fantastic: keep it happening (health advisor, Miami, 50 years old)

Exhilarating, beautiful, stimulating (insurance agent, Orlando, 56 years old)

Liked it (attorney, Basel, 47 years old)

Nice (doctor, Hamburg, 35 years old)

Agreeable thought-provoking impulse (student, Gent, 25 years old)

No surprises (student, Basel, 22 years old)

Very interesting (psychologist, Lübeck, 39 years old)

Interesting to get to know something new (information scientist, Bern, 44 years old)

Interesting, expensive (physicist, Jülich, 58 years old)

I feel the contemporary movement is very difficult to analyze. I don't understand the banana truck or the acquisitions of The Rubell Collection. I must be old school
(sales manager, Fort Lauderdale, 51 years old)

It is exciting to see what is presented here, and also sometimes annoying, when the wish to shock is in the foreground (therapist, Basel, 56 years old)

There were many items that should not be considered as art (radio moderator, Miami, 48 years old)

A brilliant fair with international flair, extremely well organized, exciting galleries and artists, but the gastronomy concept is completely wrong, Bratwurst and Raclette for an art public and far too expensive into the bargain (translator, Lucerne, 41 years old)

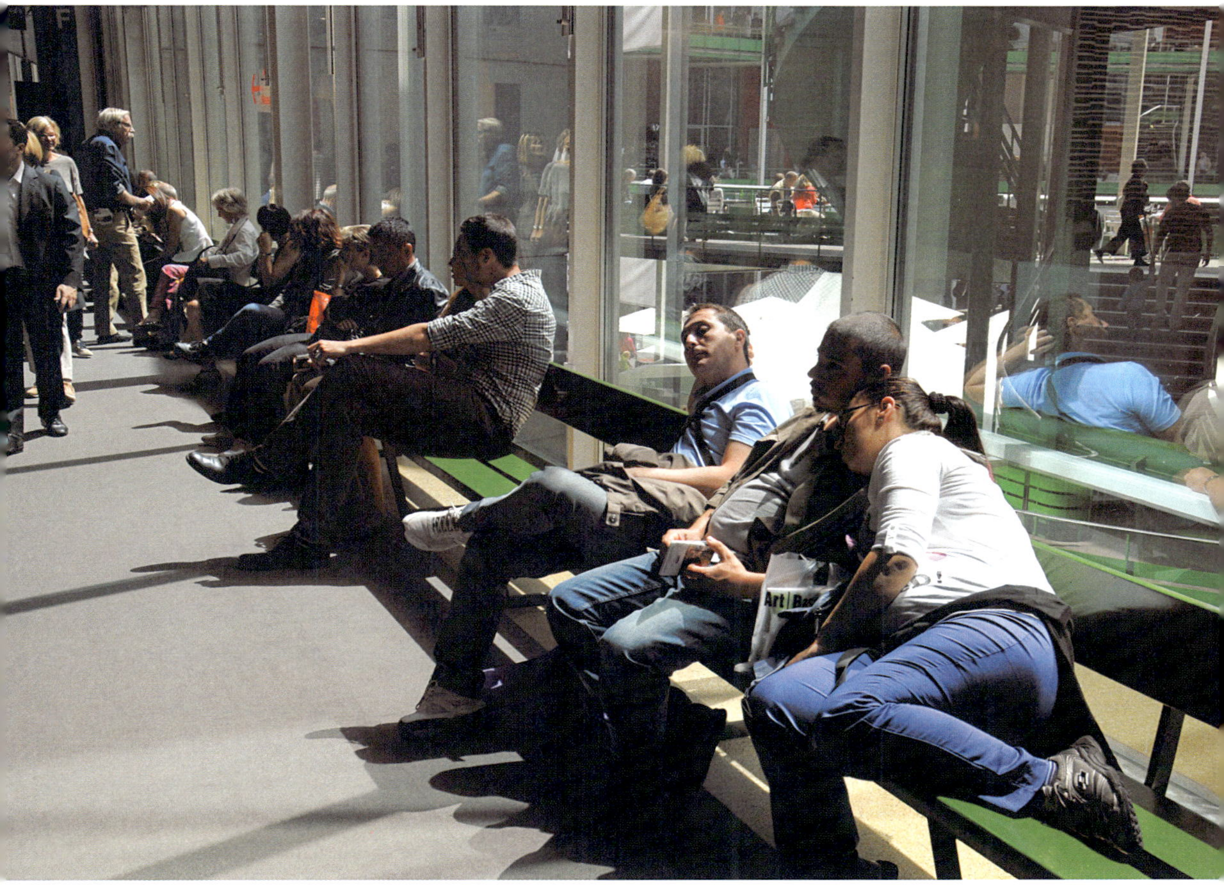

Art „is life“

A hundred confessions – one faith

If one asks the visitors to the fair what significance art has for them „personally“, a cascade of exclamations flows into the lines provided by the interview sheet. They are hymnal to lyrical confessions of faith which consistently draw the comparison between art and life – one has the impression that art is everything and can achieve everything. The entries are rare which speak of beauty, beautiful things, „well-being“, relaxation, in the sense of „equipment“ for one's own existence. Sometimes the general importance for an understanding of culture and history is emphasized; there are intellectual testimonies which invoke art as a „manifestation of historical ideas“ or point to its pedagogical effects, its contribution to „culture“, to „being human“, to „consciousness or even to „political“ perception – even though it must be doubted, in spite of all the critical references of a part of contemporary art, that even this kind of art can be an „expression of true life“. Although they are thoroughly conventional as general *assertions,* the mass of the descriptions are extremely „personal“ in a way which permits no doubts about the degree to which the collective fetish can take possession of „individual“ emotional states of mind. But for this fetish to be fully effective a *suppression of the social preconditions for access* to this emotional state is first necessary for the equation: „art is life“.

A mirror into my soul
A refined product of the human intellect
A sublime internal resonance
A way of understanding life
Access to other levels of consciousness
Art can say something that I have trouble putting into words myself, a voice for the voiceless
Art filters what is seen and what is not seen, advances knowledge, is a lasting contribution in short life spans
Art is a necessary expression for a human's emotional and spiritual well being
Art is a spiritual being
Art is an intrinsic part of life, without it we would be nothing, it is one of the elements that makes us human
Art is expression, art makes life beautiful, intimate, serious, shocking and sad, art is everything
Art is life, life is art. It is a way of seeing, of enhancing one's senses to be receptive to the world
Art is life
Art is my soul food
Beauty
Beauty as a means of increasing awareness and sensitivity, becoming more awake and alive
Beauty, emotion
Breath of Life
Cannot live without it
Changes my point of view on the world
Creativity, personal expression, spontaneity, clarification of current events
Culture, inspiration
Deepest expression
Discovery and pleasure
Elevation of the spirit
Emotion and pleasure
Enhancement of life
Enjoyment, abstraction, thought provocation
Enriching, educational
Eternal life
Everything
Everything
Everything, life, history, culture
Everything. Without it the world is a very harsh place. Art reminds us of infinite potential in all things
Expression and communication
Expression of life and experience
Expression of the time
Expression, movements, love
Food for thought, occasional bursts of brilliance, and it is a living
For me art means inspiration, reflects the moments that we feel and shows many perspectives of other worlds

Freedom... the ultimate and pure expression of being human
Fulfillment
Great way of discovering your own feelings and noticing the change of your perception over time
Growth, understanding, inspiration
Improvement of my senses
In a way, it is a very big part of my livelihood – it gives me joy but also drives my professional pursuits
Inspiration
Inspiration, experience of new perspectives
It enriches, develops personality and helps to create our own sense of aesthetics
It gives me mental pleasure to have it around
It is a form of excitement, living with works is a great privilege
It is a way to eat, sleep and breathe
It is an expression of one's self and one's imagination
It is something I do for my own personal wellbeing and fulfilment
It is the physical (sometimes virtual) manifestation of ideas via a history of aesthetics
It makes more complete; it educates me and opens my mind. It makes me smile
It's a way of life
It's just a part of my life
It's my life
Joy
Joy
Joy, Satisfaction, Entertainment, Fun !!! The only place where non-sense is fully accepted and commercialised
Just about everything
Knowledge, tranquility, stimulus and relaxation
Life
Life
Life
Life
Life
Life
Life
Life, beauty, thought, spirituality
Life enhancer, life exploration beyond oneself, life would be bleak without art
Love
Makes life culturally significant
Makes life more joyful. Makes it better
Moments of poetry in everyday life
My dream. My goal. My escape.
Passion, Challenge, Beauty
Powerful, changes the world, beauty of image and colours, personal message to the world
Recreation and joy
Reflection on history and beyond
Reflection on the world, inspiration
Sense of culture and the times
Something I love, that I want to have
Something that opens my mind and heart
Stimulation / beauty
Stimulation and political energy
The energy of life
The expression of the real life
The life of spirit in generally
To enrich my life, to express what life is doing right now to us all
Very important, personally and generally an important part of human culture
Visual dialogue at a spiritual level
Way of life!
Way of life
Wellbeing, personality
What breath is to breathing, art is to my walk on the planet
Widening of horizons
Without art, we cease to be human

The association of art and money hits the „simple“ believers hardest, and first of all those who are themselves at home in „culture“. Here an enormous tension can be felt between the *confession of faith* and the *cult* which takes on the form of idolatry at the fair, including the sale of indulgences, which permits the financially well-situated laymen to make up for their religious deficiency by purchasing relics. The fact that there is virtually no room at the fair for the „intellectual“, „critical“, „provocative“, even „political“ dimension of the artistic standpoint is only the most extreme imposition of a general test to which the faith of those working „in the cultural field“ is subjected, oscillating between unconditional devotion to art itself and its all too worldly forms of presentation.

For the „genuine“ layman, finally, the impositions are of a rather different kind. Here the *assiduous interest* in art is mixed together with a feeling of personal *incompetence* in the confrontation with artistic positions which are not yet canonical and cannot be easily interpreted. But they are mollified by the presence of Picasso and Dubuffet, Warhol, Rothko and Richter „in the original“, and a *voyeuristic curiosity* often gains the upper hand, the event, the „atmosphere“ the *participation* become the decisive factors. The presence of „money“ is not the real problem here. It is, rather, the signs visible everywhere at the fair of *exclusion* from a world which one has become accustomed to seeing as „sacred“, whose „profanity“ is, however, more clearly recognizable here than elsewhere, and for whose blessing and favour one nonetheless continuously strives.

Self-aggrandizements

How strongly the artist functions as a magnetic *model* for personal self-understanding, including that of the lover of art, can easily be gathered from the surveys among the visitors to the fair. It is easy to understand that graphic artists regard themselves as artists, designers also see themselves in this way when they are asked about their professional function in relation to art, so too the architects and photographers. In the case of gallery owners a kind of second existence is possible anyway, as it is in the case of art teachers and possibly of curators. But the more or less clear divergence between the actual profession and the statement „artist“ that can be found again and again among the lay public reveals the entirely enamored and self-enamored *dilettantism* with which the amateurs window-dress their daily professions or their existence as pensioners. We find the „creative consultant“ from Portland, the media manager from Rio, but above all the administrative officer and the optician from Miami, the doctor from Santa Barbara, an insurance agent from Orlando, a doctor from Hamburg, the graduate chemist from Freiburg, the lawyer from Zurich and the therapist from Basel – they all see themselves as „artists“, wishing to be something that makes them „different“, „special“, *extraordinary.*

But in spite of all these differences, all these temptations to which the sacred is subjected by the profane, the „love of art“ remains practically untouched, inward, „personal“. That this feeling is so important for the individual and at the same time so conventional, even conventionalistic, because it imposes moral sanctions for every breach of the rules, can only seem surprising to the lover of art – the collectively shared belief permits only such answers. And the fantasies about the omnipotence of art, the self-empowerment the lover of art believes he can draw from it, the ennoblement of mundane existence by this love of art, of the „immaterial“, whose „selflessness“ dissolves into self contemplation – nowhere else is *social narcissism* so strongly pronounced than in the sphere of a canonical „high culture“.

It is no less understandable that even here in a sphere which has left and wishes to leave the dregs of social life behind it, which truly belongs in the world of *social privilege,* „class differences" nonetheless exist. The battle for the power of ennoblement, which results from the knowledge of art, the possession of art, the demonstration of culture, necessarily gives rise to such differences. But the fact that this conflict over „true" love, which one of the „world-wide most significant fairs" for art brings to the fore, the conflict over the „right" treatment of art, the conflict between the „sacred" and the „profane", that this should take place in a social environment in which the „profane" is far removed from determining the entirety of experience, enables us to feel the class distinction and the class character which also unites the public at this fair – the veneration of art not only has a special public, but is also and for this reason its *own* public.

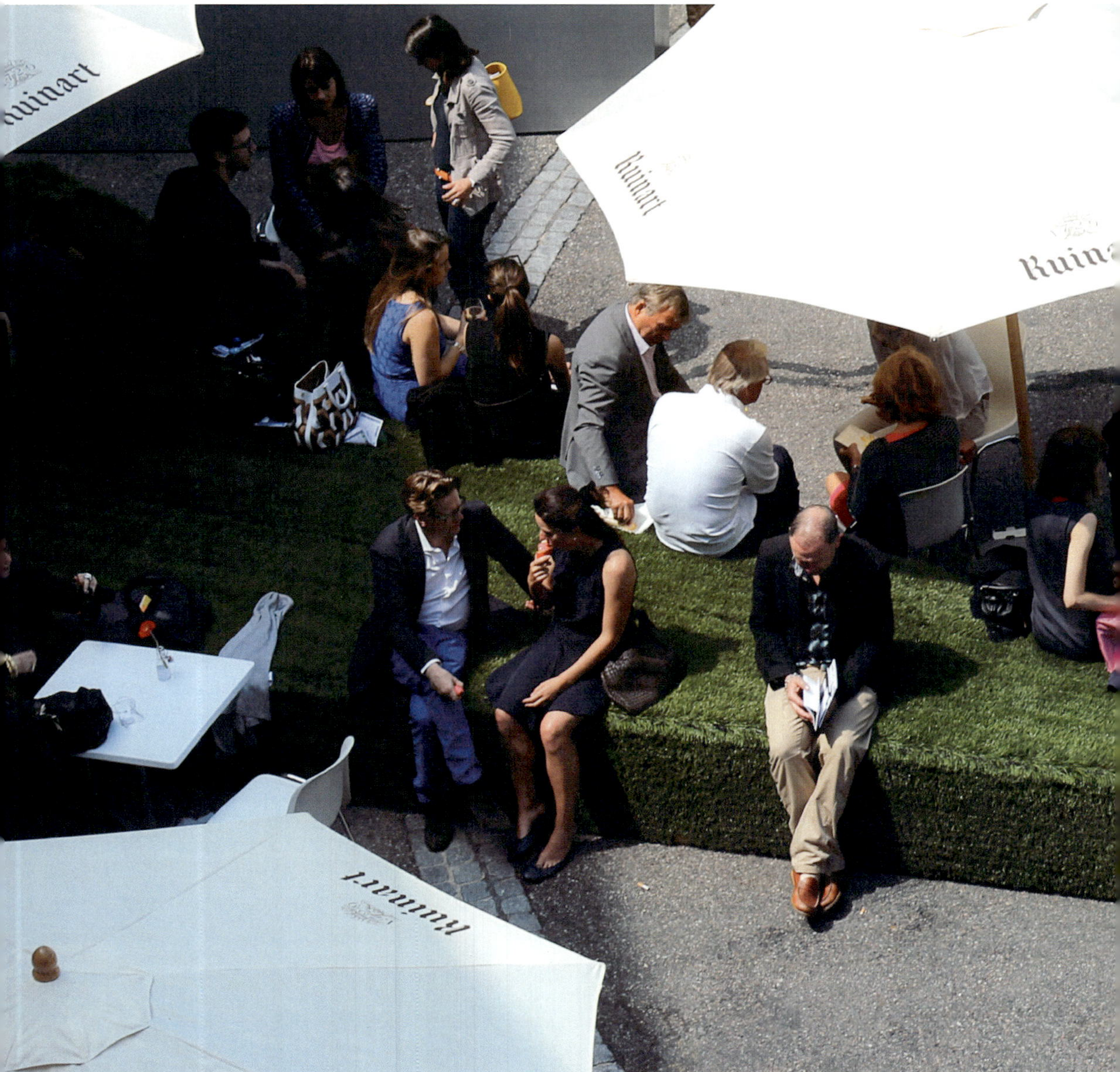
Ruinart
Ruinart
Ruinart

6 Times of Discontent

An art market without artists

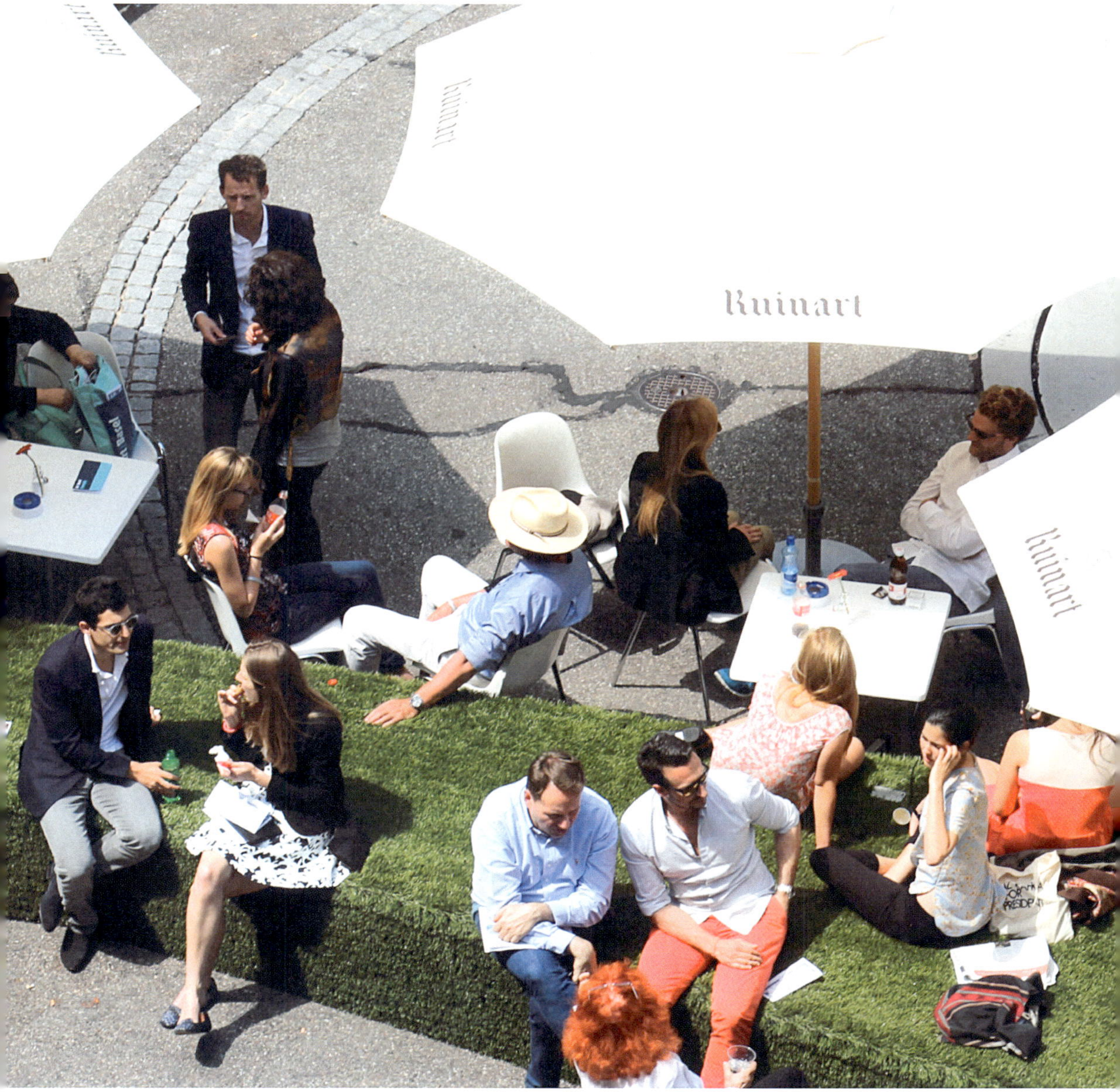

The relations the writers and artists maintain with the market, whose anonymous sanction may create unprecedented disparities among them, certainly helps to shape the ambivalent picture they have of the „public" at large, both fascinating and despised. They confuse the „bourgeois", who are enslaved by the vulgar concerns of commerce, with the „people", who are given over to the stupefying effect of productive activities.

PIERRE BOURDIEU, The Rules of Art

The „classical" artist, the protagonist of that „pure", that modern art which does not wish to satisfy the decorative needs of the rich and powerful, the ostentatious interior fittings of their existence, the external image of public institutions or the banal „beautification" of the bourgeois household, this artist has no „market", and, what is more, he is *not allowed* to have one. In the understanding of modern art deliberate production for the market is scandalous, an irreparable pandering to the preferences of a potential public which is felt to be incompetent, vulgar and profane. It destroys the „extraordinariness" of what modern art claims to be – even and just when its object subjects the „everyday" to an artistic perspective. The systematic destruction of the „ways of seeing", „ways of thinking", the provocation of „conventional" aesthetic, political and moral sensibility, which has been raised to the level of a program at least since the impressionist revolution of the 19th century, cannot „sell out" to this sensibility without losing the justification for its own existence.

This attitude of denial has been present ever since in the *social figure* of the artist; the culture of the „Bohème" seems irreconcilably opposed to the culture of the „bourgeois", and particularly in the fine arts it fully and repeatedly exploits this „extraordinary" advantage in legitimation. The dress code, the deliberate „otherness" of outward appearance, the „existentialist" or „couldn't care less" attitude, already emphasizes this refusal, but its core is the artistic work itself, not subject to the time clock or the requirement to produce specific quantities, without superior authorities, without the demands of everyday life by which „normal" people are reined in. The price the artist pays is scarcity of financial means, social „contempt" until the artistic success everyone expects occurs, a success which allows the economic returns to seem legitimate only because they were earned in a „purely" *symbolic* way.

This *structural aversion* makes it easier to understand why most artists specifically avoid art fairs, events for the sale of something that seems to have been wrested from the grasp of daily life and of working for „money" with so much difficulty. Here „dismay" is the „normal" reaction. Talking at the Art Basel Miami Beach 2013 Joseph Kosuth relates that he had met John Baldessari in a restaurant during the Art Basel a couple of years earlier. Neither of them had ever attended an art fair before. The experience evidently left them both speechless. But not quite: „So a journalist said, ‚Wow! Real artists! What do you think of the Basel Art Fair?' and I said, ‚Well, I feel like a whore at a pimps convention.' But John beat me, he said ‚It's like watching your parents fuck'" [1].

Temptations

The fair as a „market"

Art fairs are a horror especially for established artists. And although the Art Basel has issued a list with the names of forty well-known and less well-known artists who took part in the series of talks *Conversations* and *Salon* in 2014 in order to meet the objection that the fair is a more or less artist-free zone, it is totally evident that different rules apply here than in a constellation in which the art lover comes into the gallery and then accompanies the gallerist to the artist's atelier – so creating a socially intimate *ménage à trois*. At the fair this kind of intimacy is banished; buyer and seller encounter one another; they are the central figures. As the representative of one of the cultural institutions present at the Art Basel says of the most important actors at the fair: *„Well, I find that at the Art Basel itself the important actors are probably the committee which decides who can come, chooses the galleries that can come. And the galleries in turn then of course say which artist they will bring and what art. They are certainly one of the big actors. The others of course are naturally the big events which take place in and around the Art Basel. That is only natural. People fly in from all over the world... Dinner here, lunch here, dinner there, a lot of business goes on, the entire social networking. But for me the Art Basel is certainly a point where I can feel the pulse of the market. Is it all hype? Do they really buy things? Or do you only go to look? You can get an idea there about the state of the financial market in general."* Not a word about artists.

The fact that the actual leading actor in the art world, its hero, is largely notable by his absence, or that art is notably present in spite of his absence, is highly significant. It re-veals how far in the meantime the consumer of art works has moved into the center of the art world, thereby accentuating the structural aversion of the artist to the fairs. A German gallerist depicts how the artist he exhibited responded to the fair: *„Under no circumstances did the artist want to participate in the fair. That was a direct imperative – no, not to the fair. It was too commercial for them. And what we held earlier the artists have continued to hold, that they don't want to be part of a commercial scene, and definitely not of the Art. It's changed for the better nowadays. The one or the other even comes, and shows up at the fair, and a dinner is arranged for him and everything that goes with it. But I know for example of [a well known German artist] whose works I was exhibiting at the time, and then he said, but if you bring my works to the Art Basel I won't go along with that. And some of the others were just like him. It was all still very strict."*

So even if the artists in the meantime also have to make concessions to this kind of marketing, the fundamental reservations about a practice which reveals clear signs of precisely this kind of marketing remains. A younger artist on the development of the fair: *„I found it appalling the last time I was at the Art Basel. First of all how the art there was not presented in a museal space. You can really see what goes on there. Then all the different booths, they show the best one from the gallery and make a pitch for him. He's hung up there large and wide. And all the trappings. That put me off quite a bit. All that really matters there is the money. I can't compare. I don't know what it was like twenty years ago. But according to what you hear it was a bit quieter and a bit easier to overview and now it's become so blatant with all the sales pitching, and I don't know how the gallerists go about it, but everything will have changed over the years."* It is the *commodity* character of art which is manifested here and so destroys the aura which arises precisely from the tendential suspension of its commodity form: *„Art as a commodity. What matters to them is not who is really interested in the work and he then gets it, but who offers* *the most. For me it was simple. I saw the people who were walking around, the customers and the buyers, and I found the clientele pretty off-putting. It's all a question of showing yourself and being seen. That's what it's all about. It's so unbelievably superficial. That really irritated me. What goes on between them in the end, how they talk with one another, I don't know, I haven't been able to find it out yet. You probably only find it out when you're really a part of it all. I can only imagine it. It all seemed so incredibly superficial."* That this „superficiality" is not only identified with the evident practice of *market exchange* but also with the *social quality of the customers,* with a habitus more or less diametrically opposed to one's own, which reveals all the manifestations of worldliness, is also a part of the complex of aversions which the phenomenon of the art fair triggers off among the artists.

But this aversion is mixed together with a disillusioned cynicism among the established actors: *„Yes, I've been to the Art. And I was amused about all the things that were sold as art there. Well that is, for me that is already, yes, that's commerce, that's business. But I find it very interesting when the people bustle about there and claim to be experts and I find... There are good things as well, really good things, apart from that, that's there as well. But it is simply a market, business and nothing else. That's important for some, for the galleries that they are there, isn't it? They make their living from the others. Well it is simply, it is purely a market. Somehow or other everything in the world is turned into money. There's nothing left that isn't turned into money. That's the way it is. And art is a wonderful way, because you can hide so much behind it. No problem. As soon as you are in as an artist, who has a patron or a collector who buys regularly, or a gallerist who sees that you can have exhibitions, who sees that something gets into the newspaper... For me these are mediating activities you can no longer control, that means there are other people who buy you. We sell ourselves. And in this way we can sell ourselves quite precisely. Noone can sell us better than we ourselves. The interest is getting stronger and stronger because here one wants exclusiveness. That must be the case with the artist. If an artist only reproduces because he knows that this brings him success... After all there are many gallerists who say on the quiet, look, it's best if we work along these lines, because the pictures then sell like hot cakes. So it's a market like any other. The art market is like any other. And the Art Basel is of course the best example of the way art and commerce have always gone hand in hand; they are two sides of the same coin."* And a successful Swiss artist: *„It's always a question of money. Really! Greed, money, it's all business. To put it brutally, you could just as well sell cars. You could also be in a car showroom, it would give you exactly the same feeling. It really is like that. It's got nothing to do with art. You don't speak with other artists about art at such a big commercial fair. No, the talk is only about money. But that doesn't shock me. I don't have any problems with that. I have the feeling that the people could have problems with it. If they want to go into the depths, that has nothing to do with it, it really doesn't. That is brutal business. All that matters is the dough"* – the „car showroom" here focuses a moral indignation which can nonetheless stand the „shock".

But it not just the obviousness of the marketing with its negotiations and bargaining, with the „greed" as the ignoble side of what was not too long ago such a distinguished art scene, which is so painfully embarrassing for the artist and overtaxes him. There is also the show, lifestyle, bling bling and media hype. *„It's unbelievable. There are mechanisms I don't like. Nowadays people possess art the way other people have beautiful women or beautiful clothes and so on. It becomes a part of a lifestyle and a matter of prestige. Somehow I find it disgusting."* A young artist sees it in a more relaxed way. Her „disgust"

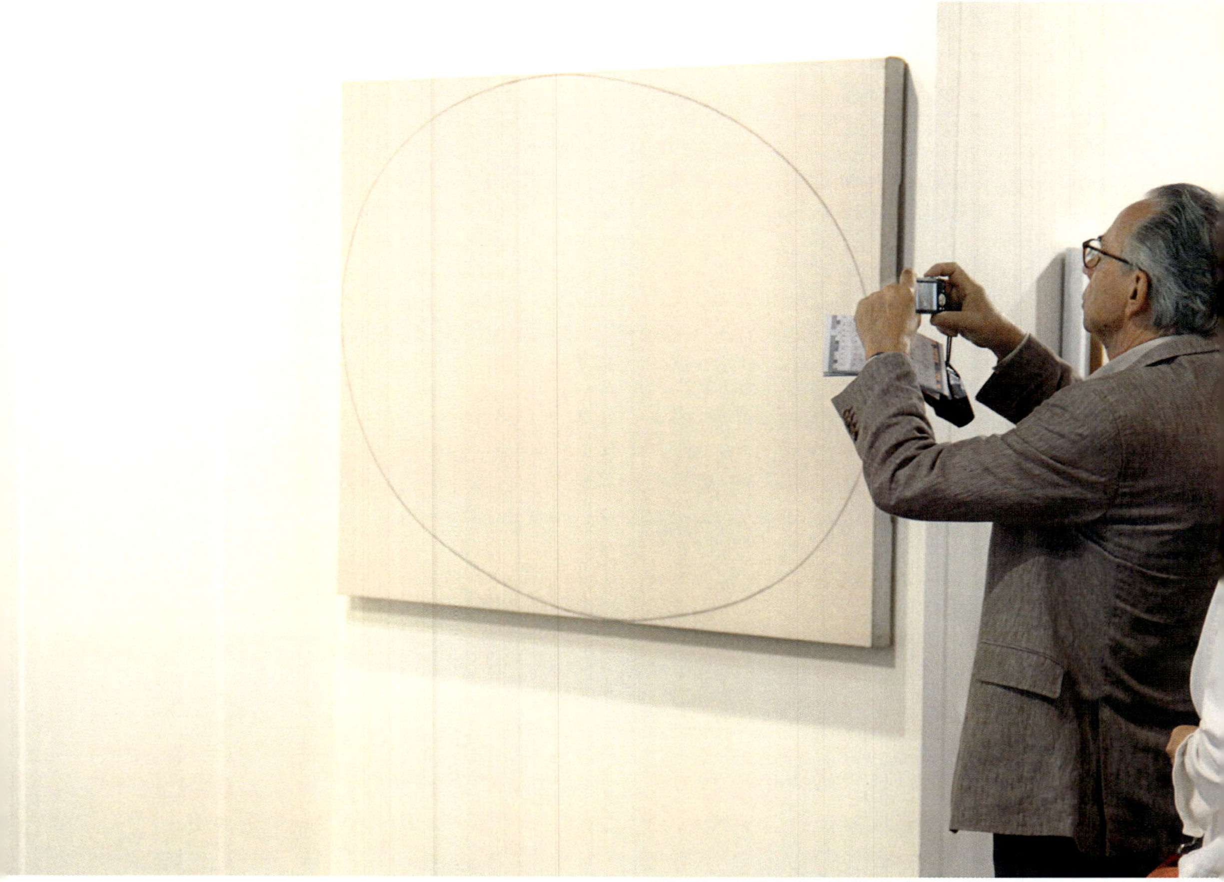

is reasonably limited and the *curiosity* of the event evokes an ironic distancing in her, although the market character remains the offending object: *„Yes, I find it amusing. And all the more so because I really enjoy observing the visitors. Because it isn't the classical visitor to a museum who shows up there. It's simply the, well, primarily the rich. Then the famous people and then another two, three... no, there are now... there are in the meantime so many subgroups at the Art. The Liste, then, the small things are more to my taste. Where, yes, where the money aspect is not so noticeable. If you feel it too strongly, just these garish things, well I prefer... I don't know. I don't know whether that's what it all should be about. But it has a very high entertainment character. There's a great deal of consumption and entertainment. And so I always have to laugh. In the meantime you buy things like trainers in a department store. Credit card or you get a bill. Well that's really, that isn't so very different. I think you also have to sign a contract. So it's not so different from buying trainers."*

At the same time this attitude reveals ambivalences in as far as the constituent economic preconditions for the artist's own „work" is shown in an embarrassing light at the fair and can never be completely denied. In all the talks with artists a skeptical to explicitly critical attitude towards the „commercialization" of art and the share of the institution „art fair" in this dynamics is expressed. One regrets the mass consumption organized for the fairs, the way of handling „cultural goods", the fast pace and the superficiality of the proceedings which contradicts one's own expectations and requirements for an „appropriate" use of art. One expresses a dislike of the ostentatious exhibition of art as a commodity and admits to an affective, almost physical aversion to the „overall package". But, on the other hand, in regard to one's own ethical and aesthetical reservations one invokes mitigating circumstances, claiming that from a pragmatic standpoint, the goings-on have become inevitable, that in spite of all the reservations one wishes to participate in order to free one's own art from the yoke of a purity requirement for art which is hostile to economic interests and so to earn the means needed to win time for the continuance of one's artistic work. A dual standard in answering the question of one's opinion on art fairs is reflected here. The formula runs: „I'm against it in principle but from a pragmatic point of view it would be advantageous."

This systematic dichotomy between the ethos of the artist and the economic constraints, the idealist claim to practice *l'art pour l'art* and the precariousness of the artist's life seems to be constitutive of the self-understanding of the artists interviewed – contradictions which can also be found among the consumers, the collectors, complaints about the vulgarity of an increasingly commercialized art scene, the dominance of the monetary, the concealment of the personal, active participation in these marketing events. It is an ambivalence resulting from the character of that „economy denied" from which the entire magic of modern art draws its strength [2].

And it is this denial of the economy which becomes a temptation here at the fair. The so clearly evident aversion of the artists towards the fair applies to its *commercial character* and it also applies to the *social environment,* which attracts all the „anti-bourgeois" reflexes inscribed in the history of modern art , because it is not so massively present in this physical form anywhere else. Whereas at other, more discreet places in the art world, at the White Cube of the galleries, the economic aspect of what is going on is skillfully disguised by the separation of front stage and back stage, and for that reason seems to be just about acceptable, it is present here in a „penetrating" and repellant form. Whereas the galleries, enact a show of sacred contemplation, organized tranquility, intimacy of the appearances, of „dialogue" with the works on exhibition, and of personal communication with the gallerist, and so protect the requirements of purity of the rules of art and contribute to the maintenance of the illusion of the pure love of art as a passion, the art fair as a whole brings the moment of disenchantment in view of the exorbitance it demonstrates with its 300 gallerists and the works of 4,000 artists. Here the market character of the art scene is so blatantly evident that the otherwise so efficient mechanisms of collective repression are rendered inoperative.

„I'd be delighted"

An artist at the Art Basel

What is the situation with the Art Basel?

Well I have to do with an incredible number of people and also with gallerists. The Art Basel is quasi... it's God. It is right, right at the top. Everyone, even if he doesn't admit it, actually wants to go there. It's always the goal. I've already told you about the one who changed the fair especially because he thought he would then have better chances to get on to the Armory Show, but that is roughly in this league... They try everything to get to the Art Basel somehow. The Art Basel has, for example they send a fax to umpteen gallerists, and that's quite amusing. I then get telephone calls from the gallerist in Vienna telling me, look, I've received a fax, I can try to register, but please don't tell anybody. Two days later I get a telephone call from my gallerist in Zurich, hey, don't tell anyone, I've received a fax... You don't have to apply yourself, they say who can apply. And they send out a couple of hundred faxes or even a thousand. I have never yet met anyone from the league of my gallerists who then actually got in. You don't get in so easily. That's a different dynamics for those who are in the game.

Which?

Well, they choose. And they choose those who on the one hand coherently... clearly and logically those who have the means, because these booths are even more expensive, even when you don't sell anything three or four times at a fair, which can also happen there if you don't happen to have blue chips to do business with at the moment. Of course they want people who don't already say second time round, sorry, I can't afford it anymore and back out. That's one reason. And the other is that they fit in well, that they don't... You must simply be at this level in the contemporary field... The people gradually come to notice it... Last time, for example, Brad Pitt came and the press asked him how many jets he had at Basel air-port... They only write that kind of rubbish because the content in the contemporary field in this Art Basel just isn't really good. There's a lot more freshness at the satellite fairs. The press probably comes because of the advertising they can print, because of the VIP tickets, because of something or other. They are only into this Art Basel shit...

And that's not only true of the Art Basel?

No, no. All the big ones... that's logical, all the big fairs protect themselves like that. It's simply a closed shop. What matters are the blue chips, the investments. In the contemporary field its only average, already well-known names, promoted names, but not really super fresh.

But if a gallery where you exhibit or which exhibits your work did get invited?

I'd be delighted as well. Obviously. It's only logical. Then I could increase my price by 20,000. You understand? All that matters is the dough. Because everything is focused on that, well, it is the most important fair and many people who have money go to the Art Basel to buy, and that's why the Art Basel keeps an eye on the satellite fairs, which they'd like to exterminate... What did you ask me? I've lost the thread.

If your gallery did get invited?

Exactly. As I said, I'd also be pleased. And the gallerist would be pleased. That's also the reason why nobody really pipes up.

Would your judgment of the Art Basel then be less negative?

It would be just the same. Whether you now work with the mafia or only look at it from the outside, well I personally... when you're in the mafia you earn more money. And I wouldn't have any problems with that. Obviously. But the chances are relatively slight anyway, because then one of the gallerists who exhibits at the fair would have to want me...

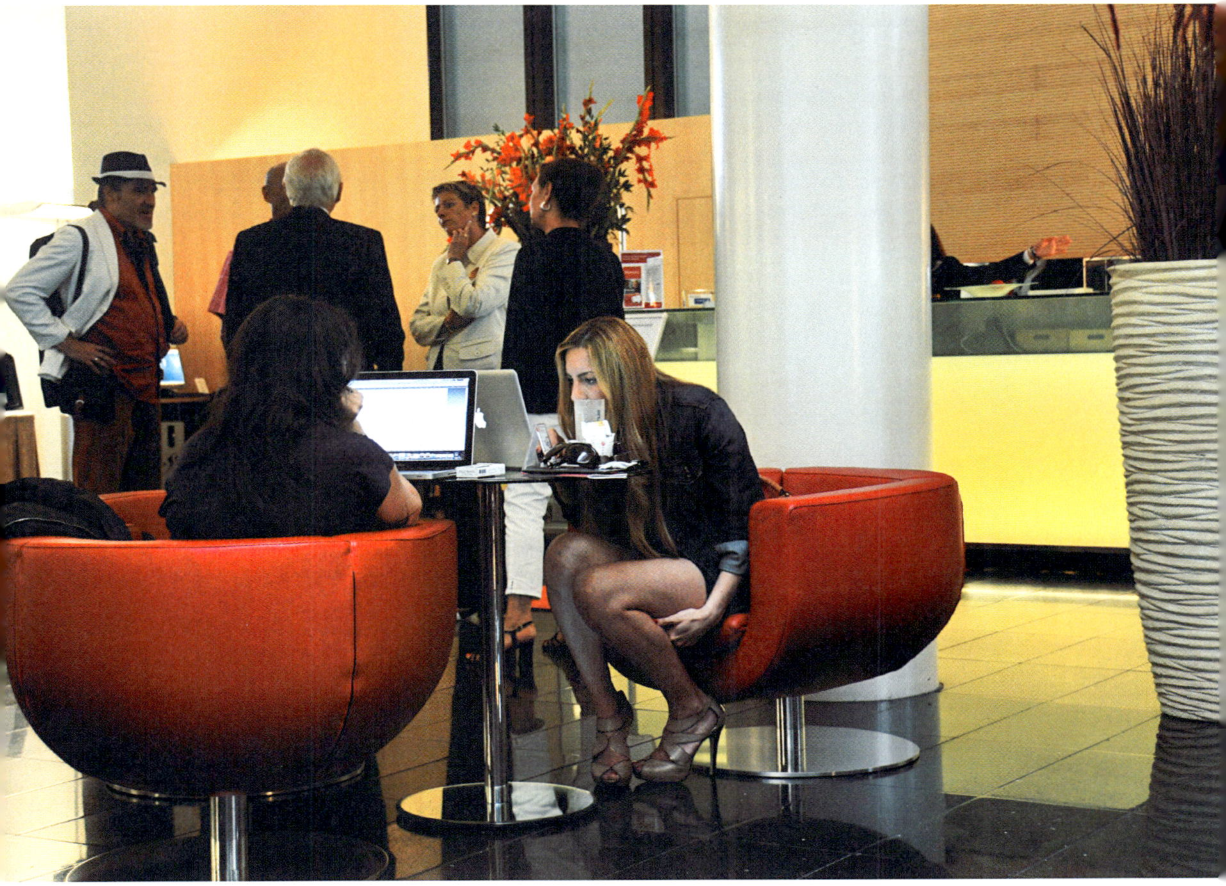

Promises

The fair as a „hub" and an „inspiration"

In spite of all the temptations for artistic self-understanding the Art Basel is also a promise. The criticism of the overstimulation and the market character is here accompanied by the thought that one owes a good part of one's own if only modest success to this „hub" of the art market: *„Actually, I find fairs disgusting when I walk around them, it's really dreadful for a person who thinks aesthetically, it's a total overstimulation. So I walk around a fair and feel pretty bad afterwards. I mostly only discover one or two works which I find exciting, perhaps because I'm so quickly overstimulated that I don't have any capacity for the rest. But on the other hand because so much rubbish is hanging there. Well I actually always go to the Art Basel and the Art Cologne and it doesn't matter which of them it is, I have the feeling every time of being so exhausted, it exhausts me more than any profit I get out of it. On the other hand, and here I have to speak from a different perspective, I know what fairs have brought me for my work, how many people have become interested in my work, how many opportunities to exhibit I had, abroad as well. An art society in Vienna saw my work at one of them and said, great, we'd like to do something with her. Those were situations where I in turn profited from the fair. Although I don't like fairs as someone who consumes art, goes into museums or to exhibitions. As a visitor I find a fair fully overloaded and exhausting, I don't like it at all. But on the other hand I know how much the fairs have changed for me and brought me profit. Profit in the sense of new opportunities for exhibitions or contacts with art societies."*

For this reason attendance at the Art Basel is not only like the stations of the cross for the established artists, who are unsparingly confronted there with the economic side of art. It is the same for those pretenders to the throne who feel excluded from this fair in its function as an instance of consecration for legitimate art which has been co-opted into the market, and are confronted with a mirror reflecting their lack of marketability. *„It's good to be there, it's good to work together with galleries which attend fairs and then sell things. And then there are fairs with a reputation and other fairs and there are, well, also fairs with a different clientele. I'm now working together with a gallery and I'm a bit dissatisfied. And I feel that it's very problematic. And notice that I have capacity and would like to work together with another gallery."*

And nonetheless, in spite of its fundamentally „repellant" nature, the Art Basel remains a place of yearning. *„My gallery never takes young artists with it to the Art Basel, that's also quite interesting. They always only take the established program, Gerhard Richter, Sigmar Polke, Blinky Palermo, and that's it. I feel I am a little bit underrepresented; I tend to say that after all I can't expect it, I'm only at the beginning and still so young, I can't make any demands now. But others also tell me I should do so."* But the yearning is very „pragmatic". Another artist: *„I believe that to be at a fair is the Alpha and Omega for a young artist. If a gallery would approach me which doesn't attend fairs, it would have no chance with me. The art market is evident there. You see that art is offered and sold there; the myth of art in a little cellar is demystified. The myth has arrived in the real world. You can quite easily see what counts; it's making money that counts. When my professor was studying the profession of the artist didn't even exist, and now, because of all the periodicals where you can read that an artist has sold a picture for 600,000 euros, all the young people have the idea of becoming an artist in order to get rich. It's absolutely idiotic, but it shows that the industry exists in the meantime and one ought to see it pragmatically.*

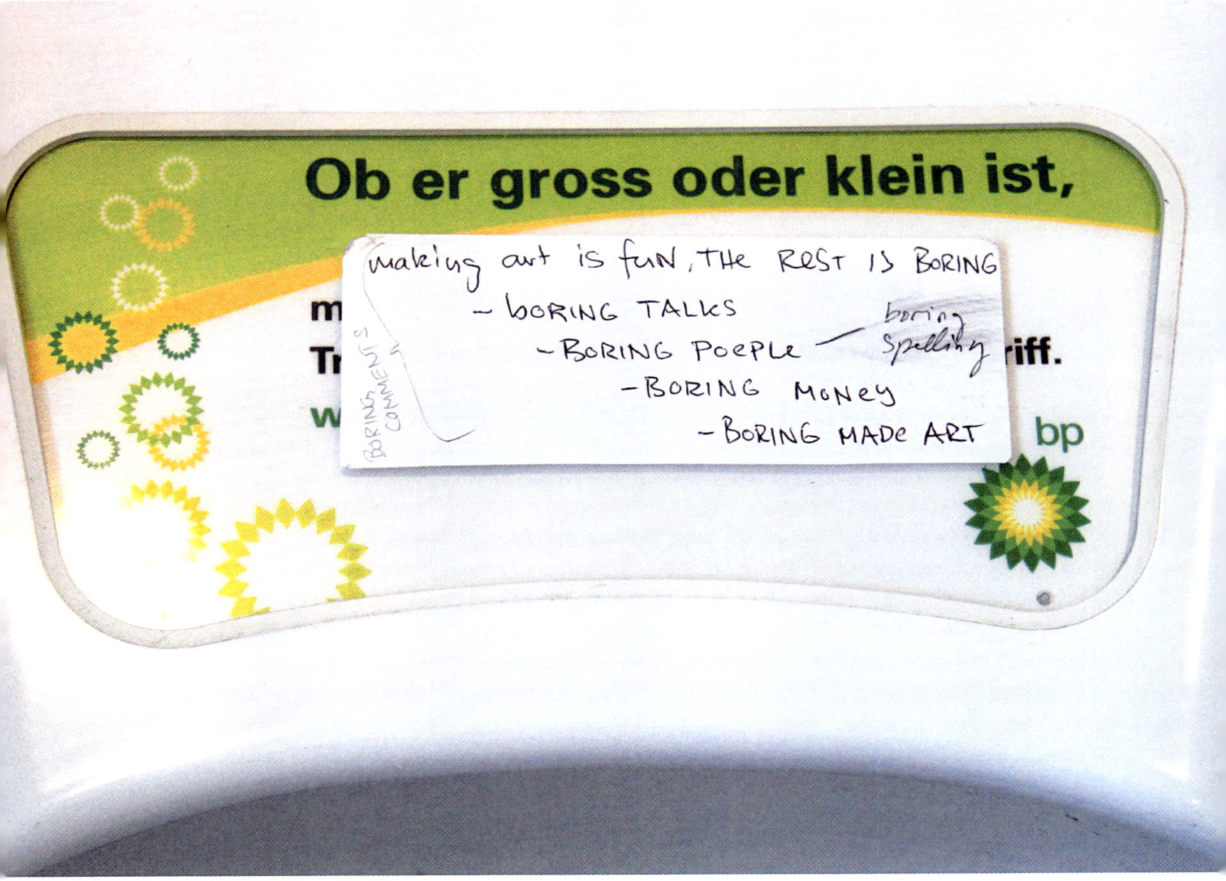
Ob er gross oder klein ist,
making art is fun, THE REST IS BORING
– BORING TALKS
– BORING POEPLE
boring spelling
– BORING MONEY
– BORING MADE ART
BORING COMMENTS
bp

I want to use it and get a foot in the door, because I want to live from art. That's my dream, plan, wish, and someday it will work out."

And the Art Basel is also „inspiration". Not necessarily the fair itself, but the various „satellite" fairs and exhibitions during the Art Basel: *„I don't know how often I really have new ideas when I go to the Art. Sometimes it's the little side exhibitions in the small art houses that stimulate me more. More than when I always see the same things, the repetitive ones that have proved their worth. And also the pictures as well, which one, well, the recognition value, that's also quite important if you want to have a place in the market. That you have a language that can be quickly recognized."* A second young artist from Basel: *„It's certainly one week in the year when I know that I'm not going to go abroad. I stay in Basel, of course. And the big thing is, it's not just the Art Basel; in this week so many other things happen. In the meantime there are about seven parallel fairs. The entire off-scene takes part. Then all of them really make their best exhibition. Then you kind of have this parcours, art films are shown in the cinema, and you go every evening to the Kunsthalle because everyone is there. And this year was really, well, I was on the go the whole week, actively, sometimes helped with projects, in the free scene, and was only once really at the Art. I finally did all this parallel stuff that I actually find much more exciting. There's a public there, a different public than otherwise. It's really, Basel is somehow the center of the art world for a week and I find it almost more exciting on the side stages than at the main event."*

In spite of all the complaints references are made again and again to the „collateral gains" one believes can be made during a visit to the Art Basel. The fair is simply seen as a mirror of the state of the art, which enables one to get an overview in a short period of time and to take impulses home. A Swiss artist: *„I personally, I definitely need it, although, or because I see it as reflection, as discussion; it's not necessarily easy, but for me it's further education. I see what's on the market, what others are doing, what is praised, what is sold, whether it's good or bad remains to be seen; both are always there. But for me it's quite clearly further education, for me myself, and I like it and I need it for myself in order to reflect. After all I also make art and so my art has something to do with all that."* And a colleague who has specialized in installations and looks for impulses at the Art Unlimited: *„Well, that's why I'm someone who works differently than someone who paints, for example, and doesn't need it. I don't believe it's a precondition for making art that you go to the Art Basel. And I also don't believe that if you go regularly to the Art Basel or compare yourself that you then make better art, that's got nothing to do with it. I myself need to visit exhibitions, quite strongly, so that I know what's there, what's up to date. What are other artists concerned with."* This standpoint is also shared by an established artist: *„Well for me it's simple, I myself go because I, really, because I find it interesting to know what these galleries are buying now or why; or it interests me, well, I'm already, how should I put it, I try to see how they think, the gallerists, or, yes, what's going through their minds or how do they look at things."*

In spite of all the skepticism and all the aversion there is obviously no way of sidestepping this „event", not for the „small players" who seek for inspiration there and above all find their own biographical fate thematized at the fair: *„In art what counts is success, isn't it? So that's very important. And on the other side stands the creative genius, the autist in his attic or wherever, who does his thing. But the moment success is involved a continuous scanning is going on, wherever you look. It can be in a conversation in an atelier, it can be at a vernissage, it can be in the train on the way back from Basel. It doesn't matter* *where."* And the importance of the art fairs for this self-assurance, the existence of a market that positivizes artistic success and creates *comparability,* sets new standards, especially among the young artists. *„Particularly in the most recent art it is also important that the artist functions at fairs. Sometimes that happens really quickly and certain booths are sold out within minutes. Then it's no longer possible a question of looking around at your leisure, of the artist being sold perhaps after conversations with the gallerist. What counts is that it really functions, that it goes off with a bang at the very first tick."*

The temptation to rationalize one's own career is all the greater the more clearly the artists are aware of the rationalities of this market: *„I think it's an interesting development, and of course it's an open question whether that's good for the individual galleries. And for the small galleries which can't or can scarcely afford to take part in fairs. On the one hand because the stand fees are so expensive and on the other because gallerists sit in the selection committees for art fairs who can then represent their own interests and arrange everything according to their own ideas, or can then deliberately exclude other galleries they regard as competition."* Certain „positions" can then fall through the cracks. *„If a gallery is interested in excluding another gallery or in making business and life more difficult for it then that's naturally a disadvantage for the artist who is represented by the gallery. And for other artists of other galleries it's an advantage. Then of course it all depends less on the quality and more on who is better able to assert his interests."*

And in spite of the unbroken belief in the quality of a position, the fair clearly reveals how much other factors play a part: *„Of course it's always difficult to put in a nutshell what makes a good work or a good artist. Perhaps that depends a little bit on how a work makes sense in its respective time. Also in regard to older and previous things and that is somehow extended, so that's perhaps another factor which makes for quality. And that then doesn't play any part at all at such an event. The artist is then in principle only a name that is offered there. So the individual work doesn't matter so much. Somehow what counts is the one who manages to work himself into as good a position as possible so that he himself profits from it and shows more presence at the moment when he can sell."*

The universal and the factual

The modern art fair as a final test

The *social role* of the artist and the self-understanding that goes with it are put to a substantial test at the Art Basel, this „Olympics of the Art World". The presentation by the media, the concentrated economic power of the market, *a visible stage* for the public negotiation of what art is and should mean, who can be a part of it under what conditions, who can claim to *represent* it: all of this goes against the grain of this self-understanding, the core of artistic self-respect – and of the repeatedly thematized *obscurity* of the „manifestation" of extraordinary significance. At this place the myths of the art field are massively shaken, the sublime notions of its independence, especially in relation to economic constraints, the mass culture of the „commodity world" and the heroic singularity of artistic existence. How can the illusion of a totally self-determined universe, which is so essential for the historical existence of the art field and the ethos of its actors, survive in a place in which the logic of the market and the power of the economic sphere so evidently dictate the rules of the game?

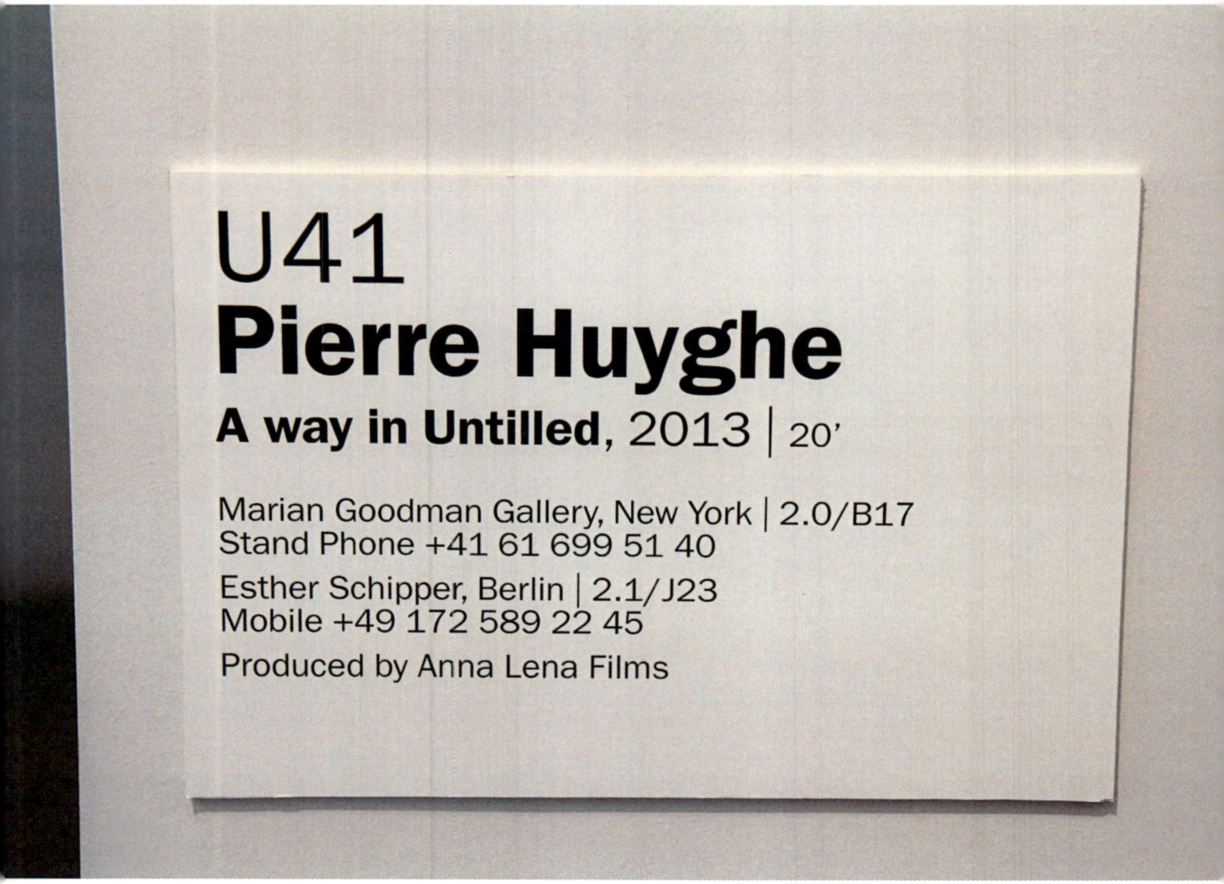
U41
Pierre Huyghe
A way in Untilled, 2013 | 20'
Marian Goodman Gallery, New York | 2.0/B17
Stand Phone +41 61 699 51 40
Esther Schipper, Berlin | 2.1/J23
Mobile +49 172 589 22 45
Produced by Anna Lena Films

The ambivalent feelings of the artist towards the Art Basel as the ultimate location of a market for art, a place where the relationship between art and world, art and money, manifests itself in such a concentrated fashion, with all its palpable and so plastic facets, a place which clearly presents this relationship itself as a kind of *social plastic,* these feelings reveal a fundamental ambivalence of the *social figure* of the modern „artist", his inner conflict between aversion and pretension, the enormous demands which he as the *other* of bourgeois society makes on himself and which are consequently made on him – and the constitutive *double standard* an economy develops in which failure for the time being in a „profane" world promises gains in another, although those gains can ultimately only be enjoyed in the profane world.

It is easy to understand why this double standard at an art fair of such a size subjects artists to a hitherto scarcely conceivable test. At the same time a *new quality* of this schizophrenia becomes clear, which is independent of status, of the *position* of the artists on their path to recognition, of the point they have reached on their „trajectory" in the art field. For the „established" artists whose works are „distributed" at the fair *absence* is a sign of „good taste" and involves an increased recourse to a symbolic credit which decisively conditions worldly success. And in the process it conceals all the biographical compromises which enabled that success. For the „debutants" who no less revere the ideology of the „quality", of the inherent value of art, the fair drives this schizophrenia to a new extreme. The undisguised *pragmatism* in dealing with the new function laws of art mediation, the provisional handing over of the universal to the factual, the *coexistence* of aversion and pretention, have all achieved new dimensions – the market becomes the standard for all those biographical compromises at the beginning of a „career" which had never been seen so openly before.

But the discomfiture remains. In an unprecedented way the modern art market renews the promise of worldly success *in flagranti,* quite concretely and visibly for everybody: it reveals the entire dishonest dimension of artistic „success". The mere fact that art can never be sufficient unto itself, that it demands and needs recognition that in the end must be *won,* so that social reputation can follow the „ideal" recognition, is very evident here. But it becomes even more clear, and, what is more, it does so in a way which ultimately denies the *collective* claim of modern art. The circumstance that here, before everybody's eyes, works of art are appropriated only in the rarest cases for public purposes but pass instead into private ownership in itself damages this universal claim. And an unvarnished look at the *social physiognomy* of the future owners destroys it totally. The market shows what is tacitly assumed but never ought to be shown if the belief is not to be shattered – the entirely worldly, the social preconditions for the success of art and the appropriation of its „immaterial" goods.

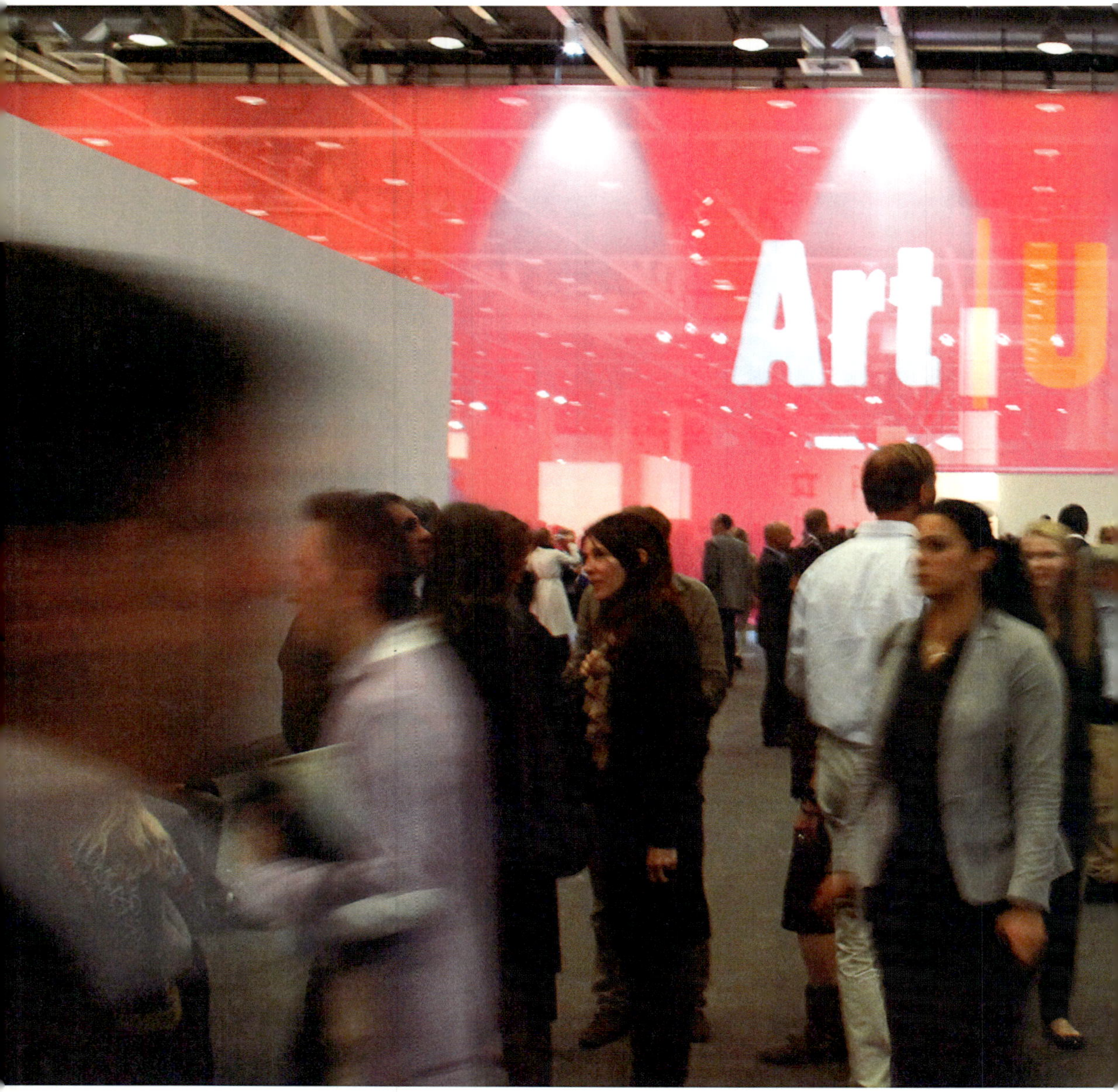
Art

7 Art in Motion

On the dynamics of an economy of symbolic goods

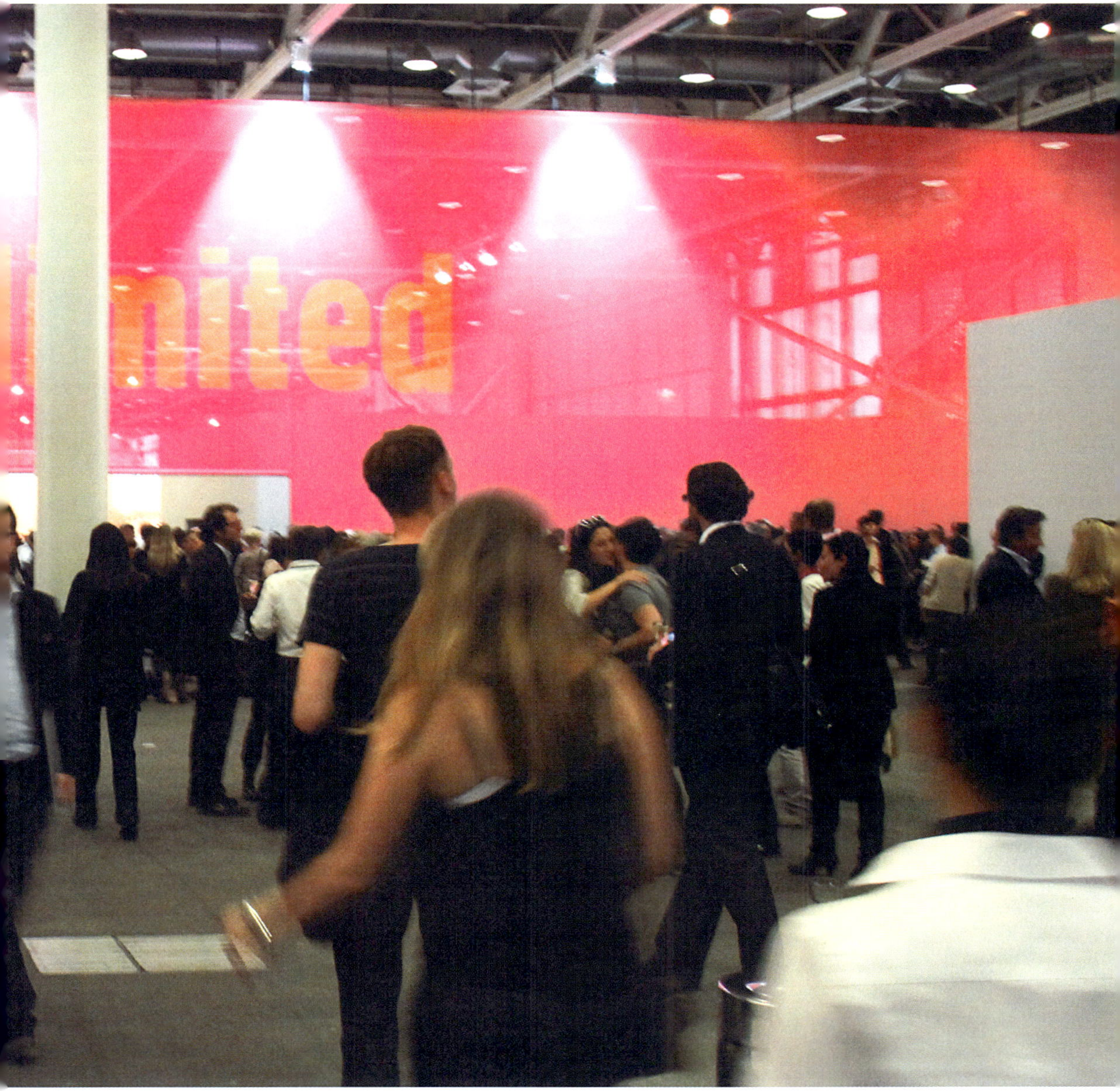

Each mill was tied, through the interplay of the exchange of services and the back-and-forth of relationships and alliances, to a stable clientele. With the decline of agriculture, use of traditional watermills decreased. People would buy milled flour rather than have their own grain milled, and motorized mills took their place, sweeping away as if by magic the whole system of conventions that governed the play of collective solidarity in the case of traditional milling.

PIERRE BOURDIEU, Algerian Sketches

What does the Art Basel tell us today about the art business today, about the presentday art market and possibly about the state of contemporary art? The fact that the mere conceptual linking of art and business, art and market can in itself be problematic is an indisputable specific feature of the modern art scene. When in the economic field turnover figures are published, return targets announced, „strategic" decisions explained, capital increases undertaken or promising mergers announced, no *moral* dissonances occur, unless the number of dismissed employees is large enough to attract attention in daily political life. It is different with modern art. Here these concepts give rise to normative tensions which cannot be excluded from the art world. And they describe a constitutive peculiarity of this world, the specific nature of an „economy of symbolic goods" in which everything which has the appearance of rationality, of „interest", of calculation, has no right to existence.

But when nowadays, in spite of this taboo, dealing with art attracts so much attention, not only among the buyers and sellers but also among the public who do not participate in this trade, it is indeed necessary to consider whether the underlying normative structure has fundamentally changed this market as a result of the sheer economic and medial power of „business" – or whether it did not. The phenomena we encounter are in many respects new: the openly carried out trade with the goods of high culture, the amazing prices involved in this trade, the tendency towards monopolization in the market, the accolades accorded to art fairs, galleries, artists – and buyers – in a cascade of mutual economic and symbolic self-assurance, the continuous and conscious *promotion* of art before the eyes of a public whose presence also seems to manifest itself in a rush of interest in the old institutions of the art scene, in the public museums.

How can these developments be pinned down? In this respect the art world is deeply split, as its „genetic code" only permits more or less shamefaced, defiant or cynical concessions to this new market. Anything else would contradict a logic which insists on a literally *exorbitant,* an „other-worldly" value of art, with which it wished to earn its paradoxical place in this world. Even an unadorned look at these changes cannot be entirely free of this perspective. But what it can see remains nonetheless remarkable. It is the disintegration of a *social configuration,* which guaranteed precisely that value whose ability to divest itself of its social connotations was its distinctive characteristic.

Art and Money

A symbolic economy under high tension

The problematic character of the relationship between „art" and „money", the consequence of an epochal emancipation of the fine arts from those direct relationships of exploitation and unmediated standards of evaluation which had characterized the European Middle Ages, the Renaissance and the Early Modern Age, has acquired a different dimension at the latest since the turn of the millennium. From this point on the modern constellation of a more or less radical antagonism between „pure" art and „commercial" art is subject to new negotiation. For it is now possible, under the impression of an historically unique boom in the art market and intensified institutional change, to observe amazing metamorphoses in the established field of art.

What is at issue, above all else, is the frequently noted penetration of „money" into the world of art, its „economization" and „financialization" [1]. And, since the 1980s, we can indeed observe a massive economic and geographical expansion of the art market, whose volume has increased threefold in the last ten years – this alone is a clear indication of the „extension of the market zone" [2]. A great amount of money is flowing into the market. Its rapid expansion corresponds to a swift increase in the circle of people with high incomes and capital. World-wide over thirty million millionaires have been counted; the population of the so-called „high net worth individuals" with an investable capital of more than a million US dollars has itself reached a two-digit million size. This group of buyers is the source of the increased demand, above all for contemporary art, and shares responsibility for the in part extraordinary increases in prices. And according to the assessments the number of private collectors has increased fourfold since the 1990s; more than half a million „mid to high level" collectors [3] devote their money to the acquisition of art.

But this is not the whole story. At the same time the „art scene" has grown rapidly in the last two decades. Apart from the biennials and the art fairs many new public and private institutions have been established which contribute to the popularization of contemporary art. The number of galleries and art dealers, museums, art exhibition halls and exhibitions has increased enormously, as have the awards and stipends for artists. A flood of young people leaves the art academies and the art schools every year [4]. An „era of artistic mass production" [5] involving the use of new media and procedures for the technical reproduction of pictures, and not least the extension of the current understanding of art – an increasing dissolution of the boundaries of the „aesthetic" since the triumph of pop art – seems to increasingly determine the contemporary art scene.

The unprecedented popularity which modern and contemporary art have experienced in the course of the expansion of the art market and the field of art in the last few decades has enabled the fine arts with their various forms of representation and discourse to take on a model function not only in the culture industry, which for a long time was the reserve of popular arts such as pop music. „Art", „design", „creativity", „projects" increasingly provide the model for the shaping of the concept of a profession, the reorganization of work relationships, and the creation of life-styles. As scarcely ever before „art" has arrived in the „real" world.

What makes art „priceless“?
The exchange of gifts and symbolic goods

In all societies there are categories of objects which are attributed a special value and are hence regarded and treated as priceless. Such „holy“, extraordinary objects, whose profane use is taboo, can take on a wide variety of forms: natural objects such as shells for the tribes of Melanesia, ceremonial stone axes in New Guinea or crown jewels in medieval Europe. They all possess the special property of lending symbolic power, a power which seems to rest upon their remoteness from the kingdom of „earthly things“.

In the modern period art is a significant example of this category of extraordinary sacred things which cannot be weighed in gold or any other earthly goods. What attributes do works of art share with the magical or religious objects in traditional societies, which allow us to make the distinction between „profane“ and „holy“? It is a shared feature of this category of exalted things that they are perceived as embodiments of extraordinary powers, that they are practically useless for the purposes of daily life, are outside the economic sphere, are instead the object of collective practices of appreciation and adoration and are kept in social spaces especially predestined for them [6]. Because of their special social status such „holy things“ are withdrawn from the sphere of „trade“, and it would be regarded as desecration if they were offered for sale like simple articles of daily use. As gifts they preserve the relationship to the person who makes a present of them; they are regarded as substitutes for this person. What constitutes the „spirit“ of an object is its material manifestation of the person of its creator or former owner, is a trace of its history – and a witness to a social bond which remains „priceless“ in its quality [7].

As unique goods in a world characterized by mass-produced commodities and anonymous market relationships between producers and consumers works of art fundamentally embody the described properties of „holy things“ of other historical social formations and in a sense present a place of retreat for these archaic forms of belief of a magical-religious origin. Art is fundamentally defined by its lack of everyday practical value and finds here the conditions of possibility for its aura and charismatic power. Strictly speaking it ought to remain remote from the profanity of the market place. But when this constitutive and essential special status is not respected in social practice a wide variety of strategies of disguise and euphemization are necessary. Like the medicine man, the sick he claims to heal and the bystanders in primitive societies, all the direct participants in the art trade, producers, sellers and buyers, have a mutual interest in maintaining this collective hypocrisy and in tacitly carrying out the breach of the taboo.

In dealing with singular and priceless goods in archaic societies anthropologists and ethnologists distinguish between agonistic and rivalizing practices on the one hand and consensual and integrative forms of behavior on the other. In analogy, in the case of trade with non-tradable objects of art we can point to the striking difference nowadays between two central institutions and social spaces for trade in the field of art: the auction house and the gallery. In an auction the socio-psychological element of public competition for symbolic goods with the help of material resources is evident. As with the archaic ritual of the potlatch the rivals ostentatiously sacrifice worldly goods in order to outdo their competitors in the struggle to acquire immaterial goods and to leave this „duel“ as the winner in terms of honor and reputation. In the case of „peaceful“ trade with such goods in the contemporary art market, however, the embedding of the commercial aspect in specific rituals and dispositives for the purposes of denial and suppression takes the form of a personal and selfless exchange of gifts and gifts in return between confidants, which seems to find an archetypical precursor, for example, in the social institution of the Kula, observed on the Trobriand Islands. In this ritualized form of the exchange of valuable goods the partners pay respect and honor to one another by the generous donation of personal values to their esteemed opposite numbers.

In social trade with non-tradable goods competition and rivalry, integration and trust, are two sides of a medal, and these two complementary aspects of symbolic goods are reflected in a great number of apparently incidental forms of social interaction and attitudes which can be observed at every turn during an art fair. But when certain actors subvert these collectively agreed forms of conduct by disregarding the tacitly assumed „rules of art“ they are severely called to order or ostracized as „spoilsports“. As one of the founding fathers of sociology, Emile Durkheim, has emphasized, we contemporaries accordingly have good reason not to search for the archaic in remote times and places, as we have it before our very eyes.

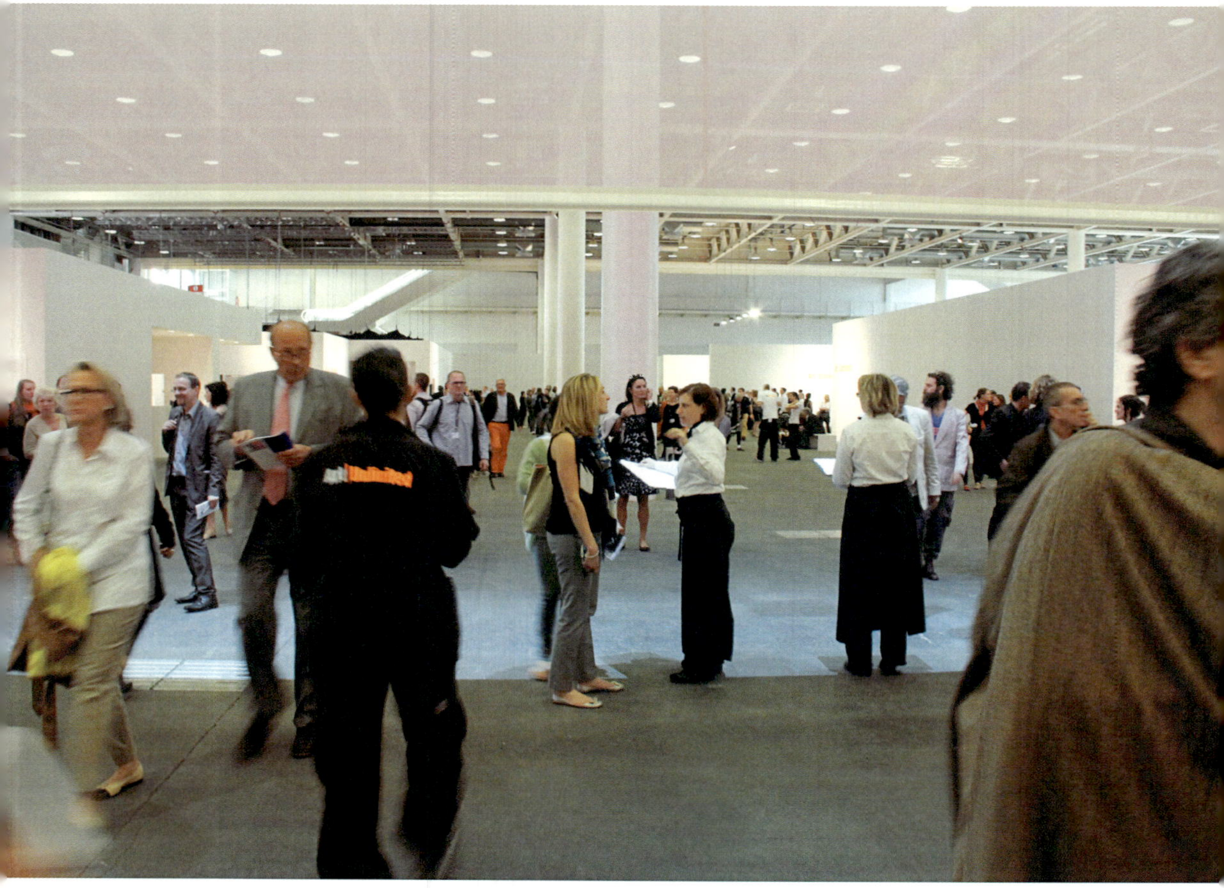

And even though these changes must not necessarily lead to transformations in the „logic" of the field of art the question of the continued validity of the old „rules of art" nonetheless arises. The penetration of alien logics of action from the economic world into the sphere of art, which was fundamentally determined by other rules for over a hundred years, does indeed mark a turning point.

Conditions of production, distribution and consumption are increasingly subjected to market forces: economic constraints, profitability, profit orientation, economic calculations, management strategies and controlling, brand messages, public relations or sponsoring have in the meantime extended far into the public cultural institutions. Even the organization of public exhibitions is increasingly oriented on economic parameters, the numbers of visitors, the donations of sponsors and current market trends. The definitional power of the art market and its actors seems to be omnipresent.

Even the classical prerogatives of art history and public museums in regard to canonization and the accumulation of value are being increasingly undermined. In particular the evaluation procedures and the reputation cascades within the art field have come under the influence of economic forces and reshape the traditional processes of value attribution, which were hitherto determined by art-historical and art-critical discourse and finally ratified by public art institutions such as museums and exhibition houses. Private institutions ranging from the huge exhibition halls of the mega-galleries to the numerous private museums and auction houses have become instances of „confirmation", accompanied by art-scientific and art-historical „evaluations" of actors from the „art world" and the increased interest of the mass media. Above all the private collectors have gained influence and importance in this process and they are a decisive factor in the increase in value of contemporary artists and their work. Through their own museums, exhibitions and loans of works to publicly financed museums the artists, works and groups of works they prefer and collect are publicly „consecrated" and their „importance", attractiveness and material value on the art market increased.

And while the dissolution of the borders between the art field and other spheres – mass culture, the culture industry, commodity aesthetics, advertising, fashion, lifestyle, the media – progresses to such an extent that the „iconoclasts" of yesterday now promote the icons of today, and Cindy Sherman ennobles the Louis Vuitton label with her name, the expansion of the art market, thirty years ago no more than a marginal niche for in-veterate art lovers and art experts, has pushed even old institutions such as museums, art history and art criticism to the periphery of the art world. The galleries-critics-system which was predominant since the nineteenth century and for a long time put its stamp on the institutional structure of the art field, has been transformed into a galleries-collectors-system, not least on account of the growing market power and resultant influence of the private collectors [8].

For its part the mass media have contributed to the popularization of the fine arts, but have also encouraged the aggressive marketing and „monetarization" of art by the use of the language of money in the feuilletons and the economics sections of the newspapers. As a result the impression has arisen among the broad public that art is no more than a flourishing business and no different from any other good investment. This can be illustrated by the endemic use in the media of the expression „blue chips" to describe high quality works of art. The expression is borrowed from the jargon of the stock exchange and, in contrast to the customary expression „masterpiece", it refers primarily to the material value of a work and less to its artistic value.

The notion of the incommensurability of artistic and economic values, which was regarded as fundamental fifty years ago, seems to have been abandoned, at least as far as the top section of art production is concerned. It is a foregone conclusion, at least for the „purists", that market success will also increase the aesthetic value of a work, although this standpoint is by no means undisputed. But we can, nevertheless, ascertain that the works of living artists are bought for the highest prices long before they have been judged by the „classical" instances of canonization. Today artists' „careers" are systematically built up like brands, and the prices achieved for their works and the development of prices itself have a resounding effect as indicators of artistic quality. They bring the works an enormous increase in value and importance, which could not be attributed to them without this extrinsic exchange value. In the meantime the majority of the artinterested public regards the market price as the criterion for artistic value [9].

The idea that „recognition" and „reputation" is nowadays less the result of artistic importance but is primarily determined by economic value within an „economy of attention", and hence largely excludes all critical discussion about artistic differences, is occasionally advocated even in the deepest recesses of the „art world" [10]. In view of this kind of discussion the notion of an art „remote from the market" seems to be a truly old-fashioned illusion. Nowhere can this „spirit" of money be so strongly perceived than at the auctions at Sotheby's and Christie's or at the Art Basel, the top events of the international art trade. These events, organized demonstrations of the role of the market, do not, so it seems, primarily serve art but the celebration of the monetary value of art, the power of money and the heating up of the art market itself. After every auction or art fair the organizers announce new sales records. Record prices, top sales and high turnovers are prominently announced, as if they were news of the highest priority. At the auctions staged by the two giants Sotheby's and Christie's new price records are in the meantime regularly greeted by the public with frenetic applause. But the ovations are scarcely a response to the works but to the staggering prices offered and paid for them.

In the exhibition halls in Basel the economic spirit is, in comparison, less blatantly present, although the mercantile character of the event cannot be denied. The art trade dominates the terrain in Basel, the discreet business dealings in the galleries yields place to the event, the presentation dominates, on the VIP days the visitors move in streams from booth to booth to enquire about the prices. The market value determines what is viewed and appraised. Here, in contrast to the galleries, an „intellectual" exchange about art only occurs on the margins, even though the management of the fair repeatedly proclaims the „great understanding of art" among the buyers. A situation, which illustrates Andy Warhol's remark: „The first thing you will see is the money on the wall" [11].

The Contemporary Art Market

A brief overview

What does the art market look like, this by no means new but now unbelievably strong player in the art field? It depends on many external factors, on economic developments, on institutional structures and on legal and taxational framework conditions – and it is extremely heterogeneous. As a genuine factor in the field of art, which transforms art into careers and capital, only the „top" sector of the market is relevant. But its relevance is growing incessantly.

Again, what does the structure of the art market today look like? Essentially the art market defines itself as a market because the works of art it deals in can be bought and sold, be personally appropriated, just like the goods at any other market. And this does not apply in the same fashion to other forms of art such as the performing arts. In this respect the fine arts differ from other forms of art. Works of art are highly valued on account of their authenticity and originality [12]. Generally a distinction is made in the art trade between the primary and the secondary market [13]. On the primary market the works of living artists are sold for the first time, either by the artists themselves in their ateliers or by mediating institutions such as commercial galleries, which usually take a percentage of the proceeds from the sales as an allowance for their expenses. The secondary market, which operates without the direct participation of the artist, comprises the further sale of the works of living and, above all, of deceased artists, by galleries, art dealers, auction houses, art consultants or private individuals. This market is largely dominated by a small number of international big galleries, fairs and auction houses such as Sotheby's and Christie's. However, the primary and the secondary markets are linked in a variety of ways – for example when the new works of an artist are sold on the primary market and older works of the same artist are offered for sale on the secondary market.

The increasing dissolution of the boundaries between the primary and the secondary market with its strong tendencies towards monopolization points to a further segmentation of marketing activities and to an increasing gap between the segments. Whereas in the „lower" areas a broad and only partly commercial art market of a local and regional kind predominates, at the top a segment has detached itself from the rest which concentrates on trading with art recognized by the professional actors of the inner circle of the „art world", and which is in turn divided up into several sub-markets according to epochs, styles, genres, dealers and buyers. Precisely this segment is the foundation on which the unique boom in the art market in the last three decades has been built.

At the same time the social structure of the art market has clearly changed. Although art dealers, galleries, auction houses and collectors have remained the central actors, their role and importance has been substantially transformed. In the 1970s, as in the entire century before, the marketing of art works was carried out almost exclusively by the classical art dealer, who maintained personal contact with his collectors and, in some of his business, cooperated with other art dealers. Some of these dealers had already specialized in the trade with contemporary art as early as the 1950s and 1960s, and had sought for new artists, whom, as „mentors", they promoted and supported financially by exhibiting their works and introducing them to interested collectors. In contrast, art auctions served until into the 1970s mainly as forums for buying and selling in the sphere of private art trading and the auction houses largely limited themselves to operating like wholesalers who provided the art dealers with works of art.

The situation changed in the 1980s, when the auction houses themselves entered the retail market, making use of modern marketing practices which had hitherto been completely unknown on the art market. Sotheby's and Christie's, above all, expanded their business activities enormously and in the course of the subsequent boom in the art market they became the most important players on the secondary market, establishing branches around the world. Their entry into the market changed both the market and its practices in a variety of ways. Art dealers and gallerists lost their dominant position on the art market and the competition between them visibly sharpened. They not only had to assert themselves against the influx of new dealers and galleries into the field, but

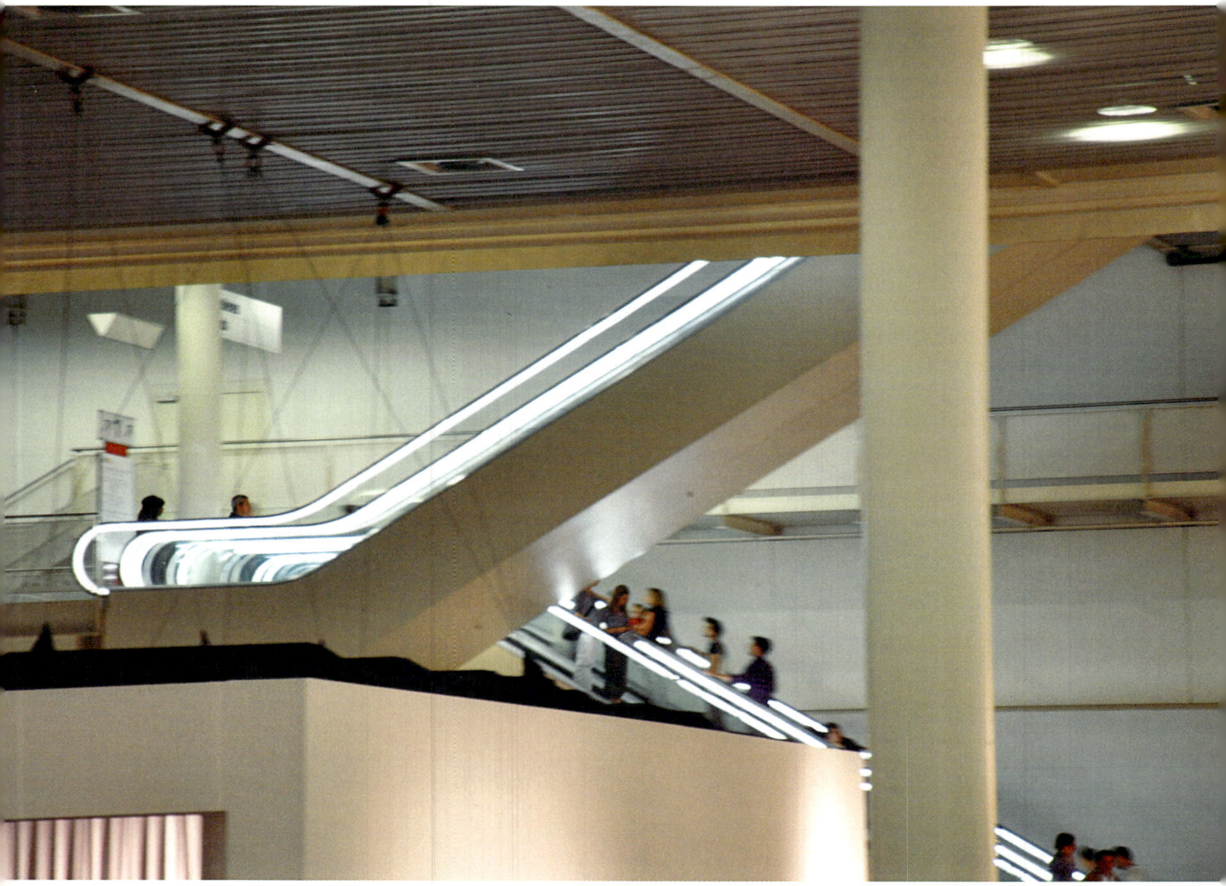

were also increasingly faced with competition for up-and-coming and acknowledged artists and for new and potential collectors. The flourishing auction market also ensured a certain degree of publicness and transparency and thus undermined the business practices of price-finding, exclusivity and discretion which had for a long time determined the conduct of the monopolistic art dealers and galleries.

The most visible sign of the incipient upswing in the art market was the rapid increase in prices, which was accompanied by an enormous increase in purchases. Growing demand and growing supply met. The increasing focus on contemporary art, which guaranteed that supplies would never dry up, first enabled the market to soar upwards, as the limited supplies of old masters or works of the classical modern period could never have had this effect. On the other hand, higher incomes, a rapidly growing population of wealthy people, new groups of buyers from Latin America, Asia, Russian and the Near East, and also higher educational levels and a growing awareness and social acceptance of the fine arts contributed to an increased demand. The „globalization" of these resources now brought about a globalization of the demand.

The current boom in the art market [14] seems, therefore, to know no limits. Although trade with works of art is only a small part of the entire culture industry, it has in the meantime become a billion dollar business. In 2013 the volume of trade in the international art market, which comprises the decorative arts and antiquities alongside old, modern and contemporary art, amounted to almost 50 billion euros, with the auction houses on the one hand and the private galleries and collectors on the other accounting for approximately fifty per cent each. Ten years earlier, in 2003, the volume amounted to almost 20 billion, so that the turnover in the last decade alone has grown by 150 per cent [15]. Since the beginning of the 1990s the turnover has even increased by more than 600 per cent [16]. The auction houses Sotheby's and Christie's, which three decades ago were still small, exclusive art auctioneers, together generated a turnover of 13 billion euros [17]. In view of these impressive figures it is scarcely possible to speak anymore of a niche market. The art market has in the meantime grown into an autonomous economic branch which, according to calculations, provides two and a half million jobs in over 300,000 enterprises, including auction houses, galleries, art dealers' shops, private art dealers, art consultancies and online sales platforms [18].

Post-war and contemporary art are among the most flourishing but also most volatile market segments. With an average increase of six per cent per year it has become the most important impetus for the auction house giants Sotheby's and Christie's. In 2013 the auction trade in post-war and contemporary art generated 5 billion euros, amounting to 46 per cent of the total turnover of the fine arts. Modern art and Impressionism and Post-Impressionism trailed far behind with figures of 29 and 13 per cent respectively [19]. In the year 2013 the growth of post-war and contemporary art even reached eleven per cent. The highest prices were also achieved in this area. In the USA this sector already accounts in the meantime for three-fifths of the values recorded at „fine arts" auctions [20]. The bitter setback during the financial crisis of 2008 and 2009, when contemporary art in particular suffered a sharp decline of 60 per cent, was quickly overcome. Subsequently this market has had an annual growth rate of 40 per cent [21]. Above all, the „blue chip" artists such as Rothko, Warhol, Bacon, Basquiat or Richter attract prosperous buyers. In 2012 the top twenty artists at the evening auctions at Sotheby's, Christie's and Philips accounted for three quarters of the total turnover of these, the biggest auction houses in the Western world [22].

However, in spite of the „hype" accompanying the market the sales figures are less spectacular than the top prices realized for individual works of art would have us believe. Only two per cent of the auction lots in 2013 realized over 200,000 euros; 42 per cent were knocked down for prices between 3,000 and 50,000 euros and 50 per cent for under 3,000 euros. Thus, all in all, 93 per cent of the works were auctioned for prices under 50,000 euros and 50 per cent for under 3,000 euros. Less than five per cent achieved prices of over a million euros, but precisely these works accounted, with 44 per cent, for almost half of the total turnover [23]. In the gallery and art dealing sector the situation is similar; three quarters of the transactions lay under 50,000 euros, 37 per cent under 3,000 euros; only four per cent achieved prices of over half a million euros [24].

Furthermore, the national art markets have developed very differently and this has led to clear regional unbalances. Whereas today the global art market is dominated by three states, the USA, China and Great Britain, which together enjoyed a share of 82 per cent of the market in 2013, the smaller markets, above all in the Western European states, have been pushed on to the margins. Europe, which had been the center of the international art trade until well into the post-war period, lost more ground in 2013 and has a market share of only one third. Great Britain accounts for 20 per cent, followed by France with six per cent. Switzerland has a share of two per cent, and Germany, Italy, Austria and Sweden with only one per cent each play scarcely any „global" role at all [25]. In view of these figures the „globalization" of the art market and the supposed boom in the art trade in the „emerging countries", often asserted by the media and art critics, turn out to be a fata morgana, if one ignores the rapid rise of China in the past few years. Only five countries, the USA, China, Great Britain, France and Switzerland, control 90 per cent of the international art market [26].

The differences between the national markets also has an effect on the gallery system. The turnover of the galleries in New York is, on average, twice as high as that of, for example, galleries in Amsterdam, and the number of their employees is also clearly greater [27], whereas galleries in countries with a stagnating art market, which represent internationally sought after artists, are forced to depend increasingly on strategies for trading abroad such as cooperation with foreign galleries or participation in foreign fairs. In Germany and Austria, for example, the galleries at home are given financial support enabling them to participate in international art fairs within the framework of the promotion of exports. In analogy to „New British Artists", „Young German Art" was created as an export label [28]. Spanish artists are also in demand worldwide with the result that in 2012 74 per cent of the volume and 90 per cent of the value was generated outside the national Spanish art market [28] – in a transnational market which has seen the establishment of the art fairs as the most important institution [29].

The art business is thus strongly dependent on social, socio-structural and economic framework conditions. From a historical point of view the parallels between the art market and the general economic development are nonetheless striking. The ups and downs of the art trade largely follow the economic cycles. This is particularly striking in regard to the coincidence with the stock market and other assets. This is also true of the most recent developments. In the 1980s there was a powerful upswing in the art market for modern art. The prices for the works of the impressionists increased in this decade by about 1,000 per cent. This boom was connected to the increasing economic and financial interweaving of the established national economies of the world and was promoted by the existing liquidity of capital. Apart from rich collectors, speculators and „amateurs" now penetrated the increasingly transnational market.

Art and Gold

Economic data in accord

In several studies the historical development of the art market has been studied by reference to price developments and comparisons have been drawn with real estate and finance markets, economic growth or income dynamics [30]. The changes from 1800 to the present day on the basis of transactions in Great Britain show how the booms and the slumps in the art market are related to prosperous phases and economic crises. The historical development also reveals striking parallels with stock exchange and income data or the data on investments such as gold [31].

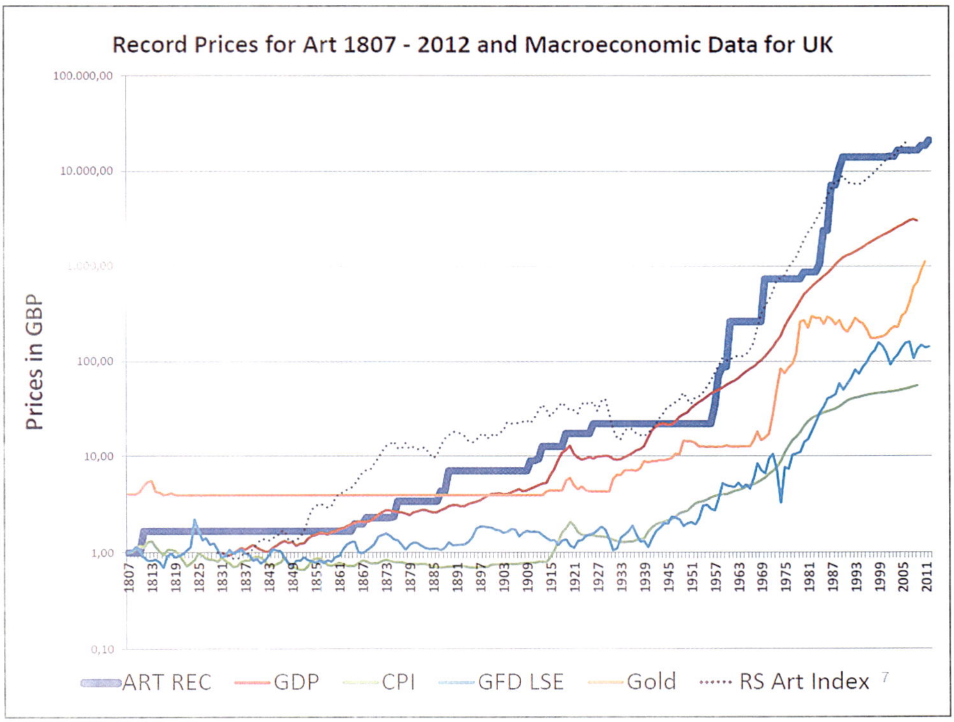

After the stock market crash in 1987 the crisis also overtook the art trade, albeit with a time lag. In the autumn of 1990 turnovers and prices slumped massively, in spite of the achievement of the highest prices at auctions as late as the spring of the same year. In the course of the severe real estate and bank crisis in Japan at the beginning of the 1990s many Japanese entrepreneurs had to divest themselves of art works, some of which had been used as securities to borrow huge sums of money („bad debt art"). Alongside the US Americans who had made fortunes in the finance sector and in the high tech and computer industry these entrepreneurs had formed one of the most important groups of buyers for this art.

The situation on the art market eased only slowly in the early 1990s. In this phase the market for „top-class" art works increasingly split off from the crisis-shaken market for art in the middle and lower price segments („flight into quality") [32]. This tendency also had an effect on the actors in the art business. Whereas the auction houses were able to increase their turnover substantially, many galleries and art dealers' shops suffered a massive reduction in turnover or even went bankrupt. At this time people first began to talk about the „dying of the galleries", a diagnosis which is still frequently made today. At the same time, contemporary art, which had not experienced such a dramatic slump, developed in the course of the 1990s into a qualitatively and quantitatively independent part of the art market. The driving force behind this process was provided by new groups of younger buyers, who had taken their place alongside an established clientele primarily interested in classical and modern art. This group brought about a generation change among collectors.

The structural change connected with these developments should not be overlooked. The increasing dissolution of the boundaries between the primary and the secondary market, the tendencies towards monopolization in the art trade with its concentration of the handling of goods and the turnover on a few big auction houses, art fairs and galleries, the division of the market into an international segment for „top-class" art and subaltern national and regional markets, which at the same time largely preserve the character of the earlier primary market, and, finally, the boom in contemporary art, not least in connection with the rise of new groups of buyers – these developments can be traced everywhere and they are accelerated by macroeconomic upheavals which to a great extent first enabled the art trade to achieve visibility as a *market activity.*

At the center of the world of pictures

The new fetishes of the art scene

The fact that top prices can only be achieved with the works of a few artists of the postwar and contemporary periods is not a new phenomenon. The division of the art market into a top segment and a broad middle sector existed in the past. Artists whose works achieved the highest prices were always a small minority, regardless of whether they were old masters, impressionists or representatives of the classical modern period. What is, however, new since the 1980s is the growing occupation of this segment by contemporary art. Among the two hundred most expensive lots on the auction market today around fifty are works by living artists. The cause for this trend should be sought not only in the changed structures of the art market, or in the scarce supply of „museal" works alone, but also in the change of taste. For the rich bourgeoisie contemporary art was for a long time scarcely attractive. The situation changed with the rise of pop art in the 1960s. It made art popular among a public outside the overseeable „art world" of the time and at the same time provided the impulse for an extension of the field of art.

But in spite of the „art fever" that pop art triggered off the prices for contemporary art stubbornly remained low; even in the 1960s the most expensive works did not cost more than a middle-class car. The auction market was still dominated by old masters, impressionists and artists of the classical modern period. Christie's reported a record year in 1965 with the auctioning of five paintings by Rembrandt, Velázquez, Dürer, Turner and Hogarth, which alone realized 1.2 million British pounds. In the same year Sotheby's in New York auctioned off impressionist and post-impressionist works worth 2.3 million dollars, including a Degas for 410,000 dollars. At the same time Sotheby's also knocked down contemporary works of art which were scarcely five or ten years old; a painting by Jackson Pollock achieved a record price of 45,000 dollars. Even in the 1970s the most

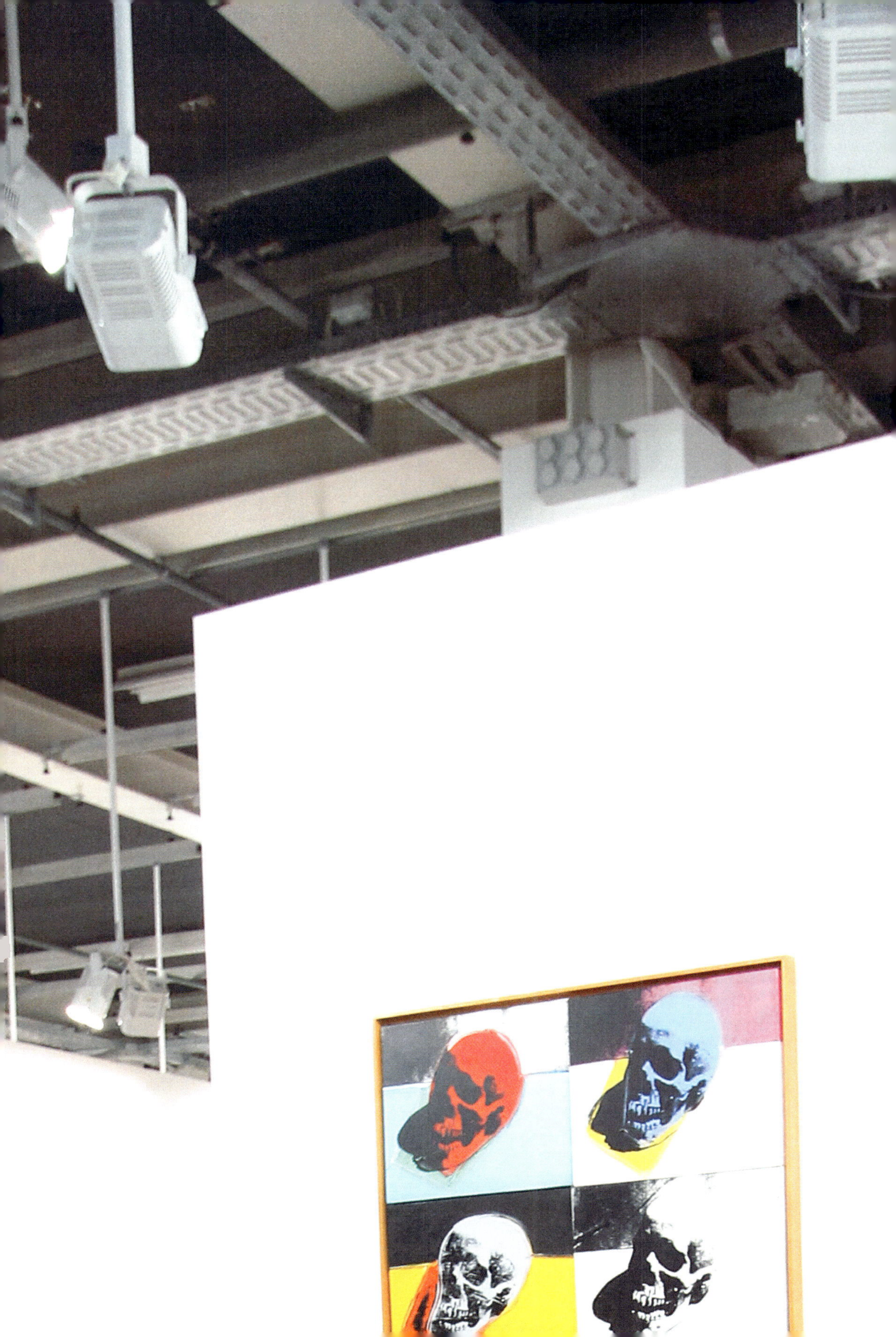

expensive work of art to be sold at an auction was a Velázquez. The first work of art by a living artists to break the million dollar barrier was sold in 1980, namely the *Three Flags* by Jasper Johns, which the New York gallerist Castelli sold to the Whitney Museum for one million dollars after it had been acquired a few years before for 900 dollars. But even in the boom phase between 1987 and 1990 no contemporary work was among the ten most expensive works of art, the list was headed by Picasso and Van Gogh.

And Picasso's *Garçon à la pipe* was, in the year 2004, also the first painting to break the „sound barrier" of 100 million dollars at an auction. Between 1980 and 1990 nine price records were registered at auctions alone, almost as many as in the entire period from 1900 to 1980 or in the eighteenth and nineteenth centuries together [33]. Whereas, at the beginning of the 1980s, the price record amounted to 2.5 million British pounds for a Van Gogh, a decade later a new record of 49 million British pounds was set up, again for a work of the Dutch painter. Although various reasons can be given for these increases, such as the scarcity of supply, social competition among collectors or the growing potential of the resale value, they are nonetheless an indication of the almost explosive expansion of the art market from the 1980s on – and of a fetishization of the market processes themselves, which find a kind of legitimation in the realization of such „top" prices. These developments seem to suggest that the old regime for the ascription of values in the field of art is heading for its demise.

At the same time the tendency towards massive monopolization in these stratospheric heights is confirmed. A current analysis of Skate shows that the most expensive transactions at auctions involve works of the same artists year after year. In the list of the 5,000 most expensive works of art we find that a quarter of the artists are represented with five or more works. There is a title race for the highest price among finalists who have already occupied the best starting positions. It is very cramped in this premium market. In 2013 only 164 artists achieved five or more sales in this segment; in 2012 the figure was 169 and in 2011 it was 174. It is becoming increasingly difficult for other artists to penetrate this market. In 2013 only 214 managed to leap into the top 5,000, whereas in 2011 250 still did so [34]. And the „C50-Index", which is based on the 50 „top artists" of the post-war and contemporary art field, has risen by more than 400 per cent since 2003 and has thus clearly outdone other asset investments such as shares or gold.

This explosion of the art market in the 21st century can only be observed in relatively few artistic „positions". And the same is true of the artistic genres. The centuries old dominant medium of the picture was already questioned as early as the beginning of the 20th century, and to this day two contrary positions exist, according to which, on the one hand, painting can continue to claim relevance, whereas, on the other hand, it is dismissed as „obsolete". And it is indeed the case that loss of importance and „renaissance" lie close together.

This kind of discourse plays virtually no part on the market. Painting continues to dominate the secondary market of the art trade – it made up 37 per cent of the lots auctioned in 2013 and generated 54 per cent of the world-wide revenues. 878 paintings were sold for a price of a million, whereas ten years earlier this mark was only reached by 205 works [35]. Only drawings, with a share of 30 per cent of the turnover from auctions, comes close to paintings. The other media trail far behind: sculptures make up 8 per cent of the global volume from auctions; photography accounted in 2013 for 4 per cent of the lots sold world-wide and for just one per cent of the turnover from auctions. Painting even remained the dominant factor in the market for contemporary art; at the auctions of July

2013 to June 2014 paintings had a share of 60 per cent, followed by drawings (19 %) and sculptures (15 %). Photography achieved a share of only 4 per cent of the turnover from auctions and the rest of the media accounted for just two per cent [36].

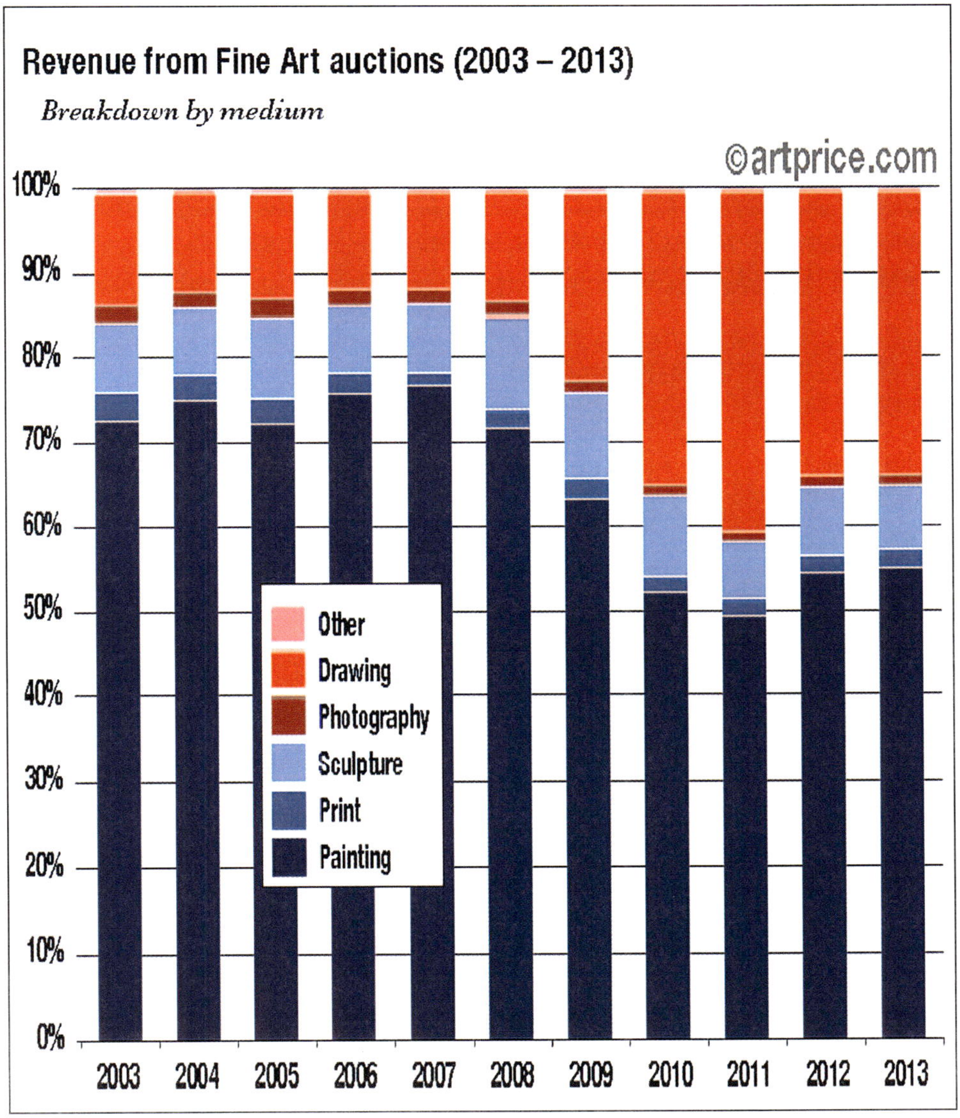

The structure of these preferences shows how close painting, or better the classical „picture" is to the „commercial" pole of the art field. It is apparently not for nothing that the battle for success on the market is particularly marked in this sector. The various currents of the „new spirit in painting", which flourished in the 1980s under a number of different labels – the neo-expressionist currents of the „new image painting", the „Transavantguardia", the „Arte Cifra", „Figuration Libre" or the „Neue Wilde" – provide clear proof of this, as do the manifestations of contemporary painting from their „post-medial" representatives to the „Leipzig School".

Many developments come together here: the massive expansion of the art market in the wake of a truly breathtaking expansion of the possibilities to acquire art; the resultant price increases; the extensive depletion of the market for classical modern art in spite of these inflationary tendencies; the increased flow of purchasing power into the field of contemporary art; the pressure of competition deriving not least from the existence of this market, with all the accompanying manifestations of monopolization of the channels of distribution, of the chances of skimming off profits, of the rationalization of self-presentation in the market and of the logics of production. All of these let us understand not only the present-day appearance of the market but also what it in fact has to offer. The symbolic and the economic values of the fine arts have seldom lain so far apart.

Artistic recognition and economic success (I)

In spite of all the reservations there are indications that the „old" mechanisms for the attribution of artistic worth continue to be effective. Even the thesis widely disseminated in the „art world" that prices in the meantime determine artistic reputation [37], can clearly be relativized by means of a comparison between the rankings of Artprice and Artfacts. The discrepancy between economic success and symbolic status – the recognition among the professional actors in the field – is still evident even among the top group of artists; many living artists with a high symbolic reputation still cannot be found among the 500 „most expensive" artists [38].

Conversely, on the list of living artists with a high turnover a whole series of names can be found of artists whose reputation is comparatively low within the art field. Jeff Koons, number three on the list of the most expensive artists, occupies only the 98th place in the list by Artfacts; Christopher Wool, who follows immediately behind Koons on the Artprice list, occupies place 246 in Artfacts, and Peter Doig is at 512. Mark Grotjahn, who came under the top ten artists of the Western world in terms of auction sales, landed way down the Artist Ranking list at place 1256. A further „media star" among the contemporary artists, the Japanese painter Takashi Murakami, takes the 25th place on the basis of auction revenues but only place 381 in the artists' ranking.

Nonetheless, the artists particularly appreciated by the art market are evidently catching up. Damien Hirst, for example, has climbed to place 17 in the ranking for artistic reputation. The decisive factor determining the improvement of his rank was probably the many exhibitions devoted to his works in recent years, some of them in renowned museums. This shows that as trend setters the market actors are in a position not only to establish their artists on the art market but also to win recognition for them in the relevant art institutions.

In the meantime many of the artists with high turnovers come from China. The fact that they have hitherto enjoyed little artistic recognition and are far down the list of the Artist Ranking is due to the fact that the ranking is decided by an art institution whose structure is still dominated by the „West". Fanzhi Zeng, the number two in the auction turnovers, occupies only place 1871 in the Artist Ranking. If figures such as Ai Weiwei or some of the artists labeled as representatives of „Chinese pop art" are left out of consideration, it can be said that little attention has been paid to Chinese artists by Western exhibitors – and that the „pure money" from the booming Chinese market is still not sufficient for the artistic recognition of Chinese painters.

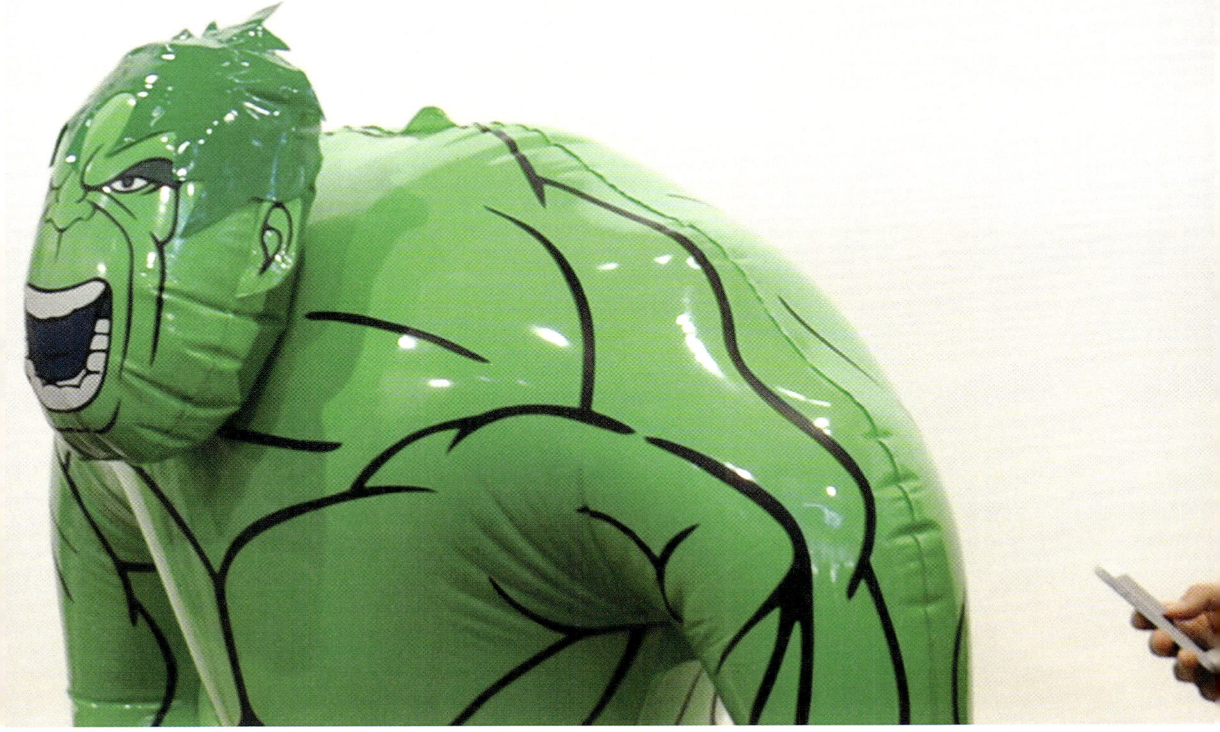

Artistic recognition and economic success (II)

Artfacts Top 50 | 2014
Living artists according to their importance

1 Bruce Nauman
2 ***Gerhard Richter***
3 Lawrence Weiner
4 John Baldessari
5 ***Cindy Sherman***
6 ***Ed Ruscha***
7 Thomas Ruff
8 Rosemarie Trockel
9 Francis Alys
10 Georg Baselitz
11 William Kentridge
12 Dan Graham
13 Fischli & Weiss
14 Erwin Wurm
15 Douglas Gordon
16 Hans-Peter Feldmann
17 ***Damien Hirst***
18 Wolfgang Tillman
19 Paul McCarthy
20 Richard Serra
21 Marina Abramović
22 Ai Weiwei
23 Harun Farocki
24 Olafur Eliasson
25 Valie Export
26 Tacita Dean
27 Carl Andre
28 Christian Marclay
29 Mona Hatoum
30 Anselm Kiefer
31 Arnulf Rainer
32 Thomas Struth
33 Nan Goldin
34 ***Andreas Gursky***
35 Yayoi Kusama
36 Rodney Graham
37 Anri Sala
38 Gilbert & George
39 Jonathan Monk
40 François Morellet
41 Jenny Holzer
42 Alex Katz
43 Thomas Schütte
44 Jasper Johns
45 Martha Rosler
46 Irmi Knoebel
47 Tony Cragg
48 Christian Boltanski
49 Thomas Hirschhorn
50 John Armleder

Artprice Top 500 | 2013
Living artists according to auction results

7 ***Gerhard Richter***
21 Fanzhi Zeng
25 Jeff Koons
30 Christopher Wool
37 Teh-Chun Chu
41 Zhiliu Xie
46 Zeng Fan
56 Peter Doig
58 Ruzhuo Cui
59 Yayoi Kusama
61 Shangyi Jin
69 Chunya Zhou
71 Pierre Soulages
72 Yongyu Huang
74 ***Ed Ruscha***
78 Mark Grotjahn
88 ***Damien Hirst***
90 Zhongli Luo
91 Jiaying He
95 Morton Thiebaud
103 ***Andreas Gursky***
104 David Hockney
105 Haixia He
116 Yidong Wang
121 Takashi Murakami
122 Xiaogang Zhang
123 Robert Ryman
125 Ye Liu
126 Anish Kapoor
136 Glenn Brown
137 Wei Liu
145 Dawei Liu
147 Rudolf Stingel
150 Xuan Ai
152 oshitomo Nara
154 Fernando Botero
155 John Currin
158 Ming Zhu
160 Enrico Castellani
168 Feiyun Yang
175 Brice Marden
176 Guolinang Shi
177 Tao Shi
184 Youfu Jia
189 Mingming Wang
196 Richard Prince
197 Frank Stella
198 David Hammons
200 ***Cindy Sherman***
203 Julie Mehretu

Without falling victim to the exaggeration structurally inherent to the art field we can safely say that the pictorial world of modern art has entered a new stage and is moving towards a new center. And it is not an exaggeration when we relate these tectonic shifts to the unfolding of a genuine market in those spheres in which art claims to have „extraordinary“ validity. The market has at one and the same time taken control of the center of these spheres of „recognized“ and „covetable“ art. It redefines the relationship between the criteria of recognition and the dimension of covetability and it rationalizes and objectifies this relationship according to its own standards – without being able to totally obliterate the profane conditions surrounding the new fetish of „top-class art“.

The measurement of art

Artist rankings and market indicators conquer the field

The rationalization of the art market is in full swing. This applies not only to production and distribution but in the meantime also to „market analyses“ which attempt to render artistic „success“ and market success measurable by means of artist rankings and art indices involving figures, prices and curves. In the „art world“ such quantitative analyses of development in the value of art works are often treated with suspicion – the ambivalent relationship of art and money can still be felt in large parts of the art scene. Those who create such data banks and others who present economic analyses of the price dynamics on the art market are regularly accused of registering only the pecuniary side of art and hence of further fostering its role as an „investment“. This „cold side“, the accusation runs, completely ignores the „emotional“ dimension of art.

But this development cannot be stopped – quite the contrary. Since the 1990s a whole series of professional data pools and information services has been established which collects and evaluates data on the art market. And in spite of all the criticism they have in the meantime become an indispensable instrument for the procurement of information for the actors in the „art world“. They ensure a certain degree of transparency in an art market which is otherwise difficult to grasp, a market for which discretion has always enjoyed top priority. Even though some of the „art lovers“ claim to strictly reject the use of such services, it is highly unlikely that any collector would acquire a work of art without comparing prices beforehand with the help of such data banks. And for the auction houses and the private art trade these instruments have become an integral part of their expertise.

Artprice, Artfacts, Artnet and Mutual Art [39] are among the most important providers but more and more providers such as Skate's Art Investment or Art Analytics are coming onto the market. The data bases vary widely but the central criteria are always economic success and/or the recognition of the professional actors and institutions in the field. Market prices, the „performance“ of artists or stock exchange listings can be followed with the help of special indices. They are based on prices realized at public sales and can be combined with many other features such as genre, medium, size and facts on a particular artist, biographical data, auction results, lists of dealers, exhibitions and awards. In addition there are diverse art market reports which appear periodically, including the prominent reports of the Maastricht Art Fair Tefaf and the London market research enterprise ArtTactic.

These developments have profoundly changed the art market. They not only involve a further rationalization of what actually happens in the market but also increasingly strengthen its influence on the process of evaluation of artistic „positions“. They contribute to a new kind of „visibility“ of the artists, whose registration has the appearance of objectivity, and they are thus in a position to create „facts“ which develop a normative force of their own.

In the shadow and in the light of popularity
Transformations of the former art scene

In spite of these striking developments the process of „economization" or „commercialization" of the art field frequently diagnosed in art criticism is not all-encompassing. These tendencies are revealed primarily at the visible peak of a hierarchical structure, in the high-price segment of the „blue chips" and the more or less „consecrated" art. This small, extremely high-selling sector, which is thoroughly infected by the „spirit" of the market and seems to be characterized by the practices of investment, „resale", speculation and the ostentatious prodigality of a tiny elite, has increasingly attracted the attention of the media and of art-theoretical discourse. In this top segment everything revolves around an overseeable group of „super-star" artists to whom the most important museums of the world devote exhibitions and retrospectives, and whose works are traded internationally for six and seven digit sums.

However, no matter how omnipresent this perspective is in media reporting, in the quantitavely much greater but in terms of turnover weaker part of the market at the opposite pole of the art field, which trades in as yet „unknown" art, the market mechanisms described above play only a subordinate role or none at all. Intrusion effects can, it is true, be found in the primary market such as, for example, an increasing professionalization of the activities of the galleries. Nonetheless – and this is a decisive point – it is scarcely possible to achieve economic or symbolic gains in this area. There is no functioning secondary market in which the products sold in the galleries could be converted with profit into hard cash. On the contrary, most of the works lose in market value as soon as they have left the gallery.

In this sphere local or regional networks of artists, galleries and buyers based on private acquaintanceships, personal relationships of trust and mutual support are still dominant [40]. The great majority of the artists cannot live off the sale of their works, and usually have to supplement their low income with „part-time work", for example in teaching, or keep their heads above water with the help of „goodwill" purchases. It has been estimated that only five per cent can make a livelihood from their work as artists [41]. The situation in most of the galleries is not much better. They also mostly work without making a profit and many are run out of a pure „love of art" as a sideline or hobby, even though the hope of making a breakthrough at some point is in the foreground when the galleries are established.

According to an enquiry of the Federal Association of German Galleries and Fine Art Dealers only five per cent of the 700 professional galleries in Germany generated a turnover of 500,000 euros and more – amounting to 80 per cent of the total turnover of all galleries [42]. But even this does not seem to be much, in view of the fact that 50 per cent of this income goes to the artists for the sale of their works and from the remainder rents, staffing costs and possibly participation in fairs must be financed. About 60 per cent of the German galleries have an annual turnover under 200,000 euros and so contribute a mere six per cent to the overall turnover of all galleries. The middle segment is apparently being ruined to the point of collapse and only a few „top dogs" are left over at the top, who can then be encountered at the leading art fairs such as the Art Basel, alongside the many practically non-commercial small galleries at the bottom end of the scale.

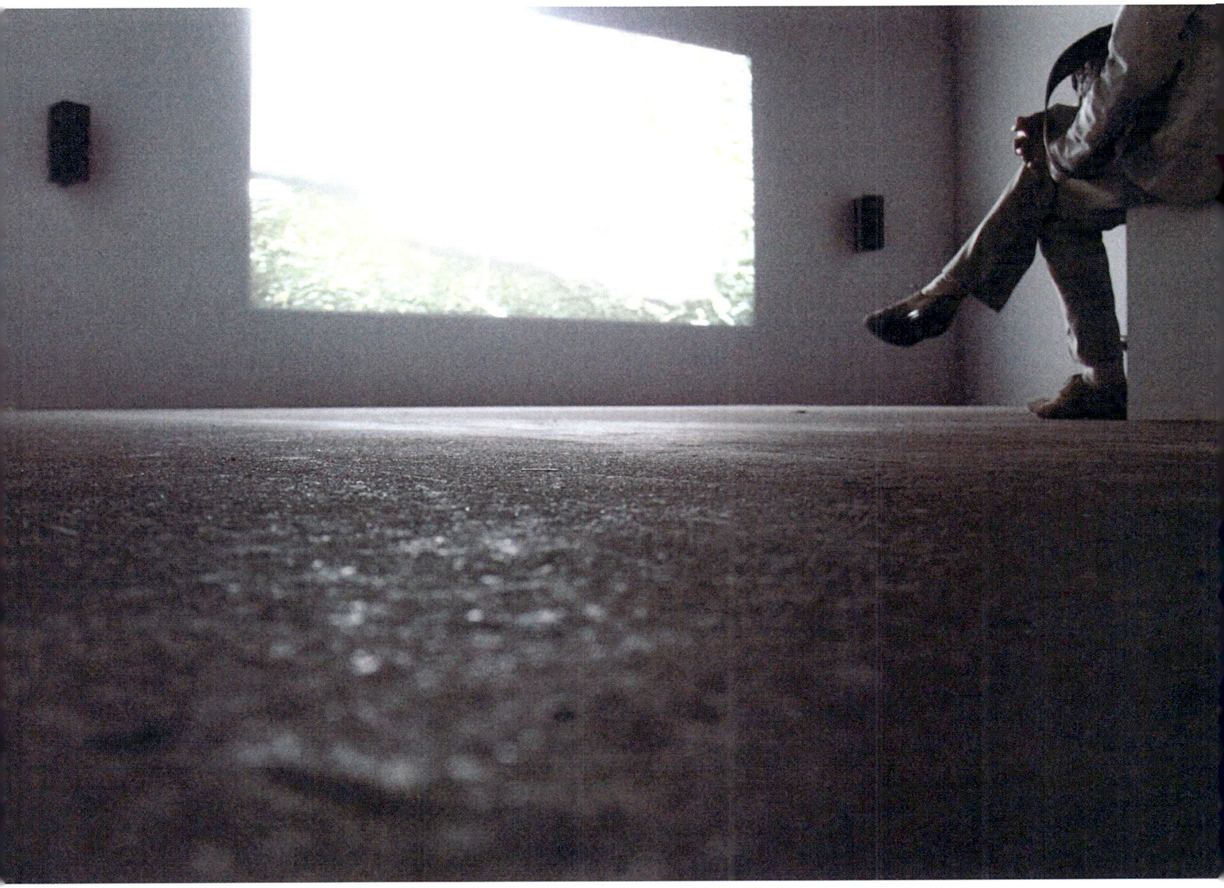

However, outside these marginal areas of the art trade, in the primary market, which is also subject to increasing marginalization, rationalization tendencies can be observed. The value creation cycles, which covered a relatively long period of time in the age of classical modern art, have shortened drastically. Galleries which formerly behaved like „culture bankers“ and relied on long-term value creation and returns have in the meantime changed their strategies and have adapted to the short cycles of the market, which they themselves create by presenting ever-new trends and artists. The market always demands new and fresh products, particularly in regard to new and contemporary art. The result is an accelerated up and down of trends and „stars“. Nowadays, in view of the large numbers of academically trained artists in the field, it is not so much a question of „discovering“ suitable artists, but rather of „placing“ them on the market with rationalized methods. More and more often the central question is: What is original enough to assert itself as a new „position“ on the market?

The short-term cycles of the market and a business conduct of the galleries oriented on short-term economic profits have not failed to have an effect on the artists themselves and on their artistic production. Many of them accept the targets set by the galleries and produce „quantities“ of items in order to satisfy the demand of the art fairs at which their galleries desire or are compelled to participate. The concept of the so-called „art fair art“ illustrates the degree to which a part of the artistic production has in the meantime been adapted to meet the expectations and the needs of the market.

Masses of artists and the artistic reserve army
The popularization of art production

The number of artists has increased substantially in the last few decades. In the USA this population grew by 78 per cent between 1980 and 2000; it virtually doubled in France between 1982 and 1999 and tripled in Germany between 1991 and 2013.

The low degree of codification in this „profession“ permits anybody, in principle, to work as an „artist“. The barriers to entry into the world of art at first seem to be low; neither a specific school finishing qualification nor a professional qualification are a precondition for a career as an artist. And the extreme diversity of the projective possibilities for future „posts“ in the art field, which accompanies the profession of the artist, makes the art field highly attractive for many young aspirants, even though, in retrospect, attendance at an art school or a university is in the final analysis a precondition for success as an artist [43].

The myth of art is at all events alive. In Germany almost 35,000 students were enrolled at art colleges in the winter semester of 2012, and at the universities almost 90,000 young people were studying art or art studies [44]. In the study year 2007-2008 the share of art students in the overall number of students amounted to almost 4 per cent; in Great Britain the figure was almost seven per cent [45].

This mounting wave of aspirants is apparently due not only to the increasing demand for art, but also to the improved social acceptance of the ideas associated with the profession of the „artist“. In post-industrial capitalism the „artist“ has become a role model, creativity a part of his self-description, a „liberated“ lifestyle a counter-project to the standardized and hierarchical work relationships and the planned and administered life of the middle classes in the Western post-war societies [46]. The impetus to rationalize deriving from capitalism has even reached the ideal of liberation from its constraints.

But the liaison between artistic and economic strategies goes even further. By deciding in favor of a certain kind of art production artists and galleries themselves choose the markets in which they see the best chance of symbolic and economic success. Artistic production is, therefore, attached in advance to different economic conditions, which are „written into“ the production itself. At the same time artists who consciously rely on alternative forms of art production which are located outside the classical art field of artists, galleries, collectors and museums attempt to set up a „distance“ between themselves and the art market and to act outside the market scene [47]. Many of these initiatives and projects are largely financed by public funds and grants. They show that on the margins of the art field a change in the relationships of art production is also taking place. The rationalization tendencies in the art market have thus not only massively transformed the distribution sector but are even penetrating into the production processes.

The strength and range of the changes triggered off by the expansive art market and the dominant actors within it can be illustrated by the example of the public art institutions. „Commercialization“ has long reached that part of the art field which was not private like the art market, but was publicly constituted and for a long time held aloof from the influence of the market and the culture industry. The museum, as the public institution which was committed to the „reflection“ of art and for a long time provided art with its „museal“ consecration, is faced by developments which increasingly question its original position and task. Although the status of the museum was never undisputed, shifts in the weighting of its role and changes in its function now point to a shift in the boundaries of cultural hegemony.

This happens in various ways. As a result of sinking subsidies and reduced budgets the museums, which are in any case already chronically underfinanced, are increasingly called upon to act as business enterprises and must generate additional income and funds from private sponsors. Blockbuster exhibitions, museum branding and the consistent „marketing“ of collections are only a few examples of the way the institutions themselves promote their „commercialization“. Through the systematic staging of exhibitions as „events“ and a diversification of the works they exhibit the museums develop into stages for art spectacles in the event culture and at the same time becomes attractions of event tourism and an instrument of city marketing.

In this process attention is paid to attracting those members of the public into the mu-seum who are not inveterate „art connoisseurs“ and cannot decipher the „museum code“. Exhibition didactics, museum pedagogics, guided tours, lectures, audio guides and similar services: all the stops are pulled out in order to fulfill the „educational mission“ of the museum. Busloads of tourists or school classes in front of the museum bear witness to the increasing „popularization“ of art and to the museum as a „destination culture“ [48].

The fact that the public museums and art exhibition halls more and more frequently show contemporary art which previously had not enjoyed museum status not only points to a further change, the transformation of the museum into a stage for contemporary art. It is also a proof of the further „economization“ of the running of public exhibitions. Apart from the museums and art halls the curated big exhibitions and the biennials must also be seen in this context.

The exhibition of contemporary works of art enables an increase in their museum valuation and their ranking on the art market. The „temple bonus“ increases the value of the works, which pays off for the galleries in hard cash, if the works are at the same time presented and sold on the art market. In the museums and exhibitions, however, this economic factor and the economic weight of the collections are largely concealed, as the separation of art and money must be maintained.

The Masses and the Museum

The popularization of viewing art

The „enjoyment of art" has become a mass phenomenon. Millions of people interested in art are attracted world-wide into the museums. In Germany alone 100 million admissions to over 6,000 museums were recorded in 2012. The number of visitors has increased steeply in the last three decades. An increase of 18 million to a total of 56 million visitors was registered in the USA between 1982 and 2002. The increase can be traced back, on the one hand, to the improved levels of education in the developed Western countries. And on the other hand the museums have strengthened their efforts to increase the number of visitors by addressing the different target groups with diversified programs and by reacting to the changed leisure behavior and the growing competition from the entertainment and leisure industries. Not without success. In particular the increased number of blockbuster exhibitions has attracted masses of visitors [49].

The „superstar" museum, above all, has become the symbol of tourist oriented art consumption; „il vaut un voyage" as a place of pilgrimage for the „amateur", who prefers to make the experience collectively with a tourist group in a bus; its type of architecture is regarded in many cases as a „lighthouse" in the industrial zones of the Western cities and its collections are mostly adorned with icons of art history which every „pilgrim" ought to have seen at least once in his life. The Musée du Louvre in Paris is a classic example; it is a must for every visitor to Paris, acclaimed in all travel guides, praised for the pyramid created by Ming Pei, and the home of probably the most famous painting in the world, Da Vinci's Mona Lisa. In 2013 the museum counted more than nine million visitors, more than 30,000 persons per day; with approximately 11 million visitors Disneyland outside Paris did not attract substantially more people. Other museums also have a public running into millions. The British Museum in London attracted almost seven million visitors in 2013, the Metropolitan Museum of Art in New York over six million and the National Gallery also six million. The Vatican museums, the Tate Modern in London, the National Palace Museum in Taipei, the National Gallery of Art in Washington, the Centre Pompidou and the Musée d'Orsay in Paris complete the top ten of the most visited museums world-wide.

The choice of the exhibitions remains „classical"; it falls primarily on pre-modern art, handicrafts and ethnographic collections. This is clear from the list of the exhibitions with the highest attendance in 2012. In the Tokyo Metropolitan Art Museum there were over 10,000 visitors daily at an exhibition of Flemish and Dutch masterpieces of the 17th century, including Vermeer's *Girl with a Pearl Earring.* In the Hermitage in St. Petersburg almost 8,000 people daily visited an exhibition of „Nineteenth Century Italian Painting". In Washington 7,600 visitors turned up every day to see an exhibition of works by Ito Jakuchu, a Japanese painter of the 18th century. There was a similar throng of 7,400 visitors daily at the Tokyo National Museum for an exhibition of Japanese masterpieces from the Museum of Fine Arts in Boston. In addition, the list includes exhibitions on the Amazon and India. In 2013 an exhibition of pre-modern art again heads the list. Eleven thousand visitors a day were counted at an exhibition on the Western Zhou dynasty held in the National Palace Museum in Taipei.

Modern and contemporary art finds a mass public when it is exhibited in popular museums. The number of visitors then reaches a peak, as in the case of the Museum of Modern Art in New York, where a retrospective on de Kooning attracted over 6,200 visitors daily and 6,600 art enthusiasts per day attended an exhibition of Cindy Sherman's work. In 2013 the Guggenheim Museum drew in a crowd of 5,600 visitors daily with an exhibition of the work of James Turrell, while 5,200 visitors daily viewed works by Claes Oldenburg at the MoMA.

Even the relatively „autonomous" pole of the art world is not immune to such huge crowds. The best example is the „Museum of 100 Days". Over 860,000 visitors attended the Documenta in Kassel between 9 June and September 16, 2012. Only the galleries were bereft of visitors.

The public museums in the USA have been primarily financed by rich patrons since time immemorial, and since the 1960s increasingly by entrepreneurs and foundations associated with enterprises whose representatives have taken their seats in the supervisory boards, advisory panels and important purchasing committees of the museums and have a decisive influence on their policies. It is, therefore, no surprise that the rise of the so-called blockbuster exhibitions coincides with the spread of culture sponsoring.

Because the galleries themselves make the works of their artists available to the exhibitions and biennials, works of art are not seldom already reserved there by potential buyers. How tightly these two spheres are in the meantime intertwined is revealed by the Documenta 13, which took place in Kassel in 2012. Of the 193 artists represented there 84 were presented at the sales booths of the Art Basel by 177 galleries in 2013. Artists shown at the Biennial in Venice also pop up regularly at the Art Basel. The collection of wooden stools installed by Ai Weiwei in the German pavilion, a work with „political" connotations at „big scale", can be acquired from the Galerie Neugerriemschneider at the Art Basel as consumable individual items of art production in manufactured form.

Thus, the private market operates below the shiny surface of the international market, the big auction houses and the global fairs, either fully beyond public visibility as an affair of more or less „amateur" actors, who remain virtually insignificant both economically and symbolically; or, in the „middle" segment, it is dependent on practices of „commercial" rationalization in order to escape this insignificance in a market which is subject to massive processes of concentration. In contrast the relatively „autonomous" regions of the art world, the big museums and the biennials, are confronted with the „misery of popularization" which precisely reflects these concentration processes. In view of the in the meantime extreme discrepancies between the market and its actors and the public institutions of art mediation in regard to their financial possibilities, the museums mostly have no choice but to flee into the arms of the mass public.

It is obvious that this strategy, to which there is often no alternative, not only contributes to a further uniformization of the „positions" acquired in the contemporary art scene, but also ratifies its monopolistic tendencies. The interpretative primacy of public art institutions continues to spiral downwards, as the erosion of their financial basis is followed by a loss of autonomy in the processes whereby value is attributed to art, and the consciously desired inrush of the masses in response to the presentation of an unconditionally iconized „program" has led to an inestimable loss of authority. The art world continues to evolve, but its driving forces have become so „hybrid" that its „commercial" manifestations call to mind times which lay before the symbolic revolution of the „modern" era.

Hegemony, autonomy and „pluralism"

The old world of art and the challenge of „post-modernism"

The talk of the „commercialization" of the contemporary world of art not only names developments which it would be difficult to describe with other concepts. This world is also itself an indisputable fact and expresses transformations to which the art field has been subjected in the past few decades. No less than „everything" is at issue: the rationalization of the structures of the art trade with its tendencies towards concentration, the changed framework conditions of artistic production, the dissolution of traditional norms and the practice of bringing art and „money" together.

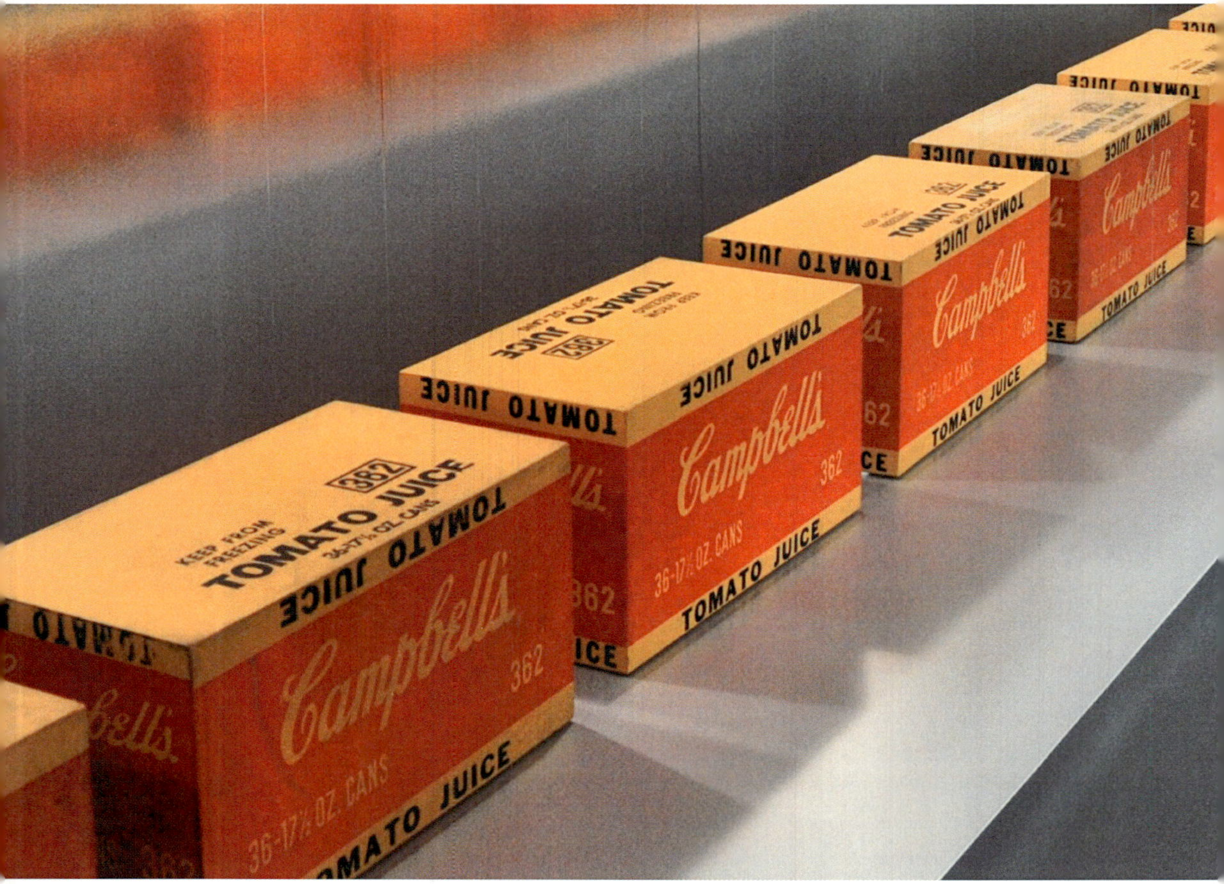
KEEP FROM FREEZING
362
TOMATO JUICE
36-17½ OZ. CANS
TOMATO JUICE
Campbell's
362
36-17½ OZ. CANS
TOMATO JUICE

It is also a question of the consequences of this transformation for the process of attributing value to art, which promises to authenticate the validity of artistic „positions" beyond the present moment. Commerce in its concrete manifestations is a „moral" issue, but that is not all. Critical discourse goes much further and puts the fundamental question as to whether another aspect, the moment of artistic „pluralism" of the „postmodern" era, which long seems to have emancipated itself from the validity criteria of the classical modern period, gives rise to the undecidability even of „autonomous" attributions of value, from which this „commercialization" of art inevitably profits. How can this constellation be objectively described?

Even in the eyes of many participants leading art fairs such as the Art Basel and big auction houses are scarcely anything other than shopping malls, department stores for luxury goods, epicenters of the „commercial art business". The works of well-known artists with a corresponding market value are traded there; the scarcity of these artistic „brand articles" guarantees exclusivity; their acquisition, so it is at least suggested by critical voices, is part of the practice of a „life-style" which requires wealth and the desire to demonstrate the possession of wealth. In this way mere money is forgotten and the desire for social recognition is realized, whereby the artistic „quality" or the „aesthetic value" of the works is a side issue. This image leads some commentators in the art world to speak of a split in the art market between „genuine" and „life-style" art. Whereas „genuine" art is here defined primarily in terms of „content" and calls for a certain connoisseurship on the part of its consumers, „life-style" art is above all defined in terms of prices, brand names of artists and galleries and current trends and fashions, and clearly requires less expert knowledge on the part of the buyers and the interested public. In this scenario the relationship between art, taste and knowledge, which had shaped the art market until the 1980s, has obviously been pushed into the background.

The problem is clear. In view of the fact that trade on the market for contemporary art is not concerned with ordinary „goods", that the prices seldom stand in any „economically" understandable relation to the „costs of production", and that the claim to artistic „quality", which has to close this obvious „gap", depends fundamentally on always disputable evaluations, it is exactly this attribution of value which decides what is and ought to be considered „legitimate art". Who then ultimately gives his blessing and what criteria form the basis for the recognition of a work as art [50]? Is it today the art market or the field of art itself in which values are laid down and confirmed?

The changes which are taking place in this regard are clear. If we argue „structurally" and refer to social configurations, we first of all see the „old" form. At the center of the „modernistic" discourse on the determination of the „legitimacy" and „value" of art stands not only the question as to what is and what is not art and how art can be separated and distinguished from everyday things. The „valorization" of artists and their work is also the outcome of a laborious discursive process, in which a small circle of experts from the inner circle of the „art world" participate – the „qualified" judges, art historians, art scholars, art critics, museum curators, acknowledged art dealers and collectors. Their „judgment of value" guides the ongoing process of canonization and in the end provisionally determines the authoritative position in art history [51].

And according to the established „rules of art" the „certification takes place in successive and largely acknowledged steps: completion of a relevant training, recognition by artists, participation in group exhibitions and then the first single exhibition in a gallery, evaluation by art critics, purchases by collectors, exhibitions in museums and finally inclusion in museum collections. With few exceptions this process of recognition lasts many years, even though individual actors or a certain spatial concentration of actors in art centers such as Paris or New York can use their power to play a central part in the „valorization" and „canonization".

If one believes the discourse on the „pluralization" of art, this „modernistic" configuration for the determination of artistic „legitimacy is, as a result of precisely this pluralization, subject to a process of progressive dissolution. The discursive questioning of the criteria for and the control over the „valorization" of contemporary works of art is indeed „multidimensional" in as far as more and more actors in the art world are involved in this evaluative process and a kind of explosion and amalgamation of the genres and approaches has taken place, which are provided with verification of their legitimacy by an entire „choir" of judges, depending on the perspectives involved.

The success of this „post-modern" art discourse over „modernism", its apparently „one-dimensional", „formalistic" and „hierarchical" approach, its search for originality and hunger for innovation, this discursive success must be attributed precisely to the structural change, the big bang in the art field since the 1980s, which has not only modernized the way the art trade functions and at the same time initiated a glut of artists, whose „modernistic" claim to originality has exploded the form-language of contemporary art. The group of so-called „qualified judges" has also expanded enormously. New players, free curators or art advisors have won power and influence in an attention economy, which intervenes more and more frequently in such processes of value attribution, by building up networks, establishing contacts and connections, becoming members of juries, trusts or advisory committees, organizing exhibitions, publishing catalogues, books and articles and so permanently casting light on new „stars" and „starlets" in the art heavens.

But this supposed dissolution of „modernism" in a new „pluralism" of the „post-modern" world itself follows a „modernistic" logic, a logic of exaggerated deconstruction which must necessarily identify its own rules with the *phenomena* against which it is directed. And its imperious iconoclasm has the best chance of itself becoming iconic – the goal and the fate of every artistic avant-garde.

The power of a „modernistic" logic can be seen in its fundamental recognition of art forms such as photography, video art, installations, performances, and also architecture and design, which had stood in the shadows of painting and sculpture or had even been regarded as „illegitimate" during the ascendancy of modernism. And this is also true of the numerous new creative practices, including even „artivism", whose legitimacy can no longer be denied. In its struggle against the existing form this „modernistic" logic pays homage to an essentialism which it at the same time wishes to deny. The fact that under the top ten of the „most important" living artists outside concept art and photography only Gerhard Richter and Georg Baselitz appear under the classical category of „painting" is for this reason not a proof of post-modern pluralism but of the never-ending revolution of the form canon of art.

To this extent the „problem" of the attribution of value to works of art can by no means be solved in a discourse on the manifestations of the „post-modern" era. The still positively connoted assertion that post-modern art has abandoned all claims to universal validity, that its questioning of the formalism of modernism, of its concept of artistic „autonomy" and „freedom from purpose", of „creation" and „work", originality and representativeness,

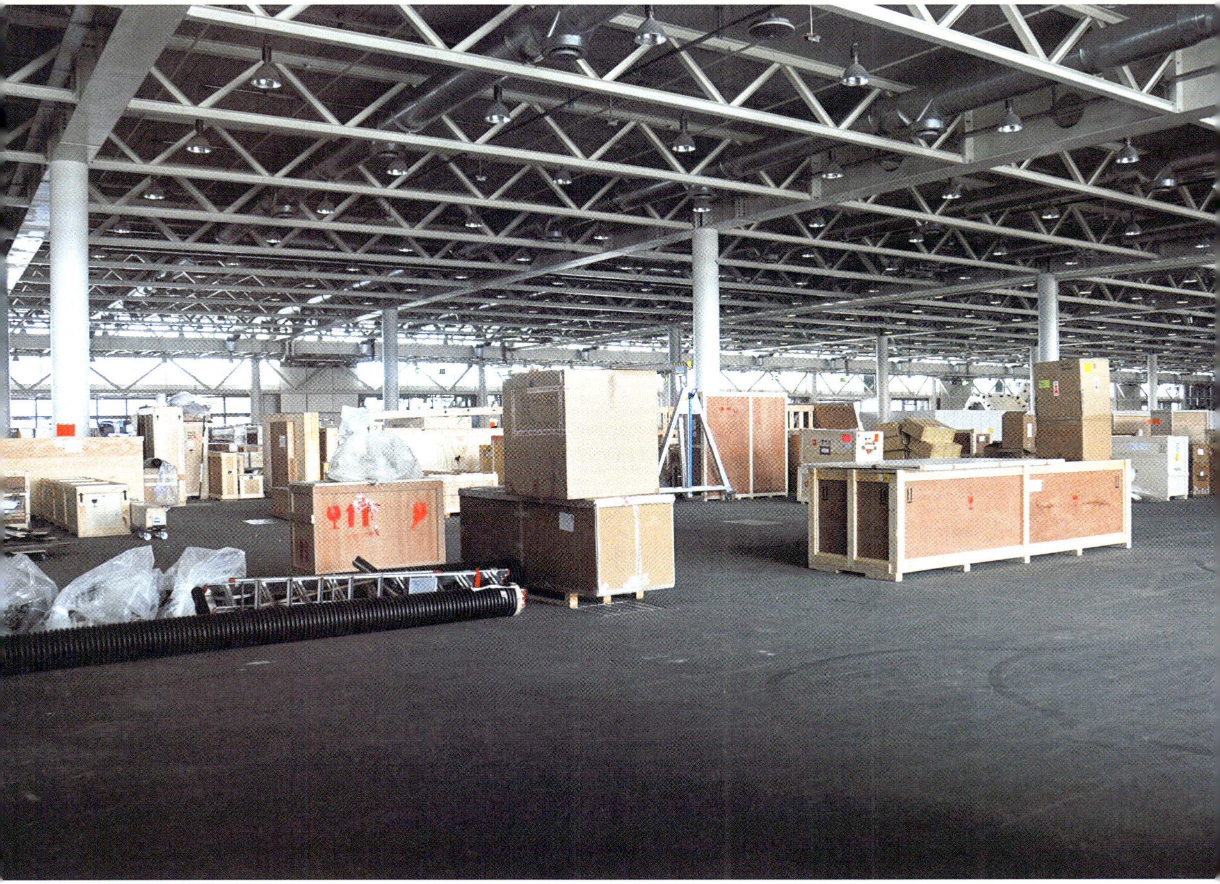

has „deconstructed“ the *Ancien Régime* of classical modernism cannot stand the test of practice. As a matter of course every artistic „production“, every artistic „position“ which nowadays distances itself from the „modernistic“ paradigm of „creation“ nonetheless makes a claim to validity; as a matter of course the „creators“ are celebrated and a „work“ is discussed as such in spite of its consciously ephemeral character; as a matter of course the essential criteria for the evaluation of this „production“ are still the modernistic criteria of „originality“ and the representativeness for the post-modern departure from representativeness frequently quoted in the discourses; and as matter of course a post-modern avant-garde, which in the meantime seems „unsuitable“ as a „conception“ [52], turns up in the contemporary „rankings“ of the „most important“ living artists. At all events the art field stubbornly resists its predicted dissolution in a discourse in which exactly that fascination resonates which announces its apparent demystification.

The accompanying negative manifestations of post-modern art, namely the fact that there can be scarcely any question of opposition to „bourgeois“ art or of any „enlightening“ spirit on which the avant-garde principle of modern art is based, that contemporary art is content with quoting itself, has nothing more to say, that its current trends are „arbitrary“ or have at least become „confusing and unclear“ [53], all of these do not belie the post-modern paradigm but rather amount to a systematically constituted denial of the actual problem, namely that the, at least imagined, intrinsic value of art – whose social constitution has never been even remotely perceived in „post-modern“ discourse, which instead simply distinguishes between „good“ and „bad“ art – can only appear to be binding when its evaluation is guaranteed by a hegemonial configuration. But just this earlier hegemonial configuration is questioned by the contemporary „commercialization“ of art. The post-modern „pluralism“ in art is an indication of an „authority gap“ which opens the door for a reevaluation of values.

Market values and value markets

Transformations of the art field after „modernism“

If one regards the movements in the „art world“ in the last few decades and particularly in most recent times it first strikes the eye how much this world has itself become a „theme“ for discussion. The relationship between „art“ and „money“ permanently accompanies the discourse on the state of the field of art. The obvious inescapability of this theme speaks volumes. It not only demonstrates that according to the notions of the participants in the art scene we are to this day dealing with two *de jure* „antagonistic“ factors. The „inner“ demands made on the actors at the Art Basel, the gallerists, collectors and curators, provide clear proof of this. But it also points to changes which have *de facto* taken place, transformations whose logic these actors can only grasp with the categories of the antagonism from which an „economy of symbolic goods“ derives its right to existence. For all concerned the visible questioning of the boundaries between „art“ and „money“ follows laws which are increasingly subject to the logic of a „genuine“ market.

What has changed? If one took only the *structural* distortions into account, the scandal would not seem as threatening as it is sometime presented. However, the essential changes occur in a segment which is decisive in regard to its *significance*. The development of an open market for works of art affects only a tiny part of the field of art, but the effect of the market activities themselves is enormous. Structurally one only sees the removal of the segment for „high-priced" art from an exchange relationship which, until a few decades ago, had been socially highly exclusive, its removal to a market whose dynamics brought the processes of production, distribution and consumption in this „visible" world of art more strongly together than had hitherto been the case, to a market which necessarily determined the visibility of these processes. These are processes of *demystification* in a world whose conditions for existence depend on the mystification of its work.

It is just as understandable that these market activities can only develop within a constellation which transports economic, social and habitual changes. The revolutions in the relationships of politics and economy, capital and labor, finance economy and industrial economy which have asserted themselves in the last few decades have not only massively extended the possibilities for the expenditure of individual wealth on „culture" and at the same time massively reduced the possibilities for the expenditure of collective wealth on „culture". They have also increasingly taken possession of the collective ambitions whose satisfaction is promised by the petit bourgeois consumption of culture. Between the new market for art which is „extraordinary" in terms of monetary value, the degradation of the institutions which hitherto had been the sole authorities for its mediation and the huge surge in popular public interest in its exhibition there exists a relationship which makes manifest the entire chain of *expropriations* which from time immemorial had provided the necessary preconditions for the *appropriation* of art.

The *staging* of a „spectacle" accompanying the acquisition of „art" is for this reason both appearance and reality. The orientation of artistic production towards the market and the mercantile strategies of its dissemination have always existed. New is the fact that the social and institutional exclusiveness of the consecration of „genuine" art is beginning to erode and is being opened up for a thoroughly rationalized trade. Like a self-fulfilling prophecy the appearance attempts to retain this exclusiveness, to present itself as the source of artistic consecration, whereas the reality does not speak of this attempt as such, but of the *rationalization* of the attempt to occupy a market monopoly position. This is the true scandal of the contemporary trade in art – that, with the erosion of the former monopoly over its evaluation, a „commodity" whose claim to timeless validity veils its character as a commodity is becoming subject to attributions of value which do not defer to the „old" criteria, but attempt to assert their own logic for the ratification of art. The monopolization effects of this development can be gathered from the data of the market, but the outcome of the conflict cannot be construed in this way. However, the „aura" of the work of art is not today dying on account of artistic attempts to destroy it, but because of the dissolution of the foundations for its evaluation, which a social and institutional configuration had guaranteed for an entire century.

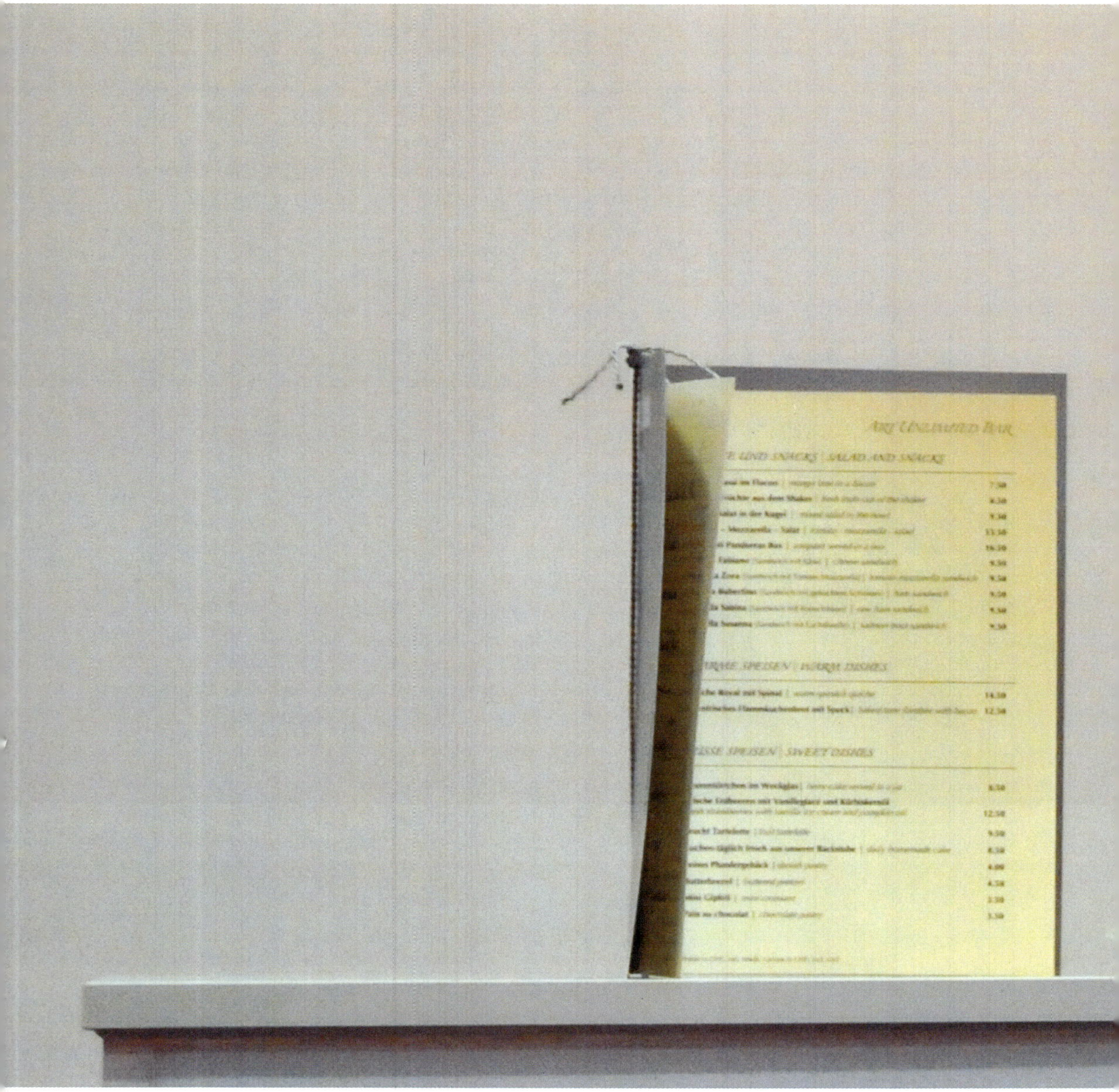
ART UNLIMITED BAR
SALAD AND SNACKS
SWEET DISHES

8 When Art meets Money

An attempt to take stock

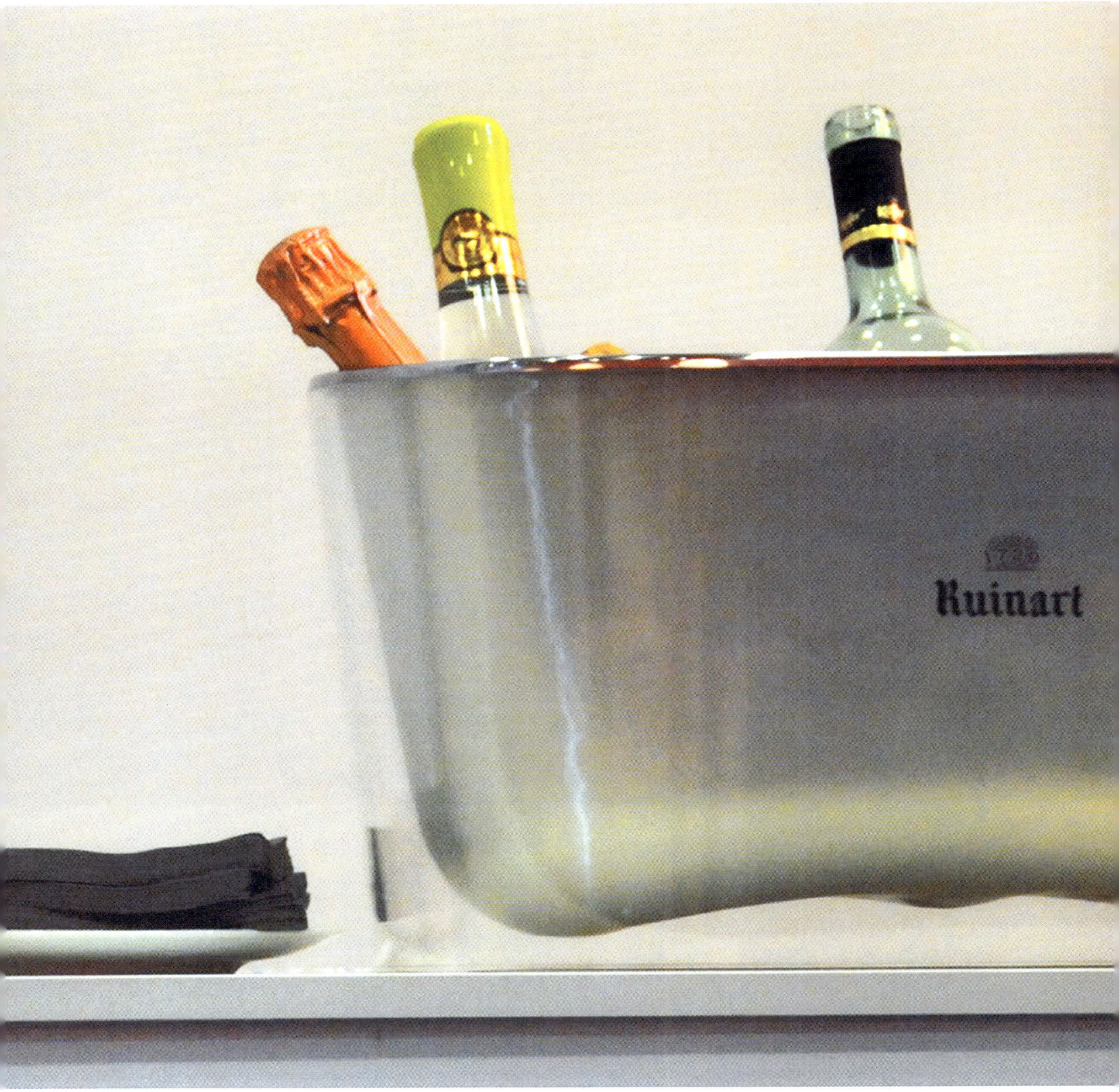

What makes a work of art a work of art and not a mundane thing or a simple utensil? What makes an artist an artist, as opposed to a craftsman or a Sunday painter? What makes a urinal or a bottle rack that is exhibited in a museum into a work of art? In order to explain this sort of miracle of transubstantiation which is the source of the work of art's existence one must replace the ontological question with the historical question of the genesis of the universe in which the value of the work of art is ceaselessly produced and reproduced.

PIERRE BOURDIEU, The Rules of Art

The world of art is quite obviously different from that of a hundred, or even fifty years ago, not only in regard to its visibility in the public sphere but also to its concrete appearance, its forms of work, its exchange processes and its exploitation cycles – quite apart from the enormous diversity of its visual language „positions". But has the result been a change in the rules of art, in the laws of the market of symbolic goods and its „reversed" economy, in the criteria for the recognition of a „work", in the autonomy of the art field in regard to establishing its own value? Are we witnesses of a fundamental change of regime or are we rather seeing contemporary metamorphoses of a historical inheritance, whose anatomy, whose construction plan remains largely untouched by these changes?

At all events it seems as if these indubitable changes in the „art world" have at least had the effect of bringing the structural ambivalences of this denied economy up to date with a hitherto unknown urgency. For just this reason it makes sense to take a closer look at the concrete context in one of the decisive locations for encounters between „art" and „money" in which the practice and the ideology of the field finds complete expression. And, indeed, at the Art Basel, above all, one can experience the tremendous „inner" tension, the need and the compulsion to justify a practice which no longer corresponds to the ideology. One encounters defiance and apology, shame and revulsion, euphemism and denunciation, frequently meets highly unsettled actors who thematize no less than a turn of the tide, the signs of the dissolution of a classical configuration; one is confronted with phenomena quite similar to those which bring about the decline of a traditional society caught in the meshes of modern capitalism. Practical constraints and social norms fall apart and the unquestioned fabric of an entire life-world disintegrates.

What is the core of this many-voiced message and what conclusions can be drawn from it? It is clear that the *realities* of this state of upheaval are not only differently perceived depending on the „position" of the actor in the art field in each particular case. The articulation of individual *confessions of faith* is also part of a collective failure to recognize the *overall* logic of the field and leads to a systematic „deformation" of these realities, which can be avoided when the systematic structure of precisely this *relationship* is understood. What then is its real core; what is the logic behind the transformation of the art field?

The norms and the rules
Signs of disintegration in a world of „values“

What we have seen at the Art Basel differs, first of all, from all the experiences one can make during a „typical“ walk around a museum or visit to a gallery. The jostling crowds, the hot dog and drink stands, call to mind the atmosphere at a funfair – even morphologically its character as a fair can scarcely be denied. But although the specific separation of the visitors into the potential buyers on the „intimate“ days and the streaming masses of the ordinary „public“ on the other days clearly reveals commercial features of a *structural* kind, and not the „disinterested“ practice of exhibitions „for all“ as in museums, an „added value“ is entered into the books here which can only be realized through a particular good, namely the immaterial, the symbolic value of art. The customers are „art lovers“, the visitors are „interested in“ art.

How deeply this *normative logic* determines the self-understanding and the actions of the participants even in the most obviously commercial aspects of an art fair can be clearly seen here. Between the permanently euphemistic and the occasionally scandalized reactions to the „goings on“ at the fair, a very special topography of „values“ comes to the fore at the Art Basel, in this „exclusive“ segment of the art world, deriving from that closeness to or distance from the „world“ with which the „law“ of the art field is historically and inseparably linked. The management of the fair actively disguises its market physiognomy and commodity character by presenting „curated“ galleries, museum-like tours, intellectual „discussions“ and regular pedagogical „frameworks“ for the „show“ or „young“ art in the *Art Statements*. All of this is designed to cloak the sale of marketable goods in the „inner“ core of the fair, while even there a „tour through a hundred years of art history“ is advertised.

The gallerists for their part occasionally shamefacedly concede the market character of the fair, undertake complicated denials of the economic aspect of their „business“ and strictly separate the „value“ of the works of art from their commercial exploitation. They repeatedly emphasize in a euphemistic way the „personal“ relationship with their clients, their understanding of art and the „quality“ of the buyer as a „collector“, which must correspond to the quality of the work of art. A mediation of art occurs whose „pedagogical“ overtones virtually ensure the disappearance of all the financial aspects. Then there are the customers who do not wish to be seen as such, buyers as „lovers“ with a passion, with an extraordinary „devotion“ to art.

They are the final goal of this chain of exploitation, which is practically denied here, alone by the fact that the „genuine“ and the „good“ collectors submit very reluctantly to what goes on at the fair, often do not even attend it personally and thus demonstrate their distance to the „market“. And finally we have the „art-interested“ visitors, who are only tolerated by the actual actors in the market as the „public“, as the visible authentication of the „extraordinary“ nature of what is on offer. But they too are equipped with cultural pretentions which shift the market character of the event into the background in spite of the high ticket prices which serve to confirm it. These are simply veiled as equivalents to an assumed „higher“ value of the goods on display. And even though many of the works which the „insiders“ regard as highly marketable must remain unintelligible to the „average public“, they nonetheless enjoy „impressive“ experiences and find their participation in the „aura“ of the event worthwhile – they are in a mental state which only the alchemy of the phenomenon of art can create.

That all of these normative justifications are and can only be „genuine" to a certain degree; that they are „stories" which must pay respect to the ideology of the art field, while behind the scenes a radically economic mechanism keeps the front stage moving; that the practices of the galleries are as a matter of course tailored to achieve the *sale* of art; that their potential clientele primarily desires to *buy* art; that the public's enjoyment of art is not least the enjoyment of a spectacle one wishes to participate in: all of this by no means damages that ideology. The ideal image of the „art world" which shines through everywhere at the fair is not only subjected to a critical test by an unbiased gaze but at the same time also functions in regard to the concrete relationships to the marketing aspect of the event as a criterion for the attribution of value. And it thus generates a *normative topography* even on the „top floor" of the art field, which corresponds to the positions taken up by the actors in this field, to their location within a space which is decisively determined by the overlapping antagonisms of „art" against „world" and „new" against „old". It speaks volumes that at the fair the „established" and hence marketable „exhibits" are crowded together in a separate space and that the price differential between the „center" and the „periphery" is extreme. This separation reflects very precisely the differing relationships to the world and the degree of consecration of the works. This structure finds eloquent expression in its normative nuances: the closer one comes to the economic, topographic and iconographic „margins" of the fair the more intensive the normative questioning of the market character of the event one is participating in becomes. A space of positions is revealed here whose normative self-understanding discloses the logic of the game as a whole, but it remains concealed from each of the actors involved. The „rules" of art, understood as *norms*, which are as valid here as they were fifty years ago, provide its „genetic" conscience [1].

Exactly this circumstance shows up the contemporary *practices* of the art world, which in the past were tightly subjected to these norms, in a highly ambivalent light. And this occurs with incomparable clarity where the closeness to the „world" takes on such strikingly concrete forms. In the field of the art fairs the Art Basel occupies a place which can claim an astounding legitimacy in regard to the goods on offer, but it reveals an unmistakable *normative deficiency* in comparison to „more dignified" fairs, because the role of „money" in its concretely perceivable manifestations is so strongly present everywhere. And as a fair it belongs to a sphere of the field of art which did not in fact exist half a century ago, could not exist, could not be allowed to exist; it occupies a space which first had to be created, a space for the more or less *open and public* marketing of art, a formerly inconceivable institution, which can never really deny its closeness to the world and, in its upper reaches, to „wealth" and „power". That in this constellation enormous dissonances must occur is both a sign of the change in the *practical rules and constraints* and a proof of the continued effectiveness of the *historical norms* of the art world.

At the Art Basel this change is rendered visible in a very vivid way, not only because of the omnipresent images of art and capital hand in hand, the huge letters advertising an international big bank in the exhibition hall, the continuous comings and goings of black limousines in front of the entrance, the collection of exoteric „signs" of the claim to social „exclusiveness" within this mirror of the social world, the wine and champagne stands, the Davidoff Lounge, the VIP sphere. It is not just this picture of a specific clientele which comes together on the days exclusively reserved for the rich and very rich customers, a picture which is, however, still even present on the visitors' days. What counts, above all, is the insight these manifestations give us into the dimensions of *calculation* behind such

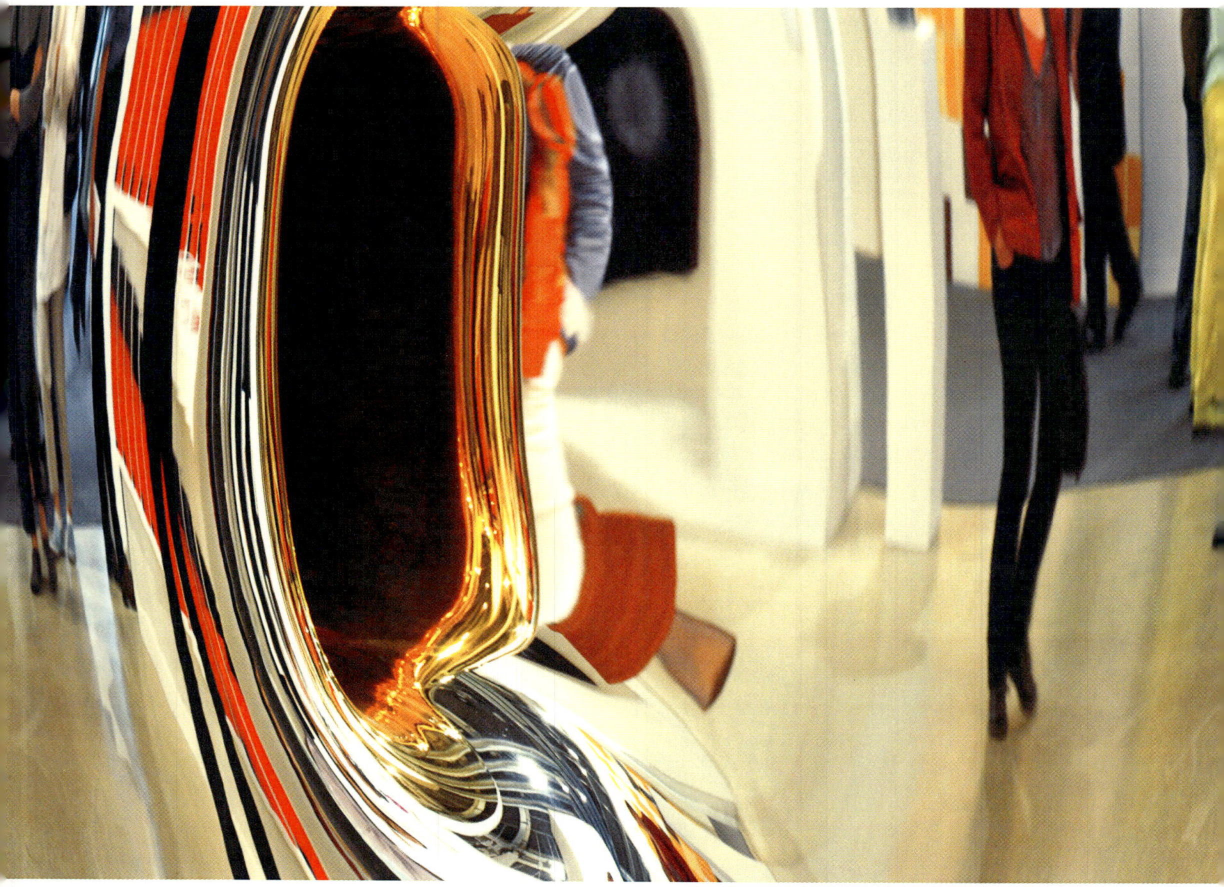

strategies – ranging from professional „marketing“ and „branding“ to the „personal“ invitations to art connoisseurs, art critics and art lovers, graded with painful precision according to social and economic importance, and from the rhetoric of „high quality meets strong sales“ to the compensatory placement of „young“ art in the peripheries of the fair. All of this, including all the scarcely perceptible logistic costs, the economic *rationalizations* with their calculation of debits and credits, which at the end of each „show“ turn out to be at least „strong“, the entire language of a „business to consumer fair“, „leading brand world-wide“, „covers the global market“, further strengthening of the position“, different „strategies for binding customers“: this entire arsenal of *mercantile techniques* is well suited to contradict the norms shared in practice by those who attend the fair.

And indeed these manifestations are a witness to a change in the regime of „art mediation“, at least in its „upper“ spheres. The important point is not that everything should be seen to be „bigger“ and „more expensive“ and, above all „more exclusive“. Decisive is rather the circumstance that all of these phenomena quite precisely bear witness to a *loss of exclusiveness,* of the exclusiveness of the museum which is not accessible to personal desires, of limited quantities and limited opportunities for acquisition, of the exclusiveness of the social circles which participate in the mediation of art, of the social and geographical space, and not least of the „other-worldly“ aura of the entire social tableau. In spite of all the assurances that the external manifestations of commercialization have left the core of what characterizes art untouched, the opening of the market and the widening of the circles entering what was formerly a genuinely exclusive constellation, the inroads of the commonplace, of a „this-worldliness“ widely felt to be a *vulgarization,* in the modern art world do in fact announce not so much the invalidation of the norms, but rather a substantial change, involving the looming *agony of a social figuration,* of its concrete „interpersonal“ commitments and obligations, its conventions, rankings, time-horizons, its intimacy and solidarity, its practicability and legitimacy. The dissonances arising from this accelerated falling apart of the norms and practices of the field of art can scarcely anywhere be so visibly grasped than at the scene of the Art Basel.

And as is always the case with such manifestations of upheaval in „traditional“ social universes, processes involving the distortion of class structures also play their part here. The fact that „Baselworld“, the fair for watches and jewelry, is assembling a strategic portfolio together with the Art Basel in a world-wide unique cooperation is certainly not only an expression of the tendency towards „commercialization“ in the art world described above but no less clearly of an extension and a regrouping of the „circles of clients“, which in turn do battle over the definition of the right to participate in this world. It is an expression of a world which grants symbolic credits that authenticate the social respectability of a life style. The *public display of luxury,* in which the fair itself consciously participates, reveals the economic power of the claimants to such participation, just as the sense of the „vulgarity“ of such attempts at usurpation reveals the normative force of inherited social capacities and the hierarchies of legitimacy in the appropriation of art, whereby the „correct“ forms of appropriation reflect and at the same time ratify the social standing. Beneath these conflicts in the circles of the ruling class a different drama of pretention takes place that does not involve millions on the bank accounts but millions of people who wish to touch the mantle of legitimate culture, a „mass public“ which has always been condemned to play the sad counterpart in this spectacle of social claims to power.

Class art and class struggle
The appropriation of art in a conflict of social pretensions

Why does art play such a visible role in the Western, in „our" contemporary society? If one ignores the increased importance attached to the „topic" in the media, whose parading of sales records and global personalities is an infallible sign of „vulgarization" in the art scene, and leaves aside the stubborn *disinterest* of „ordinary people" in its manifestations apart from these „sensations", all that is left is art as a central object for the appropriation of symbolic credit and a striving for social prestige. Art, the presence of pictures, was always a symbolization of the possibility of putting a collective existence itself in the picture, of decorating a life-style which can broadcast the practical, material and economic uselessness of these pictorial representations as an other-worldly sign of personal accomplishment. The modern period has placed this possibility in the hands of others, in the hands of the bourgeoisie, but the functions of the *appropriation* of art have scarcely changed. No matter how much the bourgeois in their passion for art see their inclinations as pure and purposeless, art fulfils a *distinctive,* a *performative* social purpose [2].

What we are experiencing today is a hitherto unknown increase in this aspect. Not only in the sense suggested by the superficial, the striking nature of the processes of appropriation, a reference to „superficiality" which, moreover, reinforces the norms of the field. We also see a change of the *phenotype,* which necessarily accompanies its normative scandalization. It points to a collapse of the social foundations of that old figuration in which the material appropriation of art had a socially exclusive character. The visible increase in the *importance* of this aspect for a normative evaluation of bourgeois appropriation, of the ways of appropriating art, first becomes intelligible when it is understood as an expression of a battle between factions of the bourgeois class for social legitimation.

The institutional opening of a genuine market for art is both an accompaniment to and a condition for the possibility of this battle for recognition. It is a possibility condition because it seems to open up communicative paths which had hitherto been more or less closed socially, economically and culturally, and at the same time it makes the *social event* of the exchange of money and art as such *public.* In the earlier constellations precisely this is objectionable; in the present constellation it is a precondition for the existence of the market. But even though the perceived self-presentation of the „rich and the beautiful" at the international art fairs rests not least on a „conservative" understanding of this self-staging – which wishes to see something „false" where what is „genuine" is simply „unfitting" and assesses the entire performance, the entire behavior on a scale of good taste – a new clientele nonetheless asserts its presence in a market which like scarcely any other can authenticate its claim to social presence. The visibility of the market participants in the „world of art" is here only a *signifier,* a „sign" of the visibility of these new class factions in the social world.

The opening of the market for art is an accompaniment to the social conflict because this opening would be inconceivable without the massive, general social upheavals which took place alongside the growing waves of prosperity since the end of the nineteenth century. The appearance of new classes of buyers in this market is the result of a fundamental *transformation of the relationships of power* between industrial and finance capital, capital and labor, politics and economy, which had shaped Fordism. It is the result of a free-market liberal reshaping of the Western welfare state, of an entire politico-economic configuration, whose dissolution opened up enormous opportunities for profit and questioned the entire earlier pattern of a slow, intergenerational, socially „vindicated", inter-related accumulation of economic and symbolic capital. And when these developments encountered the long-term effects of welfare state Fordism, the wide-spread prosperity of the petit bourgeoisie, the increased participation in education, the cultural pretention and participation – socio-historical phenomenon which played a decisive part in the popularization of the arts as a whole – a constellation arises in which the „suitability of art for the middle classes" prepared that stage for the strivings for prestige and the elitist pretentions of the economic and cultural climbers on which the public marketing of art could first be presented.

For this reason the contemporary conduct of the „rich and the beautiful" in the world of art tends to direct attention away from what is actually happening. They only operate in the entrance hall to these struggles; they are social „figures", emblems of the actual upheavals. Speculators, oligarchs, actors, models, these visible *personifications* of the ambition to participate in the world of art, conceal a logic according to which it is the *invisibility* of the ruling class which demonstrates its incomparable social position, and, conversely, the ostentatious combination of capital, art and „luxury", as it is clearly revealed in all the phases of the market activities, seems to render the claim of *new social groups* to participation deficient. In the contrast of „old" and „new" money, of heirs and upstarts, of discretion and ostentation, of cool connoisseurship and trendy superficiality, of reserve and the over-effusiveness of a non-conformism ossified in affected posing, or, from a different perspective, of saturated traditionalism and dynamic „modernity", an entire *habitus,* a *life-style* and the legitimacy of the different factions within the ruling class are subjected to re-evaluation and a field of positions within this „exclusive" market is outlined from which, once again, the tight dovetailing of the social and cultural principles governing the hierarchy of social status can be deduced. It is to these shifts within the „field of power" of the new dominant classes that the new market for art owes its ambivalent appearances.

And the conduct of the „mass public", both in the past and today, also confirms the socially distinctive character of the appropriation of art. What looks like a total capitulation of the culturally-minded public in the face of the power of the art world to define values seems so because the evidently mercantile phenomena of this „world-wide leading" fair, the blatant display of social exclusiveness and the fact that people can be observed here who have the hard cash to take possession of the art on exhibition for which one has paid an entrance fee, in order to admire, to marvel at or to reject it, this surrender can in the end only be interpreted as an attempt to *have a share* in symbolic goods which is doomed to failure. The massively extended social „circle of interested people" only injects a further contrast agent into the hierarchical conflicts of the dominant classes, which makes the antagonistic nuances of „vulgarity" and „appeal" more clearly recognizable. But the wider circle of art lovers remains a mere „public" which through its very existence devalues what it desires to appropriate.

That this „appeal", this attractive power of the art world, has in the meantime reached dimensions which none of the decisive actors would be willing to celebrate unthinkingly as a commendable love of art illuminates this insurmountable barrier between „exclusiveness" and „mass" even more succinctly and at the same time draws further boundary lines in the field of art. Where the museum formerly separated the believers from the unbelievers, the cultured from the „uncultured", but now only gathers together the rank and file as consumers in „blockbuster" exhibitions, the market for art, whose unattainable products seemingly promise participation in a cultural „community of contemporaries", also separates along different lines. And in its performance as a *market* it manifests the desirability of art sufficiently enough to transform a futile interest into a further confirmation of lack of social opportunity. And on the other side of the divide, in the „holy of holies" of the fair, in the VIP lounge protected by security guards, the representatives of banks, insurance companies and business enterprises enjoy the privilege of being served „genuine" luxury.

The central context of the phenomenon „art fair", and of the modern art market in general as a relationship of „art" and „money" is accordingly different from what a first glance at the sales records and the numbers of visitors, at the „wealth" and the „show" reveals and wishes to reveal. The *vulgarization* of the exchange between art and money which becomes visible there illustrates a tendency which is normatively highly charged but nonetheless gives every articulation of the still valid norms of the field the character of rumor mongering. This tendency can, however, only develop such normative tension because it is based upon a *real* tectonics, a drifting apart of the field, a „stretching effect" which the upheavals in the class structure bring about in a fundamentally changed social configuration. This is the root of all of the manifestations of this process which are subject to social value judgment. The appearance of new players in a game which formerly did not have to be one, not only of the personified „rich and beautiful" but also of institutional capital, global banks, insurances and business enterprises, the lining of the market with ostentatious luxury and pretended exclusiveness, the tendencies towards monopoly of artistic visibility patterns and exploitation structures, changes in museum landscapes and the nature of exhibitions, attractiveness for the masses and medialization: all of these make up *one* big context which translates the long-term shifts in the social relations of power in the Western industrial countries into a *segmentation and polarization* of its „art worlds".

Blurred boundaries, alienation, and disenchantment
Transformations of the art world in the „post-modern"

There can be no doubt that the regime of the art world has changed massively in the last few decades. The signs of change cannot be overlooked. But how can this change be interpreted? The phenomena it produces seem at first to be beyond dispute, regardless of how they are evaluated: the enormous increase in the importance of fairs and auctions; the blatant presence of „capital" in the art market; a „fair culture" with its celebrities; the deliberate „luxuriousness" of the self-presentation and the stylized character of the „events"; the astounding artistic careers made at the market; the acceleration of the „handling of goods" and the exponential increases in value; the thorough economic rationalization of this kind of „art mediation"; advertising strategies, estimates of turnover, scenarios of expansion, the observation of the market with its „facts" and „trends"; the building of private museums and aggressive patronage; the huge collections of enterprises, which are often lent out for „public" showing; the increase in institutional „sponsoring" accompanied by a corresponding depletion of the budgets of state collections, the changes in the form of their exhibitions, the „blockbusters" with public appeal and the resultant streams of visitors, the „shop" in the museum and the cafeteria alongside it; and finally the permanent attention of the media to the events in themselves.

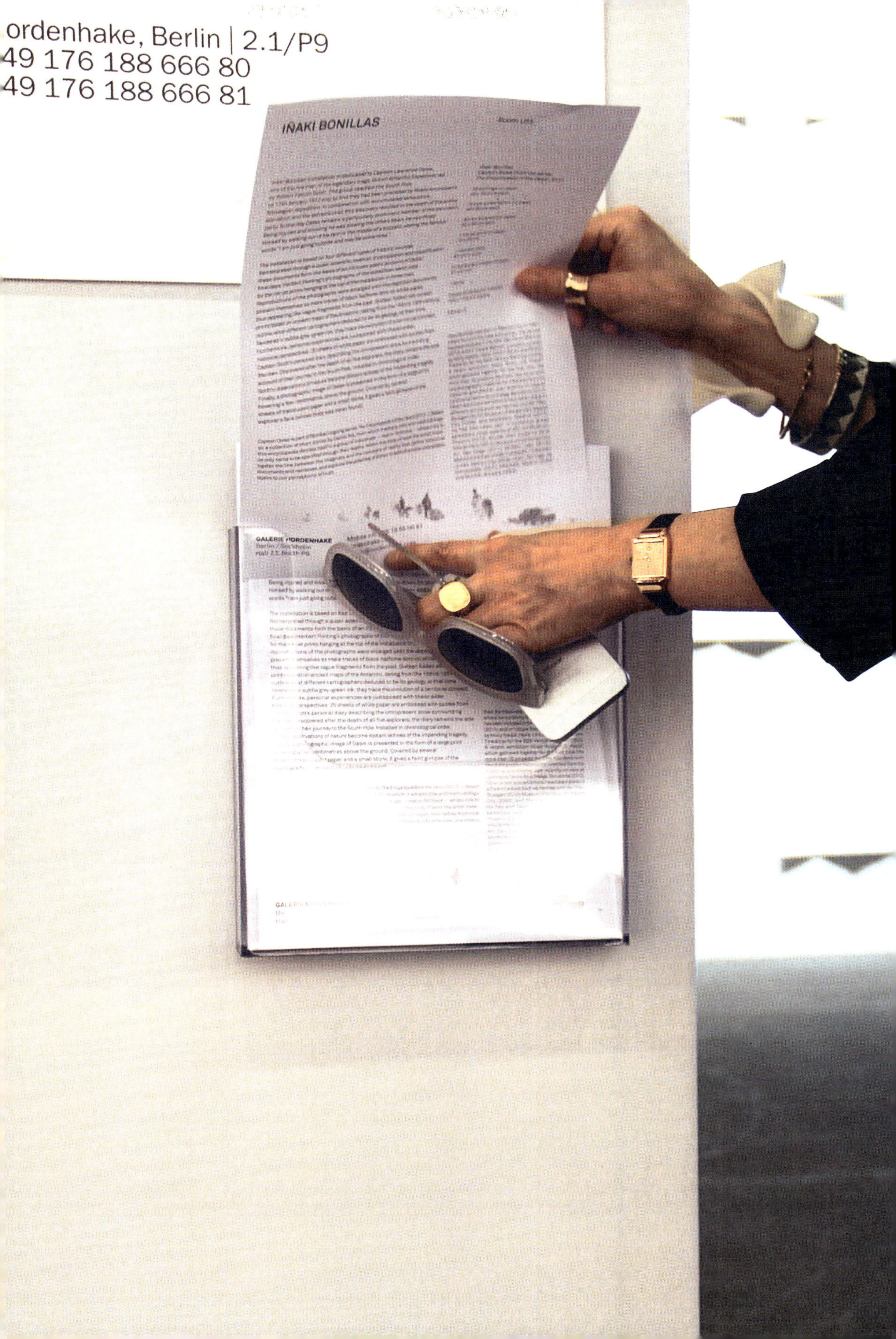
ordenhake, Berlin | 2.1/P9
49 176 188 666 80
49 176 188 666 81
IÑAKI BONILLAS
GALERIE NORDENHAKE
Berlin / Stockholm
Hall 2.1, Booth P9

On taking a closer look, however, one sees distortions under the surface whose logic only inadequately reflects these phenomena, which are at one and the same time felt to be scandalous but nonetheless worthy of spectacular reporting. The impression that above average increases in the „market value" of modern art can be observed, at least in the small segment of the art business in which the Art Basel is involved, is not mistaken, but less spectacular than one might at first assume. In October 1960 Picasso's *Femme Accroupie* of 1902 was sold by Sotheby's for 48,000 British pounds and the later work *Homme au Gant Rouge* of 1938 for 26,000 pounds, and in the same year the auction house reported revenues of 20 million dollars. Half a century later the revenues, adjusted for purchasing power, had increased tenfold. But if Ford Motors generates double the revenue of the entire global art market it is clear that the spectacular aspect of this development is not the economic significance of the market but the immeasurable growth in value of a market which hitherto was not allowed to reveal its economic side. Just here new dimensions have opened up. The art market has been booming with few interruptions for over twenty years, and particularly in the last decade it has catapulted sky high. Individual works pass into private hands for sums which no one would have been even remotely willing to pay fifty years ago, even if the financial means were available. And the works of „living artists" sell for prices which tend to render the formerly typical, long chains of value creation in the market inoperable [3].

Nonetheless these phenomena are only „place holders" for more fundamental distortions in the field of art. The financially significant but overall tiny segment of the art market in which they can be observed tells more than all the stories that are circulated. For the monetary side is by no means so decisive. Other things are spectacular in this context. In the art market the aftershocks of a revolution in the Western industrial nations can be traced, of *structural shifts in power* in the course of the transformation of the welfare state by the free-market liberal economy, which have rung in a new era. A decades-long policy of austerity as a result of which „public „art was more and more deprived of the means to play a decisive role in the „private" art market is only one link in the chain of its effects. The continuous loss in value of earned income, the mark of the new relationship of power between the market and the state, the sign of an economy whose increasingly alien face can only be shown in the *Daily Mirror* as a spectacle, as the sale of a mere „picture" for an inconceivable amount of money, is a completely different link in the chain, but this too reports on a loss of value, on the *losses in legitimation* of an entire historical configuration.

The result is a world of „finance", which can achieve hitherto inconceivable profits, wash away the historical dirt of industrial production and demonstrate its new-found power in and on that image which experiences its universally conceived publicness above all as an act of arbitrary appropriation. The exorbitantly expanded opportunities for the private accumulation of wealth in such a constellation, and the accompanying strivings for prestige in the field of art, only lend a concrete face to a development which, as the growing possibility of the privatization of the universal, describes a new regime in the distribution of collective value creation.

The coincidence of these shifts in power with the developments on the art market is less evident than the role of pure „money" in this game might have us believe. The fact that the dimensions of the *monetary* significance of art within the range of goods offered by contemporary society are rendered so *visible,* that a modern „hype" can emerge in this formerly so exclusive environment, that a market *can and should become visible* for goods claimed to be „inalienable", all of these developments indicate losses in significance which, entirely in accordance with the logic of the field, are diametrically dependent on one another. On the one hand the spectacle reported on in the media attempts to fabricate an importance which for this reason alone can be readily recognized as a *cliché,* which presents the social struggle for recognition as a *stage* on which naked interests, „worldly" investments can no longer be denied, which involves a loss of the symbolic credit the struggle is all about.

And on the other hand the factual importance of those instances disappears, which once regulated the distribution of symbolic credit, whose normative *criteria,* whose „conscience", however, continues to provide the universe of modern art even today with its gravitational forces. The fact that the Art Basel „celebrates" its „44th anniversary" with a new book, but at the same time regards a kind of „infusion" as necessary, which will bring „young" art more clearly into the foreground, reveals the total ambivalence of a market which should not be one. And the exhibition presented by the „venerable" Fondation Beyeler of Jeff Koons, whose *Balloon Dog* was acquired as „one of the most recognizable images in today's canon of art history" and later sold at Christie for 58 million dollars, indicates how porous the borders have become between the market and a canon which can scarcely ignore the factual significance of the market any longer.

This is the constellation we are confronted by today, involving a new definition of the relationship between „limited" and „large-scale" production, the *drifting apart* of the artistic field, the polarization of two worlds, phenomena which are at one and the same time indicative of *alienation* and the *dissolution of boundaries.* On the one hand we have a market which, while tending to avoid exclusively „personal" and socially highly selective preconditions of exchange, is not only clearly recognizable as such and thus establishes a *practice alien* to the formerly valid norms of the field, but also provides a social opening for a new clientele which had hitherto been inadequately supplied with symbolic credit. As a result it deepens the alienation and the antagonism between two milieus by bringing two different kinds of *habitus* on to one and the same stage. And all of the dissonances which take on concrete, tangible form for the first time on this stage serve to reinforce the normative contradiction between „art" and „money" which the non-public exchange with its reciprocal acknowledgment of social legitimation and artistic significance in the realization of social relationships could conceal.

It is a market which is perceived by all the participants in it as a „foreign body" in the field of art because it questions the existing boundaries of the previous configuration, the „guild character" of its „personal" connections and affiliations, the limits of decorum between discretion and ostentation, between „art" and „luxury". It is a market which dissolves the old time structures, the earlier spans of time between the artistic claim to symbolic credit and its complete realization in the museum; it is a market which seems capable, with increasing frequency, of generating symbolic „meaning" by economic means, which confronts the interpretational sovereignty of *public* institutions over the canonization of art with a regime of *private* accreditation, with „lobbyists" on the boards of directors of museums, with „corporate collections", „collectors' museums", retrospectives of the works of millionaires by billionaires. It is a market which supplies this kind of „large-scale production" as if it were an opera, not in a purchasable form, but as being *representative* of the „many", a production whose financial, personal and practical *costs* usurp the meaning of the work of art, whose processes of production increasingly resemble „manufacturing" procedures. It is, ultimately, a market so clearly characterized by *business management* that the former „aura" of art only comes across as an ironic claim, as a brand which calls for management.

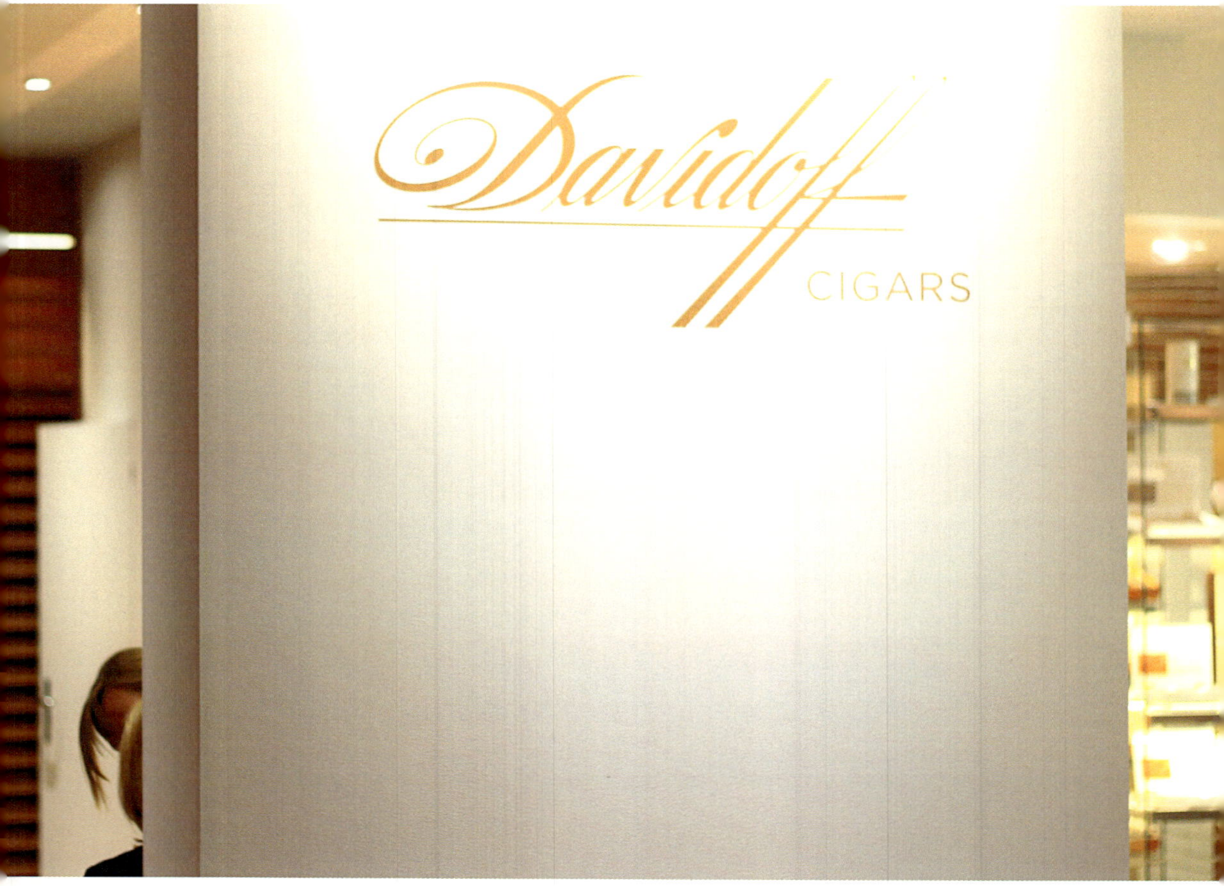
Davidoff
CIGARS

And this dialectic of the structural and practical dissolution of the boundaries of a histrical formation and of the normative and affective alienation of its participants, a social complex which must scandalize the erosion of the practices all the more clearly as a erosion of norms, and can only treat the clichéd form of modern art as a cliché of its own, this dialectic stretches, on the other hand, far into the area of cultural conflicts, the field of „limited" cultural production [4]. This field reveals a line of rapid development similar to that of the market, unfolding an enormous dynamics of reflexivity on the relationship of „art" and „world" whose „genetically" determined questioning of the traditional possibilities for artistic expression increasingly leads it to pass beyond the earlier boundaries of its formal reflexivity and even to explore the internal relationships of the „art world" in an artistic form. One end of the spectrum leads to commercialization, the other to intellectualization [5]. It is a field which can renew itself again and again in these positions, can establish the legitimate claim to be art „as such" in a moment of distancing which wishes to overcome the relationship between economic and symbolic exploitation in art at a formal level, which indulges in styles ranging from pop art and its iconography of the „ordinary" and minimalism to arte povera and „ugly" art, to strategies of antimuseal overformatting, varieties of concept art, video works, installations, to ephemeral performances consciously perceived as being unmarketable, and finally to the semantics of „institutional critique" art.

The field follows the compelling artistic logic of overbidding the existing art world by „underbidding" the works admitted to its canon. But the market catches up with this field in increasingly shorter periods of time, using its iconographic intuition to detach these innovations from their „critical" intertextual context, pocketing their symbolic credit and at the same time sorting them according to their „marketability", placing the „representative" offshoots of pop art alongside the canonical works of the postwar modern period in exhibition halls and auction houses, Rothko alongside Warhol, Richter alongside Bacon, Sherman alongside Goldin, works whose visual attraction can get by without their original points of reference. And it leaves the „unwieldy" concept arts to the museums together with innumerable „positions" of „worldly" insignificance which are indeed „beneath" the level of these forms of representation. The striking visual diversity of contemporary art is not so much the result of specific forms of development as of a genuine *deformalization,* which enables the market to set up at precisely this point its own norms and it own canonization strategies [6].

This *drifting* of the field literally „tears apart" the innovative potentials in the sphere of „limited" production, alienates its potentially most marketable products from their autochtonous origins, to which they owe their symbolic credit, and at the same time permits the norms of the field to migrate to „political" positions whose claim to legitimacy lies outside the modern transfiguration of artistic creation „as such". This is confirmed by Arthur Danto, who, in his *Transfiguration of the Commonplace* allows art to emigrate to philosophy. And the activist variations are, in turn, faced with the phenomenon of dissolving boundaries, with the dictates demanding the creation of a „public", which here, as at the other end of the art world, emphasizes the „superficial" – between Banksy, Pussy Riot and the even more transitory manifestations of „artivism" a zone of formal objection no longer exists; all that remains are longitudes of attention. The structures of the production, consumption, reception and „relevance" of art are drifting more and more widely apart.

Metamorphoses of art

A provisional outlook

Is there another truth in art than the one art itself seems to relate? For the aesthetic gaze the question is inadmissible. It only knows feelings which make this truth „accessible". But if it is openly expressed, what remains in the end behind the confessions of feeling, the awesome and exhilarating experience of art is personal value judgments, pure normativity without any claims to justification apart from the aesthetic gaze itself [7]. It is evident that this kind of „proof" must be dissatisfying from the point of view of every rational and not only social-scientific understanding. The philosophical aesthetics of the modern period has repeatedly tried to find categorical answers to this question, a „conceptual solution" of the problem at increasingly high levels of abstraction [8]. But what if all of these attempts fail to reach the core of the problem because they ignore the reality of this „pure" gaze, its conditions of possibility and the preconditions for its existence and the concrete significance it possesses for an „ascertainable" truth of art?

But even although a growing „relation to reality" has enriched the discourse in art theory since Arthur Danto and Howard Becker with the knowledge that in the *art world* and among its thousands and thousands of protagonists, its numerous institutions and „networks", we are dealing with constellations which are quite decisive for the „value" of art, with a context which at least „frames" the „inner" truth of the works [9], the question of the criteria for the judgment of such a truth still remains open – that is to say where arbitrariness ends and value begins. For this logic behind the attribution of value is unintelligible if it is not conceived of as such, as a fundamentally normative phenomenon. This same normativity is already inscribed in the „disinterested" appreciation of art formulated by Kant. And 150 years later it is expressed in a scarcely different way by Adorno – here works of art are „plenipotentiaries of things that are no longer distorted by exchange" [10]. The norms and rules of the art world follow a semantics of their own, a claim to the realization of universality divested of its origins, which wishes to leave behind it the arbitrary and concrete in the canvas and colors just as the religious vision ignores the material nature of the objects of its devotion.

But how can the contemporary developments in art and the relationship between „art" and „money" be described without resorting to a repetition of the almost inevitable stereotypes – and what opportunities do they offer for the future of the artistic field? If one believes the authoritative voices of philosophical aesthetics, art history and art criticism, we are in the middle of an „end-time" of modern art, or already beyond its end in a „post-modern" period which has not only unhinged the institutional structure of the art world, not only leveled out its special cultural status, but has also ceased to deliver valid criteria for the *evaluation* of art. In fact, however, all of these stories about the end of a story, these announcements of a „prophecy of doom" in the art field, are only a reflex of *real breaks,* of structural upheavals and changed practices and, consequently of an unpunished *violation of norms.* These eschatologies speak of an *anomy* which accompanies all the manifestations of a dissolution of fixed social configurations, and, conversely, of a *deliberate* violation of the „rules", whose institutionalization of modern art first guaranteed its authenticity. This ethical reflex shows, above all, that with the collapse of the foundations of the „old political economy" the coordinates of its symbolic economy have also disintegrated. But how is it possible to describe these changes not from the perspective of this symbolic economy but in terms of their *relationship* with one another?

Perhaps it makes sense, first of all, to take the *dimensions* of these developments into account. At first sight we are talking about an enormous upheaval in the relationship between the art field and the art market, about incredible occurrences. The breathtaking „monetary" dimensions, the contemporary treatment of art as a „commodity", the enormous increases in the price of painted canvasses, only describe the scandalous *phenotype* of this upheaval. For in fact we are not only dealing with a „branch" of the market which in *economic* terms is very modest in comparison with other „markets" but also, in the final analysis, with a very small segment of the contemporary art market. But it is one which reveals those two characteristics which bear witness to the massiveness of the break. It generates the greater part of its entire profits through evident practices of monopolization and, not least for this reason, it first makes a genuine *market* for art visible. Accordingly, the systematic scandalization of the economic side of this process is only an indication of *structural* breaks which are sweepingly suspected of having changed the *genotype* of the art field in an essential manner.

What is the nature of these structural upheavals? Even when we restrict our attention to the institutional aspect the change is unmistakable. The *relationships of power* between the „primary market" of the galleries and the market which capitalizes its products, the fairs and the auctions, have shifted radically. And even the boundaries between this now visible capitalization market and the increasingly visible institutions of public consecration, between the market and the museum, have become porous on account of the growing economic unbalance. The professionalization of the material presence of the market in the workshops of artistic production and its presence at the symbolic „acceptance" of the product by the museum, an increasingly powerless patriarch, is an unmistakable sign of this porosity. In this respect the institutional structure of the art field and its entire relationship to the „world" has doubtlessly changed [11].

But, basically, all of this is only a practical consequence of a more fundamental transformation. One of its preconditions is certainly of a *morphological* kind. According to a widely dispersed argument the rise of the middle classes and its growing cultural pretentions is associated with a *popularization* of the manifestations of high culture, which is paradigmatically expressed in pop art and its „transfiguration of the commonplace", in the dissolution of the artistic canon under the pressure of the preferences of a consumer society without any valid criteria and in an equalizing „culture industry". If we examine the structural core of this argument we find that educational expansion in the Western industrial nations has undoubtedly contributed to the creation of a *public* in the first place, of a *public sphere* without which a market cannot survive, as its commodities have a particular need of public acceptance – even when the question as to what effect this *public impact* has on the genome of the „art world" is still a long way from being answered. [12].

But the growing market for art only sees this new public in the role of a bystander. The decisive preconditions for the transformation of the relationship between art and the „world" are to be found elsewhere, in the massive general social upheavals which began towards the end of the twentieth century, in the fundamental *transformation of the political economy* and the free-market liberal reconstruction of the Western „welfare state". Neither the class conflicts for which the market for symbolic goods, the art market, provided an open stage and a showplace for the exchange of hitherto inconceivable economic profits for symbolic returns, nor the relative loss of importance of the state guaranteed institutions of public consecration are conceivable without these developments.

The dissolution of the earlier political economy is accompanied by the dissolution of the old „political economy" of art.

And it is this *structural* break which questions the existence of an entire social configuration which before not only regulated the „mediation" of art, its „discovery", its „support", but also its symbolic and economic exchange value. The scandalization of the manifestations of a „market" for art only becomes truly understandable when one takes into account the tight *factual* interweaving of the anti-economic norms of a symbolic economy with a „market" which could deny its own existence because its „clientele" with all the accoutrements of social *ancienneté* had divested itself of those properties which now appear to be all the more vulgar. The social uses of art, the social practices of its *utilization,* the entire social concealment of *relationships of power,* which was consciously questioned by modern art in its search for legitimacy, now gives way to a market which itself vainly endeavors to rescue the charismatic effects of this old social configuration with a pure form of „promotion" in which the public once again only occurs as part of the decor.

The internal dynamics of this market is so telling that there is scarcely any need for detailed examples illustrating the spectacular break which has occurred between the *norms* of the art field and the *practices involved in the appropriation* of its products. We see here a form of the socialization of the market with all the manifestations that go with it: monetary exchange, open competition, increasing monopolization, rationalization of management, quite simply a *business* in the literal sense of the word, a form of *trading* that cannot exist without *advertising.* The resultant dissonances reverberate in the art field; their structural causes subject the field to a severe test, set a process of polarization in motion, a drifting apart which, on the one hand, makes the color of money visible in every marketable „position", whereas, on the other hand, „positions" confidently declared to be „critical" only provide the normative nuances of the background to this constellation This marks the end of a configuration which was in a position to guarantee the value of modern art at a *personal* level through its social relationships and *universally* through the *arbitrary* use of its social power.

But what does the end of this story look like? Is one at least ready to tentatively admit the possibility that the validity criteria of art, that the standards for its evaluation, can never be other than „arbitrary", cannot be derived from the work alone, but require, over and beyond the indispensable art-historical contextualization of their manifestations, a recognized, socially legitimated, established constellation for their *implementation?* Then the image of „post-modern" art, whose most unsettling feature seems to be that it marks the end of a binding „canon", can be relativized in more than one respect. The *formal explosion* of modern art, dictated by the genuine laws of the field and the compulsion to outbid the established forms of art, must necessarily be described as „deformalization" because a canon can scarcely be applied to it at the *iconographic* level. But this reveals only half the truth, or better a characteristically „upside-down" truth, a truth involving the belief that the iconographic „content" of modern art provides the basis for the criteria of evaluation – and not the more or less „adequate" assessment of its relational significance, whose legitimacy has been *imposed* from „outside". The thoroughly flexible relationship between artistic *intention* and its perception as such, a relationship revealing a *systematic discrepancy* in the „classical" constellation which could only be overcome through a long and gradual *process of acknowledgment,* is certainly not completely arbitrary. To assert this would mean denying a logic of the

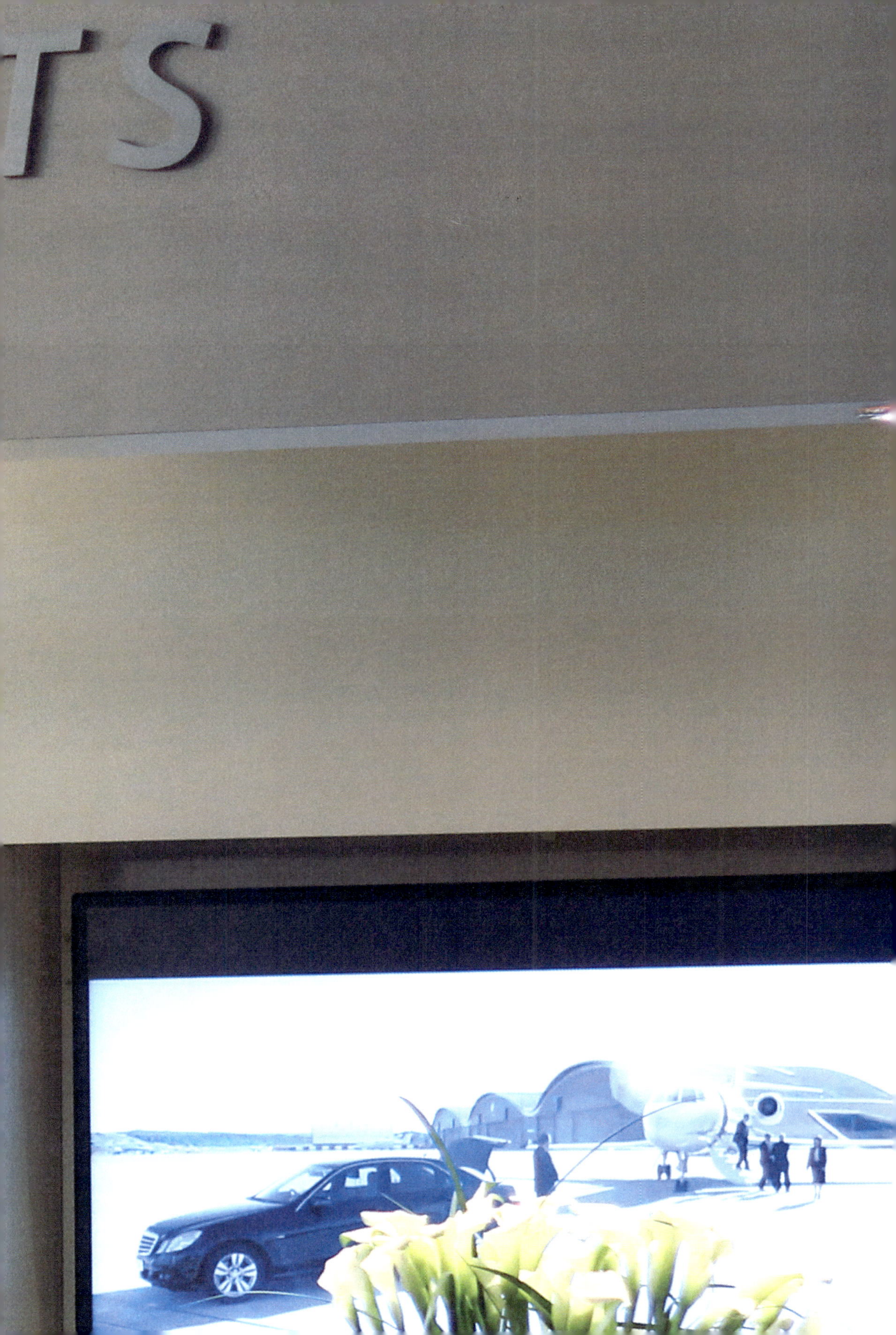
TS

relationality of artistic semantics which is to some extent *recognizable.* But the ultimate hierarchization of the *significance* of a „position" represented within this relational structure is at least just as dependent on the factual *processes of its canonization* as on its „inner", its relational content [13].

To this extent the *explosion of forms* impelled by the logic of the field, which is made responsible for the vanishing significance of the canon and of valid criteria for canonization, is not only indicative of the continuance of an essentialistically colored understanding of art but also of an *implosion of the social forms of its canonization,* of a configuration which guaranteed the implementation of the criteria. Furthermore, these criteria are always dependent on the state of the conflict over their legitimacy, on the state of virulent *conflicts over the canon,* which no longer take place between the artists and the prince, the artist and the museum, but between the artist and the *art market.* The contemporary confusion about the standards for „genuine" art is not primarily due to the enormous semantic diversity of post-modern art, but to the disappearance of „intrinsic", relational standards. They have been replaced by a volatile lack of standards, which permits the „real" market with its own real logic and institutional and social structures to enter into competition with the old forms of the canonization of artistic relevance.

It is as yet not possible to estimate how these conflicts will end. But a clear indication of the future structuring of this context can be seen in the migration of *art criticism,* which was always a key figure in the old constellation, into a sphere in which the autonomous energies of artistic production are most likely to be found – into the sphere of artistic reflexivity about the art world. For this kind of *ethnocentrism* speaks of the end of modernism in art, the end of its cult of genius, the end of „naivety" in contemporary art, which concludes from the exponential growth of the relationality and reflexivity of its „positions" that the evaluation of art is only a matter of discursive, of philosophical understanding. This bears witness, above all, to that *drifting apart* of the art field, whose continuance has left the potential protagonists in the debate on the implementation of a future canon with only one option, the cultivation of the appearance of having something to say in the „artist talks" of the „salons" of an art fair.

This further restriction of the field of limited production to purely *semantic* relationships reveals an intellectualist art criticism proclaiming the end of the avant-gardes, which imagines it is in harmony with the avant-gardes of an intellectualist art who are desperately and hopelessly attempting to overcome the spell of belief and to dissolve the magic of the field. This development, with its typically reversed structures of symbolic and canonical hierarchies, not only repeats the structures which were decisive at the beginning of modernism but accentuates them just as strongly as the loss of significance of the formerly decisive institutions of artistic consecration. The field determines its coordinates anew, but the logic of its relationships remains as modern as it was before [14].

The fact that the progressive dissolution of the old „political economy" of art, of foundations anchored in a specific social configuration, can only be perceived as a departure from the canon and from the possibility of canonizing contemporary art at all reveals the unbroken naivety of a perspective characterized by its imprisonment in the game which is being played. The assumption that the existence of a canon depends on certain properties of artistic production in which a „genuine" value is made noticeable is, according to the verdict of the „transfiguration of the commonplace" in modern art, a matter of *belief,* as is the attempt to unhinge the functional laws of art with the means of art. The „value" of modern art *was and is always* the result of a process of transfiguration, an essential precondition for the ability of the art field to survive, the existential basis of a magic on which the entire field and all its participants permanently work and must work. One aspect of this work is the self-empowerment of an intellectual critique which asserts the migration of the validity criteria of art into „discourse“ like the attempt to achieve a „deconstruction“ of the game by reproducing Duchamp‘s urinal in highly polished bronze. Arthur Danto‘s *Transfiguration of the Commonplace* became a classic work of aesthetic eschatology, without discourse ever being in a position to escape the weighty „meaningfulness“ of art, and Sherrie Levine‘s *Fountain*, exhibited among other places in Philadelphia, San Diego, Zurich, Geneva and the venerable Whitney in New York was sold at Christie‘s in 2012 for almost a million dollars. The canonization of the critique of the canon is in full swing, but the *transfigurative context* which lies behind it is ultimately not understood.

What then does the end of the story look like? Everything suggests that with the entrance of the open market into the art world a stage has been reached in which the comparatively still self-sufficient fetishization of the art of the „old“ configuration is indeed coming to an end. When even the anti-museal impulses of performance art nowadays give rise to the question, whether, apart from the artistic *intention* and the institutional context willingly provided by museums, there is any qualitative difference between Marina Abramović‘s marathon *The Artist is Present* and other kinds of human peak performance, then the work of art as a concretely *acquirable* fetish, as the un-disguised concretization of the *commodity character* of art as a fetish is in the meantime omnipresent. The growing loss of significance which thus arises endeavors to stop a thoroughly rationalized enterprise and the regions of the field which claim to be „autonomous“ struggle against their own loss of significance with statements that are only heard in „talks“. The field of conflict is vibrant and its outcome will decide how the story which cannot have any final ending ends.

Postscript

In many respects the Art Basel is a *paradigm*. It unifies everything that is connected with this concept. It wishes to be a world view and is an example, wishes to be a model and is an image of an art world which seems to be out of joint. A fair for art which presents itself in the guise of a world-embracing art exhibition, a sales event which lays claim to a higher, generally binding validity, a „happening" which engenders enthusiasm and contradiction. In view of the unspoken rule that „art" and „money" should have nothing to do with one another, such a mixture provides the stuff for many stories in this „art world". But with them it also brings to light the dimensions of a dynamics which cannot be ignored. For the fair provides a model example of the way the moral basis of enthusiasm for art makes a stand against a superstructure constructed by economic practice with which this world has been in conflict since the end of the last century. But how can the decisive characteristic of changes which are so judgmentally charged be described.

Perhaps it is the relationship of „real" transformations and the quite personal perception of them in the field of art that provides the key to the understanding of these processes. For the purely *economic* significance of the art market has grown rapidly and for precisely this reason it presents the former „political economy" of the art world with enormous challenges – but the „fine arts" are not a global economic factor and are not in a position to be one. From an economic standpoint they are „merely" one factor in the *luxury goods industry.*

It is just this point that conditions the perspectivist distortion of a perception which believes it can trace the penetrating smell of money everywhere. The *visible* global art market, a tiny segment of the exchange processes which convert art into money, provokes contradiction because its own inherent contradictions come to light there in such an undisguised form. The precondition that in the overall economy art and money were always consonant with one another, and the „cultural good" art always required the possibility for a non-economic expenditure of means made available through „worldly" profits, now becomes more than clear. In every epoch, in every social, in every economic constellation these profits will always remain incomparably greater than what art is ever in a position to exploit.

This *visibility* also leads us to the core of the actual changes we are concerned with. The monopolistic character of this constellation, a handful of art fairs, two auction houses and scarcely more than fifty artists, whose trade takes place in one „segment" of that market which in the meantime claims to stand as an example for the field of art, the prices achieved and the massive influx of *all too conspicuous* money: all of this is only one aspect of the distortions involved. For the talk of a „commercialization" of the art trade „practically" hits the nail on the head, because the concept itself already carries the pejorative connotations which must always accompany alienation through the sale of „inalienable" values. The „modernist" constellation has hitherto known how to conceal systematically the fact that in the past art was also paid for with *material* means.

But the context in which this commercialization is now taking place is broader. The open trade with art, particularly in this segment, can be seen as the beginning of a radical *rationalization* of exchange procedures which until quite recently took place predominantly at a „personal" level, as an undisguised expression of market socialization which tends to oust precisely this *personal* dimension of the exchange. This touches upon the core of a symbolic economy, whose inviolability rested on its apparently „irrational" character. It invoked a magic which drew its power to create value from the mutual ennoblement of the exchange partners, from a *social configuration* whose exclusive character acted as a guarantee for the participants in the exchange and for the value of the exchanged goods.

In the meantime the role of this configuration is being questioned, exactly in that „segment" of the market that feeds upon an exorbitant glorification of its goods. There is nothing really objectionable about the trade with art as it takes place in thousands of small galleries and hundreds of small fairs and auctions; it is disparagingly looked down upon as a market which offers „mass products" for the petit bourgeois. But as soon as „museal" pretentions are formulated for the art offered for sale the „economic" dimensions of the exchange procedure become subject to scrutiny. However the total rationalization of the market for this kind of art, its business orientation, the sums of money involved, the sponsors, the staging of the „event", the undisguised *marketing,* this „commercialization" is only the most obvious sign of the agony of a social configuration which until quite recently claimed the right to dispense the sacraments which had the power to transform a urinal into an object of meditative devotion.

It's easy to grasp that this agony has quite profane causes, that it reflects the shifts in the *relationships of power* within the circle of the chosen few who dispensed the sacrament, between the „state" and the „economy" as a whole, between the various factions of the dominant classes in our society, and that it is also closely related to the market-liberal transformation of these relationships. In spite of all the perspectivist distortions the public accompaniment of these processes remains clear enough. And the veritable *splitting off* of a „market" for museal art would be equally intelligible if it were not associated with the question repeatedly asked in the „art world" on the relationship between the values attributed by the market and the „actual" value of artistic production.

This brings us, however, to uncertain territory, in which the art theoretical discourse increasingly believes that it must lose its orientations. Our „post-modern" world is said to have experienced a departure from a „pure" aesthetics, which clung to formalistic evaluation criteria until the fine arts were drowned in the „everyday" and the „popular" manifestations of art, the syncretism of visual expression and the deconstruction of the „work", the „creator" and the „aura". It could then no longer appeal to these criteria because contemporary art had lost both „form" and „boundaries" and the explosion of artistic forms had led to a state of *undecidability.* This diagnosis burdens the „inner" development of art events with a power to explain contemporary problems in the attribution of value to art which precisely here reverberates with the echoes of a „modernistic" conception of art.

This diagnosis is neither right nor wrong, but simply misses the „problem", namely the dependence of these evaluation criteria on legitimate instances for their definition, even though the reference to contemporary realities in this regard might sound relativist.

The fact that the authority of these instances is increasingly questioned is the truly postmodern factor in a constellation in which, on the one hand, the market wins more and more definitional power over the formerly „pure“ regions of the art field, whereas, on the other hand, its „autonomous“ areas believe they can flee into the sphere of social and political art, without any guarantee that they will not also be occupied by this market.

And in fact there does not seem to be much place available for „pure“ art, the modernist paradigm, in this „contemporary“ constellation. But this is a fallacy – and a question of time. When one observes how artistic positions which three decades ago were thoroughly „outspoken“, provocative, a challenge for a taste which had just been cultivated through other challenges, have found their way into a canon which merely registers these semantic messages and instead much more willingly emphasizes their *aesthetic* features, only one conclusion is possible: that „modernism“, regardless of the damage done to it by a market which attempts to appropriate its symbolic profits as economic profits, continues to function – as a magic collectively kept alive.

Acknowledgments

We wish to express our special thanks to various institutions and persons who have contributed to the realization of this book.

The Research Committee of the University of St. Gallen provided the initial financing for a pilot study which formed the basis for the preparation and presentation of a research application to the Swiss National Science Foundation.

The SNSF funded this project for a period of one year and then approved an extension for a further six months in view of the abundance of the collected data.

Tina Willner was an indispensable colleague in the field research in Basel and Miami and carried out a great part of the interviews.

Thomas Eberle participated intensively in the field research and provided much of the photographic material presented in the book. Throughout the project he was always a close listener and a critical discussion partner.

Finally our thanks are due to the management of the Art Basel and particularly to Annette Schönholzer, who generously and uncomplicatedly opened the doors of the world of the Art Basel to us as „outsiders", in spite of the risk that the sociological radiography of this world could only be had at the expense of its demystification.

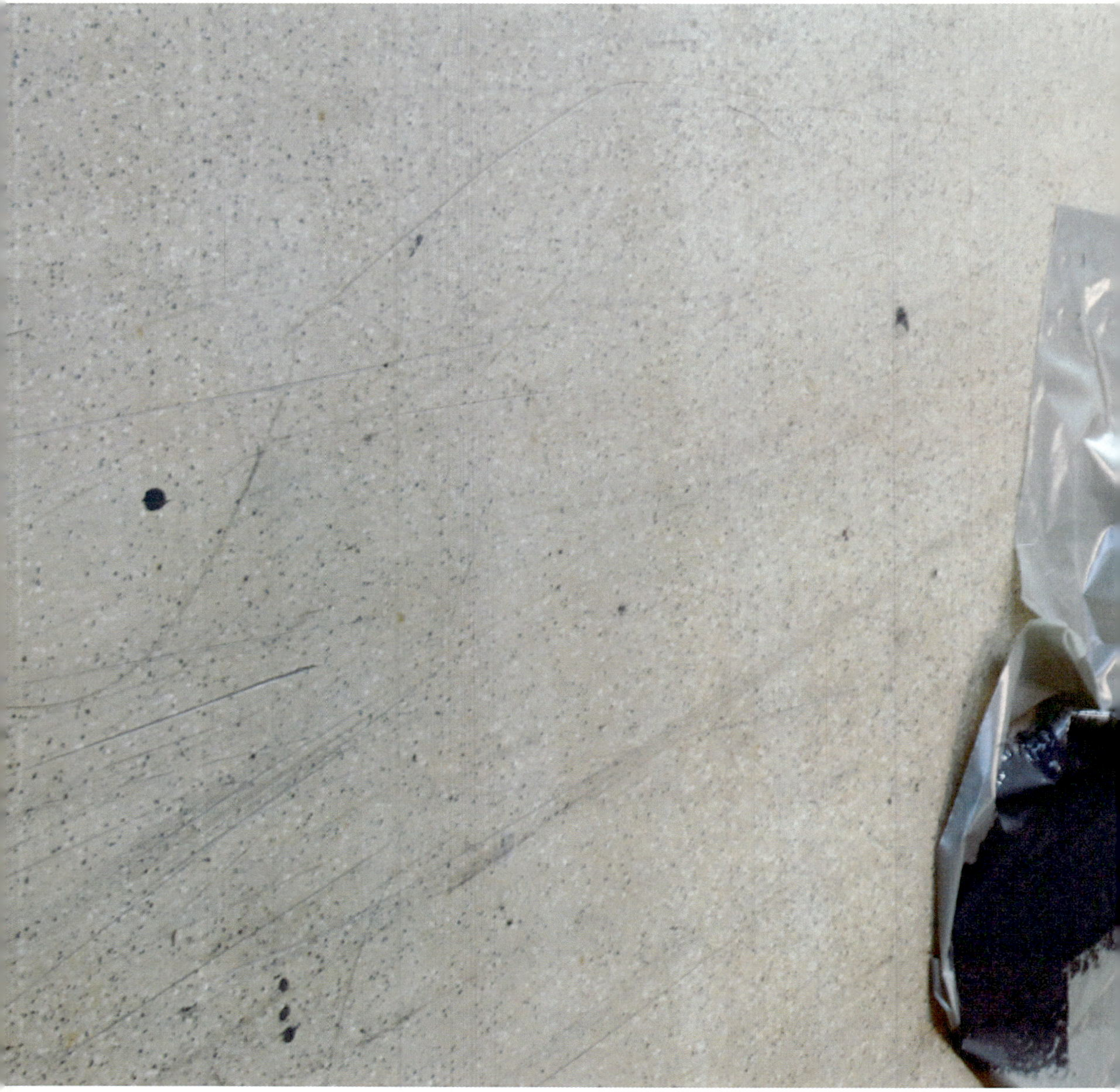

Appendix

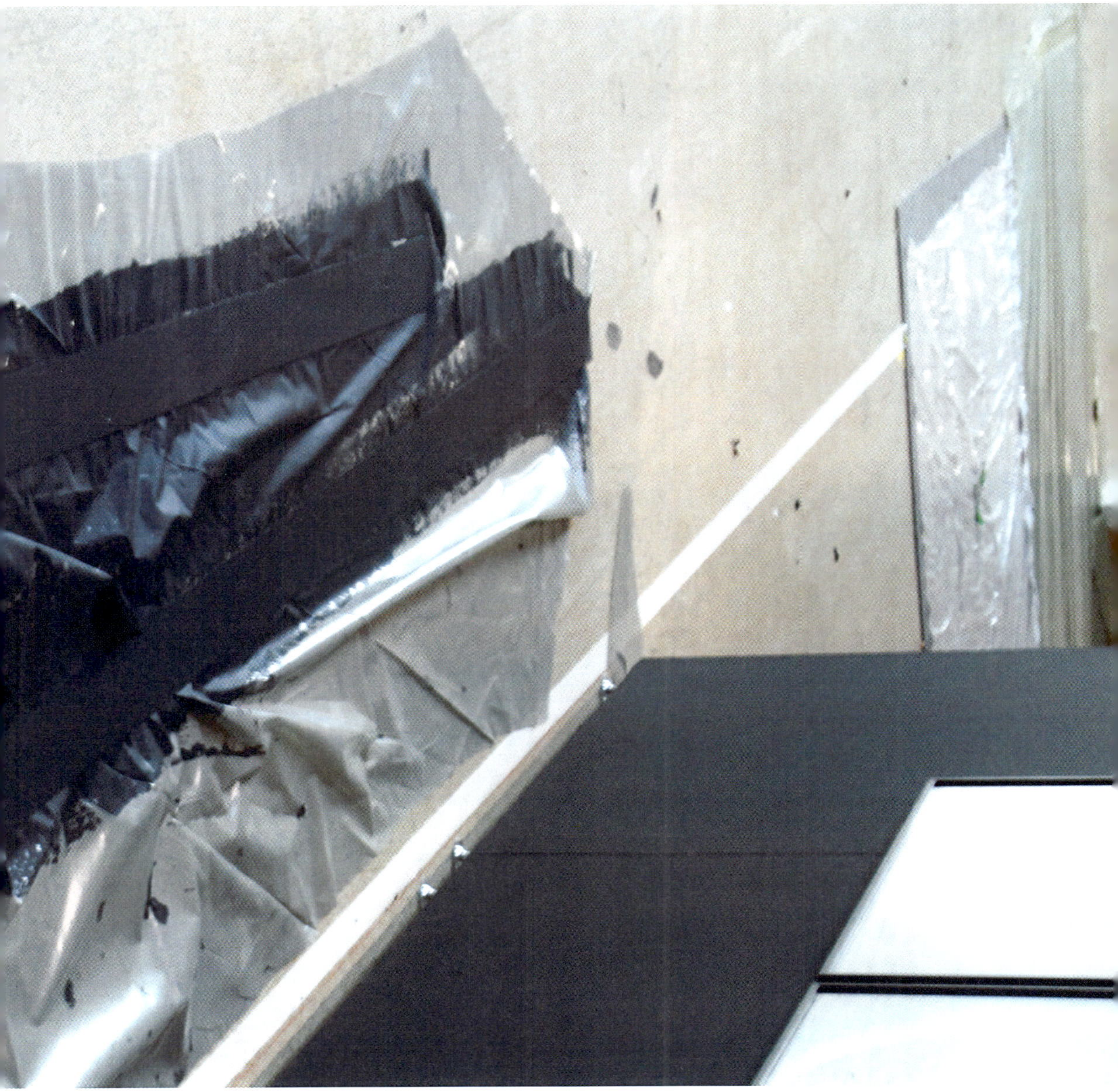

The Research Project

Perspectives

This publication presents the results of a research project which was launched with the help of a start-up financing by the Research Committee of the University of St. Gallen in 2011 and then funded for one and a half years from 2012 on by the Swiss National Science Foundation SNSF. The aim of the research project was to make a contribution to the description of the contemporary „art world" by means of a multidimensionally designed field study of the Art Basel, one of the most important events in the global art market. The Art Basel opens up a highly specific and extremely dense subject area for the understanding of the contemporary art market, its structural shifts and functional transformations.

Methods

As a still unexplored terrain the Art Basel was first of all well-suited for an open ethnographical approach. By means of participant observation of the happenings in the exhibition halls, from the time the booths were erected and the objects of art put in place to the visiting hours for the three different categories of VIPs, then to the opening for the general public and finally to the clearing of the exhibition halls after the official end of the Art Basel, it was possible to follow the entire course of the event at close range and, with the help of detailed records and photographic documentation, to collect the materials needed for an ethnographic description.

Furthermore, a broad spectrum of social-scientific methods were available for the research on this phenomenon. They extend from qualitative approaches, interviews, expert surveys or photographic documentation to the content-analytical treatment of texts, the evaluation of the literature or secondary evaluation of data to quantitative surveys based on more or less standardized questionnaires.

Interviews

In the context of the project about eighty detailed interviews were recorded. The discussions with the staff of the Art Basel in Basel and Miami Beach, with the directors of public and private museums and collections, with curators, with gallerists and collectors, art consultants, art journalists and artists provide an instructive insight not only into the „workings" of the contemporary art market but above all into the way it is perceived by the participating actors. For these discussions we are above all thankful to:

Georgina Adam • Laura Bartlett • Eva-Maria Bechter • Andreas Bicker • Elsbeth Bisig • Konrad Bitterli • Laura Blagho • Marc Blondeau • Tanya Bonakdar • Karen Boros • Paul Bürgler • Giovanni Carmine • Maike Cruse • Bice Curiger • Philippe Davet • Ulla Dreyfus • Harald Falckenberg • Sabine Folie • Patrick Forêt • Ilona Genoni • Donata Gianesi • Victor Gisler • Henrik Hanstein • Christoph Heim • Kashya Hildebrand • Gigga Hug • Fréderique Hutter • Jay Jopling • Christa Jordi-Frey • David Juda • Bernhard Knaus • Martina Kral • Ulf Küster • Simon Lamunière • Dominique Leuenberger • Gisèle Linder • Gerd Harry Lybke • Gerhard Mack • Marck • Barbara Mathes • Helmut Meier-Föllmi • Urs Meile • Pius Müller • Heike Munder • Johannes Nathan • Hans Ulrich Obrist • Patricia Ortiz Monasterio • Marlies Pekarek • Stephanie Reed • Raphael Rigassi • Michael Ringier • Mera & Don Rubell • Rudolf Sagmeister • Alain Schaer • Dennis Scholl • Annette Schönholzer • Michael Schultz • Andrée Sfeir-Semler • Uli Sigg • Marc Spiegler • Markus Stegmann • Walter Soppelsa • Benno Tempel • Ralph Ubl • Vanessa Ugobono • Marc-Jan van Laake • Monica Vögele • Jobst Wagner • Joan & Brian Washburn • Thea Westreich Wagner • Nikolai Winter • Reinhold Würth • Thomas Wüstenhagen • Nina Zimmer • Barbara Zürcher

Surveys

Within the framework of the research project standardized surveys were carried out at the Art Basel in Basel and in Miami Beach among the gallerists and visitors who attended the fairs, which had been tested by the research team in 2011 at the two locations of the fair. Questions were answered on participation in the fair, the evaluation of current developments in the art market, artistic preferences and cultural practices. The six-page survey instrument for the galleries and the four-page questionnaire for the visitors were available in both paper-based and in online format during the field phase. The material collected consists overall of the entries of 280 participants in the visitor surveys and 130 participants in the gallery interviews.

Topography

The Art Basel presents a temporal and spatial condensation of the global art market. With the help of the plans for the fair a socio-spatial structure was analyzed. The positioning of the galleries at various levels of the fair and in central or peripheral locations within the levels was compared with an abundance of secondary data on the sellers and their goods – the „age" of the galleries, their geographical location, first participation and frequency of participation in the Art Basel, the positions of artists in rankings of „importance", the prices achieved at auctions and representation at the Documenta in Kassel and the Biennale in Venice.

Photography

The field research in the years 2012-2014 was accompanied by intensive photographic documentation. First impressions were already made at the Art Basel in 2011, when more than 2,000 pictures were pooled for the visual documentation during the pilot study for the project. In the course of the project funded by the Swiss National Scientific Foundation between 2012 and 2014 over 6,000 pictures were taken. They have the character of an ethnographic documentation which focuses on spatial structures, communicative processes and the social nature of the happenings at the fair.

The Publication

The publication of research results is often beset with the problem that they are only accessible to a small circle of „insiders". In the case of social-scientific studies the case is mostly different when the „themes" they deal with are already known to „public opinion". It is not easy to find a balance in this situation, all the more so in the present case, as the „esoteric" aspect of the subject matter contrasts strongly with the way it is perceived in the media.

At the same time, an exhaustive presentation of the material collected during the project would be beyond the scope of a publication. For this reason the findings could only be presented in a selective and often summary fashion, occasionally in the way of illustration and with a strong tendency towards generalization. It was not always possible to solve this difficult problem satisfactorily, as four authors with different focus and different argumentative styles were involved. The study is a product of teamwork and for this reason alone it cannot be completely homogenous.

For chapters 3, 4 and 6 Franz Schultheis chose an approach which stayed close to the materials. The third chapter was expanded by Erwin Single, who dealt with tendencies in the gallery system. Chapter 2 is similarly oriented on findings which are not of an ethnographical kind, as is Chapter 7, which deals with transformations in the „art world". These sections were written by Erwin Single in cooperation with Thomas Mazzurana. The introductory chapter on the fair as an „event", the study of the public at the fair in Chapter 5 and the concluding survey in Chapter 8 were written by Stephan Egger.

The frequent boxes inserted into the text, to which the readers of „normal" publications may be unaccustomed, are designed to provide information, illustration and a vivid presentation. This is also true, at least to a limited degree, of the photographic design of the book. For obvious reasons only an extremely restricted selection of the visual material could be presented in this publication. In particular it was not possible to present the strongly serial character of the shots, which recorded the sequence of certain processes. The pictures thus primarily serve the purpose of illustration.

The Authors

Franz Schultheis is Professor of Sociology at the University of St. Gallen and President of the Fondation Bourdieu.

Erwin Single studied sociology, communicative sciences and journalism and works as a freelance journalist in Berlin.

Stephan Egger works at the Chair of Sociology of the University of St. Gallen and is co-editor of the „Pierre Bourdieu Schriften".

Thomas Mazzurana is a research assistant at the Intitute of Sociology of the University of St. Gallen.

Footnotes

1 At the Fair

1 The assertion of this systematic ambivalence of the actors loses none of its plausibility by reference to „counter examples". The fact that a substantial degree of „calculation" can be encountered in the „art world" which subordinates „belief" to economic considerations is just as banal as an objection as the reference to the financial operations of the Catholic Church. The decisive point is, rather, that such „critical" disclosures document a normative impetus whose juxtapositioning of „art" and „world" remains constitutive of the „art world". How would it otherwise be possible to explain why this kind of economic consideration must be concealed behind soapbox oratory which has to meet the requirements of the „official" language use and the „official" confession of faith? It is precisely this logic, the way of dealing with these rules of art and the tension created by the faults in their structural basis, which stands in the center of the present study – a description of the „big bucks" circulating in the contemporary art trade does not provide a sufficient understanding.

2 On the genesis and structure of the art field in general see Bourdieu 1996. That Bourdieu's sociology of art has in the meantime become a benchmark of art-theoretical discourse cannot belie the fact that its extremely complex argumentative structure has suffered in the process. For a discussion see below, Chapter 8.

2 The Market and the Brand

1 In her study of the international art market the cultural economist Claire McAndrew comes to the conclusion that art fairs have become the most important marketing channels alongside the classical galleries with their own sales rooms. In the meantime 14 per cent of the sales are achieved at international fairs and 19 per cent at domestic fairs (McAndrew 2014:43). This is a slight decrease in comparison to 2013 when the total figure was 36 per cent (McAndrew 2013a:59).

2 See Baja Curioni 2012:118f.

3 von Alemann 1997:233.

4 For a survey see Werner 2010.

5 On the „invention" of the art market in Cologne, the processes of institutionalization and the rise of Cologne as an art metropolis see von Alemann 1997 and Mehring 2008.

6 Although the media accepted in principle the commercial intentions of the Cologne „Art Market 67" there were critical voices which accused the organizer, the Association of Progressive German Art Dealers, of carrying art to the market. Moreover, the selection principle, according to which only a small number of galleries were invited, was criticized as being „undemocratic". The protest actions of the artists Joseph Beuys, Wolf Vostell and Klaus Staeck are legendary. For the discussion on commercialization at this time see Bongard 1967.

7 See also Boll 2005.

8 Art Basel 2014: Press Release, 22 June 2014.

9 On the origins of the Art Basel and the various factors determining its success see the detailed treatment in Genoni 2009.

10 Keller 2006.

11 Thompson 2008:235.

12 Beckert & Rössel 2004, Velthuis 2005, Yogev 2010.

13 Velthius 2012:19.

14 Bourdieu 1996:142.

15 Baia Curioni 2012:128.

16 Bourdieu 1991:30.

17 The Artfacts Ranking is used as the indicator of visibility.

18 The arrangement of the galleries changed in 2014. In 2013 the sector Statements was still located in Hall 1.0, which made its peripheral significance even clearer.

19 Velthius 2012:19.

20 Mehring 2008.

21 Bourdieu 1996:142ff.

22 „On account of its conception as a cultural experience world the Documenta today also positions itself in the field of extended production. By linking the experience orientation of the subfield of mass production to a symbolic position of power in accordance with the rules of the field of pure production it is still in a position to produce legitimate art and in this way it links the logics of the two antagonistic sub-fields." (Zahner 2006:276). For Bourdieu (1996:381) political art, which is predominantly represented at the Documenta, enjoys a special status. „The status of ‚social art', in this respect, is completely ambiguous: even if it refers artistic or literary production to external functions (for which the proponents of ‚art for art's sake' do not fail to reproach it), it shares with ‚art for art's sake' a radical challenge to worldly success and that ‚bourgeois art' which recognizes it while looking down on the values of ‚disinterestedness'".

23 Rosenberg 1964.

24 http://upstart.bizjournals.com/culture-lifestyle/culture-inc/arts/2008/11/19/Art-Basels-Funding-Woes.html?referer=sphere_search&page=3

25 http://hallandalebeachblog.blogspot.ch/2008/07/miamis-art-basels-role-in-ubs-scandal

26 Ibid.

27 Ibid.

28 http://upstart.bizjournals.com/culture-lifestyle/culture-inc/arts/2008/11/19/Art-Basels-Funding- Woes.html?referer=sphere_search&page=3

3 Liaisons dangereuses

1 Spiegler 2007.

2 Velthuis 2012, Alemann 1997, Becker 1982.

3 O'Doherty 1986.

4 Thurn 1994:78.

5 As an example see Art Basel 2012: Fair Report 2012, 10 September 2012.

6 Art Basel 2014: Press Release, 22 June 2014.

7 McAndrew 2014:43.

8 See also Mc Andrew 2011:31.

9 Bonus & Ronte 1997:149.

10 Velthuis 2012:38f.

11 „The concept of the ‚gallery' comprises (...) the most varied forms of the art trade. In the wider sense it means all kinds of trading with works of art by a private enterprise. It then also includes those businesses which sell posters and reproductions and nonetheless describe themselves as galleries. In some circumstances picture framers also describe themselves as gallerists (...) And finally the concept also includes those galleries which deal in modern art, in the art of the twentieth century" (Klein 1993:135). Other authors like Thurn (1994) associate galleries with trade in contemporary art.

12 McAndrew 2014:13.

13 McAndrew 2014:42.

14 „Serious buyers never drop into the shop" (Mc Andrew 2011:30).

15 Saltz 2013.

16 McAndrew 2011:30.

17 Von Alemann 1997:221.

18 Thompson 2008:172.

19 Art 42 Basel Exhibition Regulations, 2011, 2, and Art 43 Basel Exhibition Regulations, 2014, 3.

20 McAndrew 2011:31.

21 Herstatt 2007:29.

22 CINOA: http://www.cinoa.org/page/2858

23 Rosa 2013.

24 In view of the expansion of the Art Basel to Hong Kong it seems as if the fair in Basel will concentrate more on the European galleries, as the Asian galleries have been offered a place in the Art Basel universe at Hong Kong and must no longer necessarily come to Basel. The same applies to South American galleries in regard to Miami Beach.

25 Robertson 2011, Quemin 2012.

26 Kunstkompass 2014. For their analyses Wuggenig (2003) and Quemin (2006, 2012) use the Kunstkompass, a ranking list of the top 100 artists, which attempts to comprehend the symbolic capital of artists in terms of their visibility at international exhibitions (Wuggenig 2003:59). The ranking „is based on solo shows and artists' participations in group hangings at the most prominent venues, and on their coverage in the main contemporary art publications" (Quemin 2012:55). Art must be visible in order to be perceived, legitimated and instanced as such. In „a society which esteems what is aesthetically new the achievement and the award of attention becomes a cultural battlefield" (Reckwitz 2012:333).

27 Wuggenig 2003:61.

28 Wuggenig 2003:62.

29 Quemin 2012:57 and 61.

30 Buchholz &Wuggenig 2004.

31 Velthuis 2013.

32 Bonus & Ronte 1997.

33 Velthuis 2012:19.

4 An Art of Distinction

1 If one looks for cultural predecessors of this cultural pattern one can find it perhaps in the collective mania for collecting relics which could be observed in the Middle Ages and also during the Renaissance. It was regarded as a legitimate and even exquisite expression of piety and a guarantee for the salvation of the soul among the nobility and the emergent bourgeoisie, who invested in sometimes extremely expensive collections of religious relics. The locations where they were preserved developed into places of pilgrimage. Here material riches were transformed into a symbolic, a salvific good, and strong analogies to the function of art collecting can clearly be ascertained. Revealingly Charles de Bross used the concept of „fetishism" as early as 1709 as a criticism of this practice, which reminded him of characteristics of primitive peoples.

2 See Pety 2001:73.

3 Pety 2001:74.

4 Cembalest 2014.

5 Wuggenig 2011.

6 Moulin 1987.

7 Rauget et al. 1991.

8 Wuggenig 2008.

9 The following passage from an article in the Swiss periodical *Bilanz* shows how such symbolic struggles with their denunciatory and stigmatizing weapons have as a matter of course entered the field of public discourse and have been taken up in the medial representations of the art world: „Formerly the collection of expensive canvases was regarded as a privilege of the super-rich. But nowadays the accumulation of works of art with prospects of appreciated value has deteriorated into a social game played by a broad public. In the meantime it is good form for the middle and the upper middle class to take an interest one way or another in the manifestations of avant-gardist style. Any business executive, banker or patent attorney with a sense of self-respect, who has accumulated enough shares in companies, real estate and cars in his portfolio, now works on the creation of his own collection. And if he does not have enough small change to do so he is active as a guest who is willing to learn at vernissages and so keeps himself up-to-date in the art field. Woe betide anyone who does not even pretend to be interested in the current trends in the art market. Such a philistine is finished in better circles", see Becher 2005.

10 This is incidentally also true of the stigmatizations of an almost racist kind often expressed in the interviews by collectors in regard to the nations which have newly entered into the game of collecting contemporary art, such as the BRIC states. Here the words of a German big collector: *„He has to reach the people from Kasachstan, these few idiots in the world. I've heard that 10,000 of them are running around. 10,000 multi-millionaires who, how shall I put it, boast about their social standing by acquiring works of art which of course have to be expensive."* Here too one must call to mind that the path of the new German bourgeoisie of the post-war period into the Elysian Fields of contemporary art was stony and arduous and that they had much more time at their disposal. For this reason scientific economic analyses also take the factor „time" into account in their assessments of the art market: „One restriction derives from the different degree of maturity in the art markets. While the US and most countries in Europe show a mature art collector base, in Asia it isn't the case. For example, while in the US, 54 per cent started their collections before 1991, in China it's only 7 per cent. 55 per cent started between 2001 and 2010, compared to only 20 per cent in the US. This different maturity in collection must therefore be considered when analyzing the data", see Steiner et al. 2013.

11 With the qualities collectors like to attribute to themselves such as competence, good taste and instinct they demonstrate their command of the market in the confusing field of contemporary art – as the „heroes and sovereigns of consumption", as „secretly shimmering figures", „because they do what most people would not do even if they had the money left over for it" (Ullrich 2007). See also Ullrich 2012.

12 Moulin 1992:220f.

13 For art as a investment see Baumol & Broysen 1986, Frey & Eichenberger 1995, Worthington & Higgs 2004, Kraeussl & Lee 2010.

14 Capgemini / RBC Wealth Management 2013.

15 Mc Andrew 2014:49ff.

16 Incidentally, this type of entrepreneurial collecting reveals a clearly pronounced tendency towards a passion for art based on partnership, which even includes marital rules for the purchase of art objects, as for example in the case of an American art collecting couple who observed a „two-vote rule". That this can take on fairytale character is revealed in the account of a Turkish couple: „It all began in museums. At first she and I always met in the Guggenheim and we finally got engaged in the Whitney."

17 AXA Art 2014.

18 In this connection Thomas Mona (1997) quotes Chambon's observation: „In France one does not reveal one's name; one does not show one's treasures. Of a hundred more or less important collectors who are asked by museums, only three, perhaps four, allow their names to be mentioned."

19 Bourdieu 1984:229.

5 Commitments and Commodities

1 On the structure of the art public see the classical study published in the 1960s by Pierre Bourdieu and Alain Darbel (1991); for a reprise with very similar results after half a century see Munder & Wuggenig 2012. All the recent studies on the behavior of visitors suggest that the class character of art consumption established at that time has become even more pronounced in the last few decades. For a survey see Glogner & Föhl 2010. However, the interpretations of these trends diverge: on the discussion see Zahner 2012, and for a critical treatment Chapter 8 below.

2 The breakdown of the public at the fair into „professionals" and „amateurs", „insiders" and „outsiders", two pairs of opposites which characterize on the one hand the specific competence and on the other the degree of market integration of the actors, cannot of course do justice to the many real nuances, because the positions within these groups cannot be more specifically delimited on account of the limited empirical precision in detail of the survey instruments. But the relatively clear differences in the attitudes of the actors clearly indicate that these categories also reveal differences which determine behavior. It must, moreover, be pointed out that at least here – in contrast to everyday use even in the art world – the use of the concepts „amateur" or „dilettante" is in no way normatively intended but exclusively describes the lack of professional expertise which the professionals see as a deficiency in this context. The amateurs themselves, however, are also aware of the deficit, not least the collecting lovers of art, who read „the specialist professional literature for at least two hours every day".

6 Times of Discontent

1 See https://www.artbasel.com/en/Miami-Beach/About-the-Show/Talks/Salon

2 On the genesis and the manifestations of the social figure of the „artist“ see among others Bourdieu 1996: 54-60 and Bourdieu 2015b: 183-241.

7 Art in Motion

1 Lind & Velthius 2012, Taylor 2011.

2 Graw 2010.

3 Capgemini / RBC Wealth Management 2013.

4 Prinz & Wuggenig 2012.

5 Groys 2012.

6 Godelier 1996.

7 Weiner 1992.

8 Karpik 2010.

9 Behnke 2012:200.

10 See Crane 2009, Graw 2010.

11 „I like money on the wall. Say you were going to buy a $200,000 painting. I think you should take that money, tie it up, and hang it on the wall. Then when someone visited you the first thing they would see is the money on the wall“, see Warhol 1975.

12 For an example see Moulin 1987, Velthuis 2003.

13 See Velthuis 2011. Some authors distinguish between primary, secondary and tertiary markets, wherby the tertiary market comprises the entire auction market.

14 On the development of the art market see Mc Andrew 2012, 2013 and 2014, Artprice 2013 and 2014, Deloitte & Arttactic 2013. The volume of trade in art cannot be exactly established on account of different kinds of data, sources, statistical acquisition and classification and methods of calculation. We are, therefore, dealing mostly with estimates or calculations on the basis of empirical data. More exact data exists only for the auctioneering trade.

15 Mc Andrew 2014:20, also Mc Andrew 2013:19 and 2012:21.

16 Mc Andrew 2012:15.

17 As a comparison with other branches of the culture industry: the international music market achieved a volume of 15 billion US dollars in 2013 (http://www.musikindustrie.de/jahrbuch-international-2013/?no_ cache=1&type=1); the European book market registered a turnover of 22.5 billion euros in 2012 (http://www.fep-fee.eu/European-Book-Publishing,446). Time Warner, one of the biggest media concerns worldwide, had a turnover of 22.4 billion dollars in 2013. The turnover of Facebook in 2013 amounted to 7.9 billion dollars. The „mass markets“ for culture can thus scarcely compete economically with the extremely elitist sphere of art marketing.

18 Mc Andrew 2014:7 and 21.

19 Mc Andrew 2014:35.

20 Mc Andrew 2014:35ff and 15.

21 Mc Andrew 2014:36.

22 Deloitte & Arttactic 2013:12 and 23.

23 Mc Andrew 2014:30f.

24 Mc Andrew 2014:45.

25 Mc Andrew 2014:22.

26 Mc Andrew 2014:22.

27 Velthuis 2003.

28 Mc Andrew 2013a:8.

29 See Quemin 2008.

30 For example Groetzmann 1993, Frey & Eichenberger 1995, Mei & Moses 2002, Ashenfelter & Graddy 2006, Goetzmann, Renneboog & Spaenjers 2011.

31 From Goetzmann, Renneboog & Spaenjers 2012.

32 See also Herchenröder 2000.

33 See Goetzmann, Mamonova, Spaenjars 2014.

34 Skate 2014:2f.

35 Artprice 2014:63. The data is based on the entire auction turnover for the fine arts from old masters to contemporary art.

36 Artprice 2014a:22.

37 Crane 2009.

38 For the comparison the auction results of Artprice from 2013 (Artprice 2014) and the Artist Ranking 2014 of Artfacts were used. The data and rankings of Artprice reflect „sales success" in the shape of auction turnover; the Artist Ranking of Artfacts is primarily based upon „success at exhibitions" and „embedment in the art world". Although the data of Artfacts on exhibitions are copious and transparent, there is an element of insecurity in regard to the Artist Rankings as the method of calculation is not known. In spite of this weakness the data nonetheless provides a good insight into the discrepancy between symbolic value and commodity value.

39 Artprice has evaluated 554,523 artists, 27 million detailed results of auctions, quotations and indices since 1987, 108 million reproductions of art works from 4.500 Auction houses and details of forthcoming auctions (see http://web.artprice.com/?l=de). The data of Artfacts are based in July 2015 on information from 29,323 exhibitors worldwide, 190 countries, 609,527 exhibitions worldwide, 454,542 artists biographies, 100,011 ranked artists, 28,744 works of art, 1,965 catalogs (see http://www.artfacts.net/about_us_new). According to its own statements Artnet is, as a gallery network, the biggest of its kind. More than 1,600 galleries present 170,000 works by 35,000 artists from all over the world online. The results listed by more than 1,600 international auction houses since 1985 are evaluated; the price data base contains more than 8 million auction results on over 300,000 artists (see http://www.artnet.com/about/ abou-tindex.asp?F=1). Lastly MutualArt is an online art information service with data from „200,000 art related articles from over 250 quality magazines, newspapers and journals, and also pro-vides a conduit for galleries, museums, auction houses, art fairs and publishers" (see in detail https://www.mutualart.com).

40 See Velthuis 2013.

41 In Germany the average income of fine artists amounted to around 14,700 euros in 2013, see http://www.kuenstlersozialkasse.de/wDeutsch/ksk_in_zahlen/statistik/durchschnittseinkommenversicherte.php?navanchor=1010020

42 Institut für Strategieentwicklung 2013.

43 Prinz & Wuggenig 2012:206.

44 https://www.destatis.de/DE/ZahlenFakten/GesellschaftStaat/BildungForschungKultur/Hochschuen/Tabellen/StudierendeInsgesamtFaechergruppe.html

45 This „includes fine arts, music and performing arts, audio-visual techniques and media production, design, craft skills", http://ec.europa.eu/eurostat/documents/2995521/5035802/3-1404 2011-AP-EN.PDF

46 Boltanski &Chiapello 2007; Menger 2003; Reckwitz 2012.

47 van den Berg & Pasero 2013.

48 See Kirshenblatt-Gimblett 1998.

49 For the figures on visitors see TEA/AECOM 2013.

50 On the prices for contemporary art see Velthuis 2005.

51 Moulin 1987.

52 Bürger (1974) already declared that the avant-garde concept had failed; see also Foster 1996.

53 On the „end of art" and „end of art history" see Danto 1981 and 1997, and Belting 2003.

8 When Art meets Money

1 In his great study *The Rules* of Art Pierre Bourdieu has demonstrated with a hitherto unachieved cogency that this normative conscience can only be understood against the background of quite specific sociohistorical constellations, see Bourdieu 1996:47-140, individual preliminary studies in Bourdieu 2015a and for a socio-historical overview the early work of Hauser 1951 and 1958. This is not the place and there is also no need to deal in detail with the „genetic" line of argument developed there – on the social, economic and morphological preconditions for a „symbolic" revolution, for the qualitative break which separates the „art", the literature, music and painting, of earlier times from what today characterizes the concept, its social, material and formal detachment from traditional relationships of power and dominanty conventions, the transition from craftsmanship to „salon painting" and from there to a „free" art, see Bourdieu 1996: 54-60, 113ff, 141ff, and now also the detailed treatment in Bourdieu's *Manet. Une revolution symbolique,* 2013. The broad lines of this development, which ends in an artistic „modernism" as a new historical configuration, are undisputed.

2 The class character of „art", which describes the perception, evaluation and „way of dealing" with art and the relationship to „culture in general" as an eminently social phenomenon, has nowhere been better elaborated in detail than in the studies of Bourdieu. Here too it is impossible to deal with the complex line of argument in a footnote. But the assertion often made in the artistic field that modern art is accessible to everyman, in as far as he is willing to open the door to it, is part of the myth of its universality, although the opposite is demonstrated everywhere. The approach to art is socially contaminated to a massive degree; the differences in the ways of using art are glaring; they rigorously separate the social classes, see Bourdieu and Darbel 1991, Bourdieu 1984.

3 The repeatedly posed problem of a „market" for art must remain unintelligible as long as the specific character of this market is not taken into account. It has the character of a *denied economy,* of a market which is characterized by its unwillingness to be perceived as such, which offsets the price of art in terms of money with its „lasting" value – and this applies not only to the „work" itself but also to the nature of its acquisition. It offers a different balance of debit and credit, involving, in an ethnological sense, an „honorable", a genuine „exchange".

What is revealed here is an economy of symbolic goods, a practice in which the logic of production and the logic of consumption seem to stand in a reversed relationship to one another, in which the regime of „genuine" production indicates a „marketable" product and the codex of the „genuine" consumer honors precisely this characteristic, whereas artistic „large-scale" production generates tangible revenues which are regarded as a stain in the „pure" world of art. On the concept of an economy of symbolic goods, above all as played through in the world of „art", see again Bourdieu 1996 and 2014. The specific „value creation model" of the art market is consequently based more or less exclusively on a long-term accumulation of symbolic capital and its enormous convertibility. In no other world has the economic motto „time is money" so much substance – in the reverse sense. The art discovered for the market is an art involving wastage of time, not only of the time needed for the „production" of an object, but also of the time it takes to have its existence registered, the time for gradual recognition, in which it would be „deadly" to achieve high prices at too early a stage, to „expose" the artist to the market too soon. Finally after various stages in the accumulation of more and more „official" consecration and entry to the museum comes a generally binding approval of a process at the end of which a non-binding, unsuspicious and unobjectionable conversion into something material, into hard cash, can follow. The value-creation chains do not depend on consumption but on the processes of canonization, the authentification of the belief in the „value" of art, in a market whose consumers at the same time are given confirmation of the belief in their own social value, a market which also enables the transformation of this symbolic credit into all other possible preconditions for „creditability". This classical regime of an „economy of symbolic goods" has, however, begun to change. Its production cycles and patterns of exploitation, the institutional structure of the canonization and economization, the relationship of the market to the public sphere, to the „public", everywhere reveal manifestations of the dissolution of boundaries, of acceleration, segmentation and polarization – the phenomena of an art world in transition.

4 On the concepts of „limited" and „large-scale" production in the art field see Bourdieu 1996: 81ff., 141ff. This complex conceptual figure describes the historically established „modernistic" model of a normative classification of the relationship of the sphere of art production to the structure of its sphere of consumption. The fact that some studies in art sociology which follow Bourdieu in the meantime seem to demand an „extension" of the figure, a conception of a „sub-field of „extended production", shows, however, how strongly an „institutionalist" view is asserting itself, which increasingly weakens the actual leitmotif of Bourdieu's construction, its emphasis on the normative aspect. The misunderstanding that this ideal-typical, this, in a heuristic sense, „structure" of the art field could be perfectly defined in reality and even comprehended categorially opens up the possibility of „further development" but fails to do justice to the relational ideas behind the concept.

5 The drifting apart of the „commercial" and the „intellectual" poles of the art field in a sphere which claims „artistic" validity in the narrow sense is quite characteristic of the contemporary constellation. This constellation strongly calls to mind the triangular relationship between „salon painting", social realism and the will to produce iconoclastic forms with which the „movement" subsumed under the concept of „Impressionism" established one of the decisive dispositives of artistic modernism, albeit in a very different context. The difference is that contemporary art, on account of the enormous dynamics it has released, has in the meantime lost the secure reference points for its formulated task of violating form. The „formalism" of artistic modernism whose justification for existence was always the *overcoming of form* can nowadays only exist between the iconotopic „market art" of whatever shade and the semantics of the artistic critique of art, specifically in painting, which asserts itself both stubbornly and marketably as the traditional site and the retreat of modernism.

6 There can be no doubt that this diagnosis poses the problem of the attribution of value in the art field in a fundamental way. In this regard „intrinsic" arguments have in recent years dominated the art-theoretical discussion, colored by theses on the development of modern

popular culture, see Danto 1981, Lash 1990 and Belting 1995. There is much talk of the „interpretative openness" of contemporary art introduced following the rise of pop art and concept art with the „farewell" to the classical parameter of „creative genius", of „the work", of the primacy of „form", indeed of a „hermetic" concept of art in connection with a popularized reception aesthetics. But this not only forgets how much the attributions of value in „classical" modernism, which had incidentally always been characterized by a radical „interpretative openness", depended upon a very specific reception cartel but also that a semantics of contemporary art which does away with these forms can itself only continue to exist in a „recognized" and „acknowledged" form. The supposed „suitability for the masses" of „post-modern" art is just as much a chimera as its supposed „ambiguity". The decision on its symbolic „value" continues to be taken by a cartel of evaluating instances, in which, however, new, „private" judges of good taste have established themselves.

7 This „aesthetic gaze" simply means a supposedly competent ability to achieve distance to the morphological manifestations and the semantic content of a „work" and describes a „conscious enjoyment" in which the „inner", the „personal" appropriation of art to a large extent suppresses its intentionality. An enormous resistance to this aesthetic gaze can nowadays be encountered at every turn. A „post-modern" critique of art which believes that the concept itself is „obsolete" can only do so by disregarding its eminently social connotations. Anyone who accompanies Jerry Saltz on his tour of a Jeff Koons retrospective at the New York MoMA (see Saltz 2014) can feel this self-empowering „judgmental capacity" in every line. The „personal" sensual impression, *aisthesis*, again and again outbids the normative objection of the great critic to an artist all but impossible in the „progressive" sphere of the field.

8 For an overview see Schneider 1996.

9 Danto 1964, Dickie 1974, Becker 1982, see also White & White 1965, an „institutionalist" view-point, whose „closeness to reality" is not even approximately in a position to grasp the reality of the normative aspect of the „art world".

10 See Adorno 1997:227.

11 For a convincing and pointed account of the radical transformations which in the meantime characterize the manifestations of contemporary art see Stallabrass 2004, and for much more anecdotal attempts to sort the most recent developments see, for example, Thornton 2008, Thompson 2008 and 2014, or Adam 2014.

12 Apart from its plausibility in morphological terms the validity of the argument presented on the „mass cultural" effects in the field of the fine arts can scarcely be „verified" empirically. What at all events still seems to be comprehensible for the visual substance of contemporary art with its ostentatious attempts to „profanize" art becomes even more questionable than ever if one casts a glance at the social structure of the „public". The „popularization" of the fine arts is far removed from reaching the *populus.*

13 At this point one undoubtedly touches upon a central question of that „economy of symbolic goods" and not just one of philosophical aesthetics: the criteria for the attribution of value, for the „valorization" of products for which virtually no material parameters exist for the assessment of their value. A more cautious formulation in view of the easily offended belief of the art field should probably run as follows: that in the best case the – relationally conceived – processes in the „genesis of a work" with their „overcoming" of „traditional" forms ensure canonization. Here the thesis of the end of „formalism" in „modernism" itself seems to have become „obsolete", as it cannot grasp the re-semantization of contemporary visual languages which developed after the triumph of concept art as „form", but only very formalistically as „deformalization". Whether these works which overcome traditional forms, these „new creations" with which modern art is always concerned, are „genuine" or not cannot be unobjectionably decided in „modern" art with the categories of art history, nor is it at all possible in the case of its „post-modern" manifestations when they are accessed through

visual language alone. If art theory has had to emigrate to the sphere of philosophy since its treatment of pop art, this is not because of the explosion of forms which has taken place and certainly not because of the „transfiguration of the commonplace“, but because the tendential arbitrariness of every kind of value attribution in art has become an all too obvious problem.

14 It is evident that this finding runs counter to the predominant theses of post-modern art theory, although it by no means questions the massive transformations which the art field has experi-enced in the last few decades. On the contrary, the structural distortions of this special „econ-omy of symbolic goods“ are massive and, unless we are completely mistaken, probably also permanent. Perhaps for this reason the dissent is more of a conceptual kind. Regardless of whether they follow or depart from Bourdieu's omnipresent *Règles de l'art,* the debates in the field of art theory on „new rules“ of art can only be meant to apply to the *institutional structure* of the art world. It is indeed the case that new rules apply in this context, and their effects on processes of value attribution are totally incalculable. The „commercialization“ of the fine arts, their „medialization“, the entire complex of the rational configuration of a „market“ for art, its penetration into the public institutions of artistic consecration, cannot be denied. But no line of argument is refined enough to demonstrate that the specific modern *norms* of the art field have been fundamentally changed in consequence, their iconoclastic impulse, their attempt to achieve distance from „worldly“ constraints, be it only in the form of a „big art“ which demonstrates the hybrid lack of proportion between artistic „intentions“ and their material realization, and that these norms, even as mere *ideology,* are as effective as they were at the time of their implementation. The „rules of art“, the logic of their activation of a collective belief, which ultimately celebrates everything which originally intended to resist such celebration, not only remain intact. They continue to regulate dictatorially the symbolic cycle of contemporary artistic modernism.

Bibliography

Adam, Georgina, 2014: Big Bucks. The Explosion of the Art Market in the 21st Century. Farnham: Lund Humphries.

Adorno, Theodor W., 1997 [1970], Aesthetic Theory. London: The Athlone Press.

Alemann, Heine von, 1997: Galerien als Gatekeeper des Kunstmarktes. Institutionelle Aspekte der Kunstvermittlung. In: Gerhards, Jürgen (ed.), Soziologie der Kunst. Produzenten, Vermittler und Rezipienten. Opladen: Westdeutscher Verlag, 211-239.

Artprice, 2013: The Art Market in 2012. Saint-Romain-au-Mont-d'Or.

Artprice, 2014: The Art Market in 2013. Saint-Romain-au-Mont-d'Or.

Ashenfelter, Orley / Graddy, Kathryn, 2006: Art Auctions. In: Ginsburgh, Victor / Throsby, David (eds.), Handbook on the Economics of Art and Culture. Amsterdam: Elsevier, 909-945.

AXA Art, 2014: Collecting in the Digital Age. International Collectors Survey. Köln: AXA Art Versicherung AG.

Baia Curioni, Stefano, 2012: A Fairy Tale: The Art System, Globalization, and the Fair Movement. In: Lind, Maria / Velthuis, Olav (eds.), Contemporary Art and Its Commercial Markets: A Report on Current Conditions and Future Scenarios. Berlin: Sternberg, 115-151.

Baumol, William L. / Browen, William G., 1986 [1966]: Performing Arts – The Economic Di-lemma. A Study of Problems Common to Theater, Opera, Music and Dance. New York: The Twentieth Century Fund.

Becher, Jörg, 2005: Kunstsammler: Reich an Kunst. In: Bilanz. Das Schweizer Wirtschaftsmagazin, 29.11.2005.

Becker, Howard S., 1982: Art Worlds. Berkeley: University of California Press.

Beckert, Jens / Rössel, Jörg, 2004: Kunst und Preise. Reputation als Mechanismus der Reduktion von Ungewissheit am Kunstmarkt. In: Kölner Zeitschrift für Soziologie und Sozialpsychologie, Vol. 56, 32-50.

Behnke, Christoph, 2012: Ökonomisierung und Anti-Ökonomismus. In: Munder, Heike / Wuggenig, Ulf (eds.), Das Kunstfeld. Eine Studie über Akteure und Institutionen der zeitgenössischen Kunst am Beispiel von Zürich, Wien, Hamburg und Paris. Zurich: JRP|Ringier, 189-204.

Belting, Hans, 2003 [1995]: Art History After Modernism. Chicago & London: Chicago University Press.

Boll, Dirk, 2005: Der Kampf um die Kunst. Handel und Auktionen positionieren sich am Kunstmarkt. Dissertation. Halle: Druckfabrik Halle.

Boltanski, Luc / Chiapello, Ève, 2007 [1999]: The New Sprit of Capitalism. New York: Verso Books.

Bongard, Willy 1967: Kunst und Kommerz. Zwischen Passion und Spekulation. Oldenburg: Stalling Verlag.

Bonus, Holger / Ronte, Dieter, 1997 [1991]: Die Wa(h)re Kunst. Markt, Kultur und Illusion. Stuttgart: Schäffer-Poeschel.

Bourdieu, Pierre, 1984 [1979]: Distinction. A Social Critque of the Judgement of Taste. Cambridge/ Mass.: Harvard University Press.

Bourdieu, Pierre, 1991: Physischer, sozialer und angeeigneter physischer Raum. In: Wentz, Martin (ed.), Stadt-Räume. Die Zukunft des Städtischen. Frankfurt/M.: Campus, 25-34.

Bourdieu, Pierre, 1996 [1992]: The Rules of Art. Genesis and Structure of the Literary Field. Cambridge: Polity Press.

Bourdieu, Pierre, 2013: Manet. Une revolution symbolique. Paris: Seuil.

Bourdieu, Pierre, 2014 [2011]: Kunst und Kultur. Zur Ökonomie symbolischer Güter. Schriften zur Kultursoziologie 4, Berlin: Suhrkamp, 15-96.

Bourdieu, Pierre, 2015a: Kunst und Kultur. Kunst und künstlerisches Feld. Schriften zur Kultursoziologie 4, Berlin: Suhrkamp.

Bourdieu, Pierre, 2015b [1975]: Die Erfindung des Künstlerlebens. In: Bourdieu, Pierre, Kunst und Kultur. Kunst und künstlerisches Feld. Schriften zur Kultursoziologie 4, 183-241.

Bourdieu, Pierre / Darbel, Alain, 1991 [1967]: The Love of Art. European Art Museums and their Public. Cambridge: Polity Press.

Buchholz, Larissa / Wuggenig, Ulf, 2004: Cultural Globalization between Myth and Reality: The Case of the Contemporary Visual Arts. In: Art-e-Fact, Issue 4.

Bürger, Peter, 1974: Theorie der Avantgarde. Frankfurt/M.: Suhrkamp.

Capgemini / RBC Wealth Management, 2013: World Wealth Report 2013. Paris.

Cembalest, Robin, 2014: Good Collectors and Great Ones. The ARTnews 200 Top Collectors. In: Artnews, Summer 2014, 51-63.

Crane, Diana, 2009: Reflections on the Global Art Market: Implications for the Sociology of Culture. In: Sociedade e Estado: Vol. 24 (2), 331-362.

Danto, Arthur C., 1964: The Artworld. In: The Journal of Philosophy. Vol. 61(19), 571-584.

Danto, Arthur C., 1981: The Transfiguration of the Commonplace. A Philosophy of Art. Cambridge/ Mass.: Harvard University Press.

Danto, Arthur C., 1997: After the End of Art. Contemporary Art and the Pale of History. Princeton: Princeton University Press.

Deloitte / ArtTactic, 2013: Art & Finance Report 2013. Luxemburg.

Dickie, George, 1974: Art and the Aesthetic. An Institutional Analysis. Ithaka: Cornell University Press.

Foster, Hal, 1996: The Return of the Real. The Avant-Garde at the End of the Century. Cambridge: MIT Press.

Frey, Bruno S. / Eichenberger, Reiner, 1995: On the Return of Art Investment Analyses. In: Journal of Cultural Economics, 19 (3), 207-220.

Genoni, Ilona, 2009: Just What Is It That Makes It So Different, So Appealing? Art Basel – Von der Verkaufsmesse zum Kulturereignis. Dissertation. University of Zurich.

Glogner, Patrick / Föhl, Patrick (Hg.), 2010: Das Kulturpublikum. Fragestellungen und Befunde der empirischen Forschung. Wiesbaden: VS Verlag.

Godelier, Maurice, 1996: L'Enigme du don. Paris: Fayard.

Goetzmann, William, 1993: Accounting For Taste: Art and the Financial Markets Over Three Centuries. In: American Economics Review, Vol. 83 (5), 1370-1376.

Goetzmann, William / Renneboog, Luc / Spaenjers, Christophe, 2011: Art and Money. In: American Economic Review, Vol. 101(3), 222-226.

Goetzmann, William / Renneboog, Luc / Spaenjers, Christophe, 2012: Art and Money. Presentation. http://www.inquire-europe.org/seminars/2012/papers%20Instanbul/mo%2016.00%20Slides %20Goetzman%20Art%20final%20.pdf.

Goetzmann, William / Mamonova, Elena / Spaenjars, Christophe, 2014. The Economics of Aesthetics and Three Centuries of Art Price Records. Paris: NBER Working Paper No. 20440.

Graw, Isabelle, 2010 [2008]: High Price. Art Between the Market and Celebrity Culture. Berlin: Sternberg.

Groys, Boris, 2012: Marx nach Duchamp. In: Schweizer Monat, Nr. 995, April 2012, 74-78.

Hauser, Arnold, 1951/1958: The Social History of Art. New York: Alfred Knopf.

Herchenröder, Christian, 2000: Kunstmärkte im Wandel. Vom Jahrzehnt des Umbruchs in die Gegenwart. Düsseldorf: Verlag Wirtschaft und Finanzen.

Herstatt, Claudia, 2007: Fit für den Kunstmarkt. Ostfildern: Hatje Cantz.

Institut für Strategieentwicklung, 2013: Pilotstudie zur Situation von Galerien in Deutschland 2013. Berlin.

Karpik, Lucien, 2010: Valuing the Unique. The Economics of Singularities. Princeton: Princeton University Press.

Keller, Samuel, 2006: Ein Gespräch mit Samuel Keller. In: Lindemann, Adam, Collecting Contemporary. Cologne: Taschen, 274-277.

Kirshenblatt-Gimblett, Barbara, 1998: Destination Culture. Tourism, Museum, and Heritage. Berkeley: University of California Press.

Klein, Ulrike, 1993: Der Kunstmarkt. Zur Interaktion von Ästhetik und Ökonomie. Frankfurt: Lang.

Kraeussl, Roman / Lee, Jonathan, 2010: Art as an Investment: the Top 500 Artists. SSRN Working Paper Series, No. 1536047, VU University Amsterdam.

Krauss, Rosalind, 1985: The Originality of the Avant-Garde and Other Modernist Myth. Cambridge: MIT Press.

Lash, Scott, 1990: Sociology of Postmodernism. London: Routledge.

Lind, Maria / Velthuis, Olav (eds.), 2012: Contemporary Art and Its Commercial Markets: A Report on Current Conditions and Future Scenarios. Berlin: Sternberg.

Mc Andrew, Clare, 2011: The Role of Art and Antiques Dealers: An Added Value. London: Publications UK.

Mc Andrew, Clare, 2012: The International Art Market in 2011. Observations on the Art Trade over 25 Years. Helvoirt: The European Fine Art Foundation.

Mc Andrew, Clare, 2013a: TEFAF Art Market Report 2013. The Global Art Market, with a focus on China and Brazil. Helvoirt: The European Fine Art Foundation.

Mc Andrew, Clare, 2013b: The Global Art Market in 2013. Leaders & Laggards. Barcelona: Caixa-Forum.

Mc Andrew, Clare, 2014: TEFAF Art Market Report 2014. The Global Art Market, with a focus on the US and China. Helvoirt: The European Fine Art Foundation.

Mehring, Christine, 2008: Emerging Market. The First Contemporary Art Fair. In: Artforum International, Vol. 46 (8).

Mei, Jianping / Moses, Michael, 2002: Art as an Investment and the Underperformance of Masterpieces. In: American Economic Review, 92 (5), 1656-1668.

Menger, Pierre-Michel, 2003: Portrait de l'artiste en travailleur. Métamorphoses du capitalisme. Paris: Seuil.

Mona, Thomas, 1997: Un art du secret. Collectionneurs d'art contemporain en France. Nimes: Chambon.

Moulin, Raymonde, 1987: The French Art Market: A Sociological Perspective. New Brunswick: Rutgers.

Moulin, Raymonde, 1992. L'artiste, l'institution et le marché. Paris: Flammarion.

Munder, Heike / Wuggenig, Ulf (eds.), 2012: Das Kunstfeld: Eine Studie über Akteure und Institutionen der zeitgenössischen Kunst am Beispiel von Zürich, Wien, Hamburg und Paris. Zurich: JRP Ringier.

O'Doherty, Brian 1986: Inside the White Cube. The Ideology of the Gallery Space. Santa Monica: The Lapis Press.

Pety, Dominique, 2001: Le personnage du collectionneur au XIXe siècle: de l'excentrique à l'amateur distingue. In: Romantisme, Vol. 31 (112) 71-81.

Prinz, Sophia / Wuggenig, Ulf, 2012: Charismatische Disposition und Intellektualisierung. In: Munder, Heike / Wuggenig, Ulf (eds.), Das Kunstfeld. Eine Studie über Akteure und Institutionen der zeitgenössischen Kunst am Beispiel von Zürich, Wien, Hamburg und Paris. Zu-rich: JRP | Ringier, 205-228.

Quemin, Alain, 2006: Globalization and Mixing in the Visual Arts. An Empirical Survey of ‚High Culture' and Globalization. In: International Sociology, Vol. 21 (4), 522-550.

Quemin, Alain, 2008: International Contemporary Art Fairs and Galleries: An Exclusive Overview. In Artprice, Le Marche de l'Art Contemporain 2007-08. Saint-Romain-au-Mont-d'Or, 78-88.

Quemin, Alain, 2012: The Internationalization of the Contemporary Art World and Market. The Role of Nationality and Territory in a supposedly ‚globalized' sector. In: Lind, Maria / Velthuis, Olav (eds.), Contemporary Art and Its Commercial Markets: A Report on Current Conditions and Future Scenarios. Berlin: Sternberg, 53-83.

Rauget, Bernard / Sagot-Duvauroux, Dominique / Pflieger Sylvie, 1991: Le marché de l'art contemporain en France. Prix et strategies. Paris: La Documentation Française.

Reckwitz, Andreas, 2012: Die Erfindung der Kreativität. Zum Prozess gesellschaftlicher Ästhetisierung. Berlin: Suhrkamp.

Robertson, lain, 2011: The Art Market in Transition, the Global Economic Crisis, and the Rise of Asia. In: Harris, Jonathan (ed.), Globalization and Contemporary Art. Malden: Wiley-Blackwell, 449-463.

Rosa, Hartmut, 2013 [2005]: Social Acceleration. A New Theory Of Modernity. New York: Columbia University Press.

Rosenberg, Harold, 1964: The Anxious Object. Art Today and its Audience. New York: Horizon Press.

Rubin, Judith, 2014: TEA/AECOM 2013 Theme Index & Museum Index: The Global Attractions Attendance Report. Burbank.

Schneider, Norbert, 1996: Geschichte der Ästhetik von der Aufklärung bis zur Postmoderne. Stuttgart: Reclam.

Saltz, Jerry, 2013: Death of the Gallery Show. New York Magazine, 1. April 2013.

Saltz, Jerry, 2014: Jeff Koons, Creator and Destroyer of Worlds. In: New York Magazine, 30. June 2014.

Skate, 2014: Annual Art Investment Report 2013. New York: Skatepress.

Spiegler, Marc, 2007: Überdosis Kunstmesse. In: Monopol, 02/2007, 112-115.

Stallabrass, Julian, 2004: Art Incorporated. The Story of Contemporary Art. Oxford: Oxford University Press.

Steiner, Lasse / Frey, Bruno S. / Resch, Magnus, 2013: Home Is Where Your Art Is: The Home Bias of Art Collectors. Working Paper No. 135, University of Zürich.

Taylor, Mark C., 2011: Financialization of Art. In: Capitalism and Society, Vol. 6 (2), Article 3.

Thompson, Don, 2008: The $12 Million Stuffed Shark. The Curious Economics of Contemporary Art. New York: Palgrave.

Thompson, Don, 2014: The Supermodel And The Brillo Box. Back Stories And Peculiar Economics From The World Of Contemporary Art. New York: Palgrave Macmillan.

Thornton, Sarah, 2008: Seven Days in the Art World. New York: Norton & Company.

Thurn, Hans-Peter, 1994: Der Kunsthändler. Wandlungen eines Berufes. München: Hirmer.

Ullrich, Wolfgang, 2007: Der Sammler als „role model". Wieso Sammler Vorbild sein können. Vortrag auf dem Symposion „Leidenschaft des Sammeins" des „Private Wealth Management" der Deutschen Bank auf Schloss Münchhausen/Hameln, 5. May 2007.

Ullrich, Wolfgang, 2012. Helden des Konsums. Warum der Kunstsammler zum Vorbild des neuen Bürgers avanciert. In: Die Zeit, No. 41, 16.10.2012.

van den Berg, Karen / Pasero, Ursula (eds.), 2013: Art Production beyond the Art Market. Berlin: Sternberg Press.

Velthuis Olav, 2003: Symbolic meanings of prices: Constructing the value of contemporary art in Amsterdam and New York galleries. In: Theory and Society, Vol. 32 (2), 181-215.

Velthius, Olav, 2005: Talking Prices. Symbolic Meaning of Prices on the Market for Contemporary Art. Princeton: Princeton University Press.

Velthuis, Olav, 2011: Art markets. In: Towse, Ruth (ed.), The Handbook of Cultural Economics. 2nd Edition, Cheltenham: Edward Elgar, 33-42.

Velthuis, Olav, 2012: The contemporary art market between stasis and flux. In: Lind, Maria / Velthuis, Olav (eds.), Contemporary Art and Its Commercial Markets: A Report on Current Conditions and Future Scenarios. Berlin: Sternberg, 17-49.

Velthius, Olav, 2013: Globalization of markets for contemporary art: Why local ties remain dominant in Amsterdam and Berlin. In: European Societies, Vol. 15 (2), 290-308.

Warhol, Andy, 1975: The Philosophy of Andy Warhol. From A to B and Back Again. New York: Harcourt Brace Jovanovich.

Werner, Henry 2010: Modern Art for Sale. Die bedeutendsten Kunstmessen der Welt. Düsseldorf: Feymedia.

Weiner, Annette, 1992: Inalienable Possessions: The Paradox of Keeping-While-Giving. Berkeley: University of California Press.

White, Harrison C. / White, Cynthia A., 1965: Canvases and Careers. Institutional Change in the French Painting World. Chicago: University of Chicago Press.

Worthington, Andrew / Higgs, Helen, 2004: Random walks and market efficiency in European equity markets. In: Global Journal of Finance and Economics, Vol. 1 (1), 59-78.

Wuggenig, Ulf, 2003: Das Empire, der Nordwesten und der Rest der Welt. Die ,internationale zeitgenössische Kunst' im Zeitalter der Globalisierung. In: Raunig, Gerald (ed.), Transversal. Kunst und Globalisierungskritik. Wien: Turia + Kant, 53-67.

Wuggenig, Ulf, 2011: An der goldenen Nabelschnur. In: Texte zur Kunst, Vol. 21, No. 83, 56-75.

Yogev, Tamar, 2010: The social construction of quality: status dynamics in the market for contemporary art. In: Socio-Economic Review, Vol. 8 (3), 511-536.

Zahner, Nina Tessa, 2006: Die neuen Regeln der Kunst. Andy Warhol und der Umbau des Kunstbetriebs im 20. Jahrhundert. Frankfurt/M.: Campus.

Zahner, Nina Tessa, 2012: Inklusion und Exklusion im Konsumtionsfeld der Bildenden Kunst. In: Bernhard, Stefan / Schmidt-Wellenburg, Christian (eds.), Feldanalyse als Forschungsprogramm 2. Gegenstandsbezogene Theoriebildung. Wiesbaden: Springer VS, 339-361.

Zahner, Nina Tessa, 2015: Das Laienpublikum als Herausforderung für die Feldanalyse. In: Danko Dagmar / Moeschler, Olivier / Schumacher, Florian (eds.), Kunst und Öffentlichkeit. Wiesbaden: Springer VS, 187-210.

Picture Credits

Photographs by Thomas Eberle on pages

10/11 – 16 – 23 – 41 – 54 – 62/63 – 74 – 87 – 98 – 103 – 126/127 – 149 – 165 – 180 – 189 – 198 – 201 – 204/205 – 210

Photographs by Thomas Mazzurana on the cover and on pages

20 – 26 – 28/29 – 36 – 45 – 48 – 51 – 66 – 71 – 79 – 83 – 92/93 – 107 – 112 – 117 – 123 – 132 – 137 – 142 – 146 – 154/155 – 160 – 163 – 168 – 170/171 – 176 – 185 – 193 – 215 – 218 – 223 – 232/233